Bibliography on Economic Cooperation Among Developing Countries, 1981–1982: With Annotations

compiled and edited by Nada Verbič

Routledge
Taylor & Francis Group
LONDON AND NEW YORK

First published 1984 by Westview Press

Published 2018 by Routledge
52 Vanderbilt Avenue, New York, NY 10017
2 Park Square, Milton Park, Abingdon, Oxon OX14 4RN

Routledge is an imprint of the Taylor & Francis Group, an informa business

Library of Congress Catalog Card Number: 84-50373
ISBN: 0-86531-791-7

ISBN 13: 978-0-367-01654-8 (hbk)
ISBN 13: 978-0-367-16641-0 (pbk)

Bibliography on Economic Cooperation Among Developing Countries, 1981–1982: With Annotations

THE RCCDC SERIES ON SOUTH-SOUTH COOPERATION

Contents

Foreword

This bibliography is a part of state-of-the-art documentation prepared by the Research Centre for Cooperation with Developing Countries (RCCDC) within the first stage of the ICCDA-sponsored international research project on "Economic Cooperation and Regional Integration among Developing Countries." The project is coordinated in the name of EADI by its member RCCDC, in association with and with the support of the OECD Development Centre from Paris.

This is the third consecutive volume of the bibliography (after the 1970-78 and 1979-80 issues) and it has gained substantial interest from a wide professional public all over the world. Since this work is to be continued by RCCDC on a computerized system, we shall appreciate receiving any suggestions and entries we might have missed. This will help us in making future volumes more comprehensive and therefore more useful.

The following contributions have been made by institutions and individuals for the compilation of the present volume: an extensive bibliography on Latin American integration was provided by INTAL, Buenos Aires; Mr. V. Pregelj provided printouts from the Library of Congress, Washington D.C.; entries on Pacific Basin Cooperation were provided by Mr. M. W. Oborne of the OECD Development Centre; and the Arab League Documentation Department made available a bibliography on inter-Arab cooperation. All these contributions are gratefully acknowledged.

Under the guidance of the general editor, Nada Verbič has been responsible for the compilation, selection, and editing, assisted by Jelka Kadunc. The typesetting was done by Jelka Djukić and Slavica Jelovšek.

Also in the present bibliography some errors may have slipped in, particularly concerning the author names. We would appreciate it if readers would kindly advise us of any errors that have occurred in the work.

Dr. Boris Cizelj,
General Editor

Ljubljana, Yugoslavia

I

New International Economic Order and Co-operation Among Developing Countries

1 AFRICA, the Middle East and the new international economic order / Ed. by Jorge Lozoya, Hector Cuadra. - New York : Pergamon, 1980. XX,162p. (Pergamon policy studies on the new international economic order)

Published for UNITAR and CEESTEM.
Bibliography, statistical appendix, index.
ISBN 0 08 025117 x

2 AL-SHAIKHLY, Salah
Energy issue and negotiations for a new economic order. Development Seeds of Change, no.2, 1981, p.12-14

3 ALTMANN, Jörn
South-South cooperation : some aspects of economic order. Economics (Tübingen), vol.25, 1981, p.44-62

4 AMACHER, Ryan C.
The New International Economic Order : lessons from the real world. The Journal of Social and Political Studies (Fairfax, Va.), 5(1/2), spring/summer 1980, p.107-118. Includes bibliographical references.

5 AMERICA Latina frente al nuevo orden económico internacional : el informe Brandt. Integración Latinoamericana (Buenos Aires), no.60, August 1981, p.4., Ref.

Contents: Otra oportunidad para el Norte ? / by Barbara Ward. Qué puede hacerse (en caso de que fuera possible hacer algo) con el Informe de la Comisión Brandt ? / by Miguel S. Wionczek. Acerca del Informe de la Comisión Brandt / by Simón Teitel. El Fondo Común para los productos básicos / by Rodrigo Díaz Albónico. Mecanismos de fomento a la actividad productiva en México.

6 ANELL, L. NYGREN, Birgitta
The developing countries and the world economic order. - Andover, England : Methuen, 1980. 217p.

7 ASIA and the New International Economic Order / ed. by Lozoya, J.A., Bhattacharya, A.K. ; publ. for UNITAR and the Center for Economic and Social Studies of the Third World, CEESTEM. - New York : Pergamon, 1981. 240p. Ref. Tabs. (Pergamon policy studies on the New International Economic Order)

Eleven contributions by Thapar, Masahiro Sakamoto, Jong Youl Yoo, Lin, Anguiano, Chandra, Sarma, Vitchitrong Pombhejara, Lim Chong-Yah, and Arndt. Case studies of NIEO and resp.: Japan, South Korea, China PR, India, Southeast Asia, ASEAN, Indonesia, and Australia. Impact of NIEO on domestic development, international cooperation, industrialization, food supply, natural resources, and economic development.

8 BENACHENHOU, Abdellatif
Le Tiers-Monde en jeu. - Paris : Centre de Recherches en Economie Appliquée, 1981. 217p. Tab.

9 BELL, J. C.
In search of a Third World Order in the present global economic system. - Vancouver, B.C. : ∠University of British Colombia/, 1979. 43p.

/Economic systems/, /development policy/, /dependence/, /foreign intervention/, /developing countries/ - /IBRD/, /multinational enterprises/, /decision making/, /conference paper/

10 BOUCKAERT, L.
De Nieuwe Internationale Economische Orde (NIEO) in ethisch perspectief. Economisch en Sociaal Tijdschrift (Antwerpen), no.4, aug., 1981, p.447, Portr. Ref.

Aard van het ethisch perspectief, verduidelijkt aan de hand van 5 stellingen. Historische ontwikkeling van de Nieuwe Internationale Economische Orde (NIEO), zijn etische grondslagen.

11 BRANDT Commission papers : selected background papers prepared for the Independent Commission on International Development Issues 1978-1979. - Geneva : IBIDI, 1981. 764p. Ref.Tbs.Diagrs.

IBIDI Independent Bureau for International Development Issues

12 BUENO, Gerardo
Un nuevo orden en las relaciones financieras y technológicas con el Tercer Mundo? Foro Internacional (México, D.F.), 21(1), jul./sept., 1980, p.24-43

13 The CHALLENGE of the new international economic order / edited by (Edwin P. Reubens). - Boulder, Colorado : Westwiew, 1981. XV,298p. (Westwiew special studies in social, political, and economic development)

Includes bibliographical references and index.

ISBN 0 89158 762 4

14 CHANGING priorities on the international agenda : the New International Economic Order / edited by Karl P. Sauvant. - Oxford ; New York : Pergamon Press, 1981, XXVI,319p. (Pergamon international library of science, technology, engineering and social studies) (Systems science and world order library)

ISBN o o8 023117 9

Four contributions by Sauvant, Jankowitsch, Ruediger von Wechmar. Origins of the New International Economic Order (NIEO). Initiating role of the non-aligned countries : mobilization, organization. The Algiers summit. The NIEO program : reasons, proposals, and progress. Commodity trade. Finance and money. Industrialization. Science and technology. Food and agriculture. The position of the industrialized countries. Basic documents of the NIEO program. Statistics, mainly 1951-2000.

15 COLLOQUE latino-américain sur le nouvel ordre économique international. Tiers-Monde (Paris), vol.22, no.85, janvier/mars 1981, p.201-207

16 DAVIDSON, Nicol
Co-operation among developing countries and the New International Economic Order : address to the World Conference on the Path to Development and International Co-operation, organized by the World Peace Council, Tripoli, Libya A.P.S.J., 9-13 April 1978. - /S.l. : s.n., 1978/. 9 leaves.

17 DAVILA GOMEZ PALACIO, R.
Reestructuración industrial y el Nuevo Orden Económico Internacional. Comercio Exterior (México, D.F.), 31(6), junio de 1981, p.661-665

18 DÍAZ-ALEJANDRO, Carlos F. FFRENCH-DAVIS, Ricardo TIRONI, Ernesto
Orden económico internacional y desarrollo : investigaciones prioritarios desde una perspectiva Latino-américana. - Santiago de Chile : Cooperación de Investigaciones Económicas para Latinoamerica, 1978. 31p. (Estudios CIEPLAN ; 30)

19 ESTEVEZ, Jaime
Cancun : les limites du dialogue Nord-Sud. Amérique Latine (Paris), no.9, janvier-mars, 1982, p.5-14. Ref.

20 ESTEVEZ, Jaime PUYANA, Alicia FANON, Françoise
Del Nuevo Orden Económico Internacional a las negociaciones globales : historia de un esfuerzo. Tercer Mundo y Economía Mundial, vol.1, no.1, septiembre-diciembre de 1981, p.9-26. Incl. Ref.

21 EUROPA e America in un nuovo ordine internazionale. - Roma : Instituto per le relazioni tra l'Italia e i paesi dell'Africa, America Latina e Medio Oriente, 1981. 149p. (Atti e documenti ; 13)

22 FAULWETTER, Helmut
The struggle of developing countries against imperialism for a New International Economic Order. Wissenschaftliche Beiträge (Berlin), 16(2), 1981, p.9-23
Includes bibliographical references.

23 FRANK, Andre Gunder
Retórica y realidad del Nuevo Orden Económico Internacional. Desarrollo Indoamericano (Baranquilla, Colombia), 14(52), oct. 1979, p.17-24

The first part of this article appeared in Desarrollo Indoamericano, 14(51), agosto, 1979

24 FURTADO, Celso
Orden económico internacional y el Brasil. Trimestre Económico (México, D.F.), vol.48(3), julio-septiembre de 1981, p.523-538

25 GANGULY, S.P.
The International economic crisis and further distortion in the Third World development path. Man and Development, vol.3, no.2, 1981

26 GONČAROV, L.V.
Afrika v bor'be za novyj meždunarodnyj ekonomičeskij porjadok. Mirovaja ekonomika i meždunarodnye otnošenija (Moskva), no.6, 1982, p.49-62

27 GREMETS, Maksim
K novomu meždunarodnomu ekonomičeskomu porjadku. Problemy mira i socializma (Praga), 1, 1981, p.22-27

28 HACIA un nuevo orden económico internacional : temas prioritarios para América Latina / Comp.by Ffrench-Davis, Ricardo y Tironi, Ernesto. - México : Fondo de Cultura Económica : CIEPLAN, 1981. 305p.

29 HAQ, Khadija
Dialogue for a new order. - New York, N.Y. : Pergamon, 1980. 312p.

/New International Economic Order/, /North-South dialogue/ - /developing countries/, /regional cooperation/, /self-reliance/, /international trade/, trade negotiations/, protectionism/, /international monetary reform/, /IBRD/, /economic relations/, /development strategy/, /policy making/, /basic needs/.

30 HAQ, Mahbub Ul
The Third World and the international economic order. - Georgetown, Guayana : Ministry of Foreign Affairs, 1975. 52p., group portr.

31 HERRERA, Felipe
América Latina y el Nuevo Orden Económico Internacional. - Santiago de Chile : Universidad Católica, Instituto de Ciencia Política, 1978. 34p. (Cuadernos ; 23)

32 HOLZBERG, Bryan J.
The new world information order : a legal framework for debate. Case Western Reserve Journal of International Law (Cleveland, Ohio), 14(2), spring 1982, p.387-418

Includes bibliographical references

33 HOSKINS, Linus A.
The New International Economic Order : a bibliographic essay. Third World Quarterly (London), vol.3, no.3, 1981, p.506-527

34 JAMAR, Joseph
Organisations économiques régionales et Nouvel Ordre Mondial : quel avenir pour les intégrations régionales entre pays en voie de développement? : conclusions générales. - In: Intégrations régionales entre pays en voie de développement. - Bruges : De Tempel, 1982. p.245-274

35 JUNAC
Documentos basicos del Nuevo Orden Económico Internacional, 1978-1980. - Lima : JUNAC, Biblioteca, 1980. II,286p.

36 KAPLAN, Marcos
Características del Nuevo Orden Político Internacional. Nueva Sociedad (San José, Costa Rica), no.55, julio-agosto 1981, p.7-24

37 KEBBA-DIALLO, Florence
NIEO no-progress report. West Africa (London), no.3368, 22 February 1982, p.506

38 KIM, Samuel S.
China and the Third World in NIEO politics. Contemporary China (Boulder, Co), 3(4), winter 1979, p.10-21

39 KIM, Soo-Yong
The New International Economic Order and Korea. Korea and World Affairs (Seoul), vol.5, no.1, spring 1981, p.61-76

40 KIROS, Fassil G.
What is in the New International Economic Order for the least developed countries of Africa? Africa Development (Dakar), 6(4), 1981, p.16-34

41 KISS, Laszlo J.
Comments on the Brandt Report. Development and Peace (Budapest), vol.2, no.1, spring 1981, p.230-238

42 LAFER, Celso
Reflexiones sobre el tema del nuevo orden mundial en un orden internacional en transformación. Estudios Internacionales (Buenos Aires), vol.15, no.58, abril-junio 1982, p.127-165

43 LALL, K.B.
The Third World and new economic order : role of BBC and India. Studia Diplomatica (Bruxelles), no.4, 1980, p.411-498

44 LALL, Sanjaya
Developing countries in the international economy. - London : Macmillan, 1981, 263p.

45 LANGHAMMER, Rolf J.
Industrie- und Entwicklungsländer in der Auseinandersetzung um eine neue Weltwirtschaftsordnung. - Kiel : Institut für Weltwirtschaft an der Universität Kiel, /1981/ p.33-56. (Kieler Sonderdrucke ; 1o8)

cont.

cont'd

Veröffentlicht in: Die internationale Politik 1975/1977 : Jahrbücher des Forschungsinstituts der Deutschen Gesellschaft für Auswärtige Politik. München ; Wien : Deutsche Gesellschaft für Auswärtige Politik, 1981

46 LATIN America and the New International Development Strategy / United Nations. Economic Commission for Latin America. Projections Centre. CEPAL Review (Santiago), no.11, August 1980, p.7-30

47 LATIN America and the New International Development Strategy : goals and objectives. - New York, N.Y. : UN Economic and Social Council, 1979. 34p.
E/CEPAL/L.210

/Development strategy/, /economic and social development/, /Latin America/ - /scenarios/, /future/.

48 LATIN America and the New International Economic Order / ed. by Ffrench-Davis Ricardo, Tironi Ernesto.- London : Macmillan, 1982. 268p. Ref. Tabs.
ISBN 0 333 30074 2

Eighteen contributions by R. Ffrench-Davis, C. Diaz-Alejandro, W. Cline, E. Bacha, A.Fishlow, R. Junguito, D. Avramović, E. Tironi, S. Teitel, G. Perry, a.o., followed by comments. Latin America and the NIEO, aspects of international finance, commodity prices and export policy, industrialization in developing countries, technological change and development in Latin America, a.o. Statistics, 1949-77.

49 LATIN America and the new international economic order / ed. by Jorge Lozoya, Jaime Estevez. - New York : Pergamon Press, 1980. XIV,93p. (Pergamon policy studies on the new international economic order)
ISBN 0 08 025118 8
Published for UNITAR and CEESTEM-Center for Economic and Social Studies of the Third World.

Experts from Latin America examine the economic and social effects that the implementation of the NIEO will have on Latin America, particularly its political systems, foreign trade, industrialization and internal economics.

50 LEFF, N.H.
Beyond the international order in the Third World : premises of US policy / edited by W. Scott Thompson. - San Francisco, Ca. : Institute for Contemporary Studies, 1978

51 LEISTNER, G.M.E.
Towards a new order in Southern Africa. - Pretoria : Africa Institute of South Africa, 1979. 51p.

G.M.E. Leistner a rassemblé un certain nombre de contributions concernant le développement économique, l'interdépendence régionale, l'Union des Etats d'Afrique Australe pour un nouvel ordre économique international. Des bibliographies complètent chacun des éléments de cet intéressant dossier.

52 MAMALAKIS, M.
The New International Economic Order : centrepiece Venezuela. Journal of Inter-American Studies and World Affairs (Beverly, Cal.), vol.20, no.3, August 1978

53 LOWENTHAL, A.F. POLLOCK, D.H. MENDIVE, P.I.
A new Latin America in a changing world economy. CEPAL Review (Santiago), no.10, Apr., 1980, p.20. Ref. Tabs.

Ten contributions by Lowenthal, Pollock, Mendive, Behrman, Fishlow, Massad, Malan, Sabato, Wionczek, Cline and Bradford Jr. on the role of Latin America in a changing world economy. Export of manufactures and primary products: Latin America in a new international capital market. International monetary system. New International Economic Order. Technology transfer. Income distribution.

54 MARTIN, L.
Latin America plans new order - without U.S. Globe and Mail (Toronto), no.3, 1980

/economic relations/, /regional cooperation/, /Latin America/ - /trade relations/, /USA/, /economic development/, /member states).

55 MAYRZEDT, Hans ERNST, Mario
Perspectives of the North-South Dialogue : elements for a reorientation. Intereconomics (Hamburg), no.5, September - October 1981, p.214-220

56 MAZA ZAVALA, Domingo F.
Tercer Mundo y el Nuevo Orden Económico Internacional. Desarrollo Indoamericano (Barranquilla, Colombia), 16(65), enero de 1981, p.13-30. Incl. Ref.

With emphasis on Latin America.

57 MEXICO y el Nuevo Orden Económico Internacional. Mercado de Valores (México), 41(11), 16 marzo de 1981, p.291-296

58 MILETA, Vlatko
Zemlje u razvoju i novi medjunarodni ekonomski poredak = Developing countries and the new international economic order. Politička misao (Zagreb), no.2, 1979.

59 MINIĆ, Jelica
Some structural aspects of the New International Economic Order and of the Mediterranean cooperation. Review of International Affairs (Beograd), (32), no.754, Sept.5, 1981, p.17. Ref.

Characteristics of transformation in international relations, bringing changes in economic and social developments. Criteria for restructuring the world economy. Role of the Mediterranean countries.

60 MURPHY, Ewell E. Jr.
Decision 24, mexicanization and the New International Economic Order : the anatomy of disincentive. Texas International Law Journal (Austin, Tex.), vol.13, spring 1978.

61 NAVARRETE, Jorge Eduardo
México y el marco de negociación del Nuevo Orden Económico Internacional. Comercio Exterior (México), vol.31, no.7, julio de 1981, p.800-805

Las dos caras del decenio de los setenta. Diferencias de fondo en las negociaciones. Materias primas. Energia. Comercio. Desarrollo. Moneda y finanzas. Mexico y el Nuevo Orden económico Internacional.

62 NOVI medjunarodni ekonomski poredak : putevi ostvarenja i perspektive : finalna studija / tim autora finalne studije Tomislav Popović ... /et al./ ; redaktori Tomislav Popović, Rikard Štajner. - Beograd : Konzorcijum instituta, 1981. 456p.

Novi medjunarodni poredak - projekt / direktor projekta Tomislav Popović ; sekretar projekta Milica Uvalić.

63 NOVI medjunarodni ekonomski poredak : zbornik dokumenata : New international economic order : documents 1955-1977 / urednik zbornika Vera Jelača-Atanacković ; lektor Vukosava Mojsić ; indekse priredio Drago Vidović. - Beograd : Institut za medjunarodnu politiku i privredu, OOUR za naučnu dokumentaciju i informacije, 1979. 5 vols (1513p.)
Subject index: p.1446-1513

64 NWANKWO, G.O.
Tne new international economic and world monetary system. - Lagos : Nigerian Institute of International Affairs, 1976. 40p. (Lecture series ; 16)

Being text of a lecture delivered at the Nigerian Institute of International Affairs, Victoria Island, Lagos.

65 The OBSTACLES to the New International Economic Order / Ervin Laszlo ... /et al./. - New York : Pergamon, /1981/. XXV,143p. (Pergamon policy studies on the New International Economic Order) (UNITAR/CEESTEM library on NIEO)

Bibliography: p.127-135
Includes Index
ISBN 0 08 025110 2

A thorough investigation of the obstacles which block the creation of the new international economic order. This volume investigates the political, institutional, and legal problems as well as those resulting from present inequities: international finance, resource allocation and technology transfer.

66 OBSTACULOS al Nuevo Orden Económico Internacional / Ervin Laszlo ... /et al./; versión en español de Jaime Estévez. 1. ed. en español. - México : CEESTEM : Editorial Nueva Imagen, 1981. 182p.

Colaboradores del proyecto: p.169-182
ISBN 968 429 275 9

67 OSORIO-TAFALL, B.F.
Comentarios sobre el desarrollo y el nuevo orden internacional. Tercer Mundo y Economía Mundial, vol.1, no.2, enero-abril 1982, p.255-273

68 OSTERFELD, David
Assessing the New International Order : prospects for Third World development. Journal of Social, Political and Economic Studies (Fairfax, Va.), 7(1/2), spring/summer, 1982, p.3-26
Includes bibliographical references.

69 PAUSEWANG, Siegfried
New International Economic Order for the peasant in the Third World. Sociologia Ruralis (Assen, Netherlands), vol.20, no.1/2, 1980, p.97-115

/New International Economic Order/, /income distribution/, /peasants /, /rural development/ - /Ethiopia/.

70. PERCZYNSKI, Maciej
On the conception of the new economic order. World Marxist Review (Toronto), 23(7), July 1980, p.70-76

71 PEUPLES et états du Tiers monde face à l'ordre international / études réunies par Alain Fenet. - Paris : Presses Universitaires de France, 1978. 209p. (Publications de la Faculté de droit et des sciences politiques et sociales d'Amiens / Centre de relations internationales et de sciences politiques de l'Université de Picardie)
Incl. bibliographical references.

72 PREBISCH, Raúl
El Nuevo Orden Económico Internacional y valores culturales : dos grandes mitos del capitalismo periférico = The New International Economic Order and cultural values : two myths of peripheral capitalism. - Madrid : Instituto de Cooperación Intercontinental, 1978. 80p. (Folleto / Instituto de Cooperación Intercontinental ; 1)
ISBN 84 400 4790 8

"Preparatory document for the Colloquium on the New International Economic Order and Cultural Values, Madrid, June 12-14, 1978". Bibliography: p.53-56

73 REVUELTA LAPIQUE, José Manuel
Las comisiones regionales de las Naciones Unidas y el nuevo orden económico internacional. - Madrid : Universidad Autonóma de Madrid, Facultad de Ciencias Económicas y Empresariales, 1979. 2 vols

Thesis /doctoral/ Universidad Autónoma de Madrid, 1979.
Bibliography: p.561-617

74 RIVAS FARIAS, S.
A quién sirve realmente el Informe Brandt? Comercio Exterior (México), vol.31(7), julio de 1981, p.805-810. Ref.

75 RIVERO, Oswaldo de
Nuevo orden economico y derecho internacional para el desarrollo. - Mexico : Centro de Estudios Económicos y Sociales del Tercer Mundo, 1978, 172p. Bibl.: p.171-172

76 RUSSELL, Roberto G. CARBALLAL, Teresa
El Nuevo Orden Económico Internacional : tendencias observables en el Norte y en los países mayores de América Latina. Estudios Internacionales (Buenos Aires), 15(53), enero/marzo, 1981, p.55-88

77 RWEYEMAMU, Justinian F.
Africa and the New International Economic Order. Africa Guide, 1978

78 SANDSTROM, H.M.
"The New International Economic Order and the Caribbean : the external/internal nexus".
In: The restless Caribbean : changing patterns of international relations / edited by Millet R. and Will W.M. - New York : Praeger, 1979

79 SAUVANT, Karl P.
From economic to socio-cultural emancipation : the historical context of the New International Economic Order and the New International Socio-Cultural Order. Third World Quarterly (London), vol.3, no.1, 1981, p.48

80 SAUVANT, Karl P.
The role of transnational enterprises in the establishment of the New International Economic Order : a critical review.
In: Obstacles and opportunities in the establishment of a New International Economic order, edited by Ervin Laszlo and Jorge Lozoya.-Elmsford, N.Y. : Pergamon Press, 1981

A part of the paper has been reprinted under the title "The NIEO-Programme : a framework for restructuring the world economy? in Dieter Ernst ed., The New International Division of Labour, technology and underdevelopment : consequences for the Third World. - Frankfurt : Campus, 1980.

An earlier version had been presented at the conference on "Progress in the establishment of the New International Economic Order : obstacles and opportunities", jointly sponsored by the United Nations Institute for Training and Research and the Centro de Estudios Económicos y Sociales del Tercer Mundo, México City, January 1979.

81 SHAGARI, Sheha
On Africa and the New International Economic Order. South. The Third World Magazine (London), no.16, February 1982, p.72
Special report: Nigeria : the tomorrow game

82 SPENCE, Alan
The Middle East and the New Economic Order. Middle East (London), no.44, June 1978, p.125-131

Contents: The parting of the ways?/ A. Spence: Group of 77 : unity is vital / R.Dergham. Trade talks : few choices / B.Khindaria. TCDC : the realities behind the slogans / N.Sakr.

83 STREETEN, Paul
Approaches to a New International Economic Order. World Development (Oxford), vol.10, no.1, January 1982, p.1-17. Ref.

84 STRONG, M.F.
International development co-operation : Canada's role. - /S.l. : s.n./, 1977. 37p.
/IDRC governor/, /economic co-operation/, /foreign aid/, /New International Economic Order/, /Canada/, /developing countries/ - / statement/, /government policy/, /economic development/, /aid programmes/, /aid institutions/, /UN specialized agencies/, /IDRC mentioned/.

85 The STRUCTURE of the world economy and prospects for a new international economic order / ed. by Ervin Laszlo, Joel Kurtzman. - New York : Pergamon Press, 1980. XXI, 117p. (Pergamon policy studies on the New International Economic Order)
Published for UNITAR and CEESTEM.
ISBN 0 08 025119 6

86 ŠIROKOV, G.K.
Razvivajuščiesja strany v bor'be za novyj meždunarodnyj ekonomičeskij porjadok. Latinskaja Amerika (Moskva), 10, 1981, p.48-56

87 ŠTAJNER, Rikard
Kriza 2 : anatomija neokolonializma in (splošna) teorija nove mednarodne ekonomske ureditve / prevedel Dušan Dolinar. - Ljubljana : Cankarjeva založba, 1982. 513p. Tabs. (Misel in čas)

88 TUMLIR, J.
Evolución del concepto de Orden Económico Internacional : 1914-1980. Estudios Públicos (Santiago de Chile), 3, junio de 1981, p.85-119. Ref.

89 ULLRICH, Gabriele
An appropriate international monetary order for developing countries? Intereconomics (Hamburg), no.1, Jan./Feb., 1981, p.37-41

90 UN. ECOSOC. Commission pour l'Afrique
Plan directeur revisé pour l'installation du nouvel ordre économique international en Afrique : 1976-1981-1986. - New York : United Nations, 1978. 66p. (E/CN.14/ECO/90/Rev. 3)

91 VALE, Peter C.J.
The Lomé conventions : from Sunday charity to a New International Economic Order. - Braamfontein (Johannesburg) : South African Institute of International Affairs, 1980. /22p./. (Occasional paper / South African Institute of International Affairs)
Bibl.: p.19-22

92 VRHUNEC, Marko
Borba za nov medjunarodni ekonomski poredak : zbirka članaka i rasprava = The struggle for the new international economic order : collection of articles and discussions / Transl. Darja Jan-Salačanin; edit. Dušan Papadopolos.- Beograd : RAD, 1979. 230p. (Nesvrstanost i nesvrstani)

93 WALDHEIM, Kurt
Construyendo el orden futuro : la búsqueda de la paz en un mundo interdependiente / prólogo de Brian Urquhart ; compilador Robert R. Schiffer ; traducción de Eduardo L. Suarez. - México : Fondo de Cultura Económica, 1981. 378p. (Colleción popular ; 215)

Translation of: Building the future order world.
Includes bibliographical references.

94 WALTER, Hans-Ulrich
Das zweite Wirtschaftsabkommen von Lomé : neokoloniale Gegenvariante zur neuen internationalen Wirtschaftsordnung. Wirtschaftswissenschaft (Berlin), 29(2), Feb., 1981, p.167-184

95 WILLIAMS, Marc
Bedjaoui, Mohammed: Towards a New International Economic Order. Third World Quarterly (London), vol.2, no.4, 1980, p.782

96 WILLIAMS, Marc
The objectives of the New International Economic Order /Laszlo, Ervin ... /et al./ Third World Quarterly (London), vol.2, no.4, 1980, p.782

97 WIONCZEK, Miguel S.
Diagnóstico de los fracasos y las perspectivas del Nuevo Orden Económico Internacional. Revista de Economía Latinoamericana (Caracas, Venezuela), no.59, enero/marzo 1980, p.223-256
Summary in English

98 WIONCZEK, Miguel S.
Qué puede hacerse con el Informe Brandt? Estudios Internacionales (Buenos Aires), 14(5), abrile-junio de 1981, p.201-223

99. WIONCZEK, Miguel S.
Qué puede hacerse (en el caso de que fuera posible hacer algo) con el informe de la Comisión Brandt? Integración Latinoamericana (Buenos Aires), 60, agosto de 1981, p.11-21

100 WIONCZEK, Miguel S.
What (if anything) can be done with the Brandt Report? Development and Change (s'Gravenhagen), 12(1), January 1981, p.145-163

II

Concept of Developing Countries' Collective Self-Reliance

101 AMIN, Samir
Du Rapport Pearson (1970) au Rapport Brandt (1980) ou la crise de l'idéologie du développement. Africa Development (Dakar), 5(3), 1980, p.5-20

102 ANOTHER development perspectives for the eighties / Swedish International Development Authority. - Uppsala : Dag Hammarskjoeld Foundation, 1980. 140p. (Development dialogue ; 1980,1)

/Development theory/, /development strategy/, /aid financing/, /New International Economic Order/ - /international cooperation/ - /health services/, /breast feeding/, /infant mortality/, /multinational enterprises/, /self-reliance/, /community development/, /UN system/, /International Monetary System/.

103 ARUSHA programme for collective self-reliance and framework for negotiation. - /S.l./ : United Nations, 1979. TD/236

104 BALLANCE, Frank C.
Rural reform in Zimbabwe. Africa Report (New Brunswick, N. Jersey),vol.26,no.4, July-August 1981,p.9-14

... Zimbabwe achieved general self-sufficiency in food production during UDI-Unilateral Declaration of Independence, as farmers switched from export crops, such as tobacco to food crops and cotton. Zimbabwe is nearly self-sufficient in wheat, and expects a bumper corn harvest of over 2 million tons, with about 1.2 million tons available for reserves and exports ...

105 BASES para una estrategia de seguridad e independencia económica de América Latina. - Caracas : /SELA/, 1982. 58p. (SP/CL/VIII.0/DT ; 36)

106 BOLSOVER, Anne
The way ahead for agriculture. Africa Report (N. Brunswick), vol.27,no.1,1982,p.17-19

Nigeria's Agriculture Minister Alhaji Ibrahim Gusau says: the Green Revolution's target is self-sufficiency in food and cash crops.

107 CALL for "collective self-reliance". AED : Africa Economic Digest (London), vol.3, no.9, 26 February-4 March 1982, p.13

108 CIZELJ, Boris
Ekonomsko sodelovanje med deželami v razvoju : teorija in praksa kolektivne opore na lastne sile = Economic co-operation among developing countries : theory and practice of self-reliance. - Ljubljana : Komunist, 1982. 321p.
Select bibliography

109 CIZELJ, Boris
Kolektivni oslonac na sopstvene snage : teorija i praksa ekonomske saradnje i integracije medju zemljama u razvoju = Collective self-reliance : the theory and practice of economic co-operation and integration among developing countries. Marksizam u svetu, (Beograd), no.4, april 1979, p.5-48

110 CIZELJ, Boris
Koncept večje kolektivne naslonitve dežel v razvoju na lastne sile in njegova materializacija = A concept of greater collective self-reliance of developing countries and its materialization in the process of regional integration. - Ljubljana : CPSDR, 1979. 83 leaves.

The study constitutes the 1st phase of the research project on "Self-managing Social Planning of Foreign Economic Affairs".

111 CIZELJ, Boris
Pomen in implikacije koncepta večje kolektivne naslonitve dežel v razvoju na lastne sile s posebnim ozirom na integracijske procese = The meaning and implications of the concept of greater collective self-reliance of developing countries with special regard to the processes of integration. - Ljubljana : CPSDR, 1980. 34 leaves

The study constitutes the 4th phase of the research project "Economic Integration among Developing Countries", financed by The Research Community of Slovenia.

112 COLLABORATION for self-reliance : Canada's scientific and technological contribution to the food supply of developing countries. - Hull, Que.: Supply and Services Canada, 1981. 112p. Ill. (Science Council of Canada Report ; 32)
ISBN 0 660 10898 4

/Development aid/, /scientific cooperation/, /food production/, /self-reliance/, /science policy/, /Canada/ - /agricultural research/, /universities/, /non-governmental organizations/, /central government/, /private sector/, /CIDA/, /IDRC/, /scientists/, /training/, /institutional framework/, /recommendation/, /IDRC mentioned/.

113 COLLECTIVE self-reliance : programmes and perspectives of the Third World : introduction and documents / eds. Khan Kushi M. and Matthies Volker. - München : Weltforum, 1978. VIII,222p.

114 CO-OPERATION for development in South Asia : a programme of sub-regional collective self-reliance / by Marga Institute, Colombo. IFDA Dossier (Nyon, Suisse) 18, July/Aug., 1980, p.45-58

115 CURRENT plan geared to self-sufficiency. Arab Economist (Beirut), 13, no.136, January 1981, p.28. Tabs.

Somalia's three-year development plan, 1978-1981. Live-stock population, 1975-1977. Industrial production. Economic indicators, 1980.

116 EDGING towards self-reliance. Far Eastern Economic Review : Advertisement Supplement (Hongkong), vol.116, no. 17, April 23, 1982, p.70

117 EPHSON, Ben Jnr
Working towards self-sufficiency : Ben Ephson Jnr considers the Provisional National Defence Council's attempts to increase food production in Ghana and thereby to reduce imports. West Africa (London), no.3399, 27 September 1982, p.2503

118 FLOTO, Edgardo A. SHALABY, Ahmed A.
Economic integration and Third World collective self-reliance : two papers / preface by Ismail-Sabri Abdalla. - Nyon, Suisse : Third World Forum, 1979. 118p. (Occasional paper / Third World Forum ; 4)
Bibliography: p.83-91

119 FLOTO, Edgardo A.
Towards Third World collective self-reliance. IFDA Dossier (Nyon, Suisse), no.9, July 1979, /16p./

120 FOSTER-CARTER, Aidan
More on self-reliance. Monthly Review (New York), vol.33, no.7, December 1981, p.54-59

121 FROM dependency to development : strategies to overcome underdevelopment and inequality / edited by Heraldo Muñoz. 2nd printing. - Boulder, Colorado : Westview Press, 1982. XV,336p. (Westview special study in social, political and economic development)
Bibliography. Index.
ISBN 0 86531 079 3 pbk

122 GRASS roots of self-reliance in Shramik Sanghatana, Dhulia District, India / by P.V. Paranjape ... /et al./. - Genève : International Labour Office, 1981. 66p. (World employment programme research. Rural employment policy research programme ; 22)

123 GREEN, G.D.
Training for self-reliance in rural areas. International Labour Review (Genève), (120), no.4, Jul./Aug., 1981, p.411-423

Examination of the experience gained from an International Labor Organization (ILO) regional project which is being conducted in East and South Africa under the title of skill development for self-reliance. Main areas involved in training programmes within basic needs strategies. Role of training within the formal education system. Four types of non-formal programmes: craft training centres ; youth-training-cum-production community learning centres ; youth economic groups.

124 GUMATILLEKE, Godfrey
Cooperation for development in South Asia : a programme of sub-regional collective self-reliance. - Colombo : MARGA Institute, 1979. 24p. DDC/SACM/8.Sept.79/IFDA

/Regional cooperation/, /self-reliance/, /development research/, /South Asia/ - /conference report/, /institution building/

125 HAAS, Ernst B.
Technological self-reliance for Latin America : the OAS contribution. International Organization (Madison, Wis.), 34(4), autumn 1980, p.541-570

126 HADŽI VASILEVA, Jokica
Oslonac na sopstvene snage : važan činilac NMEP-a = Self-reliance: an important factor of NIEO. Socijalizam (Beograd), no.7/8, 1978.

127 HASHEMI, Badr
Collective self-reliance through joint industrial projects : case for the Arab countries. - /S.l. : s.n./, 1981, (102p.)
Project RAB/77/010 on behalf of the United Nations (DTCD), New York

128 HETTNE, B.
Development theory and the Third World. - Stockholm : Swedish Agency for Research Cooperation with Developing Countries, 1982. 168p. (SAREC report ; 2/1982)

/Development theory/, /economic thought/, /social sciences/ - /dependence/, /interdependence/, /self-reliance/, /developing countries/.

129 HRISTIČ, E.
Programma kollektivnoj opory na sobstvennye sily (kritičeskij analiz). Mirovaja ekonomika i meždunarodnye otnošenija (Moskva), no.6, 1982, p.120-128

130 ISLAM, Shada
ACP sets goal of self-reliance. South. The Third World Magazine (London), no.5, 15 February-March 1981, p.60. Graph.

Besides discussing with the EEC members the terms of the Lomé Convention the ACP group decides to take positive action in terms of collective self-reliance. However, a number of administrative and financial constraints must be surmounted before the organisation gets into full swing. Figures: 1975-80

ACP African, Caribbean and Pacific States

131 KERIM, Srdjan
Uloga endogenih faktora zemalja u razvoju u uspostavljanju ekonomskog poretka = The role of developing countries' endogenous factors in establishment of NIEO. (Unpublished PhD thesis defended at Economic faculty of Belgrade University). - Beograd : Ekonomski fakultet, 1981. 447p., 349 bibliogr. units.

132 LASSEN, C.A.
Reaching the assetless poor : projects and strategies for their self-reliant development. - Ithaca, N.Y. : Cornell University, Rural Development Committee, 1980. 68p. (Special series on landlessness and near landlessness ; 6)

/Rural population/, (low income/, /self-reliance/, /development strategy/, /aid coordination/ - /aid institutions/, /non-profit organizations/, /interest groups/, /self-help/, /community development/, /development projects/.

133 MACCALL, Brian
The transition toward self-reliance : some thoughts on the role of people's organizations. IFDA Dossier (Nyon, Switzerland), no.22, March/April 1981, p.37-46

134 MANDLE, Jay R.
The politics of self-reliant development. Monthly Review (New York), April 1981

135 MATTHIES, Volker
Kollektive self-reliance. - In: Handbuch der Dritten Welt: Bd 1 : Unterentwicklung, Theorien, Strategien, Indikatoren. - 2.Überarb.und erg.Ausg. - Hamburg : /s.n./, 1982. p.380-394. (Programm Wissenschaft)

136 MOREHOUSE, W.
Disengagement and Third World collaboration : neglected options in mobilizing technology for development : background paper for the Jamaica Symposium on Mobilizing Technology for Development. - Washington, D.C. : IIED, /1979/. 13p.

/Technological change/, /international cooperation/, /dependence/ - /development strategy/, /self-reliance/.

137 MORELLO, Ted
Conceiving a revolution : self-reliant population programmes prove a sound investment as South Asia's baby boom threatens to treble the population. Far Eastern Economic Review (Hongkong), vol.113, no.28, 1981, July 3, p.31

138 MRAK, Mojmir
Nafta in kolektivna naslonitev na lastne sile držav v razvoju = Petroleum and collective self-reliance of the developing countries. - Ljubljana : /s.n./, 1981. X,201p. : tab. (Magistrska dela - Univerza Edvarda Kardelja v Ljubljani, Ekonomska fakulteta Borisa Kidriča ; (8))
Bibliography: p.193-201

139 MÜLLER, J.O.
Kritische Anmerkungen zur Selbsthilfe, Fremdhilfe und Partizipation in fremdbestimmten "Selbsthilfe" : Organisationen der Entwicklungspolitik. Verfassung und Recht in Übersee (Hamburg), 13(3), 1980, p.213-225

140 NIGERIA special report : reaping the whirlwind : the oil boom has drawn attention from the need to ensure that Nigeria is self-sufficient in food. South. The Third World Magazine (London), no.16, February 1982, p.73

141 Un OBJECTIF : l'autosuffisance. Afrique-Asie (Paris), no.280, du 31 octobre 1982, p.65
"Special Madagascar"

Les grandes puissances de l'an 2000 seront-elles capables de nourrir leurs habitants et d'exporter des denrées alimentaires ?...

142 ODELL, P.R.
Latin America's energy prospects. - Rotterdam : Erasmus Universiteit Rotterdam, 1979. 43p. Ill. (Working paper series A / Economisch Geograpfisch Institut ; 79-16)

/Energy sources/, /energy consumption/, /power demand/, /Latin America/ - /petroleum resources/, /natural gas/, /geographic distribution/, /resources exploitation/, /development strategy/, /self-reliance/, /trends/.

143 PATEL, Surendra J.
Collective self-reliance of developing countries. The Journal of Modern African Studies (London), vol.4, 1975

144 PILLAI, Mohanan P.
India and world economy : a search for self-reliance : a comment. Economic and Political Weekly (Bombay), 15(44), 1 Nov., 1980, p.1904-1908

145 PROSPECTS and costs of achieving self-sufficiency in rice production in West Africa by 1990. - Monrovia : WARDA, 1979. 33p. (WARDA/SD/79/15)

/Rice/, /West Africa/ - /plant production/, /food consumption/, /agricultural market/.

WARDA West Africa Rice Development Association

146 RAHMAN, Anisur
Some dimensions of people's participation in the Bhoomi Sena movement : followed by a discussion on the issue. - Geneva : United Nations Research Institute for Social Development, 1981. VI,49p. (Popular participation programme) (UNRISD occasional paper. Report No.2/81)

147 REGIONAL SYMPOSIUM ON ENDOGENOUS INTELLECTUAL CREATIVITY, 2., 1979, México
The Second Regional Symposium on Endogenous Intellectual Creativity : cultural and intellectual creativity in Latin America : a report of proceedings, México City, México, April 1979. - Tokyo : The United Nations University, 1982. 43p. (Human and social development programme document ; 21)

148 RICHARDSON, Ron
Big brother barks : North Korea's proclaimed self-reliance is undercut by detailed evidence published in a Soviet journal. Far Eastern Economic Review (Hong Kong), vol.118, no.49, 1982, p.69-98

149 The ROLE of self-reliance in alternative strategies for development : Pugwash Symposium, Dar-es-Salam, 2-6 June 1975. World Development (Oxford), vol.5, no.3, 1977, p.257-265

150 ROUND TABLE OF ENERGY AND ECONOMIC DEVELOPMENT - STRENGTHENING OF DEVELOPING COUNTRIES' COLLECTIVE SELF-RELIANCE, 8., 1980, Zagreb
Proceedings / Eighth round table on energy and economic development - strengthening of developing countries' collective self-reliance, Zagreb, Yugoslavia, October 20 - 22, 1980. - Zagreb : Institute for Developing Countries, 1981. IX,515p.

151 ROUND TABLE ON SOCIALISM, SCIENCE, TECHNOLOGY, DEVELOPMENT STRATEGIES, 1981, Cavtat, Yugoslavia
Socialism, science, technology, development strategies / Round Table 21-26.09.1981, Cavtat. - Beograd : Medjunarodna tribina socijalizma u svetu, ∠198-/, _vols.

- : Technological self-reliance, development and social progress in developing countries : summary / Gopal Banerjee. 16 leaves

2 : Technology policy and transition towards self-reliance : some basic issues / Dieter Ernst. 32p.

22 : Problemi saradnje medju zemljama u razvoju : problemi civilizacije u strategiji razvoja i transferu nauke i tehnologije / Mounir Chafic.

66 : Development strategies along a self-reliant socialist path : the Ethiopian experience / Zelalem Wakayo. 11 leaves.

152 SADLI, Mohammad
Energy, reforms and the Third World self-reliance. Indonesian Quarterly (Jakarta), 8(4), October 1980, p.5-10

153 SAHADRI, C.V.
Self-reliant development : an IFIAS sponsored study : first status report. - Solna : International Federation of Institutes for Advanced Study, 1981. 144p. Ill.

/Agricultural engineering/, /solar energy/, /methane/, /appropriate technology/, self-reliance/, /rural communities/, /India/ - /renewable resources/, /power demand/, /systems analysis/, /systems design/, /scenarios/, /case studies/, /agroindustry/, progress report/, /statistical tables/, /references/.

154 SELF-RELIANCE als nationale und kollektive Entwicklungsstrategie / Khushi M.Khan (ed.) mit Beiträgen von: M.Bienefeld, Dieter Ernst, Carlos Fortin, Iris Freytag, Reginald H.Green, W.Hein, R.Juttka-Reisse, E.Oteiza u.A.Rahman, R.Shams, P.Streeten, W.v.Urff, K.Wohlmuth. - München : Weltforum, 1980. II,647p. (Weltwirtschaft und internationale Beziehungen: Diskussionsbeiträge ; 20)
ISBN 3 8039 0185 5

... An augmented co-operation among the developing countries (collective self-reliance) seems a possibility not only to remove bottlenecks within individual countries, but also to strengthen the bargaining position against the industrial countries. The contributions to this volume discuss various aspects of self-reliant strategies and analyse the existing empirical evidence.

155 SELF-RELIANCE : a strategy for development / edited by Johan Galtung, Peter O'Brien and Roy Preiswerk. - London : Bogle-L'Ouverture Publications Ltd, 1980. 422p. Published for the Institute for Development Studies, Geneva.
ISBN 0 904521 2006 (pbk)

A reader containing 20 texts on various aspects of self-reliance as a development policy.

156 SENEVIRATNE, Gamini
Economic co-operation among developing countries : new dimensions in the thrust for collective self-reliance. - New York : United Nations, 1980. 47p. (UNCTAD publication)

157 SHIM JAE HOON
Self-help, Seoul style : South Korean officials show the relevance of their village movement to the Asean countryside. Far Eastern Economic Review (Hong Kong), vol.113, no.29, 1981, July 10, p.44

158 SLUMS or self-reliance? : urban growth in Zambia / by H.J. Simons ... /et al./ - Lusaka : University of Zambia, Institute for African Studies, 1976. V,T29p. (Communication / University of Zambia, Institute for African Studies ; 12) Includes bibliographies.

159 SOBHAN, Rehman
OPEC's political options : case for collective self-reliance within the Third World. Alternatives. A journal of world policy (New Delhi), vol.7, no.1, summer 1981, p.43-60

Contents: Introduction. Implications of a redirection of OPEC policies. OPEC and the Third World. OPEC and the North-South dialogue. Conclusion. Notes.

160 SOMALIA : self-sufficiency eludes the settlements / by a special correspondent. AED: Africa Economic Digest (London), vol.2, no.48, December 1981, p.12-13

161 STRENUOUS efforts to achieve self-sufficiency. The Arab Economist (Beirut), vol.13, no.145, October 1981, p.18

162 SUDAN aims at self-sufficiency by 1984. The Arab Economist (Beirut), vol.13, no.147, December 1981, p.45

163 TAN BOCK THIAM
Malaysian food self-sufficiency.- Kuala Lumpur : University of Malaya Agricultural Graduates Alumni, 1976. 353p.

/Agricultural research/, /food supply/, /food production/, /agricultural economics/, self-reliance/, - /agricultural engineering/, /soil sciences/, /conference report/.

164 TECHNOLOGICAL self-reliance of the developing countries : towards operational strategies. - Wien : UNIDO, 1981. 46p. Ill. (Development and transfer of technology series ; 15)

/Technology/, /technology transfer/, /dependence/, /self-reliance/, /development policy/, /technical assistance/, /developing countries/, /foreign ownership/, /science policy/, /international cooperation/.

165 THARP, Mike
For self-reliance in Kim Il Sung's name. <u>Far Eastern Economic Review</u> (Hong Kong), vol.117, no.34, August 20, 1982, p.22

166 TOSTENSEN, Arne
Dependence and collective self-reliance in Southern Africa : the case of the Southern African Development Coordination Conference (SADCC). - Uppsala : Scandinavian Institute of African Studies, 1982. 1970p., 1 map. (Research report ; 62)
Bibliography: p.163
ISBN 91 7106 207 6

167 TOWARDS self-reliance : development, employment and equity issues in Tanzania : report to the Government of Tanzania / by a JASPA Employment Advisory Mission. - Addis Ababa : ILO, Jobs and Skills Programme for Africa, 1978. 259p. Ill.

168 VIDAS, Kazimir
Self-reliance : a precondition for the promotion of new financial and monetary relations. <u>Review of International Affairs</u> (Beograd), nos.656/657, 1977.

169 VOLLAN, Arild
Foreign aid and self-help. <u>Africa Report</u> (New Brunswick, New Jersey), vol. 25, no. 1, January-February 1980, p. 16

170 WILBANKS, Thomas J.
Energy self-sufficiency versus interdependency : implications for regional income distribution. <u>Regional Development Dialogue,</u> vol.2, no.1, Spring 1981, p.78-94

171 ZAITSEV, Nikolaj Grigorijevič
Collective self-reliance and development in Latin America. <u>Development and Peace</u> (Budapest), vol.2, no.2, 1981, p.98-116

III

Developing Countries' Multinational Enterprises

172 CAMACHO OMISTE, Edgar
Tipos de empresas en la integración económica regional : notas sobre el caso de Bolivia. Comercio Exterior (México), vol.32, no.6, junio de 1982, p.591-598

Contents: La gran empresa transnacional. El papel de la inversión extranjera. Apoyo estatal, empresas privadas y empresas públicas nacionales. Nuevas formas de empresas y servicios multinacionales.

173 CHEROL, Rachelle L. NUÑEZ DEL ARCO, José
Empresas multinacionales Andinas : un nuevo enfoque de la inversión multinacional en el Grupo Andino. Integración Latinoamericana (Buenos Aires), año 7, no.73, octubre 1982, p.42-54

Contents: El Acuerdo de Cartagena y una historia del Grupo Andino. Evolución histórica de las empresas multinacionales dentro del Grupo Andino. Elementos de una empresa multinacional (Decisión 46). Tratamiento especial de las empresas multinacionales (Decisión 46). Elementos de la empresa multinacional Andina (Decisión 169). Tratamiento especial a las empresas multinacionales Andinas (Decisión 169). Diferencias entre la Decisión 46 y la Decisión 169. Conclusiones. Bibliografía.

174 DIAZ MÜLLER, Luis
El SELA y las empresas multinacionales latinoamericanas en el marco del desarrollo regional. - México : UNAM, 1981. 113p.

175 EMPRESAS multinacionales latinoamericanas : compendio analítico de las Naciones Unidas / UNCTAD. Secretaría. - Geneva : UNCTAD, 1982. 87p.

176 INDIAN drug MNCs, backs to the wall, adapt and attack. Business Asia (Hongkong), vol.13, no.16, 1981, April 17, p.121

177 LALL, Sanjaya
The emergence of Third World multinationals : Indian joint ventures overseas. World Development (Oxford), vol.10, no.2, 1982, p.127-146

The author summarizes the current state of research in the analysis of LDCs MNCs, drawing upon specific MNC literature and other related literature on trade and technology. He deals with the evidence on Indian capital exports, placing it in the broader context of technology exports, discussing some examples of interest and drawing comparisons with foreign investment by some other LDCs.

178 LALL, Sanjaya
Third World multinationals : the Indian case. - /S.l./ : The Scandinavian Institute of African Studies, 1981. 38p. Bibl.

Presented to: Workshop on the Emergence of South-South Relations in a Changing World Order, 17-20 May 1981, Kungälv

179 LATIN AMERICAN multinational enterprises : an analytical compendium / compiled by the UNCTAD Secretariat. - Genève : UNCTAD, Trade and Development Board, Committee on Economic Co-operation among Developing Countries, 1982. V,77p. (TD/B/C.7/50)

180 LEBEN, Charles
Les modes de coopération entre pays en développement et entreprises multinationales dans le secteur de la production des matières premières minérales. Journal du Droit International (Paris), 107(3), juil./sept., 1980, p.539-604

181 MULTINATIONALS from developing countries / edited by Krishna Kumar, Maxwell G.McLeod. - Lexington Mass. : Lexington Books, 1981. XXV,211p.
Includes bibliography and index.
ISBN 0 669 04113 0

182 SE estableceran las empresas multinacionales andinas. Progreso : comercio-industria-finanzas-desarrollo (México City), June 1982, p.37-38

183 SEMINARIO SOBRE LA ADMINISTRACION Y EL FINANCIAMENTO DE LAS EMPRESAS MULTINACIONALES LATINOAMERICANAS, 1981, Lima
Empresas multinacionales latinoamericanas : versión preliminar /UNCTAD, División de la Cooperación Económica entre Países en Desarrollo. - /S.l./ : UNCTAD, 1981. 116p.

184 SVETLIČIČ, Marjan
Strategija dežel v razvoju do transnacionalnih podjetij in oblikovanje večnacionalnih podjetij dežel v razvoju = The strategy of developing countries towards the transnational enterprises and the establishment of the developing countries' multinational enterprises. Teorija in praksa (Ljubljana), nos 5-6, 1980, p.568-593

185 SVETLIČIČ, Marjan
Strategy and potentials for establishing multinational enterprises of developing countries. - In: International Workshop on the Promotion of Economic and Technical Co-operation among Developing Countries, Bled, 2-7 November 1981. - Ljubljana : Center za proučevanje sodelovanja z deželami v razvoju.

186 WELLS, Louis T.
Technology and Third World multinationals. - Genève : ILO, 1982, 31p. (Multinational Enterprises Programme working papers ; 19)

/Multinational enterprises/, /technology transfer/, /small-scale industry/, /appropriate technology/, /developing countries/, /economic implications/.

IV

Theory of Economic Integration and the Developing Countries

187 ALCALDE CARDOZA, Javier
Integración económica Europea y América Latina. Desarrollo Indoamericano (Barranquilla), 16(68), may-jun 1981, p.29-38

188 BEHRENS, Peter
Integrationstheorie : internationale wirtschaftliche Integration als Gegenstand politologischer, ökonomischer und juristischer Forschung. Rabels Zeitschrift für ausländisches und internationales Privatrecht (Tübingen), 45(1/2), 1981, p.8-50

Summary in English

189 CIZELJ, Boris
Teoretična osnova ekonomske integracije med DVR = Theoretical basis of economic integration among developing countries. - Ljubljana : CPSDR, 1980. 126 leaves.

The study constitutes the 3rd phase of the research project "Economic Co-operation among the Developing Countries", financed by The Research Community of Slovenia.

190 CLINE, William R.
El interés de América Latina en la integración económica. Integración Latinoamericana (Buenos Aires), año 6, no.62, octubre 1981, p.23-33

Contents: Estado de la integración. Base teórica. El contexto de la política. La evidencia acerca de las económias de escala. Un modelo de integración económica latinoamericana. Conclusión.

191 COHEN ORANTES, Isaac
The concept of integration. CEPAL Review (Santiago, Chile), no.15, December 1981, p.143-152

Discussion on economic and political definition of the integration process with regard to recent experience, and to integrationist measures which these two definitions are capable of generating.

192 CONESA, Eduardo R.
Conceptos fundamentales de la integración económica. Integración Latinoamericana (Buenos Aires), año 7, no.71, agosto 1982, p.2-27

Contents: Concepto de "integración". La integración como medio. Zona de preferencias. Zona de libre comercio. Unión aduanera. Mercado común y comunidad económica. La divisón del trabajo. La ventajas comparativas. La igualación de los precios de los factores. Las economías de escala. Economías de escala, planificación y regulación económica. La competencia. Los beneficios de la liberación del comercio. Protección nominal y protección efectiva. La protección efectiva en los países en desarrollo. La protección efectiva en los países desarrollados. Integración económica y tarifa óptima. Protección de industrias incipientes, ventajas comparativas y tarifas óptimas. Creación y desviación de comercio. Creación, desviación de comercio y países de menor grado de desarrollo económico relativo. Economías externas y países de menor grado de desarrollo. La limitación externa. La integración financiera y el ahorro de divisas. El remedio de las devaluaciones y la inflación estructural. La devaluación compensada. La sustitución de importaciones en bienes de capital. Tipos de cambio, tasas de interés e integración financiera. Tipos de cambio fijos o flotantes. Integración fiscal. Epílogo.

193 CONESA, Eduardo R.
La integración financiera de América Latina. Integración Latinoamericana (Buenos Aires), año 7, no.74, noviembre 1982, p.15-20.

/Versión revisada de la disertación en ocasión del "Seminario sobre aspectos monetarios y financieros de la integración en América Latina", organizado por el CEMLA y el INTAL, y llevado a cabo en México los días 25, 26 y 27 de mayo de 1982/.

Contents: La limitación externa. La demanda mundial de exportaciones tradicionales latinoamericanas. Las exportaciones no tradicionales y el endeudamiento externo. La integración financiera y el ahorro de divisas. El remedio de las devaluaciones y la inflación estructural. La devaluación compensada. La integración latinoamericana y el arancel óptimo de importación. Los subsidios a la exportación no tradicional hacia extrazona. La sustitución de importaciones en bienes de capital. Tipos de cambio, tasas de interés e integración financiera. Las razones políticas para la integración.

194 CONESA, Eduardo R.
Las nuevas formas institucionales de la integración latinoamericana. Integración Latinoamericana (Buenos Aires), año 7, no.73, octubre 1982, p.55-68

Contents: La integración: ayer, una opción. La integración: hoy, una necesidad. Los problemas: de la ALALC, del Grupo Andino, del Mercado Común Centroamericano. El margen de preferencia: arancelario. El margen de preferencia y su generalidad. Margen de preferencia y reprocidad. Margen de preferencia y soberanía tarifaria. Proyección centroamericana. Posibilidad del "veto" al margen de preferencia. El margen de preferencia y el GATT. Margen de preferencia y gradualismo. Estructura arancelaria y dependencia. Las acciones parciales. La integración y el sistema de precios. La regulación del problema de los países de menor desarrollo económico relativo. Las economías externas. El fundamento de la protección en América Latina. Cómo comenzar a implementar una tarifa externa mínima común.

195 ETIENNE, Henri
Community integration : the external environment. Journal of Common Market Studies (Oxford), vol.18(4), 1980, June, p.289-312

196 FRANCK, Tom
Why Federations fail. - New Haven : Yale University Press. /1969/.

Covers: East Africa, Malaysia, Central Africa

197 HARBORTH, Hans Jürgen
Anforderungen an eine revidierte Integrationstheorie für Entwicklungsländer. In: Integration der Entwicklungsländer in eine instabile Weltwirtschaft : Probleme, Chancen, Gefahren / hrsg. W. von Urff. - Berlin : /s.n./, 1976. 65p.

198 INFLATION, development and integration : essays in honour of A.J. Brown / edited by J.K. Bowers. - Leeds, England : Leeds University Press, 1979. VII,304p. Ill.

"Arthur Joseph Brown :a professional biography and bibliography": p.295-304. Bibliographical references.

199 INTEGRATIONS régionales entre pays en voie de développement / Joseph Jamar éditeur ; Manuel Alcantara Saez, Brigid Burns, Dominique Delaunay et Joseph Jamar ; préface Jerzy Lukaszewski. - Bruges : De Tempel, 1982. XX,274p. Ill. Tabs. (Cahiers de Bruges ; 41)

200 INTER-REGIONAL MEETING ON DEVELOPMENT RESEARCH, COMMUNICATION AND EDUCATION, 2nd, 1979, Bogotá, Colombia
Second inter-regional meeting on development research, communication ... : inter-regional co-operation in the social sciences for development, 5-8 June 1979, Bogotà. - /Paris/ : OECD Development Centre, 1980. (Liaison Bulletin between Development and Training Institutes. New Series ; 5)

Part III-2:
Mohamed Ariff: Regional economic co-operation: the ASEAN experiment, p.67-74
Eduardo R.Conesa:The experiences of integration in Latin America in the 1980 decade, p.75-86
Makhtar Diouf: Approaches to economic integration in Black Africa: assessment and suggestions, p.87-97
Helen O'Neill: Regional integration and co-operation, p.97-106
Sakr Ahmed Sakr: Economic integration and co-operation among the Arab countries, p.107-112

201 KEITEL, Hanna
Zur Theorie der regionalen Wirtschaftsintegration von Entwicklungsländern. - Heidelberg : Esprint, 1982. 161p. (Heidelberger Dritte-Welt-Studien ; 6)
ISBN 3 88326 123 8

202 LANGHAMMER, Rolf J.
"Ungleich" verteilte Kosten und Nutzen aus der regionalen Integration zwischen Entwicklungsländern : Erscheinungsbild und Bewältigungsversuche dargestellt am Beispiel der Zentralafrikanischen Zoll- und Wirtschaftsunion /UDEAC/. - Kiel : Institut für Weltwirtschaft, 1975. - 38p. (Kieler Arbeitspapiere ; 32)

203 LEDESMA, Joaquin R.
La teoría de la integración y la Asociación Latinoamericana de Libre Comercio. - Buenos Aires : Fundación para el Estudio de los Problemos Argentinos, /between 1979 and 1981/. 31,15p. (Documento de trabajo ; 18)

204 MILETA, Vlatko
Tipologija i struktura medjunarodnih ekonomskih integracija = Characteristics and structure of international economic integration. Politička misao (Zagreb), vol.18, no.4, p.139-154

205 VACCHINO, Juan Mario
Integración económica regional. - Caracas : Universidad Central de Venezuela, Facultad de Ciencias Juridicas y Politicas, Instituto de Derecho Publico Seccion Integración, 1981. 602p.

206 YOTOPOULOS, Pan.A. NUGENT, Jeffrey B.
Economic integration with special reference to customs unions. - New York : Harper and Row, 1976.

In ch. 19: Economics of development : empirical investigations

CEPAL	Comisión Económica para América Latina, Santiago de Chile
CPSDvR	Center za proučevanje sodelovanja z deželami v razvoju = Research Centre for Co-operation with Developing Countries (RCCDC), Ljubljana

V

Movement of Non-aligned Countries

207 ALGÉRIE : bilan satisfaisant du voyage présidentiel en Yougoslavie, Inde et Chine : les pays non-alignés appelés à renforcer leur cohésion. Marchés Tropicaux et Mediterranéens (Paris), 38e année, no.1904, vendredi 7 mai 1982, p.1200

208 ALTMAN, Gavro
The evolution of Yugoslavia's non-aligned foreign policy. Socialist Thought and Practice (Beograd), vol.21, no.4, 1981, p.63-79

"The principles and practice of Yugoslavia's foreign policy do not serve to preserve the prevailing state of affairs, but are in the service of development, internal and international," concludes this Yugoslav writer.

209 ANTIĆ, Zdenko
Yugoslavia celebrates 20 years of non-alignment. Munich Radio Free Europe (München), 1981. 5p. (Radio Free Europe. Research: RAD background report/257 (Yugoslavia)

"During the past 20 years, nonalignment has served as the cornerstone of Yugoslavia's foreign policy ... By pursuing this policy, Yugoslavia has certainly achieved a series of successes and was able to play a role on the world scene far beyond its economic capabilities or military potential ..."

210 ATE, Bassey M.
La no-alineación, el sistema internacional y la lucha contra el colonialismo y el racismo. Política internacional (Beograd), 32(756), 5 oct. 1981, p.9-11

211 AZIZ, Tarek
"Bagdad accueillera le 7e sommet des non-alignés en septembre, comme prévue" / un entretien de Simon Malley avec le premier vice-premier ministre irakien. Afrique-Asie (Paris), no.263, du 12 au 25 avril, 1982, p.8

212 AZIZ, Tarek
"Un nouvel élan est nécessaire pour le mouvement des non-alignés ; Bagdad reconstruira de nouvelles centrales nucléaires ; Il n'y a pas de frontières à l'esprit expansionniste d'Israël" / un entretien de Simon Malley avec le premier vice-président irakien. Afrique-Asie (Paris), no.264, du 26 avril au 9 mai, 1982, p.12

213 AZIZ, Tarek
"We are optimists" : a Ba'th Arab Socialist Party leader sees a revolution ahead against Sadat in Egypt and discusses the situation in Iraq. Third World (México City), no.3, 1979, p.34
Special issue

Earthquake ahead? What is democracy? Moving fast. /6th Summit of non-aligned countries, Havana/

214 BALOGH, András
The non-aligned movement : its evolution and current issues. Development and Peace (Budapest), 1(2), autumn 1980, p.191-199

215 BEN YAHMED, Bechir
Mort d'un système. Jeune Afrique (Paris), 22e année, no.1125, août 1982, p.26

216 BENACHENHOU, Abdellatif
For autonomous development in the Third World. Monthly Review (New York), July/August, 1980, p.43-52

217 BENACHENHOU, Abdellatif
Le tiers-monde en jeu. - Paris : CREA (Centre de Recherches en Economie Appliquée), 1981. 217p., tab.

218 BENKO, Vlado
Dejavnost neuvrščenih držav v organizaciji Združenih narodov = The activity of non-aligned countries in the Organization of the United Nations : part 1. - Ljubljana : FSNP, Raziskovalni Inštitut : Center za politološke raziskave, 1979. 155p.

219 BERENGER, Paul
Nous voulons construire le socialisme dans le cadre d'un non-alignement engagé au côté des peuples / un entretien réalisé par Devi Tolwal. Afrique-Asie (Paris), no.256, du 4 au 17 janvier, 1982, p.33

220 BOGETIĆ, Dragan
Nesvrstani i novi medjunarodni ekonomski poredak = The non-aligned and the new international economic order. Marksistička misao (Beograd), no.1, 1979

221 BONDAREVSKIJ, Grigorij L. SOFINSKY, Vsevolod
Non-alignment : its friends and adversaries in world politics. - Moskva : "Social Sciences Today" Editorial Board, USSR Academy of Science, 1978. 107p.
(Problems of the contemporary world ; 63)
Includes bibliographical references.

222 BROZ, Josip
The historical mission of non-alignment. - Beograd : Komunist, 1979.

223 BROZ, Josip
Non-alignment : the conscience and future of mankind : (speeches delivered at all six summit conferences of the non-aligned countries). - Beograd : Komunist, 1979.

224 BROZ, Josip
Non-alignment : a lasting need of mankind. Socialist Thought and Practice (Beograd), vol.18, no.7/8, 1978.

225 BROZ, Josip
Non-alignment : a united and independent factor in world politics. Socialist Thought and Practice (Beograd), vol.18, no.7/8, 1978.

226 BULAJIĆ, Krsto
Cooperation among non-aligned countries. Review of International Affairs (Beograd), no.717, 1980.

227 /CASTRO, Fidel/
"Our movement is more united than ever" : full text of the speech delivered by the President Fidel Castro at the closing session of the 6th Summit Conference /of non-aligned countries, Havana 1979/. Third World (México City), no.3, 1979, p.51. Special issue.

228 /CASTRO, Fidel/
Peace and new economic order. Third World (México City), no.3, 1979, p.18. Special issue.

At the opening session of the 6th Summit Conference, President Fidel Castro addressed the major issues before the non-aligned movement: peace for all peoples; on under-development; economic co-operation and solidarity.

229 CHANDA, Nayan
A feeler to the non-aligned : the Heng Samrin regime hopes Third World observers will visit Kampuchea and boost its international standing. Far Eastern Economic Review (Hongkong), vol.111, no.5, 1981, Jan. 23, p.9

230 CONFERENCE OF MINISTERS FOR FOREIGN AFFAIRS OF NON-ALIGNED COUNTRIES, 1978, Beograd
Basic documents / Conference of Ministers of Foreign Affairs of Non-Aligned Countries, Belgrade, July 25-30, 1978. - Belgrade : Federal Secretariat for Foreign Affairs, 1978. 155p.

231 CONFERENCE OF STATE HEADS OF NON-ALIGNED COUNTRIES, 6., 1979, Havana
Govori, dokumenti, resolucije = speeches, documents, resolutions / Šesta konferenca voditeljev neuvrščenih držav v Havani. - Ljubljana : Komunist, 1979. 256p.

232 CONFERENCE ON THE ROLE OF WOMEN IN DEVELOPMENT OF NON-ALIGNED AND OTHER DEVELOPING COUNTRIES, 1979, Bagdad
Final report / Conference on the Role of Women in Development of Non-aligned and Other Developing Countries, Baghdad, 6-13 May 1979. - /Baghdad/: General Federation of Iraqi Women, Secretariat of Studies and Researches, /1979/. 69p. Ill.

233 CONFERENCIA DE JEFES DE ESTATO O DE GOBIERNO DE LOS PAISES NO ALINEADOS, 6., 1979, La Habana
Discursos pronunciados en la 6. Conferencia de Jefes de Estado o de Gobierno de los países no alineados, La Habana, 3-9 septiembre 1979. - La Habana : Ed. de Ciencias Sociales, 1980. 1005p. Ill.

234 ČUŠIĆ, Mićo
The freedom, independence and integrity of non-aligned countries. - Beograd : Komunist, 1979.

235 DAKOVIĆ, Vojin
Blokovi, detant i nesvrstanost = Blocks, détente and non-alignment. Zbornik trećeg programa Radio Zagreba (Zagreb), no.1, 1977.

236 DAVIDSON, Nicol
The non-aligned group in the Security Council. Review of International Affairs (Beograd), no.717, 1980.

237 DEGAN, Vladimir
Temeljna načela medjunarodnog prava u politici nesvrstanih zemalja = Basic principles of international law in the policy of non-aligned countries. Zbornik trećeg programa Radio Zagreba (Zagreb), no.1, 1977.

238 DIALLO, Siradiou
La déprime : les vieux slogans, auxquels plus personne ne croit, parviennent mal à cacher la profonde division du mouvement. Jeune Afrique (Paris), no.1051, 25 février 1981, p.30-31

239 DINIĆ, Jordan
DPR of Korea and non-alignment. Review of International Affairs (Beograd), no.710, 1979.

240 DJAIDER, Kamel
Option Sud-Sud. Afrique-Asie (Paris), no.265, du 16 au 23 mai, 1982, p.17

Les non-alignés tentés par le "recentrage" ou la "neutralité négative" ? Certains le pensent. D'où la tournée du président Chadli pour relancer les principes directeurs du mouvement à la veille du sommet de Bagdad.

241 DJILAS, Aleksa
Yugoslavia after non-alignment : which way to turn. New Leader (New York), vol.64, Apr.6, 1981, p.7-9

"Although one would be wrong to equate Yugoslav communism with stalinism, it has nevertheless been an ideology with global intentions. ... Non-alignment was Tito's chosen method for spreading his revolution and gospel while at the same time remaining separate from the Soviet Union. ... The pulling apart of non-alignment has forced Yugoslavia-- albeit against its will--to return to itself, its own problems and its own interests".

242 DJUROVIĆ-BOGETIĆ, Olivera
Savremena kretanja u pokretu nesvrstanih = Contemporary trends in the non-alignment movement. Marksistička misao (Beograd), no.5, 1979.

243 DOZET, Dušan
Resistance to force : the historical basis of non-alignment. Socialist Thought and Practice (Beograd), no.9, 1979.

244 DROMNJAK, Miloš
Politika i pokret nesvrstavanja 1961-1979. = Politics and movement of non-alignment. - Beograd : Jugoslovenska stvarnost, Medjunarodna politika, 1979.

245 DRUŠTVENE snage jugoslovenske politike nesvrstanosti : naučno politička rasprava / urednici: Zoran Stojilković, Dobrica Vulović, Slobodan Stefanović. - Beograd : Centar za marksizam univerziteta u Beogradu, Marksistički centar organizacije SK u Beogradu, 1982. 204p.

246 EAST TIMOR : not forgotten. Third World (México City), no.3, 1979, p.41. Special issue
/6th Summit of non-aligned countries, Havana/

247 EXTRAORDINARY MINISTERIAL MEETING OF THE CO-ORDINATING BUREAU OF NON-ALIGNED COUNTRIES, 1979, Maputo
Extraordinary Ministerial Meeting of the Co-ordinating Bureau of Non-Aligned Countries, Maputo, 26 January-2 February, 1979. Review of International Affairs (Beograd), no.693, 1979.

248 FERNANDO, B.J.
The non-aligned movement : democratic in spirit and practice. Review of International Affairs (Beograd), no.716, 1980.

249 The FINAL declaration : the Havana Declaration sums up the progress of previous summits and sets forth decisive political and economic definitions for the non-aligned movement : document. Third World (México City), no.3, November 1979, p.53. Special issue

250 FROM Bandung to Colombo : conferences of the non-aligned countries, 1955-75. / edited with commentary by A.W. Singham and Tran Van Dinh. - New York : Third World Press Review of Books Company, 1976. 223p.

251 FURTAK, Robert K.
Lateinamerika und die Bewegung der Blockfreien : zur Frage einer Solidarisierung Lateinamerikas mit Asien und Afrika. - Hamburg : Institut für Iberoamerika-Kunde, 1980. 84p. (Arbeitsunterlagen und Diskussionsbeiträge / Institut Iberoamerika-Kunde ; 9)
Bibliography: p.66-74

252 GABON : visite du président yougoslave. Marchés Tropicaux et Méditerranéens (Paris), 38 année, no.1898, vendredi 26 mars 1982, p.857

253 GARCÍA, Inés ANDRIANZÉN, Alberto
No alineados : nueva fuerza internacional? - Lima : DESCO, Centro de Estudios y Promoción del Desarrollo, 1980. 172p. (Praxis / Centro de Estudios y Promoción del Desarrollo ; 15)
Includes bibliographical references.

254 GOLARD, Daniel
Le mouvement des pays non-alignés. - Paris : La Documentation Française, 1981. 168p. Tabl. (Notes et études documentaires ; 4613-4614)

255 GOLOB, Franc
El no-alineamiento y la distensión. Política internacional (Beograd), 32(756), 5 oct. 1981, p.21-24

256 GONČAROVA, Tatiana
Aspectos políticos e ideológicos del movimiento de países no alineados. América Latina (Moskva), vol.55, no.10, oct. 1982, p.42-54

257 GORDEEV, V.
Forum v Deli. Novoe vremja (Moskva), no.8, 1981, p.8-9
Concerns the non-aligned conference at New Delhi.

258 GRLIČKOV, Aleksandar
The non-aligned movement aspires to national independence and equality in international relations. Socialist Thought and Practice (Beograd), no.9, 1979.

259 GRLIČKOV, Aleksandar
Non-alignment and socialism as a world process. - Beograd : Komunist, 1979. 51p.

260 HUSSEIN, Saddam
Arab Unity will be achieved : the president of Iraq talks about Arab-Latin American relations, Arab Unity and the Iranian revolution. Third World (México City), no.3, 1979, p.32
Special issue. - /Sixth Summit of non-aligned countries, Havana/

261 JANKOWITSCH, Odette SAUVANT, Karl P.
The initiating role of the non-aligned countries. In: Changing priorities on the international agenda : the New International Economic Order / ed. Karl P. Sauvant. - Oxford : Pergamon, 1980

262 JEVREMOVIĆ, Pavle
Ideološka i politička strujanja u pokretu nesvrstanih = Ideological and political trends in the movement of non-aligned countries. Marksistička misao (Beograd), br. 6, 1980.

263 JEVREMOVIĆ, Pavle VLAHOVIĆ, Milena
Yugoslavia at meetings of non-aligned countries held between the fifth and sixth conferences of heads of state or government. Yugoslav Survey (Beograd), vol.20, no.4, 1979.

264 JOB, Cvijeto
Non-aligned consistently oppose all interference and intervention. Review of International Affairs (Beograd), no.719, 1980.

265 KAPETANOVIĆ, Goran
Non-alignment and the CSCE meeting in Madrid. Review of International Affairs (Beograd), 32(747), 20 May 1981, p.24-26

266 KEENLEYSIDE, T.A.
Prelude to power : the meaning of non-alignment before Indian independence. Pacific Affairs (Vancouver), fall 1980, p.461-483

267 KIM IL SUNG
The non-alignment movement is a mighty anti-imperialist revolutionary force of our times. - Pyongyang, Korea : Foreign Languages Publishing House, 1976. 322p. Portr. (No. 69487)

268 KIM, Young C.
North Korea in 1980 : the son also rises. Asian Survey (Berkeley, Ca.), vol.21, no.1, 1981, Jan., p.112-124

269 KLJUN, Edvard
The non-aligned countries and nuclear energy. Review of International Affairs (Beograd), no.731, 1980.

270 KLJUN, Edvard
Peacetime utilization of nuclear energy : cooperation among the non-aligned countries. Review of International Affairs (Beograd), no.689, 1978.

271 KOMATINA, Miljan
The messages of New Delhi : freedom and independence essential for peace and security. Review of International Affairs (Beograd), 32(741), 20 February 1982, p.1-4

272 KOMATINA, Miljan
Non-alignment : a factor of international stability. Review of International Affairs (Beograd), no.668, 1978.

273 KOMATINA, Miljan
Non-alignment : an independent global force. Review of International Affairs (Beograd), no.700, 1979

274 KOMATINA, Miljan
La política y el movimiento de los no alineados cara a las Naciones Unidas. Política International (Beograd), 32(756), 5 oct. 1981, p.11-14

275 KONFERENCIJA MINISTARA INOSTRANIH POSLOVA NESVRSTANIH ZEMALJA = Ministerial conference of foreign affairs of non-aligned countries, 1981, New Delhi
Konferencija ministara inostranih poslova nesvrstanih zemalja, Nju Delhi, 9-13. februara 1981. - Beograd : Medjunarodna politika, 1981. p.11-47

276 KONFERENCIJA RADIODIFUZNIH ORGANIZACIJA NESVRSTANIH ZEMALJA = Conference of broadcasting organizations of non-aligned countries, 2., 1980, Freetown
Druga konferencija radiodifuznih organizacija nesvrstanih zemalja, Fritaun, Sijera Leone, 1980. - Beograd : Jugoslovenska radiotelevizija, (1980), 105p.

277 KRIMS, Adalbert
Die Bewegung der blockfreien Staaten. Neue Entwicklungspolitik (Wien), H. 3, 1976

278 KURJAK, Jelica
SSSR i ostale zemlje "socijalističke zajednice" o nesvrstanosti = The USSR and other countries of the "Socialist Community" on the non-alignment. - Beograd : Institut za medjunarodnu politiku i privredu, 1981. 34 leaves

279 LIBERATION movements. Third World (México City), no.3, 1979, p.39
Special issue. /The Sixth Summit of non-aligned countries, Habana/

PLO = Palestine Liberation Organization. SWAPO = South-West African Popular Organization. Zimbabwe Patriotic Liberation Front. FRETILIN = Timorese National Liberation Front. Western Sahara's Polisario Front.

280 LIKANG, Jan
La no-alineación : factor global fuera de bloques e independiente. Política Internacional (Beograd), 32(756), 5 oct. 1981, p.15-16

281 LUKIĆ, Slobodan
The non-aligned movement and national emancipation. - Beograd : Komunist, 1979.

282 MADELEY, John
Ministers move towards unity. West Africa (London), no.3319, 9 March 1981, p.469

283 MAIRA, Luis
Latin America : strong presence at the /6th/ summit of /non aligned countries/ : the Havana Summit leaves only Chile, Guatemala, Honduras and Paraguay outside looking in. Third World (México City), no.3, 1979, p.20
Special issue.

284 MANLEY, Michael
The politics of affirmation : inaugural third world lecture, 1979. - London : Third World Foundation, 1979. 20p. (Third World Foundation monograph ; 1)
ISBN 0 906041 08 2

285 MAROVIĆ, Miodrag
Divisive attempts in non-aligned movement. - Beograd : Komunist, 1979.

286 MATES, Leo
Cometido de los fundadores en el movimiento de los países no alineados. Política Internacional (Beograd), 32(756), 5 oct. 1981, p.17-21

287 MEDJUNARODNI okrugli sto "Politika i pokret nesvrstanosti u osamdesetim godinama", 28-31. avgust 1981, Petrovaradin, Jugoslavija = International round table on "Politics and Movement of Non-aligned Countries". - /S.l. : s.n./, 1981. (various pagings)

Medjunarodni ekonomski odnosi i politička dimenzija produbljavanja jaza izmedju razvijenih i zemalja u razvoju / Ljubiša S. Adamović. 12p. Sudbina "detanta" / Gavro Altman. 11p. Legitimation patterns of the foreign military presence / Osmo Apunen. 13p. Non-alignment, the international system, and the struggle against colonialism and racism / Ate Bassey M. 10p. Razvoj odnosa izmedju velikih sila i blokovskih grupacija i reperkusije na položaj i delovanje nesvrstanih zemalja / Dimče Belovski. 11p. Nesvrstanost i problemi mira i bezbednosti na opštem svetskom planu / Vlado Benko. 16p. Developing countries' greater collective self-reliance / Boris Cizelj. 19p. Rješavanje sporova i sukoba u krilu pokreta nesvrstanih / Djuro Vladimir Degan. 12p. Strategija i taktika nesvrstanih i drugih ZUR-a u borbi za novi medjunarodni ekonomski poredak / Božidar Frangeš. 13p. Nesvrstanost i detant / Ignac Golob. 6p. Non-alignment : the need for self-scrutiny / Shaukat Hassan. 10p. Nesvrstanost i novi medjunarodni informativni poredak / Pero Ivačić. 28p. Non-alignment and its support to the conflict between north and south / Edgardo Mercado Jarren. 10p. Politika i pokret nesvrstanosti i ujedinjene nacije / Miljan Komatina. 9p. Uloga osnivača u pokretu nesvrstanosti zemalja / Leo Mates. 11p. Non-alignment and some prospective development during the '80's / K.P. Misra. 9p. Izvorni principi nesvrstanosti-nesvrstanost kao nezavisan, vanblokovski i globalni faktor u medjunarodnim odnosima / Ranko Petković. 14p. A few remarks concerning non-alignment policy and movement in the struggle for ensuring international peace, for promoting security in the world, for solving international problems in 80's / Cristian Popisteanu. 12p. The future of the non-aligned movement / Bimal Prasad. 11p. Institutionalism of the non-aligned movement : a conceptual approach / Robin Remington. 20p. Non-alignment and new international economic order / Dinesh Singh. 10p. The future of non-alignment / A.W. Singham. 31p. Non-alignment and the new international economic order / Janez Stanovnik. 17p. Kontinuitet i evolucija u borbi nesvrstanih i drugih zemalja u razvoju za nove medjunarodne ekonomske odnose / Rikard Štajner. 20p. Položaj pokreta nesvrstanosti i njegove dileme u savremenim uslovima / Bojana Tadić. 10p. Non-alignement et nouvel ordre international : perspectives. (Conclusion du rapport) / Tarajallah Boutros Samaan. 13p. Policy of non-alignment: struggle for the new international economic order and the role of women in development / Vida Tomšič. 20p. Possibilities for promoting mutual co-operation of non-aligned and other developing countries on the basis of the principle of collective self-reliance / Anton Vratuša. 13p. Konflikti medju nesvrstanim zemljama i mogućnosti njihovog rješavanja / Radovan Vukadinović. 13p. Strengthening the influence and effectiveness of the policy and movement of non-alignment / Peter Willets. 18p. List of participants.

288 MIČIĆ, Zdravko
The movement and policy of non-alignment. - Beograd : Komunist, 1979.

289 MILJUŠ, Brano
Nesvrstanost socijalističke Jugoslavije = Non-alignment of the socialist Yugoslavia. - Sarajevo : Oslobodjenje, 1977. 210p.

290 MINIĆ, Miloš
The forceful presence of the non-alignment in the world. Review of International Affairs (Beograd), vol.31, no.737, December 1980, p.1-5

291 MINIĆ, Miloš
Twenty years since the Belgrade Conference of non-aligned countries. Socialist Thought and Practice (Beograd), vol.21, Sept. 1981, p.5-21

Foresees a rising importance of the non-alignment movement with the deterioration of international relations involving two blocks alignments.

292 MINIĆ, Miloš
Unity of the authentic principles of non-alignemnt. Socialist Thought and Practice (Beograd), vol.20, no.1, 1980

293 MISHRA, Pramod Kumar
Burma's farewell to the non-aligned movement. Asian Affairs (New York), 12(pt.1), Febr. 1981, p.49-56
Includes bibliographical references.

294 MOREIRA, Neiva BISSIO, Beatriz
The nonaligned summit /Havana, September 1979/ : gathering together nearly one hundred countries and liberation movements which represent two thirds of humanity, the non-aligned movement reaffirms its vocation for unity to meet the challenges of our time. Third World (México City), no.3, 1979, p.8
Special issue

Contents: David and Frederick /hurricanes/. Tito and Castro. Egypt : under surveillance, (from the Final Declaration of the 6th Summit). Soviet plot unmasked. Kampuchea: an empty seat, (from the Final Declaration of the 6th Summit). Torpedos vs. aseptic handouts. Fighting the poison. Windy speeches. Empty seats. The case of Egypt. Scrambled history. Tito agrees. Sticking to principles. Radicalization. Bombs or people.

295 MOUSSA, Hichem
La nécessité d'un véritable non-alignement. Afrique-Asie (Paris), no.275, du 16 au 29 août, 1982, p.32

296 MUJEZINOVIĆ, Dževad
The non-aligned countries at the beginning of the 35th UN General Assembly session. Review of International Affairs (Beograd), vol.31, no.733, October 1980, p.10-13

297 NARAYANAN, K.R.
Non-alignment, independence and national interests. Review of International Affairs (Beograd), no.731, 1980

298 NAYAR, Kuldip
The Chinese view of the Third World : Han Nian-long, China's first deputy foreign minister, speaks to South about his country's role in the Third World. South. Third World Magazine (London), no.16, February 1982, p.31

... "We have declared ourselves a Third World country and we support the five principles of non-alignment..."

299 NESVRSTANI od Beograda do Beograda = The non-aligned from Belgrade to Belgrade. - Beograd : Tanjug, 1979.- . - vols. - (Svet nesvrstanih : tematsko izdanje)

Cover title: Dokumentarna hronika o stvaranju i delovanju pokreta nesvrstavanja = Documentary chronicle on the establishment and activity of the non-aligned movement.

Vol.1 - XII,291p.
Vol.2 - VI,294p.
Vol.3 - Vi,250p.

300 NESVRSTANI u Havani = The non-aligned in Habana. - Beograd : Tanjug, 1981. XIII,383p. (Svet nesvrstanih)

Dokumentarna hronika o šestoj konferenciji šefova država ili vlada nesvrstanih zemalja 3-9. septembra 1979. = Documental chronology on the third Conference of the State Heads or non-aligned countries' governments, 3-9. September 1979, Habana.

301 NESVRSTANI u Nju Delhiju = The non-aligned in New Delhi : twenty years since Belgrade. - Beograd : Tanjug, 1981. (Svet nesvrstanih ; 149, 248, 250)

302 The NEW Caribbean speaks : two strong voices at the /6th/ Summit reflect to change : Manley /Michael/ of Jamaica and Maurice Bishop of Grenada. Third World (México City), no.3, 1979, p.25
Special issue.

303 La NO-ALINEACION y el nuevo orden económico internacional : simposio Yugoslavo-Mexicano, 8-10 de noviembre de 1982. - México : CEESTEM (Centro de Estudios Económicos y Sociales del Tercer Mundo), 1982.

304 NON-ALIGNED countries push for action. AED : Africa Economic Digest (London), vol.2, no.8, February 1981, p.11

305 The NON-ALIGNED movement in World politics / edited by R.S. Smith. - Westport, Connecticut : Lawrence Hill, 1977

306 NON-ALIGNED Nicaragua : fifty years later, in Havana quite different from that of 1928, the assembly of states and peoples responds to Sandino's dramatic call. Third World (México City), no.3, 1979, p.28. - (/The 6th Summit of Non-Aligned Countries, Habana/)

/Sandino, Cesar Augusto, 1893-1934, Nicaraguan guerilla leader, one of the most controversial figures of recent Central American history/.

307 NON-ALIGNES : retour aux sources. Jeune Afrique (Paris), 22e année, no.1133, 22 septembre 1982, p.15

308 NON-ALIGNMENT in contemporary international relations / K.P. Misra, K.R. Narayanan eds. - New Delhi : Jawaharlal Nehru University, 1981. 285p.

309 NON-ALIGNMENT a victim? West Africa (London), no.3343, 24 August 1981, p.1922-1923

310 NOVAK, Andrej
The non-aligned in the 1980s. Socialist Thought and Practice (Beograd), 20(7/8), July/August 1980, p.68-93

311 NYERERE, Julius
A definition of non-alignment : "it is entirely consistent with the principles of non-alignment to respond to a plea for aid, including military aid". Third World (México), no.3, 1979, p.42
Special issue.

312 OGUNBADEJO, Oye
Non-alignment in Africa's international relations : the case of Angola. The Jerusalem Journal of International Relations (Jerusalem), 5(2), 1981, p.16-45
Includes bibliographical references.

313 PEDRONCINI, Alberto
Peaceful co-existence, the arms race and non-alignment. Review of Contemporary Law (Bruxelles), no.1, 1981, p.9-29

314 PETKOVIĆ, Ranko
Indo-Yugoslav symposium of non-alignment. Review of International Affairs (Beograd), no.724, 1980

315 PETKOVIĆ, Ranko
Kina i nesvrstanost = China and non-alignment. - Politička misao (Zagreb), no.4, 1974

316 PETKOVIĆ, Ranko
The lessons and impact of the Sixth Conference of Non-aligned Countries. Review of International Affairs (Beograd), no.708, 1979

317 PETKOVIĆ, Ranko
Nesvrstanost : nezavisan, vanblokovski i globalni faktor u medjunarodnim odnosima = Non-alignment : an independent, non-aligned and global factor of the international relations. - Zagreb : Školska knjiga, 1981. 230p. (Suvremena misao)

318 PETKOVIĆ, Ranko
Non-alignment : an independent factor in the democratization of international relations. - Beograd : Komunist, 1979.

319 PETKOVIĆ, Ranko
Oružani sukobi medju nesvrstanim zemljama = Armed conflicts among non-aligned countries. - Politička misao (Zagreb), no.4, 1980.

320 PETKOVIĆ, Ranko
Velike sile i politika nesvrstavanja = Great powers and policy of non-alignment. - Zagreb : Centar za kulturnu djelatnost SSO, 1979. 187p.

321 QURESHI, Y.
Non-aligned foreign Ministers' Conference : Delhi 1981. Pakistan Horizon (Karachi), vol.34, no.2, 1981

322 RAJAN, M.S.
Non-alignment : the dichotomy between theory and practice in perspective. India Quarterly (New Delhi), 36(1), Jan./March 1980, p.43-67
Includes bibliographical references.

323 RAM, Mohan
An echo from the Caribbean : acting blatantly in support of Moscow, Cuba attempts to sway the non-aligned movement on the Gulf issue. Far Eastern Economic Review (Hong Kong), vol.111, no.1, 1980, Dec. 26, p.16

324 REMINGTON, Robin Alison
Non-alignment as ideological transfer : the North-South dialogue. Indian Journal of Political Science (New Delhi), vol.41, no.3, 1980.

325 LA REUNION DES MINISTRES DES AFFAIRES ETRANGERES DES NON-ALIGNES, 1981, New Delhi
Désunion politique, union dans la dénonciation de l'ordre économique mondial / La réunion des ministres des affaires étrangères des non-alignés, (Nouvelle-Delhi), 6-12 février 1981). Marchés Tropicaux et Méditerranéens (Paris), 37e année, no.1840, vendredi 13 février 1981, p.347

326 SAMORA, Machel
"We must create our own future" : the president of Mosambique affirms that the emergence of socialist countries is precisely what changed the balance of power in favor of the Third World. Third World (México City), no.3, 1979, p.36
Special issue. /the Sixth Summit of non-aligned countries, Habana/.

327 SATHYAMURTHY, T.V.
Tanzania's non-aligned role in international relations. India Quarterly (New Delhi), vo.37, no.1, 1981

328 SAUVANT, Karl P.
Characteristics and availability of the documentation of the non-aligned countries and the Group of 77 : paper to be presented to the "Second World Symposium on International Documentation", Brussels, June, 1980.

329 SAVIĆ, Branko
Yugoslavia in the struggle for action unity in the non-alignment movement. - Beograd : Komunist, 1979.

330 SAXENA, Munish N.
La no-alineación en los años 80. - Moskva : Nóvosti, 1982. 66p.

331 SENGUPTA, Iyoti
Non-alignment : search for the destination. - Calcutta : Naya Prokash, 1979.

332 The SIXTH Summit of non-aligned countries /Habana/ : special reports. Third World (MéxicoCity), no.3, 1979. p.4-61
Special issue.

333 SMOLE, Jože
No-alineación y progreso social. Política Internacional (Beograd), 32(756), 5 oct. 1981, p.16-17

334 STAMBOLIĆ, Danica
Lična karta nesvrstanih zemalja. - Beograd : Rad, 1980. 54p.

335 STANIĆ, Slavko
Non-alignment and the New International Economic Order. - Beograd : Socialist Thought and Practice. 1979. 62p.

336 STANOVNIK, Janez
Le non-alignement et le Nouvel ordre économique international. Revue de Politique Internationale (Beograd), 32(757), 20 oct. 1981, p.15-20

337 STOJANOVIĆ, Stanislav
Koreni i smisao jugoslovenske politike nesvrstanosti = The roots and importance of Yugoslav policy of non-alignment. Politička misao (Zagreb), no.1/2, 1980.

338 STOJANOVIĆ, Stanislav
Tito i nesvrstanost = Tito and non-alignment. Marksistička misao (Beograd), no.3, 1980.

339 STOJILJKOVIĆ, Miodrag M.
Saradnja - put jačanja jedinstva nesvrstanih : mogućnost ekonomske, finansijske i tehnološke saradnje izmedju zemalja u razvoju = Co-operation - the way of strengthening the unity of non-aligned countries : potentials of economic, financial and technological co-operation among developing countries. Medjunarodna politika (Beograd), vol.26, no.613, 1975, p.23-26

340 STOJKOVIĆ, Momir
Društvene osnove nastanka, razvoja i afirmacije nesvrstanosti u medjunarodnim odnosima = Social basis of the establishment, development, and affirmation of non-alignment in the international relations. Socijalizam (Beograd), no.9, 1978.

341 A STUDY by experts of non-aligned coordinating countries on food and agriculture on the establishmentof a food security system including institutional agreements : (report of the meeting held in Rome, 20-22 January 1981). - /S.l. : s.n./, 1981. 6,VIp. (W/M2010)
Cover title.

342 SUBRAHMANYAM, K.
Non-alignment and defence. Strategic Analysis (New Delhi), 5(8), November 1981, p.355-359

343 THE SUMMIT CONFERENCE OF HEADS OF STATE OR GOVERNMENT OF THE MOVEMENT OF NON-ALIGNED COUNTRIES, 6., 1979, Habana
The non-aligned movement. Third World (México City), no.3, 1979.
Special issue.

344 SUMMIT CONFERENCE OF THE NON-ALIGNED COUNTRIES, 6th, 1979, Habana
Documents / The Sixth Summit Conference of the Non-Aligned Countries. - Cuba : Editorial de Ciencias Sociales, 1979. 397p.

345 ŠAHOVIĆ, Milan
Non-alignment and international law. Review of International Affairs (Beograd), no.725, 1980.

346 TADIĆ, Bojana
Klasni karakter nesvrstanosti = Class characteristics of the non-alignment. Medjunarodni radnički pokret (Beograd), no.1, 1978.

347 TADIĆ, Bojana
Nesvrstanost i neutralnost u savremenom svetu = Non-alignment and neutrality in the contemporary world. Zbornik trećeg programa Radio Zagreba (Zagreb), br.1, 1977.

348 TADIĆ, Bojana
Non-alignment's role in today's world. Review of International Affairs (Beograd), no.680/681, 1978.

349 TADIĆ, Bojana
Posición del movimiento de no-alineación y sus dilemas en las condiciones de hoy. Política Internacional (Beograd), 32(756), 5 oct. 1981, p.24-27

350 The THIRD World without superpowers : the collected documents of the non-aligned countries / Odette Jankowitsch and Karl P. Sauvant eds. - Dobbs Ferry, N.Y. : Oceana, /1978/. 4 vols.
Introduction. p.XXXL-LV. reprinted, in part, in: Problèmes Politiques et Sociaux. 22 June 1979, p.10-15

351 TRIFUNOVIĆ, Bogdan
Self-management and non-alignment. Socialist Thought and Practice (Beograd), vol.18, no.3, 1978.

352 TRPUTEC, Zoran
Nesvrstanost i novi medjunarodni ekonomski poredak = Non-alignment and the new international economic order. Zbornik trećeg programa Radio Zagreba (Zagreb), no.1, 1977.

353 TUZMUKHAMEDOV, R.A.
Neprisoedinenie : nekotorye voprosy meždunarodnogo prava. Sovetskoe gosudarstvo i pravo (Moskva), 6, 1981, p.113-120

354 VRATUŠA, Anton
Profiles of non-alignment : socialist and non-aligned Yugoslavia. - Georgetown : Ministry of Foreign Affairs, 1978. 70p.

355 VRHOVEC, Josip
The advance of non-aligned policy. Socialist Thought and Practice (Beograd), vol.18, no.7/8, 1978.

356 VRHUNEC, Marko
Borba za novi medjunarodni ekonomski poredak : zbirka članaka i rasprava = The struggle for the new international economic order : collection of articles and discussions / Transl. Darja Jan-Salačanin; edit. Dušan Papadopolos. - Beograd : RAD, 1979. 230p. (Nesvrstanost i nesvrstani)

357 VUČKOVIĆ, Čedomir
Osnove jugoslovenskog opredeljenja za nesvrstanost i uloga Josipa Broza Tita = The background of Yugoslav non-alignment and the role of Josip Broz Tito. Zbornik trećeg programa Radio Zagreba (Zagreb), no.1, 1977

358 VUKADINOVIĆ, Radovan
Nesvrstane zemlje i detant = The non-aligned countries and détente. - Beograd : Jugoslovenska stvarnost; Medjunarodna politika, 1979.

359 VUKOVIĆ, Branislav
Non-alignment and the national question in the developing countries. Review of International Affairs (Beograd), no.684, 1978.

360 VYCHODIL, František
Results of the Sixth Conference of Non-Aligned Countries. International Relations (Tokyo), 1980, p.72-90

361 WILLETTS, Peter
The non-aligned in Havana : documents of the sixth summit conference and an analysis of their significance for the global political system. - London : Frances Pinter, 1981. XIV,283p., tab, ill. (Global politics)
Appendices, abbreviations
ISBN 0 903804 80 8

362 WÜNSCHE, Renate
Die Politik der Nichtpaktgebundenheit in den internationalen Beziehungen der Gegenwart. Asien, Afrika Lateinamerika (Berlin), H.4, 1976

363 ŽARKOVIĆ, Vidoje
Reassertion of the authentic principles of non-alignment. Socialist Thought and Practice (Beograd), vol.19, no.9, 1979.

VI

Regional Co-operation Among Developing Countries

364 ADEDEJI, Adebayo
"Les conclusions des experts de la Banque Mondiale se trouvent aux antipodes de nos objectifs pour le développement du continent" / un entretien de notre envoyée spéciale à Tripoli Augusta Conchiglia avec le secrétaire exécutif de la Commission Economique pour l'Afrique de l'ONU. Afrique-Asie (Paris), no.266, du 25 mai au 6 juin, 1982, p.47

365 ALALC
Modalidades, repercusión y alternativas de una zona franca para Paraguay en territorio uruguayo. Montevideo : /s.n./, 1980. 330p.

366 ALESSANDRINI, H.
Antecedentes generales sobre planificación regional en América Latina y Chile. Revista Interamericana de Planificación (B. Aires) 15(57), marzo de 1981, p.115-123

367 BANSKOTA, N.P.
Nepal : toward regional economic cooperation in South Asia. Asian Survey (Berkeley, Ca.), vol.21, no.3, 1981, March, p.342-354

368 BARROS CHARLIN, Raymundo HALPERIN, Marcelo
Legal aspects of the establishment of a regional margin of preference. Latin American Integration (Buenos Aires), June 1982, p.64-68
(Special English edition)

Summary of a study prepared by Raymundo Barros, and Marcelo Halperin.

369 BASIC transport network for the Southern cone of Latin America. Latin American Integration (Buenos Aires), June 1982, p.20-24

370 BENITAH, Marc
Analyse des mechanismes du "Biais urbain" en Afrique et perspectives dans le cadre d'une intégration régionale. West African Economic Journal (Ibadan, Nigeria), vol.1, no.1, March 1980, p.43-50

371 BEST, Gustavo
Hacia una implementación regional latinoamericana del Programa de Acción de Nairobi. Boletin Energetico, no.22, sept.-oct. 1981, p.7-13

372 BHANDARI, Arvind BHATIA, B.M. SILVA, Dalton de
Focus on South Asia. Commerce (Bombay), (142), no.3636, Feb. 21, 1981, p.393. Tabs.

Five contributions by Arvind Bhandari, Bhatia, Dalton de Silva and Brahmanand Mishra on the economic development of South Asia. Position of India on the international money market. Role of IMF in Pakistan. Bangladesh's dependence on foreign aid. Sri Lanka's effort to emulate Singapore. Co-operation between India and Nepal in the development of hydro-electric project.

373 BHATTACHARYA, A.K.
ASEAN : a case study in regional co-operation among developing countries. - /S.l. : s.n./, 1981, /31p./ Bibl. (UNITAR pilot study)

374 CEPAL, Session, 18., 1979
Fourth regional appraisal of the implementation of the international development strategy : Report on the eighteenth session of the Economic Commission for Latin America. - /Santiago/ : CEPAL, 1979.

Vol.2 : p.199-296 (E/CEPAL/1083/Rev.1/Add.1)

/Development strategy/, /Latin America/ - /regional cooperation/, /development policy/, /regional integration/, /Third Development Decade/.

375 CEPAL, Session, 18., 1979
Preparations and contributions by CEPAL for the formulation of the new international development strategy for the Third United Nations Development Decade : report on the eighteenth session of the Economic Commission for Latin America. - Santiago : CEPAL, 1979

Vol.1, p.181-193 (E/CEPAL/1083/Rev.1)

/ECLA/, /development strategy/, /Third Development Decade/ - /recommendation/, /economic and social development/, /regional cooperation/.

376 CIAT ante al 6 conferencia interamericana de ministros de trabajo, Lima, noviembre 1978. - Lima : Inter-American Centre for Labour Administration, 1978. 32p. (CIAT-reg. 219/AT-37)

/Monograph/ describing the objectives, programmes, work methods and development potential of the Inter-American Centre for /Labour Administration/ as the instrument for /regional co-operation/ in /Latin America/n labour questions.

377 CONFERENCE OF MINISTERS AND HEADS OF PLANNING OF LATIN AMERICA AND THE CARIBBEAN, 2nd, 1978, Lima
Second Conference of Ministers and Heads of Planning of Latin America and the Caribbean, Lima, Nov. 15-18, 1978 : preliminary version. - Santiago : ILPES, 1979. 110p.

/Regional cooperation/, /economic cooperation/, /regional planning/, /Latin America/, /Caribbean/ - /leadership/, /conference report/, /list of participants/, /agenda/.

ILPES Instituto Latinoamericano de Planificación Economica y Social

378 CONFERENCE ON ASIAN PERSPECTIVES, 1978, Colombo
Minutes of the Conference on Asian Perspectives held in Colombo, 10-12 March, 1978. - Colombo : Marga Institute, 1978. 16p.

/Development strategy/, regional cooperation/, /Asia/ - /India/, /Sri Lanka/, /Thailand/, /Nepal/, /Vietnam/,

379 CONFERENCE ON REGIONALISM AND THE NEW INTERNATIONAL ECONOMIC ORDER, 1980, New York
Regionalism and the New International Economic Order / edited by Davidson Nicol, Luis Echeverria, Aurelio Peccei ; foreword by Kurt Waldheim. - New York : Pergamon, /1981/. LI,387p. (UNITAR/CEESTEM library on NIEO) (Pergamon policy studies on the New International Economic Order) (Studies in regional co-operation)
ISBN 0 08 026318 6
Includes bibliographic references and index.

Studies presented to the UNITAR-CEESTEM-Club of Rome Conference at the United Nations.

Regionalism in the past and present, regionalism in the future, regionalism and the establishment of a NIEO.

380 The CONSTELLATION of Southern African States : a new strategic offensive by South Africa / Centre for African Studies, Eduardo Mondlane University, Maputo. Review of African Political Economy (London), no.18, May/August, 1980, p.102-105

381 La CONVERGENCIA regional : cooperación entre la Argentina y el Grupo Andino. - Buenos Aires : INTAL, 1981. 356p.

382 CO-OPERATION in industrial financing in ASEAN countries : studies on regional co-operation in the field of industry. UNIDO/IS.346

383 CORRAGGIO, José Luis
Bases teóricas de la planificación regional en América Latina : un enfoque crítico. Demografía y Económia (México), 14(2), 1980, p.141-178

384 DAVIDSON, Nicol
Regionalism and the New International Economic Order. - New York : Pergamon, 1981. 387p.
UNITAR FS/17
ISBN 0 08 026331 3

/Regional co-operation/, /New International Economic Order/, /intergovernmental organizations/, /developing countries/ - /economic cooperation/, /historical analysis/, /future/, /UNCTAD/, /ASEAN/, /EEC/, /CMEA/, /Latin America/, /international development strategy/, /financial aspects/, references

385 FAO, Session, 21., 1981, Roma
Regional and national development strategies : some selected issues for the 1980s / Food and Agriculture Organization of the United Nations, twenty-first session, Rome, 7-26 November 1981. - /S.l. : s.n./, 1981. 24p. (C 81/22)

386 FRY, Gregory E.
Regionalism and international politics of the South Pacific. Pacific Affairs (Vancouver), vol.54, no.3, 1981, p.445-484

387 FUKUDA, Takeo
"Heart to heart understanding is necessary in regional cooperation". ASEAN Newsletter (Jakarta), vol.2, no.4, September 1981, p.8

388 GOLD, E.
Problems of development and ocean management in the Eastern Caribbean : economic, legal, environmental and planning aspects : proceedings of an international seminar, Kingstown. St. Vincent and the Grenadines, West Indies, 11-13 May, 1981. - Halifax, N.S. - Dalhousie Ocean Studies Programme, 1982. 184p.

/Law of the Sea/, /marine resources/, /resources management/, /regional cooperation/, /territorial waters/, /East/, /Caribbean/ - /horizontal cooperation/, /economic cooperation/, /development strategy/, tourism/, /environmental protection/, /marine pollution/, /pollution control/, /fishery development/, /industrial aspects/, /legal aspects/, /boundaries/, /recommendation/, /agenda/, /list of participants/, /conference report/.

389 GREGG, R.W.
The UN-Regional Economic Commissions and integration in underdeveloped regions. In: The UN-System and its functions / eds. R.W. Gregg, M. Barkun. - New York : /s.n./, 1973

390 GRIMAUD, Nicole
Maghreb et péninsule arabe : de la réserve à la rivalité ou à la co-opération. Défense Nationale (Paris), vol.37, décembre 1981, p.95-110

391 HANSEN, H.
Developing countries and international shipping. - Washington, D.C. : World Bank, 1981. 148p. (World Bank staff working paper ; 502)

392 HOFMAN, Alejandro Boris
Dos ensayos sobre planificación regional. - Buenos Aires : CEUR, 1982. 74p.

393 HOFMAN, Alejandro Boris
Notas en torno a un modelo alternativo de planificación regional. Revista Interamericana de Planificación (B.Aires), vol.16, no.62, junio de 1982, p.9-26

394 HUBER, Jürgen
The practice of GATT in examining regional arrangements under article 24. Journal of Common Market Studies (Oxford), vol.19, no.3, March 1981, p.281-298

Contents: The examination of the existing regional arrangements by GATT under Art. 24(7). Regional arrangements examined outside the scope of art. 24. Factors which influenced GATT in examining the regional arrangements. Special treatment for regional agreements of LDCs. Conclusions.

395 HUMMER, Waldemar HINTERLEITNER, Reinhold
Supra-regional, regional and sub-regional cooperation and integration in Africa. Law and State. Institute for Scientific Cooperation (Tübingen), vol.21, 1980, p.74-108

396 INDIAN Ocean Commission to be set up. AED : Africa Economic Digest (London), vol.3, no.31, July 1982, p.12

397 INOTAI, András
Regional economic integrations and international divison of labour : regionalism and globalism in the new period of world economic development. - Budapest : The Hungarian Scientific Council for World Economy, 1982. 85p. (Trends in world economy ; 39)
ISSN 0133 7769
ISBN 963 301 093 4

398 INTEGRACIÓN y cooperación regionales en los años 80. - Santiago de Chile : CEPAL, 1982. 174p. (Estudios e informes de la CEPAL ; 8)

399 INTER-AMERICAN CONFERENCE OF MINISTERS OF LABOUR, 6., 1978, Lima
Carta socio-laboral de Lima ; acta final / Sexta Conferencia Interamericana de Ministros del Trabajo, 26 noviembre - 1 diciembre 1978, Lima, Peru. - Lima : Inter-American Centre for Labour Administration, 1979. 32p. (Series documentos ; 78/1)

/CIAT/ILO pub./ /conference report/ and /recommendations concerning /regional cooperation/ in /labour policy/ and /manpower planning/ activities in /Latin America/. Signals /human resources/ and /employment/, /vocational training/ /migration/, /labour statistics/, /tripartite participation, etc. as priority areas of concern. /Conf./ Lima 1978 Nov. 26 to Dec. 1.

400 JUNAC
Elementos para un plan de acción destinado a reactivar el proceso de integración económica subregional. - Lima : JUNAC, 1981. 71p.

401 KAFANDO, T.
Coopération économique régionale en Afrique de l'Ouest et problématique du développement des pays enclaves : le cas de Haute-Volta, du Mali, et du Niger. - Dakar : CODESRIA, /1976/. 19p. (Document de travail / Conseil pour le développement de la recherche économique et sociale en Afrique ; 3)

402 KHAN, Robina
Caribbean victims of drug colonialism. South. The Third World Magazine (London), no.5, 15 February 1981, p.57

Transnational pharmaceutical companies in the Caribbean distribute drugs in a random way. Robina Khan describes attempts to rationalise distribution of these products.

403 KORNEGAY, Francis A. VOCKERODT, Victor A.
Arusha and regional cooperation in Southern Africa : a preliminary analysis of resources for research and study. SADEX : the Southern Africa Development Information/Documentation Exchange. (Washington, D.C.), vol.1, no.2, 1979

404 KORNEGAY, Francis A. MORTIMER, Joyce R.
Namibia's transition and regional cooperation in Southern Africa. SADEX : the Southern Africa Development Information/Documentation Exchange (Washington, D.C.), 3(1), Jan./Feb., 1981, p.1-25

405 LANDAU, Georges D.
El Grupo de Cooperación para el Desarrollo Económico del Caribe : un marco multilateral de progreso subregional. Comercio Exterior (México), vol.32, no.12, diciembre de 1982, p.1332-1337

406 LASZLO, Ervin KURTZMAN, Joel BHATTACHARYA, A.K.
RCDC, regional cooperation among developing countries : the new imperative of development in the 1980s. - New York : Pergamon, /1981/. VIII,92p. (Pergamon policy studies on the New International Economic Order) (UNITAR-CEESTEM library on NIEO)

"Published in cooperation with UNITAR". Report of the joint UNITAR-CEESTEM and Club of Rome Conference on Regionalism and the NIEO. Bibliography: p.46-87. Includes index.
ISBN 0 08 027556 7

407 LECTURAS sobre regionalización / Amat y Leon Chavez, Carlos y Bustamante Belaunde, Luis, eds. - Lima : Universidad del Pacifico, 1981. 342p.

408 LESSEDJINA IKAWAME IPU'OZIA
La coopération multilatérale interafricaine en aviation civile : les institutions africaines relatives à l'aviation civile. - Kinshasa : Presses Universitaires du Zaïre, /198-/. 156p.
Text of source materials in French or English in annexes: p.85-156
Bibliography: p.81

409 LONG, Frank
Technology transfer : the Caribbean experience. Public Administration and Development (New York), vol.1, no.2, April-June 1981, p.140-148

410 MARTNER, G.
Estrategia tercermundista para América Latina. Nueva Sociedad (San José), (51), Nov-Dec 1980, p.7-32

/Article/ identifying problems of /trade structure/ effecting /development country/s and suggesting a strategy for /regional cooperation/ within /Latin America/. Discusses the potential for /trade negotiation/, /economic integration/, development /financing/, etc. References.

411 MATSUMOTO, S.
Southeast Asia in a changing world : proceedings and papers of a Symposium held at the Institute of Developing Economies on March 15-17, 1979. - Tokyo : Institute of Developing Economies, 1980. 242p. (IDE symposium proceedings ; 5)

412 MAURITIUS and Madagascar improve ties. AED : Africa Economic Digest (London), vol.3, no.29, July 1982, p.7

413 MENNIS, Bernard SAUVANT, Karl P.
Emerging forms of transnational community : transnational business enterprises and regional integration. - Lexington : Heath, /1976/, 240p.

414 M'HARUIA, Jonathan
Un marché commun pour l'Océan Indien. Afrique-Asie (Paris), no.257, du 18 au 31 janvier, 1982, p.58

Le M.M.M. a toujours préconisé un raffermissement des liens économiques et commerciaux entre les pays de l'Océan Indien : Seychelles, Madagascar, Les Comores, la Réunion et ... Maurice.

M.M.M. : Mouvement Militant Mauricien

415 MISHRA, Pramod Kumar
Determinants of intra-regional relations in South Asia. India Quarterly (New Delhi), 36(1), Jan./March 1980, p.68-83
Includes bibliographic references

416 NECOCHEA, Andrés
Universidad y desarrollo regional : un enfoque por la via de los problemos regionales. EURE : revista latinoamericana de estudios urbano regionales (Santiago), vol.8, no.23, diciembre de 1981, p.9-28

417 NEW patterns of growth in Latin America / ed. by Hamori, J. - Budapest : Hungarian Academy of Sciences, Institute for World Economy, 1981. 130p. Refs. Tabs. (Studies on developing countries ; 107)

Eight contributions by Kollath, Kadar, Lara, and Hamori. Diversification of external economic relations and trends in regional cooperation in Latin America. Case studies on the economies in the 1970s of Brazil, Chile, Argentina, Peru, Venezuela, with prospects.

418 NNEBE-AGUMADU, Samuel
Regional experience in co-operation in transport communications in Africa. West African Economic Journal (Ibadan, Nigeria), vol.1, no.1, March 1980, p.25-42

419 NUGENT, Jeffrey B.
The cement industry in Arab countries of the Middle East : a survey of its present status and of its future prospects and evaluation of the potential benefits of regional coordination. Beirut : United Nations Economic and Social Office, 1973. (PP/73/10)

420 NUGENT, Jeffrey B.
Regional cooperation and coordination in the field of industrial development. - Beirut : United Nations Economic and Social Office, /1973/. (PP/72/39/Rev.1)

421 NUGENT, Jeffrey B.
The sugar industry in Arab countries of the Middle East : a survey of its present status, of its future prospects and an evaluation of the potential benefits of regional coordination. Beirut : United Nations Economic and Social Office, 1973. (PP/73/11)

422 NURSE, L.
Public policy and industrial relations in English speaking Caribbean : the challenge of regionalism. - Cave Hill, Barbados : University of the West Indies, Institute of Social and Economic Research, 1980. 62p. Bibl.

423 ONDARTS, Guillermo
The formation of regional economic groups and Latin American integration. Latin American Integration (Buenos Aires), June 1982, p.53-55 (Special English edition)

Summary of a study prepared by Guillermo Ondarts

424 Les ORGANISMES réginaux en Afrique / sous la dir. d'Yves Arcadias. - Paris : Ministère de la Coopération et du Développement, Service des Etudes et des Questions Internationales, 1981. -vols. (Etudes et documents ; 45)
ISBN 2 11 084469 8
vol.1. 281p.
vol.2. 195p.

425 O'SHAUGHNESSY, H. MONTAGNON, P. CHISLETT, W. (et al.)
Latin America. Financial Times (London), June 29, 1981, sect.III, p.1, Ill, Tabs. Portr.

Regional co-operation. Economic situation GNP. Inflation. Foreign policy. Finance. Balance of payments. Population. Four profiles. Food. Energy. Mining. Industry. Foreign investments. Whiskey. Museums. Military balance. Amazonia. Figures, 1960-2000.

426 PASTIZZI-FERENČIĆ, Dunja
Nesvrstanost i unapredjenje regionalne suradnje zemalja u razvoju = Non-alignment and promotion of developing countries regional cooperation. Zbornik trećeg programa Radio Zagreba (Zagreb), br.1, 1977.

427 PEÑA, Felix
Interdependencia regional, proyectos conjuntos y derecho internacional. Integración Latinoamericana (Buenos Aires), vol.6, no.64, diciembre de 1981, p.27-32

428 PIREZ, Pedro
Información y planificación regional y urbana en América Latina : a la búsqueda de los temas perdidos. Revista Interamericana de Planificación (Buenos Aires), vol. 16., no.62, junio de 1982, p.27-37

429 POSIBILIDADES de cooperación regional sobre productos farmacéuticos de alta demanda. - Caracas : SELA, 1981. (SP/CL/VII.O/DI ; 3)

430 PREBISCH, Raúl
Mayor cooperación regional : nuevo programa para el desarrollo latinoamericano. Visión. La revista interamericana (New York), vol.56, no.12, junio de 1981, p.51

431 PROGRAMME of collaborative research on cooperation for development and collective self-reliance in South Asia. - Colombo : Marga Institute, /1978/, 9p.
DOC. SACM/1.5/78

432 PROYECTO del Programa bienal de cooperación regional 1982-1983. - Caracas : SELA, 1982. (SP/CL/VIII.O/DT ; 15)

433 REGIONAL co-operation in development research and training.-Paris : OECD, Development Centre, 1981, 95p. (Liaison bulletin between development research and training institutes : new series ; 6)

434 REGIONAL plan of action on new and renewable sources of energy. - Santiago : ECLA, 1981. 29p. (E/CEPAL/Conf.73L.2)

United Nations Conference on New and Renewable Resources of Energy : pre-conference documents.

Energy sources/ renewable resources/ economic development/ Latin America, energy crisis/ development potential/ resources exploitation/ development strategy/ regional cooperation/ regional planning/ conference report/ agenda

435 REGIONALISMUS und regionale Integration : Bibliographie 1970-1980 : Afrika, Karibik, Lateinamerika, Südostasien / Von Günther Doeker /et al./. - Frankfurt a.M. : Lang 1981. 107p. (Völkerrecht und Internationale Politik ; 6)
ISBN 3 8204 6982 6

Contents: Günther Doeker, Wolfgang S. Heinz, Thomas Koll, Mark B.M. Suh et Abdullahel Masud Syed ont uni leurs efforts pour présenter une étude bibliographique sur le régionalisme et l'intégration régionale de 1970 a 1980. Dans ce travail sont présentées l'Afrique, la zone Caraïbe, l'Amérique Latine, l'Asie du Sud-Est.

436 REGULAR MEETING OF THE LATIN AMERICAN COUNCIL, 8, 1982, Caracas
Decisions nos 112, 113, 114, 115, 116, 119, 124, 125 and 127 of the 8th Regular Meeting of the Latin American Council. - Caracas : SELA, /1982/. 45 leaves

Decision no:

112: Imposition of economic measures of a coercive nature.
113: Regional economic security.
114: Economic relations between Latin America and the United States of America.
115: Support for the Republic of Panama.
116: Relations between Latin America and the European Economic Community.
119: Economic co-operation among developing countries.
124: Meetings of high-level government experts to identify projects and actions for regional co-operation.
125: Biennial programme of regional co-operation (September 1982-August 1984).
127: Constitution of the Action Committee for the establishment of the regional food security system (C.A.S.A.R.)

437 REUNIÓN DEL COMITE DE PROGRAMACIÓN, 7., 1979, México
Informe sobre la 7a Reunión del Comite de Programación, México, D.F., 22 al 25 de agosto de 1979. - Lima : Inter-American Centre for Labour Administration, 1979. III,98p.

CIAT-/ILO publ./ /conference report/, /recommendation/s and /resolution/s concerning /regional cooperation/ programmes and activities in matters of /labour administration/ in /Latin America/. Includes /list of participants/. /Conf/ México 1979 Aug 22 to 25.

438 RODRIGUEZ-ARIAS, J.C.
Assistance by the United Nations system to regional inter-country technical cooperation institutions : note by the Secretary-General / Joint Inspection Unit. - New York : United Nations, 1981. III,53p.+6p. (A/37/101) (JIU/REP/80/10)

"Presented to the Thirty-six session of the General Assembly. Item 104 of the preliminary agenda."

439 SAN GIORGI, R.
Convenio "Simon Rodriguez" de Integración Socio-Laboral y la Administración del Trabajo, Lima, marzo, 1978. - Lima : Inter-American Center for Labour Administration, 1978. 14p. (CIAT/CIAT/DT/78/15)

/CIAT-ILO publ./, /working paper/ on the objectives, instruments and functional levels of /regional co-operation/ in matters of /labour administration/ and /employment policy/ in the /Andean region/.

440 SÀNCHEZ GONZALES, Walter
Third World perspectives on regional arrangements for peace and security : the Latin American case. The Jerusalem Journal of International Relations (Jerusalem), 5(2), 1981, p.1-15
Includes bibliographical references.

441 SAQAT, Saeed Sulaiman
The Kuwait Convention for Co-operation on the Protection from Pollution of the Marine Environment of the Arabian Gulf Area, April 1978. Revue Egyptienne de Droit International (Al Qahira), vol.34, 1978, p.149-158

442 SCHEMAN, Ronald L.
Regionalism reconsidered : excerpt from Governance in the Western Hemisphere. - /Aspen, Colo./ : Aspen Institute for Humanistic Studies, June 1982, 36p.

443 SEMINAR ON STUDIES FOR COOPERATION IN DEVELOPMENT IN SOUTH ASIA, 2nd, 1979, Colombo
Second Seminar on Studies for Co-operation in Development in South Asia, Colombo, 23-28 April '79. - Colombo : Marga Institute, 1979. 14p. (various pagings) Doc.SACM.SEM/70(2)

/Regional cooperation/, /South Asia/, /national planning/ - /conference report/, /list of participants/

444 SISON, J.C.
AGRIASIA : the agro-data for Southeast Asia. - /Los Raños/ : Agricultural Information Bank for Asia, 1981. 1 vol. (various pagings). Ill.

/IDRC supported/, /data bases/, /bibliography/, /agriculture/, /South East Asia/ - /regional cooperation/, /information users/, /information dissemination/, /information retrieval/, /IDRC mentioned/, /references.

445 SOBHAN, Rehman
Regional economic co-operation in South Asia : legacy and prospects. Economic Bulletin for Asia and the Pacific (Bangkok), vol.31, no.1, June 1980, p.106-119

446 SOUTH PACIFIC COMMISSION
Regional co-operation in the South Pacific : the South Pacific Commission : history, aims and activities. - 5th ed. - Noumea, New Caledonia : South Pacific Commission, 1980. 13p.

447 SPYROPOULOS, G.
ILO SEMINARIO SOBRE PROMOCION Y COORDINACION DE ESTUDIOS E INVESTIGACIONES EN MATERIA DE CONDICIONES DE TRABAJO EN AMÉRICA LATINA, 2nd, 1979, México City
Mejoramiento de las condiciones de trabajo en América Latina : la contribución de la Organización Internacional del Trabajo. - Genève : ILO, 1979, 42p. (Documento de trabajo ; 1) (ILO-PIACT 1-0-86-3)

/ILO publ./ /conference paper/ comprising a /working paper / outlining the objectives and activities of the /PIACT/, with particular reference to the /role of ILO/ in the promotion of /working conditions/ and /regional /cooperation/ regarding/ labour administration/ in /Latin America/. Includes a resume of the preceding seminar and a panorama of /labour research/ activities in the area. /Reference/s. /Conf/ Mexico 1979 Sep to 10 to 14.

448 SURVEY of economic and social developments in the ECWA region, 1980. - Beirut : ECWA : Economic Commission for Western Asia, 1980, 154p.

/ECWA/, /petroleum/, /economic indicators/, /social implications/ - /growth rate/, /capital-output ratio/, /capital formation/, /money supply/, /national expenditures/, /agricultural production/, /industry/, /inland transport/, /science policy/, /international trade/, /export volume/, /manpower/, /multinational enterprises/, /regional cooperation/, /statistical tables/.

449 THAMBIPILLAI, Pushpa
Regional co-operation and development : the case of ASEAN and its external relations. - Honolulu : University of Hawai, 1980. 324p.

450 TIMBERMAN, David G.
In search of a Pacific Basin Community. Asian Survey (Berkeley, Ca.), vol.21, no.5, 1981, May, p.579-598

451 El TRANSPORTE en la cooperación Argentina-Grupo Andino. - Buenos Aires : INTAL, 1981. 114p.

452 TWITCHETT, K.J.
Regional linkages and the UN. Journal of Common Market Studies (Oxford), vol.18, 1980

453 UNCTAD. TDB. Committee on Economic Co-operation among Developing Countries
Economic co-operation and integration among developing countries : a review of recent development in subregional, regional and interregional organizations and arrangement : report by the UNCTAD secretariat. - Genève : UNCTAD, 1982. -vols

Vol. 1 : Latin America. 1982. X,110p. (TD/B/C.7/51)
Vol. 2 : Africa. 1982. XI,108p. (TD/B/C.7/51)

454 UNITED NATIONS. ECOSOC. CEPAL, Session, 19., 1981, Montevideo, Uruguay
Decentralization of the economic and social activities of the United Nations : the new functions of the regional commissions in regional and interregional co-operation / note by the Secretariat ; CEPAL, Economic Commission for Latin America, nineteenth session, Montevideo, Uruguay, 4-16 May 1981. - New York : United Nations, 1981. III,16 leaves. (E/CEPAL/G.1174)

455 UNITED NATIONS. ECOSOC. ESCAP, Session, 37., 1981, Bangkok
Progress reports on special regional projects and regional institutions. - New York : UN, 1981. -vols.

Item 7 : Report of the management board of the Asia and Pacific Development Centre. 1981. 36p. Tabs. (E/ESCAP/230)

456 UNITED NATIONS. ECOSOC, Session, 2., 1981, New York
General discussion of international economic and social policy, including regional and sectoral developments : regional co-operation : survey of economic and social conditions in Africa, 1979-1980 : items 3 and 6 of the provisional agenda : summary / Second regular session of 1982 ; United Nations. ECOSOC. - New York : United Nations, 1981. 23 leaves. (E/1981/76)

457 UNITED NATIONS. ECOSOC, Session, 2., 1981, New York
Regional co-operation : second regular session of 1981, agenda item 7 / report of the Secretary-General. - New York : United Nations, ECOSOC, 1981. 37p. (E/1981/80)

458 UTTLEY, Garrick
Globalism or regionalism? : United States policy towards Southern Africa. - London : The International Institute for Strategic Studies, 1979. 36p. (Adelphi papers : 154)
ISBN 0 86079 031 2
ISSN 0 567 932 x

459 VAITSOS, Constantine V.
Kriza u regionalnoj ekonomskoj saradnji (integraciji) zemalja u razvoju : pregled = Crisis in regional economic cooperation (integration) among developing countries : a survey. Marksizam u svetu (Beograd), no.4, april 1979. p.56-117
Bibliography: p.112-117

The article analyses the meaning, theory and key policy instruments of economic integration among LCDs and reviews the experience of various regional cooperation efforts in the Third World.

CODESRIA Council for the Development of Economic and Social Research in Africa

ECWA Economic Commission for Western Asia, Beirut

CEESTEM Centro de Estudios Económicos y Sociales del Tercer Mundo, Ciudad de México

CMEA Council for Mutual Economic Assistance, formerly COMECON, Moskva

IDRC International Development Research Centre, Ottawa, Canada

INTAL Instituto para la Integración de América Latina, Buenos Aires

UNITAR United Nations Institute for Training and Research, New York

VII

Economic Co-operation Among Developing Countries

VII-1. GENERAL

460 ABDENUR, R. SARDENBERG, R.
Notas sobre las relaciones Norte-Sur y el Informe Brandt. Estudios Internacionales (Buenos Aires), 14/54), abrile-junio de 1981, p.166-200

461 AFRO-ASIAN co-operation. West Africa (London), no.3395, 30 August 1982, p.2210

462 AKINSANY, Adeoye
The Afro-Arab alliance : dream or reality. African Affairs (London), 75, 1976

463 ALIMA, Jos-Blaise
Un contentieux qui vient de loin. Jeune Afrique (Paris), no.1065, 2 juin 1981, p.25

Un accord vieux de neuf ans n'a jamais réussi a dissiper une querelle frontalière à forte odeur de pétrole. /Nigeria-Cameroun/

464 ALTMANN, Jörn
South-South cooperation and economic order. Intereconomics (Hamburg), no.3, May/June, 1982, p.143-147

465 ANALYTICAL compendium of developing countries' decisions and recommendations on ECDC/TCDC, 1976-1981 / research team : Boris Cizelj, Bojan Zidarič, Metka Fuks. - Ljubljana : Research Center for Co-operation with Developing Countries, 1981. - 194p.

Prepared for the ECDC/TCDC promotion workshop, Bled (Yugoslavia), November 2-7, 1981

466 ARGENTINA-BRASIL : la potencialidad de la cooperación bilateral. - Buenos Aires : INTAL, 1981. 149p.

467 ARGENTINA-URUGUAY : cooperación jurídica. Integración Latinoamericana (Buenos Aires), 63, noviembre de 1981, p.51

468 AVRAMOVIĆ, Dragoslav
Developing countries after Cancun. Journal of World Trade Law (Oxford), vol.16, no.1, January-February 1982, p.3-26

469 AYARI, Chedly
What future for cooperation? Africa Report (New Brunswick), 27(3), May/June 1982, p.42-48. Concerns Africa and Arab countries.

470 BELHASSEN, Souhayr
En route vers une vraie coopération. Jeune Afrique (Paris), no.1061, 25 février 1981, p.35

Au-delà des difficultés soulevées par les experts, il semble que des deux côtés on ait bien l'intention d'aboutir.

471 A CALL for greater cooperation. Trade, Industry and Investments (Makati, Metro Manila), vol.2, no.5, May 1982, p.3

Keynote address of President Ferdinand E. Marcos before the 13th Meeting of the ASEAN Economic Ministers, Philippines, International Convention Center, 20 May 1982.

472 CAMEROUN : signature d'un traité et de deux accords de coopération avec la Guinée. Marchés Tropicaux Méditerranéens (Paris), 37e année, no.1843, vendredi 6 mars 1981, p.620

473 CAMEROUN : transport, agriculture, forêt et culture : renforcement de la coopération avec le Gabon. Marchés Tropicaux et Méditerranéens (Paris), 37e année, no.1836, vendredi 16 janvier 1981, p.141

474 CHHABRA, Hari Sharon MEHTA, Bairaj AGRAWAL, Ram Gopal
India and Africa. New African (London), no.159, Jan. 1981, p.47. Tabs.

Relation between India and Africa. Existing and potential co-operation: balanced trade, technology transfer, joint venture. Economic position of Indians in East Africa. Economic development of India (electrification). Statistics, 1977-1979.

475 CHI SECK CHOO
Industrial organizations and industrial estates : a case study. Tijdschrift voor economische en sociale geografie-TESG (Leiden), no.4, 1981, p.235. Figs. Ref.

Examination of the intra- and inter-organizational linkages among foreign and local firms which are a consequence of the task environment built up by organizations located in industrial estates in Malaysia. Impact of foreign firms on the production activities of domestic firms.

476 La CHINE populaire et les États africains : itinéraire d'une coopération. Marchés Tropicaux et Méditerranéens (Paris), 38e année, no.1920, vendredi 5 novembre 1982, p.2933-2973

477 CIZELJ, Boris
Ekonomska saradnja medju zemljama u razvoju = Economic co-operation among developing countries. - Beograd : Privredni pregled, 1981. 343p.

478 CIZELJ, Boris
Razvoj, značilnosti in pomen programa ekonomskega sodelovanja med deželami v razvoju = Development, characteristics and significance of the economic co-operation programme among developing countries. - Ljubljana : Center za proučevanje sodelovanja z deželami v razvoju, 1981, 39p. (Ekonomsko in tehnično sodelovanje med deželami v razvoju kot instrument kolektivne naslonitve na lastne sile : sestavni del URP "Raziskovanje mednarodnih odnosov in razvoj nove gospodarske ureditve")

479 La COMPLEMENTARITE économique syro-libyenne. L'Economiste Arabe (Beirut), vol.24, no.267, février 1981, p.19

480 CONFERENCE ON ASIA-PACIFIC IN THE 1980s, 1980, Bali
Asia-Pacific in the 1980s : toward greater symmetry in economic interdependence / /speeches and papers presented at the CSIS Conference on Asia-Pacific in the 1980s, Bali, 11-13 Jan., 1980/ - Jakarta : Yayasan Proklamasi : Centre for Strategic and International Studies, 1980. VIII, 178p.
Includes bibliographical references

481 CONVENIOS bilaterales Argentina-Uruguay / Central de Estadísticas Nacionales de la República Argentina. - Buenos Aires : /s.n./, 1982. 1 vol. (various pagings).
Se actualiza mediante hojas renovables.

482 La COOPERACION de la República Argentina a países en desarrollo : año 1980. - Buenos Aires : OEA, Ministerio de Relaciones Exteriores y Culto, 1982. 103p.
OEA Organización de los Estados Americanos

483 COOPERACIÓN económica entre países en desarrollo : análisis de la Conferencia de Caracas de 1981 y exámen de las perspectivas de la CEPD. - Caracas : SELA, 1982. 96p. (SP/CL/VIII.O/DT ; 6)

484 COOPERACIÓN entre la JUNAC y CARICOM. Integración Latinoamericana (México), año 7, no.74, noviembre de 1982, p.64

485 La COOPERACIÓN entre países en desarrollo. p.133-138. In: Documento de apoyo por: CEPAL, Comisión Económica para América Latina, decimonoveno periodo de sesiones, Montevideo, Uruguay, 4 al 16 de mayo de 1981. - /s.l./ : CEPAL, 1981. (E/CEPAL/G. 1160)
Una apreciación global. Las relaciones económicas entre América Latina y Africa; quadro 38, 39.

486 COREA, Gamani
North-South dialogue : a regular feature intended to provide eminent statesmen and scholars involved in North-South issues with an opportunity to express their views. Third World Quarterly (London), vol.3, no.4, 1981, p.603-614

487 COTE d'Ivoire : renforcement des relations économiques avec le Sénégal. Marchés Tropicaux et Méditerranéens (Paris), 37e année, no.1853, vendredi 15 mai 1981, p.1359

488 CUESTION cafetera : su impacto económico, social y político : Colombia-Costa Rica-Costa de Marfil / comp. Reveiz Edgar. - Bogotá : CEDE, 1980. 365p.
CEDE Centro de Estudios sobre Desarrollo Económico

489 DIAS, Nicia
Un modèle de coopération. Afrique-Asie (Paris),no.275, du 16 au 29 août, 1982, p.52

L'oeuvre entreprise par la Havane en vue d'établir avec l'Afrique les liens exemplaires sur les plans économique médical et culturel s'inscrit dans le cadre d'une participation effective et désinteressée à la consolidation et à la défense de l'indépendance.

490 DÖLLINGER, Carlos von
A note on the limitations to economic cooperation among developing countries : lessons from the Latin American experience.
In: Beiträge zur Industrialisierungs- und Handelspolitik der Entwicklungsländer / hrsg. V. Timmermann. - Berlin : /s.n./, 1980, p.173-184 (Schriften des Vereins für Sozialpolitik, Gesellschaft für Wirtschafts-und Sozialwissenschaften. N.F. ; 110)

491 DRAGIČEVIĆ, Vuko
Značaj saradnje zemalja u razvoju - Ministarska konferencija Grupe 77 u Karakasu = The importance of developing countries' mutual cooperation - The Ministerial Conference of the Group 77 in Caracas. Medjunarodna politika (Beograd), no.748, June 1981, p.4-6

492 DURBAN, Dorothee
Coopération afro-arabe : la relance. Afrique-Asie (Paris), no.273, du 26 juillet 1982, p.58

Elle a connu un développement qualificatif lorsque l'attitude agressive et raciste d'Israël et la crise petrolière ont crée les raisons politiques et économiques nécessaires au rapprochement.

493 ECONOMIC co-operation among developing countries. Forum. OPEC Bulletin (Wien), August 1981, 4p.

494 ECONOMIC co-operation among Latin American and Caribbean countries in the establishment of container repair and maintenance enterprises : project prepared by CEPAL / United Nations. CEPAL. - New York : United Nations, Economic Commission for Latin America, 1981. III,10p. (E/CEPAL/G.1186)

495 ECONOMIC relations between West Asia and Southeast Asia / Lee Soo Ann,editor. - Singapore : ISEAS, 1978. 236p. (Proceedings of international series ; 4)

496 ESTEVEZ, Jaime
Cancun : los limites del diálogo. Tercer Mundo y Economia Mundial, vol.1, no.2, enero-abril 1982, p.197-217

497 FUKS, Metka
Položaj dežel v razvoju v mednarodnem gospodarstvu, pomen in perspektive njihovega medsebojnega sodelovanja. - Ljubljana : Center za proučevanje sodelovanja z deželami v razvoju, 1981. 57p. - (Ekonomsko in tehnično sodelovanje med deželami v razvoju kot instrument kolektivne naslonitve na lastne sile). RSS 11-5562-523

/developing countries/ international trade/ /international cooperation/ collective self-reliance/

498 GHARBI, Samir
Vers un sommet afro-arabe. Jeune Afrique (Paris), no.1073, 29 juillet 1981, p.33

La 18e Conférence de l'OUA a permis de débloquer une situation gelée depuis les accords de Camp David.

499 GOETZ, Arturo L.
Beyond the slogan of South-South co-operation. World Development (Oxford), 9(6), June 1981, p.583-585

500 A GOING concern and a good place to live. The Arab Economist (Beirut), vol.13, no.147, December 1981, p.25

501 GUEN, Moncef
Un premier pas : l'union douanière algéro-tunisienne. Jeune Afrique (Paris), no.1075, 12 août 1981, p.12

502 GUINEE : Accord économique avec Liberia. Reorganisation du commerce et création de banques. Marchés Tropicaux et Méditerranéens (Paris), 37e année, no.1853, vendredi 15 mai 1981, p.1358

503 GUINEE : nouvelles perspectives de coopération avec l'Inde. Marchés Tropicaux et Méditerranéens (Paris), 37e année, no.1846, vendredi 27 mars 1981, p.837

504 GUINEE : renforcement de la coopération avec la Nigeria. Marchés Tropicaux et Méditerranéens (Paris), 37e année, no.1854, vendredi 22 mai 1981, p.1414

505 GUINEE-BISSAU : relance de la coopération avec l'Algérie. Marchés Tropicaux et Méditerranéens (Paris), 38e année, no.1902, vendredi 23 avril 1982, p.1091

506 GUINEA-BISSAU : relations with Cape Verde restored. AED : Africa Economic Digest (London), vol.3, no.26, 1982, p.15

507 HANSSON, Karl-Erik REVESZ, Richard
Economics of cooperation in shared water resources development. Natural Resources Forum (New York), vol.6, no.2, April 1982, p.151-166

508 HAQ, Mahbub Ul
Beyond the slogan of South-South cooperation. World Development (Oxford), vol.8, 1980, p.743

509 HAYTON, Robert D.
Cooperation in development of shared water resources. Natural Resources Forum (New York), vol.6, no.2, April 1982, p.167-181

510 HIGH LEVEL CONFERENCE ON ECONOMIC CO-OPERATION AMONG DEVELOPING COUNTRIES, 1981, Caracas, Venezuela
Final report of the High level conference on economic co-operation among developing countries, Caracas, 13-19 May, 1981. - Caracas : Group 77, 1981. IV,55p. tab., ann.

511 HOSSAIN, Ishtiaq
Bangladesh-India relations : issues and problems. Asian Survey (Berkeley, Cal.), vol.21, no.11, nov. 1981, p.1115-1128

512 ILE Maurice : coopération plus étroite avec les Seychelles. Marchés Tropicaux et Méditerranéens (Paris), 38e année, no.1915, vendredi 23 juillet 1982, p.2103

513 INTERNATIONAL ROUND TABLE ON ECONOMIC CO-OPERATION AMONG DEVELOPING COUNTRIES, 2nd, 1982, México Ciudad
CEESTEM/UNCTAD/RCCDC round table on economic co-operation among developing countries, México City, 22-29 November 1982. - México City : CEESTEM, UNCTAD, RCCDC, 1982.

Contents: Towards a global system of trade preferences among developing countries / Nassau A.Adams. 29p. Cooperación económica entre los países en vias de desarrollo en el area de los productos primarios / José-Miguel Benavente. 39p. Industrialization via sub-regional integration : the tourtuous road / Oswaldo Davila Andrade. 36p. Planned and balanced preferential trade : a demonstration of its feasibility / Peter C. Elkan. 9p., tabs. The role of newly industrialized countries in the promotion of co-operation among developing countries / Metka Fuks and Mitre Koliševski. 25p., tabs. Monetary and financial co-operation among developing countries : preliminary review of progress, problems and prospects / A.Inostroza. 10p., ann. 1,2. Latin American energy co-operation : problems and perspectives / Cornelio Marchán. 29p. Financial co-operation among developing countries : a note / Mojmir Mrak. 12p. Agricultural foodstuffs and raw materials : South-South co-operation, an inevitable requirement / Belfor Portilla and Silvia del Valle. 35p. South-South co-operation : background / Paper prepared by the Core of Assistance to the Chairman of the Group 77. 6p. The APEC Secretariat (Action Programme for Economic Co-operation) / Lloyd Searwar. 15p., att.1: The work of the APEC Secretariat; att.2: List of APEC studies and reports. Trade among developing countries by main commodity groups and regions : statistical note / Maciej Tymovski. 12p., tabs. A discussion note on Institutional aspects of ECDC / Raúl Uranga. 20p., ann. 7p. Report of the UNCTAD-CEESTEM-RCCDC round table on economic co-operation among developing countries. 23p., ann. 8p.

514 JOHNSON, W.R.
Africans and Arabs : collaboration without co-operation change without challenge. International Journal (Toronto), vol.35,no.4, autumn 1980, p.766-793

/Economic cooperation/, /bilateral relations/, /motivations/, /Arab organizations/, /OAU/ - /petroleum/, /prices/, /financial aid/, /scenarios/, /political aspects/, /economic implications/.

515 JUGOSLOVENSKO SAVETOVANJE "EKONOMSKA SARADNJA SA ZEMLJAMA U RAZVOJU" = YUGOSLAV CONFERENCE ON ECONOMIC CO-OPERATION AMONG DEVELOPING COUNTRIES, 31., 1981, Bled, Slovenia
Tretje jugoslovensko savetovanje "Ekonomska saradnja sa zemljama u razvoju", Bled, 11.-12.06.1981 / Center za proučevanje sodelovanja z deželami v razvoju. - Ljubljana : CPSDvR-Center za proučevanje sodelovanja z deželami v razvoju, 1981. Various pagings.

Contents: Tendencije u razvoju zemalja u razvoju i neke implikacije tih kretanja na ekonomske odnose Jugoslavije sa zemljama u razvoju / D.Despot & M. Staničić. 20p. - Položaj ZUR u medjunarodnoj privredi i značaj njihove medjusobne saradnje u svetlu realizacije politike većeg kolektivnog oslonca na sopstvene snage / Boris Cizelj and Metka Fuks. 28p. 5 ann. Iskustva u poslovanju mešovitog poduzeća BOKYU / I. Patarčić. 4p. Prioritetna pitanja medjusobne ekonomske saradnje zemalja u razvoju / M. Sokić. 12p. Mesto ZUR u pojedinim dokumentima sistema ekonomskih odnosa sa inostranstvom i dogradjivanje sistema mera za unapredjenje privredne saradnje sa zemljama u razvoju / G. Božović. 21p. Skupne naložbe jugoslovanske lesne industrije v proizvodnjo in predelavo tropskega lesa v podjetju v tujini SLOVENIA BOIS BANGUI, Centralnoafrička republika / P. Olip. 4p. Strategija zajedničkih ulaganja kao poslovno-tehnološka saradnja sa ZUR i specifičan oblik uklapanja u medjunarodnu podelu rada / Marjan Svetličič. 52p. Aktivnost Novosadskog sajma na povezivanju organizacija agroindustrijskog kompleksa Jugoslavije sa ZUR. / I. Gros. 5p. Kofinansiranje razvojnih projekata u ZUR i mogućnosti uključivanja Jugoslovenske banke za medjunarodnu ekonomsku saradnju / G. Cetinić. 10p. Značaj investicione saradnje u našim ekonomskim odnosima sa zemljama u razvoju / Marko Verbič. 15p. Analiza tokova i problema privredne saradnje Jugoslavije sa ZUR / Mitre Koliševski. 23p.+ 4 ann. Oblici i mehanizmi usmerovanja petrodolara u razvoju zemalja u razvoju i položaj Jugoslavije / M. Crnobrnja. 17p. Karakteristike planiranja Arapskih zemalja kao okvir za uključivanje Jugoslavije u privredni razvoj ove grupe zemalja u razvoju / Mojmir Mrak. 19p.

516 KENYA : vers un développement de la coopération et des échanges entre l'Indie et le Kenya. Marchés Tropicaux et Méditerranéens (Paris), 37e année, no.1843, vendredi 6 mars 1981, p.625

517 KENYA : vers la normalisation des relations ougando-kényanes. Marchés Tropicaux et Méditerranéens (Paris), 37e année, no.1836, vendredi 16 janvier 1981, p.147

518 KILGORE, Arthur
ACP-G77 : a common interest? South. The Third World Magazine (London), no.9, July 1981, p. 67-69

519 The KOREAN connection : president Chun Doo Hwan of South Korea is due this week in Nigeria (August 19-22, Gabon (August 22-24) and Senegal (August 24-26) : a correspondent looks at the links between Korea and Africa and what Korea can offer to Africa. West Africa (London), no.3393, 16 Aug 1982, p.2099

520 KRIEGER MYTELKA, Lynn
Common Market with some uncommon problems. Africa Report (New Brunswick, N.J.), vol.10, no.7, October, 1970, p.12-17, reprinted in Development Digest, 1972

521 KÜCK, Gert
Economic co-operation among developing countries : a brief account on the Arab scene. Wissenschaftliche Beiträge (Berlin), 16(2), 1981, p.24-28

522 KÜCK, Gert
Ekonomska saradnja i integracija : slučaj zemalja u razvoju = Economic co-operation and integration : the case of the developing countries. Marksizam u svetu (Beograd), no.4, april 1979, p.149-157

523 LATIN America and the Caribbean. World of Information (Essex, England), 1980-Annual

524 LATIN AMERICAN SEMINAR ON HORIZONTAL CO-OPERATION FOR THE INTERNATIONAL DRINKING WATER SUPPLY AND SANITATION DECADE, 1st, 1981, Santiago de Chile
Report of the First Latin American Seminar on Horizontal Co-operation for the International Drinking Water Supply and Sanitation Decade, (Santiago de Chile, 9-13 March 1981) / United Nations. ECOSOC. Economic Commission for Latin America. - New York : United Nations, 1981. III,19p. (E/CEPAL/G.1171)

525 LECHINI, Gladys
Evolución de la relación argentino africana. Revista de Derecho Internacional y Ciencia Diplomática (Rosario), año 29, no.50/51, 1981, p.73-87

526 LECHINI, Gladys
Una politica Argentina para Africa. Estrategia (Buenos Aires), no.69, 1981, p.82-91

527 LIBYE : accord de coopération avec les Seychelles. Marchés Tropicaux et Méditerranéens (Paris), 37e année, no.1854, vendredi 22 mai 1981, p.1509

528 LISICA, D.
The subject and the possible organized forms of co-operation on the questions of standardization between developing countries : Group Meeting on standardization and quality control in the industrialization process of developing countries, Arandjelovac, Yugoslavia, 1981. - Wien : UNIDO, 1981. 9p. Tabl. (UNIDO-ID/WG.346/8)

/UNIDO pub/ on /cooperation/ in /standardization/, with special reference to the/ role of developing countries/ - covers (1) the need for co-operation (2) the present state of co-operation between the DCs ; /institutional framework/ : /ISO/, ARSO, DEVCO, IEC, ASMO, /CMEA/, COPANT (3) the possibilities of using the experience of the /developed countries/ (4) further possible ways in finding solutions for an optimal development of standardization. /Statistics/.

529 MANSOUR, Fawzy
Ekonomska saradnja izmedju zemalja "trećeg sveta" : smernice za povelju = Economic co-operation among Third World countries : guidelines for a charter. Marksizam u svetu (Beograd), no.4, april 1979, p.48-55

530 MODELING the multiregional economic system : perspectives for the eighties / ed. by F.G. Adams and N.J. Glickman. - Lexington, Mass. : Lexington Books, /1980/, 10, 310p. Charts, figs, tabs, bibl.

531 MORAN, Theodore H.
Modeling OPEC behavior : economic and political alternatives. International Organization (Madison, Wis.), 35(2), spring 1981, p.241-272

532 OECD (Organisation for Economic Cooperation and Development) : trilateral cooperation : Arab development funds and banks. Third World Quarterly (London), vol.1, no.1, 1979, p.168

Vol.1 : Approaches to trilateral cooperation
Vol.2 : Special approaches to trilateral cooperation

533 OKRUGLI STO ZEMALJA U RAZVOJU = ROUND TABLE OF DEVELOPING COUNTRIES, 9., 1981, Zagreb
Saradnja u oblasti transporta i komunikacija izmedju zemalja u razvoju = Co-operation in the field of transport and communication among developing countries / 9. okrugli sto zemalja u razvoju, Zagreb, 21.-23. april 1981 ; organizator Institut za zemlje u razvoju, 1981. various pagings.

534 OLADE. Meeting of Ministers, 12., 1981, Santo Domingo
Latin American Energy Cooperation Program : PLACE / report of the Committee of Ministers to the Twelfth/!/ Meeting of Ministers, Santo Domingo, Nov. 13/14, 1981. - Santo Domingo : OLADE, 1981. 15 leaves

OLADE Organización Latinoamericana de Energía

535 ORGANIZACION DE LOS ESTADOS AMERICANOS. Grupo de trabajo conjunto CEPCIES/CEPCIECC Cooperación hemisferica y desarrollo integral / texto preparado y aprobado por el Grupo de Expertos Felipe Herrera ... /et al./ - Washington : Organización de los Estados Americanos, Secretaría General, 1980. XII,141p. (Informe para la Secretaría General de la Organización de los Estados Americanos). OEA/Ser.T/II. GTC/15-80

536 ORREGO-VICUÑA, Francisco
Perspectivas de la cooperación entre América Latina y los países de ASEAN. Estudios Internacionales (Buenos Aires), vol.15, no.58, abril-junio 1982, p.190-204

537 OTAYEK, René
La coopération arabo-africaine : esquisse d'un bilan. Année Africaine. Centre d'Etude d'Afrique Noire de Bordeaux (Paris), 1979, p.288-318

538 PALANKAI, Tibor
Lomé Convention : is it a "new deal" for the developing countries? Development and Peace (Budapest), vol.1, no.2, autumn 1980, p.72-92

539 POPESCU, Ion C.
The co-operation among developing countries. Revue Roumaine d'Etudes Internationales (Bucureşti), vol.12, no.2, 1981, p.133-141
Includes bibliographical references.

540 PROSPECTS for economic complementarity with Lybia. The Arab Economist (Beirut), vol.13, no.138, March 1981, p.18-19

541 PROSPECTS for production cooperation between India and Tanzania. New Delhi : Indian Institute of Foreign Trade, 1979. 146p. Ill.

542 PUYANA, Alicia
Cooperación económica Sur-Sur. Tercer Mundo y Economía Mundial, vol.1, no.1, septiembre-diciembre de 1981, p.125-151

543 RAMPHAL, Shridath S.
South-South : parameters and pre-conditions. Third World Quarterly (London), vol.4, no.3, July 1982, p.460

544 RAO, N.
Economic co-operation among developing countries. OPEC Bulletin (Vienna), vol.12, no.8, 1981

545 REGULATION of business co-operation in Latin America : present situation and outlook. Latin American Integration (Buenos Aires), June 1982, p.79-86

Summary of the report prepared by Carlos M.Correa under the supervision of Guillermo Ondarts.

546 REICHEL, Hans-Christian
Multilaterale Aspekte von ECDC. Aussenpolitik. Zeitschrift für internationale Fragen (Stuttgart), vol.32, no.1, 1981, p.52-57

547 Las RELACIONES económicas entre el Grupo Andino y los países del Caribe. Integración Latinoamericana (Buenos Aires), año 7, no.75, diciembre 1982, p.74-80

Contents: Marco general de las relaciones internacionales del Grupo Andino con los países del Caribe. Principales caracteristicas de los países del Caribe. Análisis de las relaciones comerciales entre el Grupo Andino y el Caribe. Consideraciones finales.

548 Les RELATIONS économiques egypto-soudanaises. Marchés Tropicaux et Méditerranéens (Paris), 37e année, no.1851, vendredi 1er mai 1981, p.1238

549 RÉUNION : la coopération économique avec Maurice. Marchés Tropicaux et Méditerranéens (Paris), 37e année, no.1856, vendredi 5 juin 1981, p.1554

550 REUNION ORDINARIA TECNICA ESPECIALIZADA SOBRE INTERCONEXION DE CUENCAS. 1, 1981, Lima
Documentos. - Lima : Comisión Nacional Coordinadora para la Interconexión de las Cuencas, 1981. - 2vols.

551 ROUND TABLE UNCTAD/CEESTEM/RCCDC ON ECONOMIC CO-OPERATION AMONG DEVELOPING COUNTRIES 1982, Ciudad de México
Informe de la Mesa Redonda UNCTAD/CESSTEM/RCCDC sobre Cooperación Económica entre Países en Desarrollo, (Ciudad de México, 22 a 29 de noviembre de 1982). - Genève : UNCTAD, 1982. II,/34/p. (UNCTAD/ECDC/TA/15)

552 RWANDA : accord de coopération avec la Zambie. Marchés Tropicaux et Mediterranéens (Paris), 38e année, no.1901, 16 avril 1982, p.1040

553 SARAN, Ammu Joseph
Obote (Uganda) seeks Indian "transfusions". AED : Africa Economic Digest (London), vol.2, no.48, December 1981, p.15

554 SAUDI Arabia. Mineral exploitation close to realisation. Arab Economist (Beirut), 12, no.134, Nov., 1980, p.20

Mineral deposits in Saudi Arabia. Iron, gold, silver, copper and zinc. Participation of foreign exploitation companies. Saudi-Sudanese co-operation.

555 Le SENEGAL et ses relations avec les pays voisins. Marchés Tropicaux et Méditerranéens (Paris), 37e année, no.1852, vendredi 8 mai 1981, p.1297

556 SENEGAL : Tunisia agrees economic co-operation. AED : Africa Economic Digest (London), vol.3, no.8, February 1982, p.23

557 SENÉGAL : vers un développement de la coopération bilatérale avec le Ghana. Marchés Tropicaux et Méditerranéens (Paris), 37e année, no.1842, vendredi 27 février 1981, p.483

558 The SOCIAL and economic impact of tourism on Pacific communities / edited by Bryan H. Farrell. - Santa Cruz, Cal. : University of California, Center for South Pacific Studies, 1977. IX,141p. Ill.
Bibliography: p.140-141

559 SOMMET ISLAMIQUE, 3., 1981, Taïf
Une solidarité arabo-africaine renforcée / Le 3e Sommet islamique, (Taïf, 25-28 janvier). Marchés Tropicaux et Méditerranéens (Paris), 37e année, no.1839, vendredi 6 février 1981, p.287

Les décisions économiques du Sommet islamique de Taïf. Abstention de la Libye. Contact algéro-marocain fortuit. Présence de l'Afrique au "Sommet islamique".

560 SOUTH-SOUTH dialogue : a brief report. Third World Quarterly (London), vol.1, no.2, 1979, p.117

561 SOUTH-SOUTH meeting : consultations close, text of conclusions adopted / International Foundation for Development Alternatives. - Geneva : IFDA, 1982. 14p.

562 SOUTH-SOUTH : a necessary alliance. South. The Third World Magazine (London), no.9, July 1981, p.13-18

Economic cooperation among developing countries (ECDC) was the focus of a top-level conference in May. But whether the meeting will result in effective action remains to be seen. Andrés Federman analyses why South-South is so necessary and examines the constraints on such policies.

563 SUHARTONO, R.B.
Economic relations between Northeast and Southeast Asia : a view from Indonesia. Indonesian Quarterly (Jakarta), 9(1), Jan., 1981, p.18-63

564 SYLVESTER, Anthony
Arabs and Africans : cooperation for development. - London : Bodley Head, 1981. 252p. + index, 1 map, photographs.
ISBN 0 370 30332 6
Real name Karl Lavrenčič, born in Ljubljana 1921.

565 TALBOT, Ross B.
Four world food organizations : influence of the Group of 77. Food Policy (London), vol.7, no.3, August 1982, p.207-221

566 TOGO : renforcement de la coopération avec la Tunisie. Marchés Tropicaux et Méditerranéens (Paris), 37e année, no.1854, vendredi 22 mai 1981, p.1417

567 TOGO : vers un accroissement de la coopération avec le Koweit. Marchés Tropicaux et Méditerranéens (Paris), 38e année, no.1888, vendredi 15 janvier 1982, p.145

568 TUNIS accentue sa coopération avec des pays du Golfe. Marchés Tropicaux et Méditerranéens (Paris), 38e année, no.1899, vendredi 2 avril 1982, p.884

569 TUNISIE : la coopération avec l'Arabie séoudite connaît un développement favorable. Marchés Tropicaux et Méditerranéens (Paris), 36e année, no.1868, vendredi 28 août 1981, p.2210

570 UHLIG, Christian AHN, Doo Soon
Vorschläge für ein entwicklungspolitisches Instrumentarium zur Förderung der wirtschaftlichen Zusammenarbeit der Entwicklungs-länder untereinander.- Bochum : /s.n./, 1981, p.90

571 UN. ECOSOC. Economic Commission for Europe, Session, 36., 1981, Genève
Economic co-operation in the Mediterranean in the light of the final act of the CSCE : (Commission decision J(XXXV) / report by the Executive Secretary. - Genève: /s.n./, 1981. /9/p. (E/ECE/1026)

572 UNCTAD, Session, 5., 1979, Manila
Economic co-operation among developing countries : priority areas for action : issues and approaches : item 18 of the provisional agenda / report by the UNCTAD Secretariat. - Genève : UNCTAD, 1979. II,/39/p. (TD/244)

573 UNCTAD, Session, 5., 1979, Manila
Economic co-operation among developing countries : supplementary material and considerations relating to priority areas for action : item 18 of the provisional agenda / report by the UNCTAD Secretariat. - Genève : UNCTAD, 1979. IV,56p. (TD/244/Suppl.1)

574 UNCTAD. TDB. Session, 24th., 1982, Genève
The role of UNCTAD in support of economic co-operation among developing countries / report by Hassan Ali Debbagh. - Genève : UNCTAD, 1982. /7/ leaves. (TD/B/892)

575 UNCTAD. TDB. Working Party on the Medium-Term Plan and the Programme Budget, Session, 1st, 1980, Genève
Review of the UNCTAD Medium-Term Plan 1980-1983 : UNCTAD Medium-Term Plan 1980-1983 (updated) / report by the UNCTAD secretariat. - Geneva : UNCTAD, 1980- . -vols
Programme 6 : Economic co-operation among developing countries. 1980. 10p. (TD/B/WP/3/Add.4)

576 UNIDO
The UNIDO programme for economic co-operation among developing countries. - Wien : UNIDO, 1979. 25p. Tabs. (UNIDO-ID/CONF.4/15)

/UNIDO pub./ on promotion of special reference to the/role of UNIDO/ in expanding the /role of developing countries/ - covers (1) activities of /UNIDO/ (2) /energy/ and economic co-operation (3) round-table ministerial meetings on industrial and /technology/cal co-operation (4) the system of industrial /financing/. Additional references: /investment promotion/, /technical assistance/. Annexes summary of UNIDO TCDC /aid projects.

577 UNITED NATIONS. General Assembly, Session, 36th, 1981, New York
Development and international economic co-operation : thirty-six session, item 69 of the preliminary list. - New York : United Nations, 1981. IV,67p. Tabs. (A/36/333)

578 UNITED NATIONS. General Assembly, Special Session, 11., 1980, New York
Assessment of the progress made in the establishment of the New International Economic Order and appropriate actions for the promotion of the development of developing countries and international economic co-operation : economic co-operation among developing countries : item 7 of the provisional agenda / report of the Secretary-General. - New York : UN, 1980. 14p. (A/S-11/5/Add.3)

579 VOSS, Harald
Kooperation in West Afrika : multilaterale Institutionen und bilaterale Zusammenarbeit. Afrika Spectrum (Pfaffenhofen/Ilm), H.2, 1979

580 WALTER, Hans-Ulrich
Some aspects of economic co-operation among developing countries in Sub-Saharan Africa. Wissenschaftliche Beiträge (Berlin), 17(1), 1982, p.39-58
Includes bibliographical references.

581 WALTER, Hans-Ulrich
Wirtschaftskooperation im südlichen Afrika im Kampf gegen das Apartheid-Regime : Notwendigkeit, Probleme, Tendenzen. Asien, Afrika, Lateinamerika (Berlin), 6, 1981, p.1053-1064
Includes bibliographical references.

582 ZEHENDER, Wolfgang
Development policy in crisis : the case of Sub-Saharan Africa and its consequences for cooperation. Intereconomics (Hamburg), no.3, May/June, 1982, p.138-142

VII-2. TRADE

583 AGNIHOTRI, V.
India's trade with developing countries. Foreign Trade Review (New Delhi), 14(3), Oct./Dec., 1979. p.220-248

584 ALSINA, Mario A.
Armonización de los sistemas aduaneros latinoamericanos. Integración Latinoamericana (Buenos Aires), no.75, diciembre de 1982, p.61-73

585 AMSDEN, A.H.
The industry characteristics of intra-third world trade in manufactures. Economic development and cultural change (Chicago), 29, no.1, Oct., 1980- p.1. Ref. Tabs.

Job generation of LDC-exports to developed and developing countries. Commodity composition of export to LDCs, 1973.

586 ARMAS, A.
Philippines intra ASEAN trade liberalization.-Quezon City : University of the Philippines, Institute for Economic Development and Research, 1978. 55p. (Discussion paper / University of the Philippines, Quezon City. Institute of Economic Development and Research ; 78-13)

/trade liberalization/, /Philippines/- /import volume/, /import promotion/, /tariff reductions/, /international trade/, /Indonesia/, /Malaysia, /Singapore, /Thailand/.

587 BANDERJI, Ranadev
The development impact of barter in developing countries : the case of India. - Paris : Development Centre of the Organisation for Economic Co-operation and Development, /1977/. 205p. (Technical studies / Development Centre of the Organisation for Economic Co-operation and Development) (Document / Development Centre of the Organisation for Economic Co-operation and Development)
Bibliography: p.202-205
ISBN 92 64 11677 x

588 BRAZIL and Cuba court Africa. South. The Third World Magazine (London), no.2., Nov., 1980, p.15. Graphs. Map. Tabs.

Trade between Latin America (Cuba, Brazil) and Africa, 1979. Oil supplies to Brazil. Economic indicators, 1974-1977.

589 CENTROAMERICA : las recientes medidas económicas y su repercusión en el comercio intraregional. Integración Latinoamericana (Buenos Aires), año 7, no.66, marzo 1982, p.60-62

Contents: Descripción de las medidas. Probables efectos de las medidas sobre el comercio intraregional.

590 CHILESHE, Jonathan Hannock
The challenge of developing intra-African trade. - Nairobi : East African Literature Bureau (EALB), 1977. XVII,257p. incl.references, selected bibliography and index.

591 CONESA, Eduardo R.
Las exportaciones intralatinoamericanas como motores del desarrollo. Integración Latinoamericana (Buenos Aires), no.52, noviembre de 1980

592 CONFERENCE ON TRADE PROSPECTS AMONG THE AMERICAS : LATIN AMERICAN EXPORT DIVERSIFICATION AND THE NEW PROTECTIONISM, 1980, Sao Paolo
Export diversification and the new protectionism : the experiences of Latin America / ed. by Werner Baer and Malcolm Gillis. The Quarterly Review of Economics and Business (Urbana, Ill.), 21(2), summer 1981, 301p.

Special issue

593 COUNTRY profile : Malaysia. Chamber News. Metropolitan chamber of commerce and industry (Dacca), Dec., 1980, p.41. Tabs.

Geography. The domestic economy. Prices. Credit. GDP. Agricultural production. Mineral production. Energy. Foreign trade. Balance of payment. Economic prospects. Trade with Bangladesh. Economic Plan 1981-85. Figures 1971-85.

594 DOCUMENTOS presentados a la "Conferencia sobre Perspectivas de Comercio entre las Américas". Estudos Económicos, vol.11, no.2, abril-junio de 1981, p.1-185

595 DODWELL, David
Developing countries' trade "will increase". Financial Times (London), July 31, 1981

596 FITZGERALD, M.A. HOWARD, C. HECHT, R.
Hard times push neighbours together. Zambia : a budget for all seasons. Natural rubber : one of Africa's best bets. Africa Economic Digest : AED. Weekly Business News, Analysis and Forecast (London), no.6, Feb. 6, 1981, p.2. Ill. Portrs. Tabs.

Economy development. GDP. Foreign and intraregional trade of East Africa, namely Uganda, Kenya, Tanzania, Zambia. Impact of Zambia's 1981-budget. World Bank opinion about Africa's rubber.

597 FUKS, Metka
Možnosti substitucije uvoza industrijskih proizvodov iz EGS z uvozom iz dežel v razvoju = Possibilities of substituting (Yugoslav) import of manufactures from EEC by imports from developing countries. - Ljubljana : RCCDC-Research Center for Cooperation with Developing countries, 1981, 78p.

598 GUIA para exportar a Ecuador. - Lima : Fondo de Promoción de Exportaciones no Tradicionales, 1981. 46p.

599 GUIA para exportar a Venezuela. - Lima : Fondo de Promoción de Exportaciones no Tradicionales, 1981. 66p.

600 HALPERIN, Marcelo
América Latina y el comercio interregional de productos agropecuarios. Integración Latinoamericana (Buenos Aires), 61, septiembre de 1981, p.82-83

601 HAVRYLYSHYN, Oli WOLF, Martin
Trade among developing countries : theory, policy issues and principal trends. - Washington, D.C. : World Bank, 1981, IV,112p. Tabl. Diagr. (World Bank staff working paper ; 479) References

/International trade/, /commodities/, /theory/, developing countries/ - /trade structure/, /trends/, /trade barriers/, /export value/, /statistical tables/, /references/.

602 HELLEINER, Gerald K.
Intra-firm trade and the developing countries. - New York : St. Martin's Press, 1981. X,110p.
Bibliography: p.99-106. Includes index.
ISBN 0 321 42538 4

603 INDIA as a world trading partner : speakers papers : a Financial Times Conference in association with the Federation of Indian Chambers of Commerce and Industry, New Delhi, 21 and 22 January, 1981. - London : Financial Times Conference Organisation, 1981. 131p. Tabs.

Twenty-two contributions by Modi, Mukherjee, Okita, Ariffin, Raghavan, Ram, Bajaj, Malhotra, Arunachalam, Biffen a.o. on India as a world trading partner. Trade with Japan, ASEAN and EEC. Investment opportunities in Malaysia. Role of public and private sectors. Joint ventures. Trade between developed and developing countries. India's development and technological potential. Energy development plans. Overseas banking in India. Development of oil and gas to selfsufficiency. Industrial development. India in the 1980's.

604 INTAL
Incentivos a la exportación y comercio intralatinoamericano : elementos para una propuesta de armonización. - Buenos Aires : INTAL, 1981. 107 leaves

605 INTERNATIONAL TRADE CENTRE/UNCTAD/GATT
Analysis of actual and potential trade flows between developing countries / International Trade Centre. - Genève : UNCTAD/GATT, 1980. (ITC/TD/16/C)

606 INTERNATIONAL TRADE CENTRE/UNCTAD/GATT
The profiles and potential of external trade of members of the Economic Community of West African States. - Genève : UNCTAD/GATT, 1979.

607 INTERNATIONAL TRADE CENTER/UNCTAD/GATT
The scope for increased trade between developing countries in vegetable oils and other oilseed products / ITC UNCTAD/GATT. - Genève : UNCTAD/GATT, International Trade Centre, 1981. XX,282p. Tabs. (ITC publications)

608 INTERNATIONAL trade documentation : annotated list of publications received by the International Trade Centre. - /Geneva/ : International Trade Centre UNCTAD/GATT, Documentation Section, 1983. IVp, 32 leaves. (ITC/TD/DS/61)
Appendix: ITC publications issued in 1982.

609 INTRA-LAFTA trade registers sharp gains over past five years. Business Latin America (New York), October 29, 1980, p.351-352

610 JEPMA, Catrinus
An application of the constant market shares technique on trade between Associated African and Malagasy States and the European Community (1958-1978). Journal of Common Market Studies (Oxford), vol.20, 1981, p.175

611 KIM SHEE POON
The politics of Thailand's trade relations with the people's republic of China. Asian Survey (Berkeley, Ca.), vol.21, no.3, 1981, March, p.310-334

612 KRAVIS, Irving B.
Aranceles aduaneros óptimos, integración y otras estrategias comerciales para América Latina. Integración Latinoamericana (Buenos Aires), año 6, no.64, diciembre 1981, p.2-13

613 KUWAIT and Singapore to expand trade. The Arab Economist (Beirut), vol.13, no.146, November 1981, p.5

614 KUWAITI securities market needs better organization. The Arab Economist (Beirut), vol.13, no.147, December 1981, p.30

615 LALL, Sanjaya
Vertical inter-firm linkages in LDCs : an empirical study. Oxford Bulletin of Economics and Statistics (Oxford), 42, no.3, Aug., 1980, p.203. Tab. Ref.

It is argued that direct relationship established by firms in complementary activites which are external to pure market transactions, are essential to the functioning of any normal industrial market, their role for industrial diversification in developing countries. Economic factors which cause linkages to be established and the form they take. Experience of two principal firms.

616 LANGHAMMER, Rolf J.
The importance of "natural" barriers to trade among developing countries : some evidence from the transport cost content in Brazilian imports. - Kiel : Institute of World Economics, 1982. 22p. (Kieler Arbeitspapiere. Institut für Weltwirtschaft an der Universität Kiel ; 136)

617 LANGHAMMER, Rolf J.
Der Süd-Süd-Handel : Substitut oder Komplement zum Nord-Süd-Warenaustausch? : Substitutions- und Komplementaritätsprozesse im Handel von Entwicklungsregionen 1963-1975. p.141-171
In: Beiträge zur Industrialisierungs- und Handelspolitik der Entwicklungsländer / von Heinz Ahrens ... /et al./. - Berlin : Duncker & Humblot, 1980.

618 LOUSTANAU, Cherie A. COHEN, Jesse B.
An introduction to contract procedures in the Near East and North Africa. 2nd edition. - Washginton, D.C. : US Department of Commerce, International Trade Admi-ministration, 1980. XI,89p.

619 MACQUEEN, Matthew
Lomé and the protective effect of rules of origin. Journal of World Trade Law (London), vol.16, no.2, March-April 1982, p.119-132

620 MADAGASCAR : Libya signs for commercial agreements. AED : Africa Economic Digest (London), vol.2, no.49, 11-17 December 1981, p.10

621 MESA REDONDA UNCTAD/CEESTEM/RDCC SOBRE COOPERACION ECONOMICA ENTRE PAISES EN DESARROLLO, 1982, México
Informe / Mesa Redonda UNCTAD/CEESTEM/RDCC sobre Cooperación Económica entre Países en Desarrollo, México, 22-29 nov. 1982. - Geneva : UNCTAD, 1982. 26,8p.

622 NATH, U.R.
India offers trade and industrial know-how. Africa Economic Digest: AED. Weekly business news, analysis and forecast (London), (2), no.26, June 26, 1981, p.2. Ill. Tabs.

Indian trade with Africa, south of the Sahara. Indian trading stores, traditional and important part of many African countries. Indian technology know-how to Africa. Commodity trade. Indian joint ventures. Tables, 1977-'79.

623 Les PHILIPPINES s'intéressent aux marchés arabes. L'Economiste Arabe (Beirut), vol.24, no.275, octobre 1981, p.13

624 PIZZNO SALAZAR, Diego
Incentivos a la exportación y comercio intralatinoamericano. Comercio Exterior (México), vol.14, nos 3-4, marzo-abril 1982, p.5-40

625 RAVEN, J.
Stream lining the export process. Chamber News. Metropolitan Chamber of Commerce and Industry (Dacca, Bangladesh), Febr. 1981, p.1

Sectors of international trade facilitation, and ways in which developing countries can benefit from them. Standardization of trade documents. Mutual and technical assistance between LDCs. Automatic data processing. Role of national organizations. Examples.

626 POLIĆ, Mario
Suradnja medju nesvrstanim zemljama u razvoju u oblasti trgovine = Cooperation among non-aligned countries in the field of trade. Zbornik trećeg programa Radio Zagreba (Zagreb), no.1, 1977.

627 POLLINS, B.
Breaking trade dependency : Third World proposals for alternative trade regimes in a global simulation. - Berlin : /s.n./, 1981

628 PROTOCOLO modificatorio del Convenio de Cooperación Aduanera peruano-columbiano de 1938, suscrito en Bogotà el 9 de enero de 1981. - Bogotà : /s.n./, 1981. 145 leaves.

629 RANIS, Gustav
Desafíos e oportunidades colocados pelos superexportadores de Asia : implicacoes para o exportaçao de manufacturados de America Latina. Estudos Económicos (San Paulo, Brazil), vol.11, no.2, abril-junio de 1981, p.51-84

630 Las RELACIONES económicas entre el Grupo Andino y los países del Caribe. Integración Latinoamericana (Buenos Aires), año 7, no.75, diciembre 1982, p.74-80

Contents: Marco general de las relaciones internacionales del Grupo Andino con los países del Caribe. Principales caracteristicas de los países del Caribe. Análisis de las relaciones comerciales entre el Grupo Andino y el Caribe. Consideraciones finales.

631 RUIZ NAPOLES, Pablo
El comercio entre países desarrollados y subdesarrollados : algunos aspectos teóricos y de política económica. Comercio Exterior (México), vol.31, no.10, octubre de 1981, p.1173-1178

Los terminos del debate. La teoría de las "ventajas comparativas". Puntos de vista basados en teorías del imperialismo. Elementos para una teoría del intercambio internacional. Replanteamiento del debate político sobre el intercambio.

632 SIERRA-LEONE : Intra-Union trade approved. West Africa (London), no.3404, 1 November 1982, p.2860

633 SOBHAN, Rehman
Enhancing trade between OPEC and the developing countries of Asia. Third World Quarterly (London), vol.4, no.4, October 1982, p.719

634 STEWART, Frances STEWART, Michael
A new currency for trade among developing countries. Trade and Development. UNCTAD review (Genève), no.2, autumn 1980. p.69

635 TAKEUCHI, Kenji
Tropical hardwood trade in the Asia-Pacific region. - Washington, D.C. : World Bank : The Johns Hopkins University, 1974. XVIII, 90p. + 3 annexes, stat. app., references. (World Bank Staff occasional papers ; 17)
ISBN 0 8018 1627 0

Suggests that the Philippines, Malaysia, and Indonesia could industrialize remote areas and more than triple foreign exchange earnings through expansion of wood-processing operations.

636 TERMINOS de intercambio, tarifa óptima e integración. Integración Latinoamericana (Buenos Aires), año 6, no.62, octubre 1981, p.1

637 TRADE and economic integration among developing countries. Finance and Development (Washington, D.C.), (2), June 1982, p.24-27

638 TRADE prospects among the Americas : Latin-American export diversification and the new protectionism, Sao Paulo, Brazil , 1980. Papers and comments. Quarterly review of economics and business (Urbana, Illinois), vol.21, summer 1981 : whole issue.

Contents: Exports and policy in Latin American countries: prospects for the world economy and for Latin-American exports, 1980-90 / by D. Kessing. Commodity exports and NIEO proposals for buffer stocks and compensatory finance: implications for Latin America. Effects of changes in consumption and trade patterns on agricultural development in Latin America / by A. Figueroa. State-owned enterprises in Latin-American exports / by R. Vernon. The Mexican oil syndrome; early symptoms, preventive efforts, and prognosis / by A. Del Rio. Policy responses to external shocks in selected Latin-American countries / by B. Balassa. The burden of exchange rate adjustment in Brazil / by E. Cardoso. Columbia and the Andean group : economic and political determinants of regional integration policy / by M. Urrutia. Challenges and opportunities posed by Asia's superexporters: implications for manufactured exports from Latin America / by G. Ranis. Gains to Latin America from trade liberalization in developed and developing countries / by R. MacCullough. The industry-country incidence of "less than fair value" cases in US import trade / by J. Finger. External debt and the trade imperative in Latin America / by M. Long.

639 TYLER, William G.
Advanced developing countries as export competitors in Third World markets : the Brazilian experience. - Washington, D.C. : Center for Strategic and International Studies, 1980. 87p. (Significant issues series ; vol.2, no.8)

640 TYLER, William G.
Growth and export expansion in developing countries : some empirical evidence. Journal of Development Economics (Amsterdam), vol.9, no.1, August 1981, p.121-130

641 UNCTAD
Trade among developing countries by main SITC groups and by regions. - Genève : UNCTAD, 1980. (UCTAD/TD/B/C.7/45)

SITC Standard International Trade Classification

642 UNCTAD. TDB. Committee on Economic Co-operation among Developing Countries. Session, 2nd, 1981, Genève
Updated information on trade among developing countries by main SITC groups and by regions : statistical note by the UNCTAD secretariat. - Genève : UNCTAD, 1981. /22/ leaves. (TD/B/C.7/45)

643 UNCTAD. TDB. Session, 21., 1980, Genève
Report of the Committee on Economic Co-operation among Developing Countries on its first special session held at the Palais des Nations,Genève, from 23 June to 2 July 1980. - Genève : UNCTAD, 1980. II,26 leaves. (TD/B/818)(TD/B.C.7/44 Suppl.4)

644 La VINCULACIÓN entre los países centroamericanos y la Asociación Latinoamericana de Integración. - Buenos Aires : INTAL, 1981. 41 leaves, 32 tabs.

645 WORTZEL, L.H. WORTZEL, H.V.
Export market strategies of NIC and LDC-based firms. Columbia Journal of World Business (New York), (16), no.1, spring, 1981, p.51. Ref.

Identification of five stages of export marketing. Present status of newly industrialized countries (NIC) exporters and circumstances contributing to this status. Presentation of strategic alternatives for developing countries exporters. Analysis of the major considerations involved in choosing a particular option.

646 YEATS, Alexander J.
Valuación de aranceles, costos de transporte y establecimiento de preferencias comerciales entre países en desarrollo. Integración Latinoamericana (Buenos Aires), no.67, abrile de 1982, p.3-10

647 YELPAALA, K.
The Lomé Conventions and the political economy of the African-Caribbean-Pacific countries : a critical analysis of the trade provisons. Journal of International Law and Politics (New York), vol.13, no.4, 1981

VII-2.1. Global System of Trade Preferences Among Developing Countries

648 GLICK, Leslie Alan, MOCTEZUMA BARRAGAN, Javier
Aspectos jurídicos del Sistema General de Preferencias de Estados Unidos y sus efectos para México. Comercio Exterior (México), vol.31, no.10, octubre de 1981, p.1119-1128

649 KORAK po korak - do slobodne trgovine = Step by step - to the free trade. Glasnik Privredne komore Jugoslavije (Beograd), no.18, 1981, p.22

Globalni sistem preferencijala medju zemljama u razvoju treba da učini njihove proizvode konkurentnijim i tako doprinese njihovom razvoju. Pripremna faza za pregovore je gotovo završena i oni mogu da otpočnu. Medjutim, zbog različitog nivoa razvoja trgovine pojedinih zemalja ne mogu se očekivati brzi i potpuni rezultati.

650 PEÑA, Felix
Système global de préférences commerciales entre pays en développement : l'expérience recueillie, en matière de préférences, dans les systèmes d'intégration en Amérique latine : analyse destinée à en dégager des suggestions applicables à un système global de préférences entre pays en développement. - Genève : UNCTAD, 1979. 83p. (TD/B/C.7/22/Add.1)

651 SHUKLA, Shrirang Purushottam
A global system of trade preferences among developing countries : non-tariff preferences and direct trade measures within a Global System of Trade Preferences : measures and possibilities in the context of the Asian experience, with special reference to manufactures and semi-manufactures. - Geneva : UNCTAD, 1979. II,71p. (Project RAS/78/036/UNCTAD/UNDP)
UNCTAD/ECDC/TA/7

652 SISTEMA Generalizado de Preferencias (SGTP). - Lima : FOPEX-Fondo de Promoción de Exportaciones, 1982. 34p.

653 El SISTEMA Global de Preferencias Comerciales (SGPC) entre países en desarrollo. - Caracas : SELA, 1982. (SP/CL/VIII.O/DT ; 14)

654 THIRD World preferences. West Africa (London), no.3392, 9 August 1982, p.2064

Mr Bhagirath Lal Das, Indian Trade Ambassador in Geneva, told a news conference that representatives of some 70 nations in the Group of 77 had recommended negotiations on a new system of preferences to increase trade among developing countries.

655 UN. General Assembly, Session, 37., 1982, New York
Launching of global negotiations on international economic co-operation for development : development and international economic co-operation / report of the Economic and Social Council ; United Nations. General Assembly, thirty-seventh session, agenda item 12,38 and 71. - New York : United Nations, 1982. 16 leaves. (A/37/544)

656 UNCTAD. Committee on Economic Co-operation among Developing Countries. Session 1st, 1979, Genève
A global system of trade preferences among developing countries (GSTP). - Genève : UNCTAD, 1980. -vols.

TD/B/C.7./36/Add.1:
Statistics of trade among developing countries by country and product : note by the UNCTAD Secretariat. 34p.

TD/B/C.7/36/Add.2:
Trade of developing countries in selected agricultural products and basic commodities by main origins and destinations. 93p.

TD/B/C.7./36/Add.3:
Trade of developing countries in selected manufactures and semi-manufactures by main origins and destinations. VI,201p., 1 ann.

657 UNCTAD. Committee on Economic Co-operation among Developing Countries
A global system of trade preferences among developing countries (GSTP). - Genève : UNCTAD, 1981. -vols.

TD/B/C.7/46:
Measures to counterbalance the loss of customs and fiscal revenues that might ensue for least developed countries from the introduction of the GSTP / report by the UNCTAD Secretariat. II,/18/p.

TD/B/C.7./48:
Relationship between the GSTP among developing countries and the subregional and regional integration groupings of those countries / study by the UNCTAD Secretariat. II,8p.

TD/B/C.7./48/Add.1:
detto : annex: List of members of subregional and regional integration and economic co-operation groupings of developing countries. 2p.

658 YADI, Melchiade
A global system of trade preferences among developing countries : The trade preferences on the African economic co-operation and integration groupings. - Genève : UNCTAD, Committee on Economic Co-operation among Developing Countries, 1979. II,28p.
TD/B/C.7./32

VII-2.2. State Trading Organizations

659 ANOUS, Mohamed K.
Co-operation among State Trading Organizations of Arab Countries / report prepared at the request of the UNCTAD Secretariat. - Genève : UNCTAD, Committee on Economic Co-operation among Developing Countries, 1979. 69 leaves (TD/B/C.7/37)

660 BHANDARI, Basant Raj
Expanding trade through STOs : the Asian experience. International Trade Forum (Genève), December 1979, p.11

661 GORJAN, Božo
Possibilities of co-operation between state trading organizations (STO) of Malta and other developing countries with special reference to the ESCAP countries and to selected product groups : paper submitted to the Meeting of the Asian G-77 Countries on Promotion of State Trading, Djakarta, 1981. - Djakarta : /s.n./, 1981. 21p. + 4 annexes

662 INTERNATIONAL SYMPOSIUM OF STATE TRADING ORGANIZATIONS OF DEVELOPING COUNTRIES, 1982, Ljubljana, Yugoslavia
Report / International Symposium of State Trading Organizations of Developing Countries, Ljubljana-Yugoslavia, 29 March-2 April 1982 ; jointly sponsored by United Nations Conference on Trade and Development (UNCTAD), International Trade Centre UNCTAD-GATT (ITC), International Centre for Public Enerprises in Developing Countries (ICPE), with the financial support of the UNDP Interregional Programme. - Ljubljana : International Centre for Public Enterprises in Developing Countries, 1982. 40p.

663 KOSTECKI, M.M.
State-trading in industrialized and developing countries. Journal of World Trade Law (London), vol.12, 1978, p.187

664 MUKHERJEE, S.K.
Possibilities for co-operation among state trading organizations of developing countries in fertilizer trade. - Genève : UNCTAD, 1982. 3p. (TD/B/C.7/52)

665 POSSIBILITIES for co-operation among state organizations of developing countries in fertilizer trade : addendum, statistical annex. - Genève : UNCTAD, 1982. 121p. Tabs. (TD/B/C.7/52/Add.1)

666 RAHMAN, M.A. BHUYAN, A.R. REZA, S.
The trade effects of South Asian customs union : an expository study. Pakistan Development Review (Islamabad), (20), no.1, spring 1981, p.61. Bibl. Ref. Tabs.

Estimation of the static trade effects of a customs union comprising Bangladesh, India, Nepal, Pakistan and Sri Lanka. Specific form of integration considered here. Factors which effect the magnitude of the effects of the elimination of tariffs on trade in a commodity following the establishment of a customs union. Trade effects on the individual countries and on the region as a whole. Estimated welfare gains.

667 SY, Ibrahim
Co-operation among state marketing companies in French-speaking Africa South of the Sahara / UNCTAD. TDB. Committee on Economic Co-operation among Developing Countries. - Genève : UNCTAD, 1978. III,/27/p. (TD/B/C.7/18/Add.2)

668 STATE trading and development : a perspective view of state trading organizations in developing countries as instruments of national development and channels of international cooperation / edited by Praxy Fernandes. - Ljubljana : International Centre for Public Enterprises in Developing Countries, 1982. 277p.
ISBN 92 9038 070 5

VII-3. INDUSTRIAL CO-OPERATION

669 ALGÉRIE/KOWEIT : association d'investissement. Marchés Tropicaux et Méditerranéens (Paris), 38e année, no.1897, vendredi 19 mars 1982, p.781

670 ALI, Salamat
The gulf narrows : Mrs Gandhi tries to sell her views on regional problems to Saudi Arabia and to improve economic relations. Far Eastern Economic Review (Hongkong), vol.116, no.18, April 30, 1982, p.11

671 ALI, Salamat
Indira's profitable trip : the Indian prime minister wins assurances of aid and investment interest from Saudi Arabia. Far Eastern Economic Review (Hongkong), vol.116, no.20, May 14, 1982, p.95

672 ARAB investments are welcomed in Tunisia. The Arab Economist (Beirut), vol.13, no.138, March 1981, p.26-27

673 AVRAMOVIĆ, Dragoslav
Bridging the gap with joint ventures. South. The Third World Magazine (London), no.20, June 1982, p.69-71

674 AWANOHARA, Susumu
Getting it together - privately : frustrated by red tape and nationalist bickering, Asean businessmen propose a new form of industrial cooperation. Far Eastern Economic Review (Hongkong), vol.11, no.3, 1981, Jan. 9, p.42

675 BAZ, Freddie
La part des sociétés d'investissement dans l'économie arabe. L'Economiste Arabe (Beirut), vol.24, no.277, décembre 1981, p.12-13

676 CHRISTELLER, Christian
Une nouvelle stratégie arabo-iranienne de gestion pétrolière : étude de cas. - Paris : Economica, 1980. IX,295p. Tabl. Diagr.

677 CONTRATACIONES del sector publico en América Latina /INTAL. Integración Latinoamericana (Buenos Aires), no.70, julio de 1982, p.34-36

678 COOPERATION industrielle syro-séoudienne. L'Economiste Arabe (Beirut), vol.24, no.267, février 1981, p.20

679 DAVILA ANDRADE, Osvaldo
Industrialización vía integración subregional : un escarpado camino. /S.l. : s.n./, 1982. 2p.

Documento presentado al 2do Taller Internacional sobre Cooperación Económica entre Países en Desarrollo, México, 22-29 nov. 1982

680 ENTREPRENEURIAL interchange of productive resources among Latin American countries. Latin American Integration (Buenos Aires), June 1982, p.44-46. Tabs. Special English edition.

Summary of a study prepared by Jaime Campos, under the supervision of Guillermo Ondarts.

681 GRANT, K. KENDALL, S. BUCHANAN, R.
Latin America and the Middle East. Middle East Economic Digest : MEED. Weekly news, analysis and forecast (London), Sept. 1981, p.1. Ill. Maps. Ports. Tabs.
Special issue

Role of Cuba's "Uneca". Oil. OPEC. Problems of Venezuela, Mexico, Ecuador. Banking. "Arlabank". Arab investments into Latin America. Brazil and Iraq. Political ties. Figures, 1961-'80.

682 GREEN light for Bolivia-Brazil gas deal. Latin America Weekly Report (London), no.5, Jan., 1981, p.9. Graph. Map.

Construction of gas pipelines from Bolivia and Argentina to Brasil. Industrial projects.

683 INDUSTRIJSKI razvoj i medjusobna suradnja zemalja u razvoju : od male privrede do transnacionalnih kompanija / Deseti okrugli stol zemalja u razvoju, Zagreb, 15.-17. 09.1982 = Industrial development and mutual co-operation among developing countries : from the small-scale economy to the transnational enterprises / The Tenth Round Table of the Developing Countries, Zagreb : /s.n./, 1982.

Contents: Neki aspekti djelovanja višenacionalnih privrednih jedinica u razvoju / Mladen Andrlić. 6p. Raznovrsnijim putevima do progresa / Bogdan Crnobrnja. 9p. Suradnja zemalja u razvoju u izobrazbi industrijske radne snage / Biserka Cvjetičanin. 10p. Mobilizing additional financial resources through greater use of national currencies of developing countries / Ante Čičin-Šain. 16p. Koncepti i institucije medjusobne industrijske suradnje zemalja u razvoju i novi medjunarodni ekonomski poredak/ Djuro Despot. 9p. Novosadski sajam - mesto unapredjenja poslovnih aktivnosti i povezivanja agroindustrijskog kompleksa Jugoslavije i zemalja u razvoju / Ivan Gros. 6p. Institucije za razvoj medjusobne saradnje u oblasti finansiranja privrednog razvoja i realizacija programa iz Karakasa u toj oblasti / Mojmir Mrak. 19p. Suradnja "Rade Končara" sa zemljama u razvoju / Ivo Mučić. 8p. Mutual co-operation of developing countries in technology and human resources development for industrial development in developing countries / Y. Nayudamma. 28p. Human resources development. 13p. Financial co-operation for industrial development of developing countries / Augustin Papić. 13p. Aktivnost farmaceutsko-hemijske proizvodnje "Galenika" Beograd-Zemun na formiranju Centra za bio-tehnologiju i genetičko inženjerstvo u saradnji sa UNIDOM / Vlatko Rukavina. 6p. Suradnja sa zemljama u razvoju na planu transfera tehnologije - jugoslavenska iskustva / Višnja Samardžija. 9p. Industrial co-operation among developing countries : chain approach and some strategies from Indian experience / Nirmal Singh. 8p. Neka iskustva saradnje jugoslovenske inžinjering organizacije i privrede zemalja u razvoju / Dušan Stanojlović. 7p. Contribution to studies of presence and of effects of presence of transnational corporation /TNC/ in developing countries / Srboljub Stojanović. 10p. Internalisation of international economic relations, development and economic co-operation among developing countries / Marjan Svetličić. 21p. Tehnička suradnja medju zemljama u razvoju (TCDC) i nove forme suradnje u industrijskom razvoju / Nada Švob-Djokić. 9p. Problemi kontrole transnacio-

cont.

cont'd

nalnih kompanija / Milan Vojnović. 17p. Business association RUDIS Trbovlje : construction of shoe factories in Algeria. 12p. The Inter-American Development Bank and its activities in Latin America's industrial sector. 16p. Metalurški kombinat "Železara Sisak". 5p. The special unit for TCDC of UNDP and the potential of promoting industrial development. 7p. Tripartite forms of industrial co-operation. 33p.
Annex 4p.

684 JOINT ventures and public enterprises in developing countries : proceedings of an international seminar held in Ljubljana, 4-12 December, 1979 / edited by V.V. Ramanadham, convened by the International Centre for Public Enterprises in Developing Countries in collaboration with the UN Department of Technical Co-operation for Development. - Ljubljana : International Center for Public Enterprises in Developing Countries, 1980, 231p.

685 JOINT ventures through technical co-operation among developing countries and their economic potential / team leader Marjan Svetličič. - Ljubljana : Research Center for Co-operation with developing countries, 1981. 64p.
(UNDP project INT/80/910) (TCDC/2/INF.6)

686 KRIEGER MYTELKA, Lynn
Restructuration de l'industrie textile et relations franco-africaines. Repères. Cahiers du C.E.R.E.S. (Paris), no.67, Nov.-Dec., 1979, p.34-41

687 LIFSCHITZ, Edgardo
Comportamiento y proyección de la industria de automotores en América Latina : los casos de Argentina, Brasil y México. Comercio Exterior (México, D.F.), vol.32, no.7, julio 1982, p.775-785

688 MUTALIK-DESAI, P.V.
Opportunities for joint ventures in Africa. Commerce (Bombay), (143), no.3660, Aug. 8, 1981, p.256. Tabs.

Discussion of the role and experience of Indian industrialists in setting up industries, and transferring skills and technology to Africa. Joint ventures by name of the Indian party, country of location, fields of collaboration and Indian equity. Examples of joint ventures in Tanzania, Nigeria and Libya. Causes of some failures. Recommendations.

689 PATERNO, Vicente T.
South-East Asian experience in industrial joint ventures. Public Enterprise Quarterly Journal (Ljubljana), vol.2, no.3, 1982, p.87-91

690 PAVLIČ, Breda
Joint investments among developing countries and their financing. Public Enterprise Quarterly (Ljubljana), vol.2, no.3, 1982, p.81-86

691 RIEDEL, J. OSTERKAMP, Rigmar SEIBERT, T.
Multilaterale Industriekooperation. - München : /s.n./, 1979, 251p.

692 SVETLIČIČ, Marjan
Joint ventures among developing countries with special emphasis on the role of public enterprises. - Ljubljana : International Center for Public Enterprises in Developing Countries, 1982. 17p.
In: ECA/OAU Regional conference on the role of the public sector in national and regional development in the context of the implementation of the Lagos Plan of Action. 2-9 September 1982, Addis Ababa (Ethiopia)

693 UNIDO
MEETING OF THE AD HOC COMMITTEE ON CO-OPERATION AMONG DEVELOPING COUNTRIES IN THE FERTILIZER INDUSTRY, 1., 1980, Nairobi
Report /of the/ Meeting in Co-operation in Fertilizer Industry, 1980. - Wien : UNIDO, 1980. 18p. (UNIDO-ID/WG.322/2)

/UNIDO pub./ /Report/ of a /meeting/ on /cooperation/ in /fertilizer industry/, with special reference to the relevant /role of developing countries/ - covers (1) implementation of action programme recommended by UNIDO's 2nd consultation (2) additional areas of co-operation (3) mechanisms for implementing co-operation. Additional references: /training assistance/, /advanced skills and technology/, /financing/, /establishment of new industry/, /information service/, /role of UNIDO/, /technical assistance/.
Annexes outline of steps required for setting up viable fertilizer industry. /Recommendation/s, /list of participants/, /list of documents/.

694 UNIDO
REUNION DE SOLIDARITE DES MINISTRES DE L'INDUSTRIE EN VUE DE COOPERER AU DEVELOPPEMENT INDUSTRIEL D'HAITI, 1979, Port-au-Prince
Rapport / Réunion Développement industriel d'Haiti, 1979. - Wien : UNIDO, 1979. 54p. (UNIDO-UNIDO/EX.109) (UNIDO-UNIDO/EX.109/Corr.1)

/UNIDO pub./ /Report/of a ministerial /meeting/ to promote /cooperation/ for/industrial development/ in /Haiti/ (reference: /role of developing countries/) - covers (1) meeting background ; ways to implement /bilateral/ and /multilateral/ /technical assistance/ (2) situation of the /industrial sector/ (3) potential /project selection/ : bilateral discussions between Haitian officials and delegates of /Argentina/, /Barbados/, /Benin/, /Brazil/, /Colombia/, /Mexico/, /Peru/, /Dominican Republic/, /Senegal/ and /Venezuela/. Additional references: /international cooperation/, /industrial project/s, /institutional framework/, /legal aspect/s, /role of UNIDO/. /Recommendation/s. /List of participants/.

695 UNIDO
MEETING ON CO-OPERATION AMONG DEVELOPING COUNTRIES, 1981, Morocco
Report /of a/ Meeting on Cooperation among Developing Countries /organized by the National Council of Pharmacists, Morocco, 1981. - Wien : UNIDO, 1982. 5p. (Meeting on Pharmaceutical Industry, 1981) (UNIDO-UNIDO/PC.34)

/UNIDO publ./ /Report/ on a /meeting/ regarding /TCDC/ in development of /pharmaceutical industry/ -summarizes discussions, mentioning especially issues of production, /choice of technology/, /information exchange/, /training/, and the role of UNIDO/ /technical assistance/ in /cooperation/

696 UNIDO
WORKSHOP ON THE REGIONAL PROJECT FOR CO-OPERATIVE RESEARCH AMONG METALLURGICAL RESEARCH AND DEVELOPMENT CENTRES IN ASIA AND THE PACIFIC, 1981, Jamshedpur, India
Report. - Wien : UNIDO, 1982. 22p. Tabs. (Workshop on cooperative research in metallurgy, Asia and the Pacific, 1981) (UNIDO-ID/WG.361/18)

/UNIDO publ./ /Report/ of a/meeting/ on regional cooperation/ among /metallurgy/ research centre/s in the /ESCAP/ region covers (1) background of the workshop (2) deliberation regarding (a) /research and development/ /technical personnel/ /requirements to 1990/ (b) large scale /cooperation/ to strengthen capabilities of R&D centres (c) "twinning" of metallurgical centres in the region, /list of participants/, /list of documents/, list of centres established with assistance from /UNDP/ and /UNIDO/. Additional references: /technical assistance/, /financing/, /TCDC/, /Asia/

697 UNIDO/ESCAP GROUP MEETING ON REGIONAL CO-OPERATION IN THE VEGETABLE OILS AND FATS INDUSTRY, 1979, Bangkok
Report of the UNIDO/ESCAP Group Meeting on Regional Cooperation in the Vegetable Oils and Fats Industry. - Wien : UNIDO, 1979. 8p. (UNIDO-UNIDO/EX.106)

/UNIDO publ./ /Mission report/ on a /meeting/ regarding /ESCAP/ /regional cooperation/ in the vegetable oil/ industry - (1) covers meeting of major /oil seed/ producing countries in the region with a view to establishing a coordination committee ; comments on relevant /UNIDO/ proposals (2) gives findings and /recommendation/s relative to a proposed "Regional Consultative Forum on the Vegetable Oils Industry". /Agenda/.

698 VÄYRYNEN, Raimo
The Arab Organization of Industrialization : a case study in the multinational production of arms. Current Research on Peace and Violence (Tampere, Finland), 2(2), 1979, p.66-79

699 WHITE, Eduardo
Latin American joint ventures : a new way to strengthen the bargaining power of developing countries vis-a-vis transnational corporations? / with the collaboration of S. Feldman. - New York : United Nations Centre of Transnational Corporations, 1981. 142p. (A technical paper)

VII-4. FINANCIAL-MONETARY CO-OPERATION

700 AFRICAN Development Bank asks for ECOWAS support. AED : Africa Economic Digest (London), vol.2, no.22, May 1981, p.16-17

701 AFRICAN DEVELOPMENT BANK, Abidjan
Agreement establishing the African Development Bank as amended on the seventh day of May, nineteen hundred and eighty two in Lusaka, (Zambia); date of entry into force of Resolution 05-79 of the Board of Governors adopted at Abidjan (Ivory Coast), on the seventeenth day of May ninteen hundred and seventy nine. - Abidjan : African Development Bank, 1981. 38p.

702 AFRICAN DEVELOPMENT BANK GROUP, Abidjan
Report by the Boards of Directors of the African Development Bank Group covering the period from 1st January to 31st December 1980 / ADB seventeenth annual meeting and ADF eighth annual meeting, Lomé May 11-15, 1981. - Abidjan : African Development Bank : African Development Fund, /1981/. 133, 136p. Ill. (ADB/BG/XVII/2)(ADF/BG/VIII/2)
Includes selected abbreviations
Cover title: Annual report 1980

703 AFRICAN DEVELOPMENT BANK GROUP, Abidjan
Report by the Boards of Directors of the African Development Bank Group covering the period from 1st January to 31st December 1981 / ADB eighteenth annual meeting and ADF ninth annual meeting, Lusaka, May 5-8, 1982. - Abidjan : African Development Bank : African Development Fund, /1982/. 133,136p. Ill. (ADB/BG/XVIII/2)(ADF/BG/IX/2)
Includes selected abbreviations
Cover title: Annual report 1981

704 ALI, Sheikh R.
Petropolitics and the Third World. Korea and World Affairs (Seoul), 4(1), spring 1980, p.70-86

705 ALIDE. Asamblea General. Reunión Ordinaria, 10., 1980, Panama
Banca de fomento en la promoción de proyectos y financiamientos multinacionales : anales de la Décima Reunión Ordinaria de la Asamblea General de ALIDE. - Lima : ALIDE, 1980. 367p.

|ALIDE| Asociación Latinoamericana de Instituciones Financieros de Desarrollo

706 ARAB finance for OMVS. AED : Africa Economic Digest (London), vol.3, no.15, April 1982, p.12

707 ARAB monetary integration / edited by Khair El din Haseeb and Samir Makdisi. - London : Croom Helm, 1982. 475p. incl. index.

708 ARIZA, Rafael
La cooperación financiera entre los países latinoamericanos. Integración Latinoamericana (Buenos Aires), 55, marzo de 1981, p.3-19

709 AYARI, Chedly
BADEA (Banque Arabe pour le Développement Economique en Afrique) : de la necessité d'être unis. Jeune Afrique (Paris), 22e année, no. 1118, 9 juin 1982, p. 73

710 AYARI, Chedly
La B.A.D.E.A. est un forum de prédilection pour la coopération entre pays africains et pays arabes. Afrique-Asie (Paris), no. 278, du 27 séptembre au 10 octobre, 1982, p.33

711 BACHA, E. DIAZ ALEJANDRO, Carlos F.
Financial markets : a view from the semi-periphery.- Santiago de Chile : CIEPLAN, 1981. 57p. (Notas técnicas ; 29)

712 BADEA : Banque Arabe pour le Développement Economique en Afrique, /Khartoum/. Jeune Afrique (Paris), 22e année, no. 118, 9 juin 1982, p. 75-80

713 BEAC : Banque des Etats de l'Afrique Centrale : /Yaoundé/ : Cameroun, Centrafrique, Congo, Gabon, Tchad : une institution au service de cinq économies. Jeune Afrique (Paris), 22e année, no.1106, 17 mars 1982, p. 35-54

Neuf ans déjà. Le "franc suisse" del l'Afrique. Quand le franc francais est malade. Vie et mort d'un billet de banque. Au carrefour de cinq économies. "La" banque vue par les banquiers. Un outil d'intégration économique régionale. Une institution qui repose sur une volonté de vivre ensemble / Une interview de Casimir Oye Mba, gouverneur de la BEAC. Qui trace la route et qui pilote? Les services centraux. Les principaux responsables. Décentralisation : former les hommes. Le budget de la BEAC.

714 CONESA, Eduardo R.
La integración como factor de disciplina monetaria. Integración Latinoamericana (Buenos Aires), 55, marzo de 1981, p. 35-42

715 La COOPERACION financiera entre los países Latinoamericana. Integración Latinoamericana (Buenos Aires), (55), marzo 1981, p. 3-19

716 EAST AFRICAN DEVELOPMENT BANK, Kampala (Uganda)
The East African Development Bank and the industrial development of East Africa : ten year report 1967-1977. - Kampala, Uganda : The Bank, /1977/, 45 p. Ill.
At head of title: Partners in development.

717 ECHEGARAY SIMONET, Alfredo
Evolución y perspectivas de la cooperación financiera en América Latina. - Buenos Aires : INTAL, 1982

718 El ENFOQUE monetario de la balanza de pagos. - México : Centro de Estudios Monetarios Latinoamericanos, 1980. XII, 147p. Ill. (Reuniones y seminarios / CEMLA)
Bibliography: p.143-146

719 L'EXPANSION des banques arabes depuis 1973. Syrie et monde arabe. Etude mensuelle économique, politique et statistique (Damascus), (27), no.331, sept. 25, 1981, p.11. Tabs.

Caractéristique du système bancaire. Renforcement. Consolidation. L'extérieur du système bancaire. Banques commerciales. Marché monétaire et financier au Koweit. Système bancaire Séoudite. Développement en Liban. L'internationalisation des activités bancaires arabes. Coopération financière. Activités sur le plan international. Chiffres, 1974-80.

720 FAISONS la connaissance de la BOAD. Jeune Afrique (Paris), no.1068, juin 24, 1981, p.95. Figs. Tabs. Graphs. Portrs.

Rôle de Banque Ouest Africaine de Développement (BOAD) et l'Union Monétaire Ouest Africaine (UMOA) en Afrique de l'Ouest. Structure du capital. Cinq projets. Contrôles. Interview avec le directeur de la BOAD par l'avenir. Chiffres, 1980-'81.

721 FINANCIAL integration in Latin America. Integración Latinoamericana (Buenos Aires), año 6, no.55, marzo 1981.

722 GHARBI, Samir
BADEA : le chaud et le froid : décidés a développer la coopération avec l'Afrique, les Arabes restent intraitables sur toute compromission avec Israël. Jeune Afrique (Paris), 22e année, no.1114, 12 mai 1982, p.25

BADEA Banque Arabe pour le Développement en Afrique

723 HARIK, Antun F.
Problems and prospects of financial integration. The Arab Economist. Center for Economic, Financial and Social Research and Documentation (Beirut), vol.14, no.149, 1982, p.26-31

724 HIGH-LEVEL CONSULTANTS MEETING ON FINANCIAL CO-OPERATION AMONG DEVELOPING COUNTRIES, 1982, Geneva
Hihg-level Consultants Meeting on Financial Co-operation among Developing Countries, Geneva, 8-10 February. - Geneva : UNCTAD, 1982. - 10 vols. (ECDC Staff Group) (various pagings)

1 : The Jamaica Meeting on Finance : major questions / by Dragoslav Avramović, - 12 leaves
2 : Joint ventures among developing countries / by J.D.A. Cuddy. - 13 leaves
3 : Energy investment / by F. Abbate. - 9 leaves
4 : Export credit / by J.D.A. Cuddy. - 10 leaves
5 : Commodity finance / by J.D.A. Cuddy.-5 leaves
6 : The financing of regional credit arrangements among developing countries / by F. Abbate. - /5/ leaves
7 : Payments arrangements for oil imports / by F. Abbate. - 3 leaves
8 : The Caracas Programme on Finance : substance and implementation / by Dragoslav Avramović. - 6 leaves
9 : The non-aligned movement and the Group of 77 : issues in monetary and financial co-operation, with a case study of the non-aligned solidarity fund for economic and social development / by Leelananda de Silva. - 27 leaves
10 : Review of proposals for Third World financing co-operation /by R. Stamenković. - III,43 leaves

725 JAMAICA MEETING OF EXPERTS OF THE GROUP 77 ON ECDC FINANCE, 1982, Kingston, Jamaica
Report by the Rapporteur General on the Jamaica Meeting on ECDC Finance, Kingston, 26-31 March 1982. - Geneva : UNCTAD, 1982. 26 leaves. (GP77/JAM/Finance) (UNCTAD/PSS/TCS/44)

726 KITCHEN, Richard L.
Alternative possibilities for handling balance of payments and debt crises : a Third World Monetary Fund. IFDA Dossier (Nyon, Suisse), no.25, Sept.-Oct. 1981, p.86-88

727 KITCHEN, Richard L.
The development and expansion of south-based financial arrangements and institutions. In: International Financial Flows. - Wien : UNIDO, 1979. p.112-126. (UNIDO-UNIDO/IOD. 324)

/UNIDO publ./ on south-based financial arrangements and institutions, with special reference to the /role of developing countries/ in /export/ /credits/ - covers (1) medium term/ export credit arrangements between /developing country/s : proposed /credit insurance/ scheme, export credit fund to be set up, /regional/ credit systems (2) debt organization: existing systems for debt rescheduling, possible arrangements for handling /balance of payments/ and debt crises. Additional references: /international cooperation/, /institutional framework/, /industrial development/, /capital market/, /trade policy/, /monetary policy/, /South-South/, cooperation.

728 KUWAIT Fund comes first in Arab lending. The Arab Economist (Beirut), vol.14, no.152, May 1982, p.33

729 LEJAVITZER, Moisés
Evolución y estructura de la balanza de pagos de América Latina y el Caribe. - México : Centro de Estudios Monetarios Latinoamericanos, 1979. 177p. Ill. (Series estudios / Centro de Estudios Monetarios Latinoamericanos)

730 MODALIDADES operativas : publicación informativa de la CAF, agosto de 1980

CAF Corporación Andina de Fomento, Caracas /est.1970/

731 MONEY, banking and finance in Africa : bibliography / Association of African Central Banks. - Dakar : African Centre for Monetary Studies, 1979. 257p.

732 MULTILATERAL clearing agreements, economic cooperation and promotion of trade among countries : document prepared by the Ankara Centre for the Third Meeting of Governors of Central Banks and Monetary Authorities, held on September 1-2, 1980 in Riyad, Saudi Arabia. Journal of Economic Cooperation among Islamic Countries (Ankara), Oct., 1980

733 NASR, Z.A.
A proposal for establishing an Arab Fund for Scientific and Technological Development. - /Kuwait/ : Kuwait Fund for Arab Economic Development, 1978. 138p. Ill. Includes bibliographical references.

734 NGABISSIO, Noël Ngouo
Banque du Développement des États de l'Afrique Centrale (BDEAC) : un outil d'intégration économique et d'harmonisation du développement / photos André Lepage. Jeune Afrique (Paris), 22e année, no.1121, 30 juin 1982, p.41-56

Contents: Capital confiance. Le fonctionnement. Un personnel hautement qualifié. Les managers. Des locaux esthétiques et fonctionnels. Comment intervient la Banque. Des règles de prêts rigoureusement définies. 21 projets financés en 6 ans. La coopération internationale. De multiples services. Enoch Derant Lakoué: "Une nouvelle croissance". Répondre aux préoccupations des Etats membres. La Banque en bref.

735 Le NIGERIA recevrait une aide financière d'un milliard de dollars des pays du Golfe. Marchés Tropicaux et Méditerranéens(Paris), 38e année, no.1904, vendredi 7 mai 1982, p.1213

736 OYE MBA, Casimir
Réflexions sur l'évolution et les problèmes monétaires dans la zone de la BEAC : Banque des États de l'Afrique Centrale. Marchés Tropicaux et Méditerranéens (Paris), 38e année, no.1899, vendredi 2 avril 1982, p.885

737 La PROCHAINE entrée du Mali dans l'Union Monétaire Ouest-Africaine : à la veille des réunions ouest-africaines de Dakar. Marchés Tropicaux et Méditerranéens (Paris), 37e année, no.1883, vendredi 11 décembre 1981, p.3279

738 REUNION DE LA BANCA COMERCIAL, 1., 1982, Buenos Aires
La aceptación bancaria latinoamericana (ABLA). - Montevideo : ALADI, 1982. 11p. (ALADI/BC/I/di3)

739 REUNION DE LA BANCA COMERCIAL, 1., 1982, Buenos Aires
Informe / Reunión de la Banca Comercial, 1., Buenos Aires, nov. 28-dic. 1, 1982. - Montevideo : ALADI, 1982. 19p. (ALADI/BC/I/Informe)

740 REUNION DE LA BANCA COMERCIAL, 1., 1982, Buenos Aires
La participación de la Banca Comercial en la promoción y financiamiento de las exportaciones latinoamericanas. - Montevideo : ALADI, 1982. 19p. (ALADI/BC/dt 1)

741 SADDY, Fehmy
OPEC capital surplus funds and Third World indebtedness : the recycling strategy reconsidered. Third World Quarterly (London), vol.4, no.4, October 1982, p.736

742 SAFDAR AKHUND, Erik
Monetary and financial integration. The Arab Economist (Beirut), vol.14, no.153, June 1982, p.33

743 SIMONNOT, Philippe
De nouveaux géants. Jeune Afrique (Paris), no.1055, 25 mars 1981, p.42-43

"Ils" n'ont que le pétrole. Désormais, les pays du Golfe disposent aussi d'un nouvel atout: leur formidable puissance bancaire.

744 SINTESIS de la evolución financiera de América Latina y el Caribe en el año 1979. CEMLA Boletín (México), 26(3), suppl., mayo/jun. 1980, p.181-205

745 SINTESIS de la evolución financiera de América Latina y el Caribe en el año 1980 / CEMLA. - Montevideo : Banco Central del Uruguay, 1981. v.4

CEMLA Centro de Estudios Monetarios Latino-Américanos, México

746 SKULLY, Michael T.
ASEAN regional financial co-operation : developments in banking and finance. Singapore : ISEAS, 1979. 78p. (Occasional paper series ; 56)

ISEAS Institut of Southeast Asian Studies

747 SOBHAN, Rehman
Institutional mechanisms for channelling OPEC surpluses within the Third World. Third World Quarterly (London), vol.11, no.4, October 1980, p.722-745

748 TUNISIE: appel à la coopération financière des pays arabes du Golfe. Marchés Tropicaux et Méditerranéens (Paris), 38e année, no.1895, vendredi 5 mars 1982, p.674

749 UMOA : éléments statistiques de la situation économique et financière de l'Union. Marchés Tropicaux et Méditerranéens (Paris), 38e année, no.1895, vendredi 5 mars 1982, p.678

UMOA Union Monétaire Ouest-Africaine, Paris

VII-5. TECHNICAL CO-OPERATION AND TRANSFER OF TECHNOLOGY

750 ADMINISTRATIVE COMMITTEE ON CO-ORDINATION. Consultative Committee on Substantive Questions. Session 2, 1981, Genève
Economic and Technical Co-operation among Developing Countries : item 6(a) of the provisional agenda / Administrative Committee on Co-ordination. Consultative Committee on Substantive Questions (Operational Activities), second regular session of 1981, Genève, 7-9 July, 1981. - /S.l./: ACC, 1981. 10 leaves. (ACC/1981/OP/7)

751 ALVAREZ SOBERANIS, Jaime
La nueva ley sobre transferencia de technología : aciertos y limitaciones de la política gubernamental. Commercio Exterior (México), vol.32, 1982, p.1117

752 AMIROUCHE, H.
Transfer of technology and inter-arab co-operation = Le transfert de technologie et la coopération interarabe. Acier Arabe. Union Arabe du Fer et de l'Acier (Alger), no.89, 1980, p.24-31; no.90, 1981, p.44-53
Titel u.Text engl.u.franz.

753 ARAOZ, Alberto
CINTERFOR y el Sistema Latinoamericano de Cooperación Tecnica en Formación Profesional. - Montevideo : ILO. CINTERFOR, 1980. 115p. (Estudios y monografias ; 55)

/CINTERFOR pub./ /monograph/ presenting a survey of the networks and mechanisms of /regional cooperation/ in /Latin America/ in the field of technology and /vocational training). Describes the role of /ILO/, /activities/ of /CINTERFOR/ as the nucleus of an /information network/, and the prospects of /self-reliance/, etc. References.

754 ARAOZ, Alberto
Cooperación técnica en América Latina : sugerencias para su fortalecimiento. Comercio Exterior (México), 31(5), may 1981, p.540-550

755 ARAOZ, Alberto
Cooperación técnica entre países en desarrollo : hacia una ampliación de conceptos tradicionales. - Buenos Aires : CISFA, 1976. 17p. (Serie ciencia y tecnología ; 1)

Cooperación internacional/, /asistencia técnica/, /países en desarrollo/ - /relaciones comerciales/, /consultores/, /proyectos de desarrollo/.

756 BASES para la reunión del Grupo de Trabajo ad-hoc del Consejo Latinoamericano sobre Cooperación Técnica. - Caracas : /SELA/, 1982. 16p. (SP/CL/VII.0/DT ; 7)

757 BIBLIOGRAPHY on Technical Co-operation among Developing Countries : /documents of the organizations of the United Nations Development System and other international organizations/. - New York : /United Nations/, 1981. 28 leaves

758 BLAHO, Andras
Transfer of technology and the developing countries. Utafiti (Dar es Salaam), 3(2), 1978, p.283-296

759 CARIBBEAN SEMINAR ON SCIENCE AND TECHNOLOGY POLICY AND PLANNING, 1st, 1973, Bridgetown, Barbados
First Caribbean Seminar on Science and Technology Policy and Planning, Bridgetown, Barbados, Dec. 10-14, 1973. - Washington, D.C. : Regional Scientific and Technological Development Program, General Secretariat of the Organization of American States, 1977. 154p. (Studies on scientific and technological development ; 21)

/Science policy/, /science/, /technology/, /Caribbean/ - /national policy/, /regional cooperation/, /agricultural research/, /technology transfer/, /employment/, food technology/, /foreign trade/, /planning/, /conference report/.

760 COLOMBO PLAN CONSULTATIVE COMMITTEE, Meeting, 26th, 1977, Kathmandu
The transfer and adaptation of technology... : the special topic of the 26th Consultative Committee Meeting, Nepal, 29 November-7 December 1977. - Colombo : Colombo Plan Bureau, 1978. 274p.

At head of the title: The Colombo Plan for Co-operative Economic and Social Development in Asia and the Pacific.

761 COMMONWEALTH Caribbean directory of old agencies : charities, trusts, foundations and official bodies offering assistance in Commonwealth countries in the Caribbean region / consultant editor Norman Tett, assistant editor Ronald Macfarlane. - London : Commonwealth Foundation, 1978. 128p. Map. Bibliography: p.121-122
Includes index.
ISBN 0 903850 15 x

762 CONTRERAS QUINA, Carlos
Transferencia de tecnología a países en desarrollo. - Caracas : Instituto Latinoamericano de Investigaciones Sociales, 1979. 262p. Ill.
Includes bibliographical references.

763 La COOPERACION técnica entre países en desarrollo en los foros internacionales. - Caracas : SELA, 1982. (SP/CL/VIII.O/Di ; 3)

764 COOPERATION technique entre pays en développement : potentionalités tunisiennes. - Tunis : Ministère de l'Economie Nationale, /1981/. 32p. Ill.

765 CORREA, Carlos Maria
El derecho latinoamericano y la propuesta de regulación internacional de la transferencia de tecnología : un análisis preliminar. Integración Latinoamericana (Buenos Aires), 57, mayo de 1981, p.31-58

766 CORREA, Carlos Maria
Regímenes de control de la transferencia de tecnología en América Latina. - Quito : Banco Central del Ecuador, División Técnica, 1980. 174p. (Serie Monografías / Programa Jurídico-Económico sobre Inversiones Internacionales en América Latina ; 5)

Issued jointly with: Inter-American Development Bank, Institute for Latin American Integration and Programa Jurídico-Económico sobre Inversiones Internacionales en América Latina. Includes bibliographical references.

767 CORREA, Carlos Maria
Transfer of technology in Latin America : a decade of control. Journal of World Trade Law (London), vol.15, no.5, Sept./Oct., 1981, p.388-409

768 CORREA, Carlos Maria
El trato preferencial de la consultoría e ingeniería locales en América Latina. Integración Latinoamericana (Buenos Aires), no.70, julio de 1982, p.21-33

769 DELOCALISATION du capital et discipline du travail. Critique de l'Economie Politique (Paris), no.14, janv./mars 1981, 149p.
Special issue.
Concerns Latin America and Asia.

770 La DEPENDANCE et le transfer de technologie : 3ème journée d'étude du CEDAF (Centre d'étude et de documentation africaines). Les Cahiers du CEDAF, no.5-6, 1981

771 DIRECTORY of focal points for TCDC = Répertoire des centres de promotion de la CTPD = Catalogo de centros de coordinación para la CTPD. - /New York/: UNDP, 1981. 194p.

772 FLIT, Isaias
Integración tecnológica en América Latina y el Caribe : un plan de acción. Socialismo y Participación, no.15, septiembre 1981, p.105-116

773 GREEN, Reginald Herbold
Technical cooperation among developing countries : notes towards an action prospectus. International Problems (Tel Aviv, Israel), 1976/1977

774 GROUP OF 77, 1981, Wien
Report of the Technical Meeting of Experts of the Group of 77 on Technology and Industrialization in preparation for the High-level Conference on Economic Cooperation among Developing Countries, Vienna, 1981. - Wien : UNIDO, 1981. 14p.

/Report/ of the /meeting/ on promotion of /technology/ and /industrialization/, with special reference to the /role of developing countries/ in /cooperation/ - gives experts' /recommendations/ regarding creation of /technological institute/s and agencies as focal points for /industrial services/ ; facilitating access to technology ; sectorial services ; monitoring technology use in DCs ; /innovation/s and research/ ; increasing negotiating capacities ; /technology transfer/ ; research and development /concerning energy source/s ; /industrial information/ ; /industrial project/s ; /training/. Additional references: /advanced skills and technology/, /industrial institutions/, South-South/.

775 HANSEN, Barbara
Economic aspects of technology transfer to developing countries. International Review of Industrial Property and Copyright Law (Weinheim, F.R.G.), 11(4), 1980, p.429-440

776 HIGH-LEVEL POLICY MEETING ON THE REGULATION OF TECHNOLOGY TRANSFER, 1981, Wien, Lisboa
The possibilities and feasibilities of ASEAN regional co-operation in technology transfer. - Wien : UNIDO, 1981. 6p. (UNIDO-ID/WG.349/1)

/UNIDO pub/ on potential of /ASEAN/ /regional cooperation/ in /technology transfer/ - covers (1) purposes of ASEAN establishment (1967) ; /administrative aspects/ (2) /import/ of technology promoting /industrialization/ into member countries ; /import volume/ and value ; /prices/ paid ; /technology policy/ and control ; need for indigenous development of technological capabilities (3) some suggestions for co-operation. Additional references: /economic integration/, /Malaysia/, /Thailand/, /Singapore/, /Indonesia/, /Philippines/, /role of UNIDO/, /TIES/, /information system/.

777 HODARA, Joseph
Se reunió la Comisión de Ciencia y Tecnología del Clacso. Comercio Exterior (México), vol. 32, 1982, p.146

CLACSO Consejo Latinoamericano de Ciencias Sociales, Buenos Aires /1967/

778 HUSSEIN, Aminu
The Group of 77, the United Nations and the quest for a new international technological order : political-economic analysis of issues, processes and evolving policies. - Ann Arbor, Mich. : University Microfilms International, 1982. X, 309p.

Thesis (Ph.D.) - Case Western Reserve University, Cleveland, Ohio, 1981. Bibliography: p.278-292

779 INFORME sobre cooperación técnica entre países en desarrollo (CTPD). - Caracas : SELA, 1981. 5p. (SP/CL/VII.O/Di ; 4)

780 INTEGRATION of science and technology with development : Caribbean and Latin American problems in the context of the United Nations Conference on Science and Technology for Development / edited by D. Babatunde Thomas, Miguel S. Wionczek. - New York : Pergamon, /1979/, XII, 278p. (Pergamon policy studies ; 22)
ISBN 0 08 023881 5

Proceedings of a Symposium in Miami, April 6-8, 1978, sponsored by Florida International University, the Institute of Social and Economic Research, University of the West Indies and the Institute of Development Studies, University of Guyana. Includes bibliographical references and index.

781 INTER-COUNTRY institutional arrangements for economic and technical co-operation among developing Asian and Pacific countries. - New York : United Nations, Economic and Social Commission for Asia and the Pacific, 198-- . - vols. (ESCAP TCDC Publications)

Vol. 1 : Intergovernmental institutions. - 1980. IX, 196p. (ST/ESCAP/102/TCDC/IIA/1)
Vol. 2 : Non-governmental and national institutions. - 1980. XVII, 182p. (ST/ESCAP/132/TCDC/IIA/2)
Vol. 3 : Pacific institutions / prepared in co-operation with the Institute of Pacific Studies, the University of the South Pacific, Suva, Fiji. - 1981. XXIII, 206p. Map. Ill. (ST/ESCAP/168/TCDC/II/A3)

782 INTERNATIONAL WORKSHOP ON THE PROMOTION OF ECONOMIC AND TECHNICAL CO-OPERATION AMONG DEVELOPING COUNTRIES WITH PARTICULAR REFERENCE TO DEVELOPING COUNTRIES' JOINT INVESTMENTS AND THEIR FINANCING, 1981, Bled, Yugoslavia
Report of the International Workshop on the Promotion of Economic and Technical Co-operation among Developing Countries with Particular Reference to Developing Countries' Joint Investments and their Financing, (Bled, Yugoslavia, 2-7 November 1981) /Organized jointly by RCCDC, Ljubljana, and UNCTAD Secretariat, sponsored by UNDP, UNIDO, FAO, UNCTC and the Yugoslav and Dutch Governments/. - Genève : UNCTAD, 1982. /32/p. (UNCTAD/ECDC/TA/14)

Proceedings of the Workshop published under the title: Challenges of South-South Co-operation. - Boulder, Colorado : Westview Press, 1983. XII,455p. Tabs.

783 JOINT OAU/UNIDO SYMPOSIUM ON INDUSTRIAL TECHNOLOGY FOR AFRICA, 1980, Khartoum
Intra-African co-operation in industrial technology = Coopération intra-africaine en matière de technologie industrielle. - Wien : UNIDO, 1980. 12p. (UNIDO-ID/WG. 332/7)

/UNIDO pub/ on /Africa/n /regional cooperation/ in industrial /technology/ - covers (1) antecedents and present situation ; concepts of collective /self-help/ and mutual assistance ; relevant /recommendation/s ; specific programme (2) a framework for action. Additional references: /technology policy/, /technology transfer/, /research and development/, /industrial information/, /science/, /education/, /role of UNIDO/, /INTIB/, /TIES/

784 JUNAC
Inventarios de capacidades tecnológicas : fabricantes de bienes de capital de la Subregión Andina, 1981. - Lima : JUNAC, 1981. 584p.

785 KATZ, Jorge ALBIN, Eduardo
Da industria nascente a exportaçao de tecnología : a experiencia argentina. Estudos Económicos, vol.11, no.2, abril-junio 1981, p.103-121

786 KHERA, Inder P.
Technology transfer from Third World countries : opportunities and problems. Foreign Trade Review (New Delhi), 14(4), Jan./March, 1980, p.333-348.

With some emphasis on the role of multinationals.

787 MEETING OF HEADS OF NATIONAL AGENCIES OF TECHNICAL COOPERATION AMONG DEVELOPING COUNTRIES, 1st, 1982, Tunis
Final report / First meeting of heads of national agencies of technical cooperation among developing countries, Tunis, 25-29 October, 1982. - Tunis : Technical Cooperation Agency of Tunisia ; Geneva : International Club of Cooperation, 1982. 1 vol. (various pagings)
Abbreviations

788 MEETING ON ECONOMIC AND TECHNICAL CO-OPERATION AMONG LATIN AMERICAN MULTINATIONAL ENTITIES, 1981, San José, Costa Rica
Conclusions of the Meeting on Economic and Technical Co-operation among Latin American Multinational Entities, (San José, Costa Rica, December 3 to 4, 1981). - Caracas : SELA, 1982. 5 leaves (SP/CL/VII.O/Di.5)

789 MENCK, Karl W.
Economic and technical co-operation among the developing countries. Economics (Tübingen), vol.24, 1981, p.88-108

790 MISION de cooperación técnica a la Comunidad Económica del Africa Occidental (CEAO) - Caracas : SELA, 1981. (SP/CL/VII.O/Di ; 6)

791 NAIROBI recommendations for a Programme of Technical Co-operation among African Countries = Recommendations de Nairobi pour un Programme de Coopération Technique entre Pays Africains. - /S.l. : s.n., 1980/, 23p.

Contents: The Nairobi Recommendations emerged from the Conference on African Government Experts of Technical Co-operation among African Countries, organized in Nairobi, Kenya, 12-20 May 1980, by the UNDP's Regional Bureau for Africa. Representatives of 45 African countries and 52 international intergovernmental and non-governmental organizations participated in the Conference.

792 NECESIDADES de cooperación técnica subregional en el Istmo Centroamericano, 1982-1986 / Comite de Cooperación Técnica del Istmo Centroamericano. - México, DF : CEPAL, 1981. 18p.

793 ORGANISATION of the Islamic Conference : technical co-operation among member states of the Islamic Conference : a résumé of the activities of the Ankara Centre. Journal of Economic Cooperation among Islamic Countries (Ankara), vol.2, no.2, 1981

794 OTEIZA, Enrique RAHMAN, Anisur
Technical co-operation among developing countries as a dimension of a New International order. - /S.l. : s.n./, 1978. 31 leaves

This report was prepared by the authors at the request of the UNDP, in connection with the UN Conference on Technical Co-operation among Developing Countries. It has been submitted to the UNDP as agreed.

795 OTEIZA, Enrique RAHMAN, Anisur
Technical co-operation among Third World countries and the international order / edited by Leelananda de Silva. - México : Third World Forum, 1978. 72p. (Occasional paper / Third World Forum ; 3)

796 PIÑEIRO, Martin TRIGO, Eduardo
Cambio técnico y modernización en el sector agropecuario de América Latina : un intento de interpretación. Desarrollo Económico (Buenos Aires), vol.21, no.84, enero-marzo 1982, p.435-468

797 RADWAY, Robert J.
Comparative evolution of technology transfer policies in Latin America : the practical realities. Denver Journal of International Law and Policy (Denver, Colo.), 9(2), summer 1980, p.197-215

798 RADWAY, Robert J.
Transferencia de tecnología a Colombia : un análisis específico del sector procesador de alimentos. Revista ANDI, no.53, 1981, p.55-86

799 REDES de cooperación técnica multilateral en América Latina : análisis de algunas experiencias. - Caracas : SELA, 1982. (SP/CL/VIII.O/Di ; 4)

800 REGIMEN de la transferencia de tecnología en los países de América Latina : textos legales y procedimientos administrativos. - Buenos Aires : Instituto para la Integración de América Latina : Banco Inter-Americano de Desarrollo, 1977- . -vol. Ill.

Subjects: License agreements -- Asociación Latinoamericana de Libre Comercio countries / technical assistance / patent licenses -- Asociación Latinoamericana de Libre Comercio countries.

801 REGIMEN legal del regalías : transferencia de tecnología, propriedad industrial. - Bogotá : Cámara de Comercio, 1982. 190p.

802 REGIONAL COORDINATION AND CONSULTATION MEETING ON TECHNICAL COOPERATION AMONG DEVELOPING COUNTRIES, 2., 1981, New York
Final report of the Second Regional Coordination and Consultation Meeting on Technical Cooperation among Developing Countries, /New York, May 27-29. 1981/ / 8th Regular Meeting of the Latin American Council Caracas, July 19-28, 1982. - /S.l./: SELA, 1981. /17/p. (RC/II/DF/1) (SP/CL/VIII.O/DT No.10)

803 REGULAR MEETING OF THE LATIN AMERICAN COUNCIL, 8., 1982, Caracas
Multilateral technical co-operation networks in Latin America : analysis in some experiences. - /S.l./ : SELA, 1982. 135p. (SP/CL/VIII.O/Di 4)

804 REMICHE, Bernard
Le transfert de technologie en Amérique Latine : rapport présenté dans le cadre du séminaire organisé à Louvain-la-Neuve par le Centre d'Etudes Européennes de l'Université Catholique de Louvain. - /S.l. : s.n./, 1979. 59p.

Les aspects juridiques et économiques de l'intégration en Amérique Latine.

805 RENEWABLE sources of energy. - New York : United Nations, Economic and Social Commission for Asia and the Pacific, 198-- . - vols. (ESCAP ECDC-TCDC Publications)

Vol.1 : Solar energy, 1980
Vol.2 : Biogas, 1981
Vol.3 : Wind energy, 1981
Vol.4 : Small hydropower development / prepared in co-operation with the United Nations Industrial Development Organization (UNIDO), Vienna. - 1980. II,309p. Ill. (ST/ESCAP/208)
Vol.5 : Draught animal power (under preparation)

806 REUNION CONJUNTA DE EXPERTOS GUBERNAMENTALES DE AFRICA Y AMERICA LATINA SOBRE COOPERACION ECONOMICA Y TECNICA, 1982, Addis Ababa
Informe / Reunión Conjunta de Expertos Gubernamentales de Africa y América Latina sobre Cooperación Económica y Técnica, Addis Ababa, 1-4 junio 1982. - Santiago de Chile : CEPAL, 1982. 25p.

CEPAL Comisión Económica para América Latina

807 REUNION CONSULTIVA SOBRE MECANISMOS DE COOPERACION TECNICA ENTRE PAISES DE LA REGION, 1977, Bogotà
Reunión consultiva sobre mecanismos de cooperación tecnica entre países de la región, Bogotà, septiembre de 1977, Proyecto 150 / Servicio Nacional de Aprendizaje. - Montevideo : ILO, 1978. 100p. (Informes ; 80)

/CINTERFOR pub./ /conference report/ and /recommendation/s concerning /regional cooperation/ in matters of /vocational training/ in /Latin America/. Examines /training programme/ requirements, /financing/ mechanisms, problems, etc. in context with Cinterfor project 150. /Conf/ Bogotà 1977 sep 7 and 8.

808 REUNION DE COORDINACION Y CONSULTA REGIONAL SOBRE COOPERACION TECNICA ENTRE PAISES EN DESARROLLO, 2, 1982
Informe final. - Caracas : SELA, 1982. (SP/CL/VIII.O/DT ; 10)

809 REUNION SOBRE COOPERACION ECONOMICA Y TECNICA ENTRE ORGANISMOS Y MULTINACIONALES LATINOAMERICANOS, 1981, San José, Costa Rica
Conclusiones / Reunión sobre Cooperación Económica y Técnica entre Organismos y Multinacionales Latinoamericanos, San José, Costa Rica, 3-4 diciembre 1981. - Caracas : SELA, 1982. 6p. (SP/CL/VII.O/Di ; 5)

810 SABATO, Jorge A.
Nueva ley de transferencia de tecnología de Argentina. Comercio Exterior (México), 31(8), agosto de 1981, p.888

811 SABATO, Jorge A.
Procura nueva ley de transferencia de technología de Argentina : marcha atrás. Interciencia (Caracas), vol.6, no.6, noviembre-diciembre de 1981, p.415-416

812 SAGASTI, Francisco R.
Autodependencia tecnológica y cooperación entre los países del Tercer Mundo. Estudios Internacionales (Buenos Aires), vol.9, no.33, enero-marzo 1976, p.47-61

/Personal CIID/, /autodesarrollo/, /política científica/, /cooperación científica/, /países en desarrollo/ - /marco institucional/, /bibliografía/.

813 SALAM, Abdus UDGAONKAR, B.M.
Science and technology capability building in the Third World countries : some issues. - IFDA Dossier (Nyon), no.29, May-June 1982

814 SELECT bibliography of documents on transfer and development of technology that have been prepared by or for the UNCTAD secretariat/ United Nations Conference on Trade and Development. Trade and Development Board. Committee on Transfer of Technology. - Genève : UNCTAD, 1980. 18p. (TD/B/C.6/INF.2/Rev.2)

815 TRAINING courses available in developing ESCAP countries 1979. - New York : United Nations ; Bangkok : Economic and Social Commission for Asia and the Pacific, 1979. III,402p. (ESCAP TCDC publications) ST/ESCAP/80

Index of training courses

816 UNCTAD. TDB. Committee on Transfer of Technology, Session, 4., Genève
Conclusions and recommendations adopted by the meeting of governmental experts on the transfer, application and development of technology in the energy sector : item 3(2)(ii) of the provisional agenda / note by the UNCTAD secretariat. - Genève : UNCTAD, 1982. 4p. (TD/B/C.6/L.41)

817 UNCTAD. TDB. Committee on Transfer of Technology, Session, 4., 1982, Genève
A strategy for the technological transformation of developing countries ; item 3 of the provisional agenda / report by the UNCTAD secretariat. - Genève : UNCTAD, 1982. III,35 leaves. (TD/B/C.6/90)

818 UNCTAD. TDB. Committee on Transfer of Technology, Session, 4., 1982, Genève
Strengthening the domestic technological capacity of developing countries : technical and operational assistance by the Advisory Service on Transfer of Technology : item 3(a) of the provisional agenda / report by the UNCTAD secretariat. - Genève : UNCTAD, 1982. V,/36/p. (TD/B/C.6/93)

819 UNDP/UNCTAD Programme of Economic and Technical Co-operation among Developing Countries : list of on-going UNDP assisted projects and projects in the pipeline according to the main programme areas of the UNDP/UNCTAD Programme. - /Genève : UNCTAD, 1980/. 11 leaves

820 UNITED NATIONS. General Assembly, High-Level Committee, Session, 36., 1981, New York
Report of the High-Level Committee on the review of technical co-operation among developing countries. - New York : United Nations, 1981. IV,35p. (Official records : thirty-sixth session / General Assembly : suppl. 39, A/36/39)

821 WHITE, Eduardo FELDMAN, Silvio
Organizational forms of transfer of technology to developing countries by small and medium-sized enterprises : a case study of equity joint ventures and technology agreements in Latin America /presented to the/ Trade and Development Board, Committee on Transfer of Technology, fourth session, Geneva, 29 November 1982. - Geneva : UNCTAD, 1982. VIII,62p. Tabs. (TD/B/C.6/77)

UNCTAD United Nations Conference on Trade and Development, Geneve

UNDP United Nations Development Programme, New York

VII-6. CO-OPERATION IN THE FIELD OF INFORMATION AND COMMUNICATION AMONG DEVELOPING COUNTRIES

822 AGUIRRE-BIANCHI, Claudio HEDEBRO, Göran
The challenge of co-operation : a study of alternative communication in Latin America . - Stockholm : University, Institute of Latin America, 1980. 68p. (Research paper series ; 17)
References

823 AHCENE-DJABALLAH, Belkacem
Aspect du nouvel ordre international de l'information : étude et documents. - Alger : Office des Publications Universitaires, 1980. 217p. Tabl.

824 AIYPEKU, W.O.
Global, African and Nigerian efforts to develop information systems for socio-economic development. - Ottawa, Ontario : Information Sciences Division, IDRC, 1981. 14p.
IDRC-Doc.276

/IDRC personnel/, /DEVSIS/, /Africa/ - /information policy/, /regional level/, /national level/, /Nigeria/, /libraries/, /IDRC mentioned/

DEVSIS Development Science Information System

825 ARBOLEDA-SEPULVEDA, O.
Visión general de la documentación e información agricola en los países de la Zona de las Antillas. - San José : CIDIA, 1977. 19p.

/Subvención CIID/, /servicios de información/, /AGRIS/, /Caribe/, /Guyana// - /documentación/, /agricultura/, /encuestas/

826 ARRIAGA, Patricia
Publicidad, economía y comunicación masiva : Estados Unidos y México. - México : CEESTEM : Editorial Nueva Imagen, 1980. 324p.
Bibl. p.291-324

827 ARRIETA ABDALLA, Mario
Obstáculos para un Nuevo Orden Informativo Internacional. - México : CEESTEM : Editorial Nueva Imagen, 1980. 415p.
Bibl. p.399-415
ISBN 968 429 273 2

CEESTEM Centro de Estudios Económicos y Sociales del Tercer Mundo

828 AUBRAC, R.
Information systems and services in the UN family of organisations : information for development planning. - Bangkok : Asian and Pacific Development Institute, 1979. p.250-254

/IDRC personnel/, /information systems/, /information services/, /UN/ - /INIS/, /AGRIS/, /data banks/.

829 AWANOHARA, Susumu
The computer society : Singapore's bid to become a regional leader in data processing attracts swarms of salesmen. Far Eastern Economic Review (Hongkong), vol.113, no.36, 1981, Aug. 28, p.73

830 BAJRA, Ismail
The non-aligned and the New International Information System. Review of International Affairs (Beograd), no.700, 1979.

831 BAJRA, Ismail
The non-aligned countries and the new system of information and communications. Review of International Affairs (Beograd), 32(750/1), 5/20 July 1981, p.7-9

832 BARTOLOVIĆ, Dragan
The contemporary world, underdeveloped countries and communication. Socialist Thought and Practice (Beograd), vol.19, no.3, 1979.

833 CAPRILES ARIAS, Oswaldo
Reflexion sobre las políticas de communicación. Nueva Sociedad (Caracas), no.52, 1981, p.67-83

834 CATHERINET, M.D.
Étude du plan d'opérations de RESADOC. - /Ouagadougou/ : Comité Inter-états de Lutte contre la Sécheresse dans le Sahel, 1980. 1 vol. (paginations diverses)

/Subvention CRDI/, /réseau d'information/, /services d'information/, /information scientifique/, /information technique/, /Sahel/ - /plan d'opération/, /base de données/, /coopération régionale/, /mise en place des encadrements/, /budget/, /aspects financiers/, /recommendation/.

835 CEDEAO : télécommunications : appel d'offres international. Marchés Tropicaux et Méditerranéens (Paris), 38e année, no.1894, vendredi 26 février 1982, p.613

836 CLADES : its role and functions. - Santiago : CLADES, 1977. 14 leaves. (CLADES information ; 5)

CLADES Centro Latinoamericano de Documentación Económica y Social, Santiago

837 COMMUNICATION economics and development / ed. by Jussawalla M., Lamberton D.M. - New York : Pergamon, 1982. 355p. Figs. Graphs. Ref. Tabs. (Pergamon policy studies on international development)

Sixteen contributions by M.Jussawalla,D. Lamberton, P. Streeten, C. Jonscher, H. Dordick, M. Porat, R. O'Brien, G. Helleiner, J. Galtung, K. Uno, a.o. on integrating the areas of communication and economics. Information, communication and division of labour. Communications in international trade theory. International economic order. Role of communication in Japanese economic development. Development benefits from telecommunication. Telecommunication in developing countries. Impact of telecommunication on agricultural development in Nepal. Use of economic concepts in communicating planning practice ; analysis of six agencies in the USA, Canada, Thailand, Malaysia and the Philippines. Statistics, 1960-1980.

838 COMMUNICATIONS in the rural Third World : the role of information in development / edited by Emile G. McAnany. - New York : Praeger, 1980. XVI,222p. (Praeger special studies) (Praeger scientific)
Bibl. p.201-219. Includes index
ISBN 0 03 052986 7

839 COMPUTERS in developing nations / J.M. Bennet, and R.E. Kalman, editors. - Amsterdam : North-Holland, 1981. XVI, 272p.
ISBN 0 444 86270 6
/Proc. of IFIP TC-9 Int.Seminar, Melbourne, Australia, 13. October 1980/

Contents: Preface. Opening and closing session / Papers by Y. Paker and O. Rateau. Session: Strategies and policies for development / Papers by R.E. Kalman, M.E. Müller, B. Nag, H. Sackman. Computer policies in India: Relevance for the Third World / Papers by A. Balasubrahmanian, S.V. Deodhar, P.P. Gupta, T.V. Natarajan. Computer futures in the ASEAN/PNG region / Papers by P.F. Baraoidan, N.G. Cook, R. Lau, C.F. Lau, R.J. Pesik. Computer advances and applications of relevance to developing countries / Papers by D. Chevion, S.-C. Loh, O. Longe, B.D. Pradhan. Realities of computer and satellite use in developing nations / Papers by U.K. Banerjee, R. Buhler, S.G. Kingan, J. Moo, I.B. Sulaiman. Computers and cooperation : aids to development in the 1980s / Papers by C.C. Gottlieb and D.D. Cowan, V.G. Jorssen, N. Sharif.

840 CONFERENCE OF BROADCASTING ORGANIZATIONS OF DEVELOPING COUNTRIES, 2nd, 1980, Freetown
Druga konferencija radiodifuznih organizacija nesvrstanih zemalja, Fritaun, Sijera Leone, 1980. - Beograd : Jugoslovenska radiotelevizija, /1980/. 105p.

841 CONSULTATION ON THE CO-OPERATION DEVELOPMENT OF NATIONAL INFORMATION SYSTEMS IN THE CARIBBEAN REGION, 1980, Kingston
Consultation on the Co-ordinated Development of National Information Systems in the Caribbean Region, Kingston, 19-23 May 1980 : working paper. - Paris : Unesco, 1980. 14p.
PGI-80/CS/14/5
PGI-80/WS/4

/Information systems/, /information services/, /regional cooperation/, /Caribbean/ - /pilot projects/.

842 COTE d'Ivoire information : coopération avec Sénégal. Marchés Tropicaux et Méditerranéens (Paris), 38e année, no.1895, vendredi 5 mars 1982, p.681

843 CUSICANQUI VELASCO, J.
Servicio de información y documentación sobre juventud rural : un instrumento para el desarrollo. - San José : IICA, Secretaria Interamericana de Juventudes Rurales, 1980, 11p.

/Subvención CIID/, /servicios de información/, /juventud rural/, /América Latina/ - /elaboración de proyectos/, /implementación de proyectos/, /publicaciones/, /documento de reunión/.

844 CVIJETIČANIN, Biserka
Novi kulturni poredak i kulturna suradnja medju nesvrstanim zemljama = The new cultural order and cultural co-operation among non-aligned countries. Zbornik trećeg programa Radio Zagreba (Zagreb), no.1, 1977

845 DIZDAREVIĆ, Faik
Saradnja radio-difuzija nesvrstanih zemalja : stanje i mogućnosti = The co-operation among broadcast organizations of non-aligned countries : achievements and prospects. Zbornik trećeg programa Radio Zagreba (Zagreb), no.1, 1977.

846 ESCAP. Study Group on the Co-ordination of Government Information Systems, Session, 2., 1981, Bangkok
Technology transfer to developing countries / Economic and Social Commission for Asia and the Pacific, Study Group on the Co-ordination of Government Information Systems, second session 2-7 February 1981, Bangkok / paper submitted by Owe Salomonsson. - /S.l. : s.n./, 1981. 7p. (ADM/CGIS (2)/4

847 GALILEA,Sergio O. NUÑEZ,Benjamin M.
Modelo de desarrollo nacional y regional y el sistema de información en el periodo 1964-1970. - Santiago de Chile : CIDU : IPU, 1981. 79p.

848 HAMELINK, Cees J.
The new international information order : development and obstacles. Occasional Paper. Vienna Institute for Development (Wien), no.2, 1980, /26p./

849 INFORMATION for development in Latin America and the Caribbean : summary of a meeting held in Cali, Colombia, 23-28 October 1977. - Ottawa : IDRC, 1979. 28p.

Summary of a meeting on information for development and problems related to the implementation of national information systems in Latin America and the Caribbean. Discusses AGRIS, AGRINTER, UNDP and the role of CLADES in the possible regional implementation of DEVSIS.

850 INFORMATION system for planning in Latin America and the Caribbean : a basic instrument for coordination and cooperation among developing countries. - Santiago : CLADES, 1979. 97p. (E/CEPAL/CLADES/G.2)

851 INTERGOVERNMENTAL CONFERENCE ON COMMUNICATION POLICIES IN AFRICA, 1980, Yaoundé
Final report / Intergovernmental Conference on Communication Policies in Africa, 1980, (Yaoundé). - Paris : Unesco, 1981. 81p.

852 INTERNATIONAL SERIALS DATA SYSTEMS. Regional Center for Southeast Asia
Final report covering February 1977 - December 1979. - Bangkok : ISDS-SEA Regional Centre, 1980. 1 vol. (various pagings)

853 JAWORSKI, Helan C.
Development information network for co-operation among developing countries : multi-regional feasibility study. - New York : UNDP, 1980. 56p. Illustr.

854 JUNAC. Expertos gubernamentales. Reunión, 2., 1980
Informe final de la segunda reunión de expertos gubernamentales sobre el sistema andino de información tecnológica. (JUN/REG.SIT/II/Informe final.Rev. 1, 16 de junio de 1980)

855 JUNAC.
Propuesta de la Junta para la creación del sistema andino de información tecnológica y del programa para su establecimiento progresivo. (JUN/Propuesta 112, 30 de enero de 1980)

856 KUHENGA, Makwaia
Africa and the NIIO. Third World (México City), no.3, nov. 1979, p.108
Special issue.

NIIO New International Information Order

857 Lista de publicaciones de CLADES disponibles / Centro Latinoamericano de Documentación Económica y Social. - Santiago : CLADES, 1980. 5p. (E/CEPAL/CLADES/L.4)

858 MANY voices, one world : towards a new more just and more efficient world information and communication order / /report by The International Commission for the Study of Communication Problems/. - London : Kogan Page ; New York : Unipub ; Paris : Unesco, /198-/. XX,312p. Bibl. Ref. Index

At head of the title: Communication and society : today and tomorrow. President of the Commission, Sean MacBride.

859 MARTELANC, Tomo
Nesvrstani u borbi za novi medjunarodni informativni poredak = The non-aligned in the struggle for a new international information order. Zbornik trećeg programa Radio Zagreba (Zagreb), no.1, 1977

860 MEETING OF LIBRARIANS AND DOCUMENTALIST, Port of Spain
Report on Meeting of Librarians and Documentalists, Port of Spain, Trinidad and Tobago / Caribbean Development and Cooperation Committee. - Port of Spain : ECLA, Office for the Caribbean, 1977. 9p. (E/CEPAL/CDCC/24)

/IDRC supported/, /information services/, /information systems/, /libraries/, /regional cooperation/, /Caribbean/ - /conference report/, /obstacles to development/, /development strategy/, /recommendation/, /list of participants/, /list of documents/

861 MEETING OF THE RESEARCH AND INFORMATION SYSTEM OF THE NON-ALIGNED AND OTHER DEVELOPING COUNTRIES, 1st, 1979, Beograd
Final report of the first Meeting of the Research and Information System of the Non-aligned and other Developing Countries, held in Belgrade, January 23-25, 1979. /S.l. : s.n 1979/. 1 vol. (various pagings)

862 MEYER, Reinhold
Africa : the role of mass media in promoting rural development : reality and myths. - Bonn : /S.n./, 1979. 33p.
(Arbeiten aus der Abteilung Entwicklungsländerforschung) (Forschungsinstitut der Friedrich-Ebert-Stiftung ; 78)

863 NAIR, Basskaran
Mass media and the transnational corporation : a study of media-corporate relationship and its consequences for the Third World. - Singapore : Singapore University Press, /1980/, VIII,172p. Ill.
Bibliography: p.160-169. Includes index
ISBN 9971 69 005 5

864 NATIONAL sovereignty and international communication / edited by Kaarle Nordenstreng, Herbert I. Schiller. - Norwood, New Jersey : Ablex, 1979. XV,286p. (Communication and information science / ed. by Melvin J. Voigt)
Includes bibliographies and index
ISBN 0 89391 008 2

865 NDIAYE, G.D.
RESADOC : vers la réalisation du premier système international africain d'information documentaire régionale. Documentaliste (Paris), vol.17, no.2, mars-avril 1980, p.54-58

/Personnel CRDI/, /système d'information/, /niveau national/, /coopération régionale/, /réseau d'information/, /Sahel/ - /cadre institutionnel/

866 NICHOLS, John Spicer PIERCE, Robert N.
Keeping the flame : media and government in Latin America. New York : Hastings House, 1979. XVI,270p. (Studies in public communication) (Communication arts books)
Includes bibliographical references and index
ISBN 0 8038 3950 2

867 OKRUGLI STO ZEMALJA U RAZVOJU, 9., 1981, Zagreb = Round table of developing countries
Saradnja u oblasti transporta i komunikacija izmedju zemalja u razvoju = Co-operation in the field of transport and communications among developing countries / Deveti okrugli sto zemalja u razvoju, Zagreb, 21.-23. aprila 1981 ; organizator / Institut za zemlje u razvoju, Zagreb. - Zagreb : Institut za zemlje u razvoju, 1981. (Various pagings)
Set of papers

868 PACIFIC TELECOMMUNICATIONS CONFERENCE, 1981, Honolulu, Hawaii
PTC'81 : Pacific Telecommunications Conference / edited by Dan J. Wedemeyer. - Honolulu, Hawaii : Pacific Telecommunications Council, 1981. 1 vol. (various pagings). Ill. Maps.

Papers and proceedings of a conference held January 12-14, 1981, at Ilikai Hotel, Honolulu, Hawaii. Includes bibliographies.

869 PADIS : Pan American Documentation and Information System. - New York : United Nations, Economic Commission for Africa, 1981. 14p. Ill.

870 PADIS INTERGOVERNMENTAL MEETING OF AFRICAN COMPUTER, DOCUMENTATION AND INFORMATION SCIENTISTS, 1981, Salisbury
Report of the PADIS Intergovernmental Meeting of African Computer, Documentation and Information Scientists, Salisbury, Zimbabwe, 19-23 Oct., 1981. - Addis Ababa : ECA, 1981. 38p. (various pagings)

/IDRC supported/, /information systems/, /information network/, /regional cooperation/, /economic and social development/, /Africa/ - /institution building/, /training/, /obstacles development/, /occupational qualifications/, /conference report/, /list of participants/, /resolution/, /IDRC mentioned/

PADIS Pan-African Development Information System

871 PAVLIČ, Breda
Informaciono-komunikacijska moć kao element transnacionalizacije i novog medjunarodnog poretka = The power of information and communication as an element of transnationalization and of a New International Economic Order. Marksizam u svetu (Beograd), vol.8, nos 11-12, 1981, p.5-18

872 PAVLIČ, Breda
Information-communications policies and development strategies : critical questions for developing countries. - [S.l. : s.n.], 1978. 24 leaves

873 PAVLIČ, Breda
Tendence v mednarodni delitvi dela v informatiki, procesi transnacionalizacije in politika neuvrščenosti. - Ljubljana : Center za proučevanje sodelovanja z deželami v razvoju, 1980. 22 leaves, tabs

Študija je sestavni del raziskovalne naloge: "Transnacionalna podjetja in interesi dežel v razvoju", ki jo financira RSS

874 POLLOCK, D.H.
Caribbean and issues of communication and development. - Ottawa, Ont. - Carleton University, Norman Paterson School of International Affairs, 1980. 224p. Ill. ISBN 0 7709 0111 5

/Economic and social development / trends / Caribbean / - /petroleum resources/, /Trinidad and Tobago/, /development aid / CARICOM /, /imports/, /food/, /food production/, /press/, social influence/, /television/, /cultural development/, USA / cultural identity/, /literature/, /research/, /Canada/.

875 PRELIMINARY study on the Latin American Center for Information on Petroleum. Latin American Integration (Buenos Aires), June 1982, p.56-59. Tabs.
Special English edition

Summary of a study prepared by Guillermo Ondarts, Rafael Cornejo, Guido Schammas and Néstor Farias, B.

876 QUIRINO-LANHOUNMEY, J.
DEVSIS : une philosophie de la documentation et de l'information : international cooperative information systems : proceedings of a seminar held in Vienna, Austria, 9-13 July, 1979. - Ottawa : IDRC, 1980. p.54-58

/Subvention CRDI/, /DEVSIS/, /Afrique/ - /coopération internationale/

877 REDŽEPAGIĆ, Faruk
Sistem za istraživanje i informisanje nesvrstanih i drugih zemalja u razvoju: opći dio = Research and information system for non-aligned and other developing countries : general. - Zagreb : Institut za zemlje u razvoju, 1980. 167 leaves. (Medjunarodni ekonomski poredak = International Economic Order ; 70)

878 REYES MATTA, Fernando
Transnational communication and the alternative communication answer. Current Research on Peace and Violence (Tampere, Finland), 2(2), 1979, p.96-103

Paper presented to the 8th General Conference of IPRA

879 SARAČEVIĆ, T.
Progress in documentation : perception of the needs for scientific and technical information in less developed countries. Journal of Documentation (London), vol.36, no.3, Sept. 1980, p.214-267

/Information needs/, /scientific information/, /technical information/, /developing countries/ - /information systems/, /access to information/, /information dissemination/, /information network/, /information users/, /information policy/.

880 SARDAR, Z.
Between GIN and TWIN : meeting the information needs of the Third World. ASLIB Proceedings (London), vol.33, no.2, Febr. 1981, p.53-61

/Information needs/, /information systems/, /information policy/, /development countries/ - /information network/, /IDRC mentioned/.

881 SATELLITE options for rural telecommunications in developing countries / prepared by Academy for Educational Development. AID Rural Satellite Program, Applications Management. - Springfield, Va. : Reproduced by National Technical Information Service, U.S. Department of Commerce, 1981. 180p. Ill. Maps.

"Prepared ... for the U.S. Agency for International Development, under contract no. AID/DSPE/C-0081". The study will be updated periodically.
DOC. NO.: AED/RSP-81/01

882 SCHAETZEN, Y. de RAS-WORK, T.
Dossier Télécommunications. Afrique Industrie Infrastructures (Paris), 11. no.221, déc., 1980, p.40. Map. Portrs. Tabs.

Le rôle du PANAFTEL (Panafricain des télécommunications) en développement des télécommunications en Afrique. Interview avec le Secrétaire-général de l'Union internationale des télécommunications sur la pénétration en milieu rural. Le réseau PANAFTEL. Des organisations financières et fournisseurs de matériel. Chiffres. 1970-87.

883 SCHILLER, Herbert
Will advanced communication technology create a new order? Media Development (London), no.4, 1980, p.22

884 SERVAN-SCHREIBER, Jean-Jacques
L'informatique et les pays en développement. Marchés Tropicaux et Méditerranéens (Paris), 37e année, no.1840, vendredi 13 février 1981, p.351

885 SILVA, V.P. de
Information for development planning : report of the Seminar on Information for Development Planning, Pattaya, Thailand, 23-27 Jan. 1978. - Bangkok : Asian and Pacific Development Institute, 1979. 261p. Ill.

/IDRC supported/, /information/, /information needs/, /development planning/, /South East Asia/, /electronic equipment/, /information exchange/, /decision making/, /information systems/, /scientific cooperation/, /case studies/, /conference report/, /agenda/, /list of participants/, /recommendation/

886 SINDCAP : Sistema de Información y Documentación Centroamericana de Administración Pública. - San José, Costa Rica : ICAP, 1981, 15p.

887 SOURCES of African and Middle-Eastern economic information / ed. by Euan Blauvelt and Jennifer Durlancher. - Aldershot : Gower, 1982. 2 vols.

888 SPASIĆ, Aleksandar
Funkcija i oblici suradnje nesvrstanih u oblasti informisanja = The role and forms of the non-aligned co-operation in the field of information. Zbornik trećeg programa Radio Zagreba (Zagreb), no.1, 1977

889 TALUKDER, A.
Development of a socio-economic information network in South Asian region : the case of Bangladesh. - /Dacca : Bangladesh Institute of Development Studies/, 1982. 17p.

/IDRC supported/, /information network/, /economic information/, /social information/, /institution building/, /Bangladesh/ - /conference paper/.

890 TEORETIČNE osnove nove mednarodne informacijsko-komunikacijske ureditve : (s posebnim ozirom na novo mednarodno gospodarsko ureditev in načelo naslonitve na lastne sile) = Theoretical background of the NIICO : (with special regard to the NIEO and the concept of self-reliance) / Breda Pavlič, Slavko Splichal. - Ljubljana : Center za proučevanje sodelovanja z deželami v razvoju, 1981. 100p. Select bibliography: p.6-33.

Research of the international relations and the development of the NIEO, RSS C5-0210-523/81

891 THAIRU, P.W.
Development of information : an African approach : proceedings of the Third International Standing Conference of Eastern, Central and Southern African Librarians held at Kenya Science Teachers' College, Nairobi, Aug. 27- Sept. 2, 1978. - Nairobi : Kenya Library Association, 1979. 143p. Ill.

/Information services/, /information systems/, /Africa/ - /information dissemination/, /rural areas/, /obstacles to development/, /libraries/, /archives/, /regional cooperation/, /books/, /publishing/, /training/, /conference report/, /agenda/, /list of participants/.

892 TOWARD a new world information order : consequences for development policy : an International Conference sponsored by the Institute for International Relations and the Friedrich-Ebert-Stiftung Bonn, Federal Republic of Germany, December 4-6, 1978 / Dieter Bielenstein, editor. - Bonn : Institut für Internationale Begegnungen und Friedrich-Ebert-Stiftung, 1979. 119p.

893 TRANSPORT and telecommunication in Africa : the role of the African Development Bank. - Abidjan : African Development Bank, Information Division /1981/. /12p./ Ill.

894 TURNBULL, A. YOUNG, P. PARRY, J. et al.
Telecommunications survey. African Business (London), no.29, Jan., 1981, p.41. Maps. Tab.

Europe leading in telecommunications, Africa following. Telephones in African countries. Targets of PANAFTEL (Pan-African Telecommunications). Progress and network. Submarine cables. Telecommunication: development in Zimbabwe, Kenya, Sierra Leone, Egypt, Sudan, Botswana, Nigeria. Scope of telecommunication firms in Africa. Projects. Figures 1973-79.

895 UNIDO
Directory of industrial information services and systems in developing countries / prep. for Industrial and Technological Information Bank INTIB by UNIDO technology programme, Industrial Information Section. Wien : UNIDO, 1981. /121/p.

List of information services, arranged by country in alphabetical order, with information on: address, telephone/telex, language used, type of activity, services provided, subject coverage, geographic scope, publications. Indexes of subjects, acronyms and institutions.

896 UNITED NATIONS. ECLA.
Infoplan : información basica / UN. Latin American Centre for Economic and Social Documentation. Economic Commission for Latin America. - Santiago : UN, 1980. 6p. (UN-E/CEPAL/CLADES/R.2)

/ECLA/-/UN pub./, /report/ describing INFOPLAN objectives concerning the establishment of an /information system/ for /regional cooperation/ in respect of /development planning/ in /Latin America/ and the /Caribbean/. Covers /data collecting/, /data processing/ /information dissemination/, implementation of strengthening of /national/ information centre/s, /financial aspect/s, etc., and outlines /pilot project/ activities and results.

897 VINOGRADOV, V.A. ROBERTS, S.A. BRITTAIN, J.M. et al.
Socio-economic information : systems, uses and needs. International Social Science Journal (Paris), (33), no.1, 1981, p.7. Map. Ref. Tabs.

Eleven contributions by Vinogradov, Roberts, Brittain, Ennals, Scott, Seisuke Komatsuzaki, Lefort, Luhmann, Phlipponneau, Drechsler a.o. Towards an international information system. Demand and supply patterns in the United Kingdom. Need for a systematic communications network. Impact on the communication theory of the evolution of the media. Improbability of communications. Use of applied geography. Case studies of Singapore, Malaysia, the Philippines, Indonesia, Hungary and South Africa.

898 WOOLSTON, J.E.
Position paper by Information Science Division, International Development Research Centre (IDRC) / Inter-organization Consultation on Scientific and Technical Information Activities in Latin America and the Caribbean. - Ottawa : IDRC, Information Sciences Division, 1980. 5p. IDRC-doc-250

/IDRC personnel/, /Latin America/, /Caribbean/, /technical information/, /scientific information/, /information systems/, /information services/

899 WORKSHOP ON TECHNIQUES FOR EFFECTIVE PARTICIPATION IN THE CARIBBEAN INFORMATION SYSTEM - PLANNING (CARISPLAN), 1981, Wildey, Barbados
Report on the Workshop on Techniques for Effective Participation in the Caribbean Information System - Planning (CARISPLAN), 9-13 Mar., 1981, Wildey, Barbados. - Port of Spain : ECLA, Office for the Caribbean, 1981. 16p.

/IDRC supported/, /information system/, /training centres/, /Caribbean/ - /technical aspects/, /list of participants/, /agenda/.

900 YOUNG, F.W. BERTOLI, F. BERTOLI, S.
Design for a microcomputer-based rural development information system. Social Indicators Research (Dordrecht), 9(3), September 1981, p.283-312

901 ŽAGAR, Vlatko
Tehnološka osnova informacionih sistema i nesvrstanost = Technological basis of information systems and non-alignment. Zbornik trećeg programa Radio Zagreba (Zagreb), no.1, 1977

VIII

Process of Economic Integration Among Developing Countries

VIII-1. GENERAL

902 ALTMANN, Jörn
South-South cooperation and economic order. Intereconomics. Review of International Trade and Development (Hamburg), vol. 17, no. 3, May/June 1982, p. 143-144

Regional associations between developing countries have so far often proved to be less than successful. This, Professor Altmann points out, is hardly surprising in view of the lack of homogeneity of socio-political and economic systems among member countries, without which any integration process is bound to stagnate.

903 BERTONE, Luis E.
Los procesos de integración y la protección de la innovación tecnológica. Integración Latinoamericana (Buenos Aires), año 7, no. 69, junio 1982, p. 75-87

904 HAMED, Osama
Egypt's open door economic policy : an attempt at economic integration in the Middle East. International Journal of Middle East Studies (London), vol. 13, Febr. 1981, p. 1-9

Notes Egypt's attempts at economic growth in the 1970's and the country's uncertain economic future because of its economic dependence on the Arab world.

905 SALGADO PEÑAHERRERA, Germánico
Viable integration and the economic co-operation problems of the developing world : part 2. Journal of Common Market Studies (Oxford), 19(2), December 1980, p. 175-190
Part 1 of this article appeared in: Journal of Common Market Studies, Sept. 1980

906 VACCHINO, Juan Mario
Integración económica regional. - Caracas : Universidad Central de Venezuela, Facultad de Ciencias Juridicas y Politicas, Instituto de Derecho Publico, Sección Integración, 1981, 602p.

907 VAITSOS, Constantine V.
Crisis en los procesos de integración económica. Trimestre Económico (México), 46 (181), jan-mar, 1979, p. 35-128

/Article/ on the pitfalls of /economic integration/, with particular reference to /Latin America/. Examines the various internal e.g. /interest group/s and external (incl. the /role of USA/ and /multinational enterprise/s causes of the /failure/ of /common market/s, and sets out conditions for /success/ful /regional cooperation/, /bibliography/ p. 117 to 128, /reference/s and /statistical table/s.

908 WIRTSCHAFTSORDNUNG, sozio-ökonomische Entwicklung und weltwirtschaftliche Integration in den Entwicklungsländern : eine primär empirische Analyse von Zusammenhängen und Auswirkungen. Ein Forschungsauftrag des Bundesministeriums für Wirtschaft durchgeführt von Axel J. Halbach, Rigmar Osterkamp, Hans-Gert Braun, Anton Gälli. - Bonn : Bundesministerium für Wirtschaft, 1982. XII, 336p. (Studien-Reihe ; 36)

909 La AGRICULTURA en la integración latinoamericana / obra editada bajo la dirección de José Garrido Rojas. - Santiago de Chile : Editorial Universitaria, 1977. 183p. (Nuevas perspectivas de la integración latinoamericana ; v. 2, Estudios internacionales)

Subjects: produce trade--Latin America /Agriculture and state--Latin America/ Latin America--Economic integration
Includes bibliographical references.

910 ALENDAR, Branislava
Prekretnica u razvoju regionalnih ekonomskih integracionih grupacija u Latinskoj Americi. Medjunarodni problemi (Beograd), vol.32, no.2, april/jun 1980, p.261-281
Summaries in English and Russian

911 ALTERNATIVAS de vinculación entre Panamá y los esquemas de integración latinoamericanos. - Buenos Aires : INTAL, 1982. 202p.

912 ANDRES PEREZ, Carlos
La geopolítica de la integración en la América Latina. Integración Latinoamericana (Buenos Aires), año 7, no.75, diciembre 1982, p.29-35

913 ANDRIEU, Pedro Enrique
Integración desarrollo regional en América Latina. Ciencias Administrativas (La Plata, Argentina), 20(56/57), mayo/dic. 1978, p.33-47

914 AVANCES del proceso de integración latinoamericano. - Lima : Ministerio de Integración, 1977. 161p. (Informe de coyuntura ; 4)

/Report/ on the /economic integration/ process in /Latin America/. Covers background, objectives, mechanisms and present situation with regard to the /LAFTA/, the /Andean region/ development corporation, /trade agreement/s, social/treaty/s, etc. /bibliography) p.145 to 148/, /reference/s and /statistical table/s.

915 BARCELO, Victor Manuel
Obstaculos a la integración latinoamericana. Desarrollo Indoamericano (Baranquilla, Colombia), vol.16, no.69, Octubre 1981, p.45-49

916 CAMINOTTI, Jorge R.
La integración latinoamericana ... ahora sí? Novedades Económicas (Cordoba), año 3, no.25, dic. 1982, p.10-13

917 CAMPOS, Jaime AROCENA, Martin MAYORGA QUIROS, Román et al.
El proceso de integración en América Latina durante 1980. Integración Latinoamericana (Buenos Aires), (6), no.59, julio, 1981, p.1. Ref. Tabs.

Four contributions by Campos, Arocena, Quiros and Gonzales Cano on the integration process in Latin America during 1980. Creation of the Latin American Integration Association (LAIA). Institutional aspects of the integration. Mechanisms for carrying out the basic activities. Recommendations. Statistics, 1970-1980.

918 CLINE, William R.
Las economias de escala y la integración económica en América Latina. Integración Latinoamericana (Buenos Aires), año 7, no.69, mayo 1982, p.3-33, tabs.

Contents: Reseña selectiva de literatura : concepto y medición. Economías de escala, costos de monopolio e integración económica : estimaciones para América Latina. Estimaciones empiricas de los costos potenciales del monopolio. Costos combinados de una escala inferior a la óptima y del monopolio. Conclusión.

919 CLINE, William R.
El interés de América Latina en la integración económica. Integración Latinoamericana (Buenos Aires), 62, octubre 1981, p.23-33

920 CLINE, William R.
Latin American stake in economic integration. - Buenos Aires : INTAL, 1981. 27p.

Documento presentado al Seminario sobre Politicas Comerciales Optima, Buenos Aires, 22 al 24 junio 1981.

921 CONESA, Eduardo R.
Evolution of world and Latin American Economy in 1979.
Latin American Integration (Buenos Aires), no.1, April 1981, p.23-48 (Special English edition)

Latin American growth in the context of the world recession. Problems of world economy in 1979. Adjustment in Latin America. Integration as the axis of Latin American development policy. Integration in the events of 1979.

922 CONESA, Eduardo R.
La integración económica de Argentina y Chile.
Integración Latinoamericana(Buenos Aires), año 7, no.75, diciembre 1982, p.36-48

Contents: La sustitución de importaciones. Integración latinoamericana vs. integración económica mundial. Chile frente al mercado del cobre. Argentina frente al mercado mundial de granos y carne. La tarifa óptima para Chile y Argentina. La variante latinoamericanista. La desviación y la creación del comercio. La infraestructura de transportes y energia. Gradualismo e integración latinoamericano.

923 COOPERACIÓN e integración económica entre países en desarrollo : examen de la evolución reciente en las organizaciones y acuerdos de ámbito subregional, regional e interregional / informe de la secretaría de la UNCTAD. - Geñeve : UNCTAD. Junta de Comercio y Desarrollo. Comisión de Cooperación Económica entre Países en Desarrollo, 1982- . (TD/B/C.7/51)

Vol.1 : América Latina. 1982. IX,117p.

924 CORRAGGIO, José Luis
Sobre la problemática de la planificación regional en América Latina. Revista Interamericana de Planificación (Buenos Aires), 13(52), dic. 1979, p.52-69

925 DE la dependencia a la liberación : política exterior de América Latina / Juan Carlos Puig ... /et al./. - Buenos Aires : La Bastilla, 1973, 309p. (Serie sin límites)
Includes bibliographical references.

926 EL DERRUMBE de Urupabol : golpe a la integración subregional. Visión. La Revista Interamericana (New York), vol.59, no.8, 18 octubre 1982, p.61

URUPABOL Uruguay, Paraguay y Bolivia, Caracas /1963/

927 DIAZ MÜLLER, Luis
Latinskoamerička ekonomska integracija. Medjunarodni problemi (Beograd), vol.32, no.2, apr./juni 1980, p.189-217
Summaries in English and Russian

928 ECONOMIC and social progress in Latin America : 1979 report / publ. by Inter-American Development Bank. - Washington : IDB, 1979. Tabs.

Economic and social development of Latin America since 1970 with emphasis on 1978 and 1979 : general trends, external sector, financing of the development, economic integration, population growth, urbanization. Country case studies : sectoral development, fiscal situation, foreign trade, balance of payments, development planning and other aspects. Statistics 1960-79.

929 ECONOMIC and social progress in Latin America : 1980-81 report. - Washington : Inter-American Development Bank, 1981. 455p.

Contents: General economic trends - the external sector - financing and development - economic integration - social development trends - country summaries.

930 ESTABILIDAD y flexibilidad en el ordenamiento jurídico de la integración / obra edita bajo la dirección de Rodrigo Díaz Albónico. - Santiago de Chile : Editorial Universitaria, /1977/. 1972p. (Estudios internacionales / Instituto de Estudios Internacionales de la Universidad de Chile) (Nuevas perspectivas de la integración Latinoamericana / Instituto de Estudios Internacionales de la Universidad de Chile ; 1)

Published jointly with the Institute for Latin America Integration of the Inter-American Development Bank. Includes bibliographical references.

931 FFRENCH-DAVIS, Ricardo
Terminos del intercambio reciproco y efectos distributivos de la integración económica. - Santiago de Chile : Corporación de Investigaciones Económicas para Latinoamérica, 1978. /16p./. (Notas técnicas / Corporación de Investigaciones Económicas para Latinoamérica ; 10, 1978).
Bibliografía: p./15-16/.

932 FREI MONTALVA, Eduardo
America Latina : opción y esperanza. - Barcelona : Pomaire, 1977. 299p.
Includes bibliographical references.
ISBN: 84 286 0215 8

933 GANNON, Francis X.
La agonía de Nicaragua : el contexto Centroamericano. Américas (Washington), vol.31, no.9, septiembre 1979, p.2

Contents: Centroamerica sigue en busca de la integración regional, a pesar de terremotos, inundaciones y agitaciones políticas.

934 GEICOS: El Grupo Empresario Interregional del Centro-Oeste Sudamericano : a business experiment in subregional integration. Latin American Integration (Buenos Aires), June 1982, p.30-32
(Special English edition)

Summary of a study done by Juan Carlos Blanco, within the framework of activities done by the Technical Assistance Division of INTAL.

935 GOLBERT, Albert S. NUN GINGOLD, Jenny
Latin American economic interpretation: an overview of trade and investment developments in ANCOM, CACM and LAFTA. Syracuse Journal of International Law and Commerce (Syracuse, N.Y.), vol.7, no.2, 1979/80, p.183-211

936 HERRERA, Felipe
Frei Eduardo / y la integración latinoamericana : arar en la tierra y no en el mar para enfrentar el desafío de las próximas décadas. Visión (New York), vol.59, no.2, julio 1982, p.30

937 HOFMAN, Alejandro Boris
Administración regional en América Latina : seminario del Centro Latinoamericano de Administración para el Desarrollo. - Buenos Aires : Ediciones STAP, 1976. 328p, Ill.

/Desarrollo regional/, /integración regional/ /administración publica/, /teoría/- /planificación regional/, /planificación urbana/ /aspectos financieros/, /sector publico/, /proyectos de investigación/.

938 La INDUSTRIA en la integración latinoamericana / obra edita bajo la dirección de Raymundo Barros Charlin. - Santiago de Chile : Editorial Universitaria, /1977/. 149p. (Estudios internacionales / Instituto de Estudios Internacionales de la Universidad de Chile) (Nuevas perspectivas de la integración Latinoamericana / Instituto de Estudios Internacionales de la Universidad de Chile ; 3)

Published jointly with the Institute for Latin American Integration of the Inter-American Development Bank.

939 INDUSTRIA ferroviaria latinoamericana : análisis de la integración sectorial. Integración Latinoamericana (Buenos Aires), enero-febrero 1981, p.31-36

940 INFORME mensual de la integración Latinoamericana. Comercio Exterior (México), vol.31, no.10, octubre 1981, p.1689-1173

Grupo Andino: nuevas esperanzas para el Pacto.

941 INTAL
Reuniones de los esquemas de integración y del SELA en apoyo de la Argentina. Integración Latinoamericana (Buenos Aires), no.72, sept. 1982, p.53-56

942 INTAL and Latin American integration during 1980. Latin American Integration (Buenos Aires), June 1982, p.1-7, diagr.
(Special English edition)

943 El INTAL y la integración latinoamericana durante 1980. Integración Latinoamericana (Buenos Aires), (6), Jan/Feb. 1981, p.1-11

944 Integración Latinoamericana. Revista mensual INTAL (Buenos Aires), no.51, oct. 1980
Dedicado a Centroamerica, redefinición integracionista

945 INTEGRATION of science and technology with development : Caribbean and Latin American problems in the context of the United Nations Conference on Science and Technology for Development / edited by D. Babatunde Thomas, Miguel S. Wionczek. - New York : Pergamon, /1979/. XII,278p. (Pergamon policy studies ; 32)
Proceedings of a Symposium held in Miami, April 6-8, 1978, sponsored by Florida International University, the Institute of Social and Economic Research, University of the West Indies and the Institute of Development Studies, University of Guayana. Includes bibliographical references and index.

946 The INTEGRATION process in Latinamerica during 1980. Integración Latinoamericana (Buenos Aires), año 6, no.59, julio 1981, p.1-2

947 INTER-AMERICAN DEVELOPMENT BANK, Washington
Annual report : 1980. Washington, D.C. : IADB, 1981. Graphs. Tabs. Ill.
Economic development trends in Latin America. GDP. Technical cooperation. Economic integration. Loans and projects. Financial statements.

948 El INTERES de América Latina en la integración ecónomica. Integración Latinoamericana (Buenos Aires), (62), Oct 1981, p.23

949 INVESTING : licensing and trading abroad : released June 1980 : Latin America. /S.l./ : Business International Corp., 1980. 20 leaves.
/Covering LAFTA, ANCOM, CARICOM .../

950 JURIDICAL issues of economic integration : collection of legal texts : update. Latin American Integration (Buenos Aires), June 1982, p.86-88.
(Special English edition)
Summary of a study prepared by the Legal Studies Division of INTAL.

951 KÖNIG, Wolfgang
Zu den Möglichkeiten der wirtschaftlichen Integration Lateinamerikas. In : Lateinamerika : Herrschaft, Gewalt und internationale Abhängigheit. - Bonn, 1982, p. 217-227

952 KOSAREV, Evgenij Apollinar'evič
Ekonomičeskaja integracija Latinskoj Ameriki i SŠA.-Moskva : Nauka, 1979. 229p.
Bibliography: p.221-/230/

953 KRAVIS, Irving B.
Aranceles aduaneros óptimos, integración y otras estrategias comerciales para América Latina. Integración Latinoamericana (Buenos Aires), año 6, no.64, diciembre 1981, p.2-13

Contents: Marco económico para la búsqueda de políticas comerciales óptimas en América Latina. Estrategias alternativas para una política comercial óptima. Integración regional. El procedimiento de la negociación. Protección de la industria incipiente. Retorno a un sistema comercial abierto. Las opciones por las que habrá que decidirse. Cuadros. Bibliografía.

954 LATEINAMERIKA will Wirtschaftsinteressen gemeinsam vetreten. Nachrichten für Aussenhandel (Köln), (44), no.87, Mai 7, 1981, p.5

Rolle des "Sistema Económica Latinoamericano-SELA" in Möglichkeiten für vertiefte Integrierung und Selbsthilfe und für eine einheitliche Vertretung durch das SELA gegenüber internationalen Interessengruppen. Koordinierung regionaler Kapazitäten. Dialog mit Regionalgruppen. Daten, 1974-81.

955 LATIN American integration. - Buenos Aires : The Institute for Latin American Integration (Intal), 1982. 88p., tab.

956 LATIN American Integration. 1st special Engl.ed. - Buenos Aires : INTAL, 1981. 124p.

Contents: The United States and the Third World in the 21st century / Cecilio J. Morales. Evolution of world and Latin American economy in 1979 / Eduardo R. Conesa. Evaluation of the Treaty of Acapulco and the outlook for the partial actions of the Latin American Integration Association (LAIA) / Miguel S. Wionczek. United States direct investment in Latin America, 1966-76 : an empirical analysis of the impact of the Andean code (decision 24) / Michael C. Aho and José Nuñez del Arco. The social and economic outlook for Central America in the 1980's / Román Mayorga Quiros. Economic integration in the Caribbean / Ross Murray. 1980 Montevideo Treaty : Montevideo, August 1980. Chronology of the main events and of the cooperation taking place within the integration schemes during 1979 :
1 : LAFTA
2 : Andean Group
3 : Central American Common Market
4 : CARICOM
5 : Latin American Economic System (SELA)
6 : Amazon Cooperation Treaty

957 LATIN America's railroad industry : analysis of its sectorial integration. Latin American Integration (Buenos Aires), June 1982, p.25-29, Tabs. (Special English edition)

Summary of a study prepared by Jorge Iturizza, Eduardo Rodriguez Ardila, Nelio R. van Boekel, Angel Ceci, Diego Feliú and Ramón de Bouza.

958 LEGISLACIÓN relacionada con el tratamiento a la inversión extranjera en los países centroamericanos. - /Guatemala/ : SIECA. 1978. 177p.

SIECA Secretaría Permanente del Tratado General de Integración Económica Centroamericana

959 LIZANO, Eduardo
Disparidades nacionales e integración económica. Integración Latinoamericana (Buenos Aires), año 7, no.69, junio 1982, p.34-48

960 MALDONADO, Victor Alfonso
Le marché commun latino-américain : aspects de l'intégration économique en Amérique Latine. - Paris : Institut des Hautes Études de l'Amérique Latine, 1968. 293p. Tabl. (Travaux et mémoires de l'Institut des Hautes Études de l'Amérique Latine ; 19)

961 MELGAR, A.
Integración latinoamericana : balance y perspectivas. Montevideo : CLAEH, 1980. 72p. (Serie investigaciones / Centro Latinoamericano de Economía Humana ; 10)

Integración regional/, /organizaciones americanas/, /América Latina - ALALC/, /convenios comerciales/, /marco institucional/.

962 MENDEZ-AROCHA, Alberto
La integración energetica de América Latina : trabajo complementario -- tema VI, 14. convención de UPADI, Rio de Janeiro, octubre de 1976 / con la colaboración de Carmen de Calderaro ... et al. - Caracas : Colegio de Ingenieros de Venezuela, 1976. XII,290p. Ill.

963 El MOMENTO actual de la cooperación e integración Latinoamericana / obra edita bajo la dirección de Raymundo Barros Charlin. - Santiago de Chile : Editorial Universitaria, /1978/. 179p. (Estudios internacionales / Instituto de Estudios Internacionales de la Universidad de Chile) (Nuevas perspectivas de la integración Latinoamericana / Instituto de Estudios Internacionales de la Universidad de Chile)

Published jointly with the Institute for Latin American Integration of the Inter-American Development Bank. Includes bibliographical references.

964 ORREGO VICUÑA, Francisco
Auf dem Wege zu neuen Formen der Wirtschaftsintegration in Lateinamerika. Europa Archiv. Zeitschrift für internationale Politik (Bonn), (36), no.14, Juli 25, 1981, p.428. Ref.

Krise der Wirtschaftsmodelle und die mangelnde Abstimmung der Integration im Lichte der Lateinamerikanischen Erfahrungen. Notwendigkeit des Pluralismus. Utopismus vs. Pragmatismus. Supernationalität vs. nationale Entscheidungen. Zentralismus und Liberalismus.

965 O'SHAUGHNESSY, H. RAPPORT, C. MONTAGNON, P. (et al.)
Inter-American Development Bank. Financial Times (London), April 2, 1981, 5p. Graphs. Ill. Portr. Tabs.

Impact of the Inter-American Development Bank on the finance of Latin American countries. IDB operations. Search for new funds. IDB' members and lending. Profile of IDB-president. Borrowing on fixed lines. USA and IDB. Funds coming under pressure. Ecuador as a target. Latin American Integration. Figures, 1960-82

966 PEÑA, Félix
La experiencia institutional de la integración económica de América Latina. Integración Latinoamericana (Buenos Aires), 4(42), dic. 1979, p.56-69

967 El PROBLEMA de la convergencia de las acciones parciales en el marco de la integración latinoamericana. Integración Latinoamericana (Buenos Aires). (6), Jan/Feb. 1981, p.86-92

968 El PROCESO de integración en América Latina en 1980.·Buenos Aires : INTAL, Tratado de Cooperación Amazonica, 1981. p.282-287

969 El PROCESO de integración en América Latina en 1981. - Buenos Aires : INTAL : BID, 1982. XII,311p. Tabs.
Chronology : p.291-311

970 The PROCESS of integration in Latin America in 1979.
(Summary of "the Process of Integration in Latin America during 1979", INTAL, August 1980. Latin American Integration (Buenos Aires), June 1982, p.16-19
(Special English edition)

971 El PROTECCIONISMO de los países industriales y las políticas de integración de América Latina. Integración Latinoamericana (Buenos Aires), año 6, vol.61, septiembre 1981, 128p.

Contents: Los países en desarrollo de industrialización reciento después de la crisis petrolera / Béla Balassa. Barreras comerciales que enfrentan los países en desarrollo : medidas de política comercial y fletes / J. Alexander. Prácticas restrictivas y discriminatorias de la CEE en el comercio internacional de productos agropecuarios / Marcelo Halperin. America Latina y el comercio interregional de productos agropecuarios.

972 RADWAY, Robert J.
The next decade in Latin America : anticipating the future from the past. Case Western Reserve Journal of International Law (Cleveland, Ohio), 13(1), Winter 1981, p.3-35

973 REPRESAS, José
Perspectivas de Latinoamerica (II) : el desarrollo de la región dependerá del éxito de la integración. Visión (New York), vol.57, no.12, diciembre 1981, p.55

Relaciones externas. Balanca comercial. Fluyo de capitales. Energía. Integración económica. Campo de prueba. Dificultades políticas.

974 REUNION sobre una nueva América Latina en la cambiante economía mundial. Revista de la CEPAL (Santiago), no.10, abr. 1980, /127p./
Special issue. Journal also available in English.

975 REUNIONES de los esquemas de integración y del SELA en apoyo de la Argentina. Integración Latinoamericana (Buenos Aires), año 7, no.72, septiembre 1982, p.53-56

Contents: Grupo Andino : reuniones de la Comisión Andino-Argentina. ALADI: reunión de alto nivel gubernamental de los responsables de la integración de los países miembros. SELA: reunión del Comite de Acción de Apoyo a la Argentina.

976 SALAZAR PAREDES, Fernando
Integración multinacional en función de la integración nacional. - Lima : Secretaría General de Integración, 1980. 154p. Tab. Anexos p.101-154

977 SALAZAR SANTOS, Felipe
The problem of the convergence of the partial actions within the framework of Latin American integration. Latin American Integration (Buenos Aires), June 1982, p.69-73. (Special English edition).

Summary of a study done by Felipe Salazar Santos.

978 SOCIEDAD, política e integración en América Latina / ed. by Manfred Wilhelmy. - Santiago de Chile : CINDA : Centro Interuniversitario de Desarrollo Andino. 1982. 210p.

979 TIRONI, Ernesto
Integración en presencia de corporaciones transnacionales. - Santiago de Chile : Corporación de Investigaciones Económicas para Latinoamerica, 1979. 54p. (Estudios CIEPLAN ; 3)
Bibliography: p.51-54

980 TRADE and credit in Latin America : problems and resolutions. 2nd ed. - New York : Chase Trade Information Corporation, 1981. 353p. Bibl. Graphs. Ill. Maps. Tabs.

Trade and credit in Latin America by country. Regional free trade associations : Latin American Integration Association (LAIA). Andean Common Market (ANCOM). Central American Common Market (CACM). Free trade zones. List of ports. Import and exchange regulation. Tariff rates. Patterns of import. Latin American and foreign investments. Balance of payments. Credit terms and collection of payments for US exports. Interest rates on non resident accounts. Outlook on economic trends collection experience for documentary drafts covering US shipment to Latin America. Collection charges and letter of credit charges. List of banks and financial institutions.

981 UNCTAD. TDB. Committee on Economic Co-operation among Developing Countries
Economic co-operation and integration among Developing countries : a review of recent development in subregional, regional and interregional organizations and arrangement : report by the UNCTAD secretariat. - Genève : UNCTAD, 1982.-vols

Vol.1 : Latin America. 1982. X,110p. (TD/B/C.7/51)
Vol.2 : Africa. 1982. XI,108p. (TD/B/C.7/51)

982 The VALUE added tax in the financing of social security and the Latin American integration process. Latin American Integration (Buenos Aires), June 1982, p.11-13 (Special English edition)

Summary of a study by consultants Adolfo Atchabahian, Ricardo Moles, Jorge Macon and Gonzalo Arroba.

983 WIONCZEK, Miguel S. MAYORGA QUIROS, Román
Intentos de integración en el marco de la crisis latinoamericana / estudios preparados por iniciativa de INTAL. - México : El Colegio de México, 1981. 235p.

984 WIRTSCHAFTLICHE Integration in Lateinamerika und der Karibik / erstellt von Waldemar Hummer ; im Auftrag der Auslandsabteilung der Oberbank, Linz. - Linz : Bank für Oberösterreich und Salzburg, /1977/. 47p., tabs.

VIII-2.1. Latin American Economic System—SELA

985 ACTUALIZACION de la Decisión 12. - Caracas : SELA, 1981. 2 leaves. (SP/CL/VII.O/DT ; 16)

986 ACUERDO de cooperación entre el Sistema Económico Latinoamericano (SELA) y el reino de España. - Caracas : SELA, 1981. (SP/CL/VII.O/DT ; 6)

987 AGENCIA Latinoamericana de Servicios Especiales de Información "ALASEI". - Caracas : SELA, 1981, 3p. (SP/CL/VII.O/Di ; 9)

988 AMERICA Latina frente al problema alimentario. - Caracas : SELA, 1981. 56p. (SP/CL/VII.O/DT ; 4) Add.1

989 ASCARRUNZ, Eduardo
La estrategia de seguridad económica del SELA consagró la nueva dinámica de unidad regional. - Caracas : SELA, Servicio de Informaciones Especiales, 1982. 5 leaves. (Crónicas)

990 CARMONA, Pedro
La estrategia del SELA es históricamente valedera para el futuro de América Latina. - Caracas : SELA, Servicio de Informaciones Especiales, 1982. 4p. (Crónicas)

991 CODIGO de conducta para las empresas transnacionales y código internacional de conducta para la transferencia de tecnología. - Caracas : SELA, 1981. (SP/CL/VII.O/Di ; 2)

992 COMITE de Acción de Apoyo Financiero a Bolivia : (propuesta) / Bolivia. Gobierno. - Caracas : SELA, 1982. (SP/CL/VIII.O/DT ; 40)

993 COMUNICACIÓN al Secretaría Permanente del Sistema Económico Latinoamericano / Argentina, Gobierno. - Caracas : SELA, 1982. (SP/CL/VIII.O/DT ; 29)

994 DATOS básicos, objetivos y situación actual de los Comités de Acción. - Caracas : SELA, 1981. (SP/CL/VII.O/DT ; 14) Add.1

995 DECISIONES del Consejo Latinoamericano / SELA. - Caracas : Secretaría Permanente del Sistema Económico Latinoamericano, /1977/- . (SELA documentos)
Irregular.

996 DIAZ MÜLLER, Luis
El SELA y las empresas multinacionales latinoamericanas en el marco del desarrollo regional. - México : UNAM, 1981. 113p.

997 ECONOMIA y cooperación en Africa : elementos para acciones de colaboración del SELA. - Caracas : SELA, 1982. (SP/CL/VIII.O/Di ; 6)

998 ESTUDIO preliminar sobre un mecanismo de coordinación entre países productores de carne no aftósica. - Caracas : SELA, 1981. (SP/CL/VII.O/Di ; 10)

999 GARZON VALDES, Ernesto
SELA : eine Organisation der lateinamerikanischen Entwicklungspolitik. Die Dritte Welt (Koenigstein, F.R.G.), vol.8, no.1, 1980, p.86-101

1000 GROWING co-operation of SELA and support for Nicaragua confronted with US hostility. Comercio Exterior (México), April 1981, p.158-160

1001 GRUPO LATINOAMERICANO DE JEFES DE MISION (GRULA), Bruxelles
Informe de evaluación de las relaciones entre las Comunidades Europeas y la América Latina presentado al octavo Consejo Latinoamericano. - Caracas : SELA, 1982. (SP/CL/VIII.O/Di ; 8)

1002 IDEAS para conformar posiciones de América Latina en las negociaciones sobre la cooperación internacional para el desarrollo. - Caracas : SELA, 1981. (SP/CL/VII. O/DT ; 4)

1003 IGLESIAS, Enrique V.
La crisis económica mundial y las opciones de América Latina.-Caracas : SELA, Servicio de Informaciones Especiales, 1982. 8p. (Crónicas)

1004 INFORMACION general sobre los Comités de Acción del SELA/MULTIFERT Y OLAVI. - Caracas : SELA, 1982. (SP/CL/VIII.O/Di ; 7)

1005 INFORME annual de actividades de la Secretaría Permanente. - Caracas : SELA, 1980. p.67-88 (SP/CL/VI.O/DT ; 4)

1006 INFORME sobre los centros de investigacion y capacitación de alcance multinacional : (Decisión 60 del Consejo Latinoamericano) : informe preliminar. - Caracas : SELA, 1982. (SP/CL/VIII.O/DT ; 9)

1007 Los MECANISMOS automáticos de cooperación intraregional para casos de emergencia producidos por desastres de la naturaleza / Honduras, Gobierno. - Caracas : SELA, 1982. (SP/CL/VIII.O/DT ; 37)

1008 MULTIFERT
Informe del presidente de la Asamblea de accionistas a la séptima reunión ordinaria del Consejo Latinoamericano. - Caracas : SELA, 1981. 6p. (SP/CL/VII.O/DT ; 13)

1009 POSIBILIDADES de reorientación del comercio exterior argentino hacia los países latinoamericanos. - Caracas : SELA, 1982. (SP/CL/VIII.O/DT ; 34)

1010 POSIBLE programa para la ejecución de las acciones previstas en la Declaración de Panamá. - Caracas : SELA, 1982. 7p. (SP/CL/VIII.O/DT ; 4)

1011 POSIBLES acciones futuras de las redes de cooperación técnica multilateral en el marco del SELA. - Caracas : SELA, 1982. (SP/CL/VIII.O/DT ; 8)

1012 POSICIÓN conjunta latinoamericana : beneficiosas negociaciones globales. Visión. La Revista Interamericana (New York), vol.56, no.10, mayo de 1981, p.75

Control tecnológico. Las alternativas. Nueva presencia.

1013 PROYECTO de Acuerdo de Cooperación de España con el Sistema Económico Latinoamericano (SELA). - Caracas - SELA, 1982. 6p. (SP/CL/VIII.O/DT ; 5)

1014 REGULAR MEETING OF THE LATIN AMERICAN COUNCIL, 8., 1982, Caracas
Bases for an economic independence and security strategy for Latin America / 8th Regular Meeting of the Latin American Council, Caracas, August 16 to 25, 1982. - /S.l./ : SELA, 1982. 52 leaves. (SP/CL/VIII.O/DT ; 36)

1015 RELACION de documentos presentados a la séptima reunión ordinaria del Consejo Latinoamericano. - Caracas : SELA, Secretaría Permanente, 1981. 6p. (SP/CL/VII.O/Di ; 11)

1016 RESOLUCION del SELA (Sistema Económico Latinoamericano). Integración Latinoamericana (Buenos Aires), año 7, no.70, julio 1982, p.65-66

1017 REUNION DE EXPERTOS GUBERNAMENTALES DE ALTO NIVEL PARA LAS AREAS DE AGRICULTURA Y ALIMENTACIÓN, 1, 1981, México
Informe de Relatoría / Reunión de Expertos Gubernamentales de Alto Nivel para las Areas de Agricultura y Alimentación, 1, México DF, 24-29 agosto de 1981. - Caracas : SELA, 1982. 160p. (SP/CL/VIII.O/DT ; 17)

1018 El SELA entra en nueva era : la guerra de las Malvinas lo vigorizó. Visión . Revista Interamericana (New York), vol.59, no.7, 4 de octubre de 1982, p.51

1019 SELA : una estrategia común : se fortalece la capacidad negociadora latinoamericana. Visión (New York), vol.58, no.1, 11 de enero de 1982, p.42-43

"A nuestros pueblos no les interesa que les hagan donaciones", afirmó el presidente panameño, Aristides Roy.

1020 SELA : quinto aniversario y logros recientes. Comercio Exterior (México), vol.31, no.3, marzo de 1981

1021 El SELA también apoya. Visión (New York), vol.58, no.12, 28 de junio 1982, p.32

1022 El SELA y la cooperación regional : (cumplimiento de la Decisión 73). - Caracas : SELA, 1981. 176p. (SP/CL/VII.O/DT ; 14)

1023 SELA. Comité de Acción de Apoyo a la República Argentina. Reunión ordinaria, 1., 1982, Caracas
Acuerdos alcanzados en la Ia. reunión ordinaria del Comité de Acción de Apoyo a la República Argentina. - Caracas : SELA : 1982. (SP/CL/VIII.O/DT ; 36) Add.1, 14p.

1024 SELA. Comité de Acción de Apoyo a la República Argentina. Reunión Ordinaria, 1., 1982, Buenos Aires
Informe del relator. - Caracas : SELA, 1982. (SP/CL/VIII.O/DT ; 28)

1025 SELA. Comité de Acción de Artesanías
Informe del Secretario a la octava reunión ordinaria del Consejo Latinoamericano. - Caracas : SELA, 1982. 19p. (SP/CL/VIII.O/DT ; 20)

1026 SELA. Comité de Acción de los Organismos Empresariales de Comercio Exterior de Carácter Gubernamental de América Latina del Sector Alimenticio
Acta constitutiva. - Lima : /s.n./, 1981. 9 leaves

1027 SELA. Comité de Acción de los Organismos Empresariales de Comercio Exterior de Carácter Gubernamental de América Latina del Sector Alimentarion (OECEG). - Caracas : SELA, 1981. (SP/CL/VII.O/DT ; 15)

1028 SELA. Comité de Acción de los Organismos Empresariales de Comercio Exterior de Carácter Gubernamental (OECEG)
Informe del Secretario a la octava reunión ordinaria del Consejo Latinoamericano. - Caracas : SELA, 1982. (SP/CL/VIII.O/DT ; 26)

1029 SELA. Comité de Acción de Productos del Mar y de Agua Dulce
Informe a la séptima reunión ordinaria del Consejo Latinoamericano. - Caracas : SELA, 1981. /40/p. (SP/CL/VII.O/DT ; 9)

1030 SELA. Comité de Acción de Productos del Mar y Agua Dulce
Informe del Secretario a la octava reunión ordinaria del Consejo Latinoamericano. - Caracas : SELA, 1982. 39p. (SP/CL/VIII.O/DT ; 22)

1031 SELA. Comité de Acción de Productos del Mar y de Agua Dulce
Informe sobre sus actividades correspondientes al año 1981. - Caracas : SELA, 1981. 6 leaves

1032 SELA. Comité de Acción de Productos del Mar y de Agua Dulce
Publicación periódica en Colección. - Lima : [s.n.], 1981

1033 SELA. Comité de Acción de Promoción y Comercialización de Productos Artesanales
Informe a la séptima reunión ordinaria del Consejo Latinoamericano. - Caracas : SELA, 1981. 24p. (SP/CL/VII.O/DT ; 7)

1034 SELA. Comité de Acción de la RITLA
Informe a la séptima reunión ordinaria del Consejo Latinoamericano. - Caracas : SELA, 1981. (SP/CL/VII.O/DT ; 10)

1035 SELA. Comité de Acción de la RITLA
Informe del Secretario a la octava reunión ordinaria del Consejo Latinoamericano. - Caracas : SELA, 1982. (SP/CL/VIII.O/DT ; 23)

1036 SELA. Comité de Acción de la RITLA
Informe del Secretario a la octava reunión ordinaria del Consejo Latinoamericano. - Caracas : SELA, 1982. 11p. (SP/CL/VIII.O/DT ; 23) Add.1

1037 SELA. Comité de Acción de Turismo
Informe a la séptima reunión ordinaria del Consejo Latinoamericano. - Caracas : SELA, 1981, 43p. (SP/CL/VII.O/DT ; 12)

1038 SELA. Comité de Acción de Turismo
Informe del Secretario a la octava reunión ordinaria del Consejo Latinoamericano. - Caracas : SELA, 1982. (SP/CL/VIII.O/DT ; 25)

1039 SELA. Comité de Acción para la creación de la Agencia Latinoamericana de Servicios Especiales de Información
Informe del Secretario a la octava reunión ordinaria del Consejo Latinoamericano. - Caracas : SELA, 1982. 15p. (SP/CL/VIII.O/DT ; 27)

1040 SELA. Comité de Acción para el Establecimiento de la Agencia Latinoamericana de Servicios Especiales de Información (ALASEI)
Acta constitutiva. - Panamá : [s.n.], 1981. 7 leaves

1041 SELA. Comité de Acción para la Reconstrucción de Nicaragua
Informe a la séptima reunión del Consejo Latinoamericano. - Caracas : SELA, 1981. (SP/CL/VII.O/DT ; 11)

1042 SELA. Comité de Acción para la Reconstrucción de Nicaragua
Informe del Secretario a la octava reunión ordinaria del Consejo Latinoamericano. - Caracas : SELA, 1982. (SP/CL/VIII.O/DT ; 24)

1043 SELA. Comité de Acción sobre Viviendas y Edificaciones de Interés Social
Acuerdos del CAVEIS. - Quito : /S.n./, 1980. 1 vol.

1044 SELA. Comité de Acción de Viviendas y Edificaciones de Interés Social
Informe a la séptima reunión ordinaria del Consejo Latinoamericano. - Caracas : SELA, 1981. (SP/CL/VII.O/DT ; 8)

1045 SELA. Comité de Acción sobre Viviendas y Edificaciones de Interés Social
Informe del Secretario a la octava reunión ordinaria del Consejo Latinoamericano. - Caracas : SELA, 1982. 29p. (SP/CL/VIII.O/DT ; 21)

1046 SELA. Comité de Acción sobre Viviendas y Edificaciones de Interés Social, Reunión ordinaria, 4., 1981, Caracas
Sistema latinoamericano de cooperación integral para la vivienda y los asentimientos humanos : propuesta a nivel de prefactibilidad. - Caracas : SELA, 1981. 68p.

1047 SELA. Comité de Alto Nivel. Período de Sesiones, 2., 1982
Informe sobre la labor realizada. - Caracas : SELA, 1982. (SP/CL/VIII.O/DT ; 11)

1048 SELA. Consejo Latinoamericano. Reunión ordinaria, 7., 1981, Caracas
Final report / SELA. Consejo Latinoamericano, reunión ordinaria, 7, Caracas, 23 mar.-1 abr. 1981. - Caracas : SELA, 1981. 331p.

1049 SELA. Consejo Latinoamericano. Reunión ordinaria, 7., 1981, Caracas
Informe final / SELA. Consejo Latinoamericano, reunión ordinaria, 7. Caracas, 23 mar.-1 abr. 1981. - Caracas : SELA, 1981. 325p.

1050 SELA. Consejo Latinoamericano. Reunión ordinaria, 8., 1982, Caracas
Informe final / SELA. Consejo Latinoamericano, reunión ordinaria, 8. Caracas, 16-26 agosto de 1982. - Caracas : SELA, 1982. (CL/VIII.O/DF ; 1)

1051 SELA. Consejo Latinoamericano. Reunión ordinaria, 8., 1982, Caracas
Temario provisional / SELA. Consejo Latinoamericano, reunión ordinaria, 8. Caracas, 18-25 agosto de 1982. - Caracas : SELA, 1982. (SP/CL/VIII.O/DT ; 1) Rev.1

1052 SELA. Secretaría Permanente
Ante-proyecto de agenda para la séptima reunión ordinaria del Consejo Latinoamericano a Nivel Ministerial. - Caracas : SELA, Secretaría Permanente, 1981. (SP/CL/VII.O/DT ; 2)

1053 SELA. Secretaría Permanente
Comentarios al temario provisional. - Caracas : SELA, 1982. 29p. (SP/CL/VIII.O/Di.10)

1054 SELA. Secretaría Permanente
Estados financieros de la Secretaría Permanente : ejercicio presupuestario 1980. - Caracas : SELA, 1981. (SP/CL/VII.O/Di ; 1)

1055 SELA. Secretaría Permanente
Informe a la 8. Reunión Ordinaria del Consejo Latinoamericano sobre el avance de los trabajos encomendados por la Decisión 103. - Caracas : SELA, 1982. (SP/CL/VIII.O/DT ; 16)

1056 SELA. Secretaría Permanente
Informe a la 8. Reunión Ordinaria del Consejo Latinoamericano sobre el avance de los trabajos encomendados por la Decisión 103 : (financiamiento de proyectos de cooperación regional). - Caracas : SELA, 1982. (SP/CL/VIII.O/DT ; 16) Add.1

1057 SELA. Secretaría Permanente
Informe al Consejo Latinoamericano sobre la primera Reunión de expertos gubernamentales de alto nivel para tratar los temas de agricultura y alimentación. - Caracas : SELA, 1982. (SP/CL/VIII.O/DT ; 18)

1058 SELA. Secretaría Permanente
Informe sobre cooperación latinoamericana en materia de bienes de capital : Decisión 72. - Caracas : SELA, Secretaría Pernamente, 1981. (SP/CL/VII.O/Di ; 7)

1059 SELA. Secretaría Permanente
Informe sobre el exámen de los estados financieros - año finalizado el 31 de diciembre de 1981. - Caracas : SELA, 1982. (SP/CL/VIII.O/DT ; 33)

1060 SELA. Secretaría Permanente
Latinoamerica hacia la consecución de su seguridad alimentaria. - Caracas : SELA, 1982. (SP/CL/VIII.O/Di.11)

1061 SELA. Secretaría Permanente
Lista de documentos de trabajo e informativos presentados a la 8. Reunión ordinaria del Consejo Latinoamericano. - Caracas : SELA, 1982. (SP/CL/VIII.O/Di.12)

1062 SELA. Secretaría Permanente
Proyecto de organización de los trabajos de la Reunión Preparatoria de la séptima Reunión Ordinaria del Consejo Latinoamericano. - Caracas : SELA, Secretaría Permanente, 1981. (SP/CL/VII.O/DT ; 17)

1063 SELA. Secretaría Permanente
Proyecto de organización de los trabajos de la Reunión Preparatoria de la octava Reunión Ordinaria del Consejo Latinoamericano. - Caracas : SELA, 1982. (SP/CL/VIII.O/DT ; 41)

1064 SELA. Secretaría Permanente
Proyecto de presupuesto administrativo y costo por actividades para 1982. - Caracas : SELA, 1981. 48p. ((SP/CL/E.II/DT ; 1)

1065 SELA. Secretaría Permanente
Proyecto de presupuesto administrativo y costo por actividades - 1983. - Caracas : SELA, 1982. (SP/CL/VIII.O/DT ; 32)

1066 SELA. Secretaría Permanente
Proyecto de presupuesto para 1981 : ejercicio 1ro de enero de 1981 - 31 de diciembre de 1981 : anteproyecto de presupuesto para 1982 : ejercicio 1ro de enero de 1981 - 31 de diciembre de 1981. - Caracas : SELA, 1981. (SP/CL/VII.O/DT ; 1)

1067 SELA. Secretaría Permanente
Quinto informe anual. - Caracas : SELA, 1981. (SP/CL/VII.O/DT ; 3)

1068 SELA. Secretaría Permanente
Sexto informe anual. - Caracas : SELA, 1982. (SP/CL/VIII.O/DT ; 2)

1069 SELA. Secretaría Permanente
Sugerencias recibidas de los gobiernos de los estados miembros sobre aspectos inclúdos en el artículo 1º de la Decisión 8. - Caracas : SELA, 1982. (SP/CL/VIII.O/DT ; 12)

1070 SISTEMA Económico Latinoamericano (SELA), p.193-231. In: El proceso de integración en América Latina en 1981.-Buenos Aires : INTAL, 1982.

SELA Sistema Económico Latinoamericano

VIII-2.2. Latin American Free Trade Association—LAFTA/Latin American Integration Association—LAIA

1071 The AIMS of the Latin American Integration Association.
IDB News. Inter-American Development Bank (Washington D.C.), Dec. 1980
LAIA Latin American Integration Association

1072 ALADI
Comercio exterior global de los países miembros : comparación años 1980-1981. - /S.l./ : ALADI, 1982. 9p. (ALADI/SEC/di 82.9)

1073 ALADI
Compensación multilateral de saldos y convenios de crédito recíproco : segundo cuatrimestre de 1982 : fecha de liquidación : 31 agosto 1982. - Montevideo : ALADI, 1982. 28p. (ALADI/SEC/di 52.1)

1074 ALADI
Estudio / ALADI, Asociación Latinoamericana de Integración. Secretaría General. - /S.l./ / ALADI, 1981- . - vols.

ALADI/SEC/Estudio 1 Rev.1	:	Consideraciones sobre la apreciación, multilateral prevista en la Resolución 1 del Consejo de Ministros. 1981. 15p.
ALADI/SEC/Estudio 3	:	Estudio sobre puesta en vigencia de la preferencia arancelaria regional. 1982. 52p.
ALADI/SEC/Estudio 5	:	Evolución y estructura del intercambio comercial de los países que integran la ALADI, 1952-1980. 1983. 70p.
ALADI/SEC/Estudio 6	:	La facilitación del comercio internacional. 1983. 29p.

1075 ALADI
Instrumentos financieros vigentes. - Montevideo : /s.n./, 1982. 1 vol. (var. pagings)

1076 ALADI
Participación de la Secretaría General en la reunión ministerial del Grupo de los 77. - /S.l./ : ALADI, 1983. 88p. (ALADI/SEC/Memorándum 28)

1077 ALADI
Programa de trabajos de la Asociación para 1983 / ALADI. Comité de Representantes. - /S.l./ : Asociación Latinoamericana de Integración, 1982. 8p. (ALADI/CR/Resolución 23)

1078 ALADI. Secretaría General
Guía de discusión para el Seminario Técnico sobre la Preferencia Arancelaria Regional. - Montevideo : ALADI, 1982. 35p. (ALADI/SEC/di 73)

1079 La ALADI en el futuro de Occidente. Futurable (Buenos Aires), 8, 1980, p.70-83

1080 ALADI: nuevo "acto de fe" : tendrá mayor flexibilidad negociadora que la ALALC. Visión (New York), vol.56, no.8, 20 abril 1981, p.49

1081 ALADI : el proceso de renegociación del patrimonio histórico / INTAL. Integración Latinoamericana (Buenos Aires), año 6, no.56, abril 1981, p.38-39

1082 ALADI : Reunión de la Conferencia de Evaluación y Convergencia en Bogotá. Integración Latinoamericana (Buenos Aires), año 7, no.69, junio 1982, p.88-91

1083 ALADI's pipedream of economic integration. Latin America Weekly Report (London), no.46, Nov.21, 1980, p.9. Tab.

Economic integration of Latin American Free Trade Association (LAFTA) into Associatioń Latinoamericana de Integración (ALADI). Main functions of ALADI. Manufactured exports by LAFTA countries.

1084 ALALC : La Asociación Latinoamericana de Integración : un análisis comparativo. - Montevideo : /Secretaría de la ALALC/, septiembre 1980, 59p.

ALALC Associación Latinoamericana de Libre Comercio, Montevideo, Uruguay

1085 ALGUNAS consideraciones sobre la "convergencia" de las acciones parciales en el marco de la ALADI / INTAL. Integración Latinoamericana (Buenos Aires), año 6, no.55, marzo 1981, p.56-59

1086 ALICA : acuerdos de alcance parcial en el marco de la ALADI. Integración Latinoamericana (Buenos Aires), año 7, no.65, enero-febrero 1982, p.37-38

Contents: Proyecto de acuerdo de alcance parcial de complementación económica entre Brasil y Uruguay en la industria carnica. Proyecto de acuerdo de alcance parcial comercial en la industria alimentaria entre Argentina y Colombia. Proyecto de acuerdo de alcance parcial comercial sobre productos de la industria alimentaria entre Colombia y Chile.

ALICA Asociación Latinoamericana de Industriales y Cámaras de Alimentación

1087 AMPLIACION de los acuerdos de complementación industrial. Sintesis (Montevideo), (137) Sept-Dec. 1980, p.10

1088 ANÁLISIS comparación de los Tratados de Montevideo 1960 y 1980. Integracioñn Latinoamericana (Buenos Aires), (50), 1980, p.30-48

1089 AROCENA, Martín
El surgimiento de la Asociación Latinoamericana de Integración. Integración Latinoamericana (Buenos Aires), año 6, no.59, julio 1981, p.11-24

1090 ASOCIACION LATINOAMERICANA DE INTEGRACION, Montevideo
La Asociación Latinoamericana de Integración : un análisis comparativo / Asociación Latinoamericana de Libre Comercio. - /Montevideo/ : ALALC, 1980. 59p.

1091 ASOCIACION LATINOAMERICANA DE INTEGRACIÓN (ALADI) In: El proceso de integración en América Latina en 1981.- Buenos Aires : INTAL, BID, 1982. p.27-63

1092 BARROS CHARLIN, Raymundo
Análisis comparativo de los Tratados de Montevideo 1960 y 1980. Integración Latinoamericana (Buenos Aires), año 6, no.54, ene-feb. 1981, p.93-100

1093 BARROS CHARLIN, Raymundo
Análisis comparativo entre los Tratados de Montevideo de 1960 y 1980. Comercio Exterior (Bogotá), vol.13, nos 6-7, junio-julio 1981, p.3-16

1094 BARROS CHARLIN, Raymundo
Participación empresarial en la ALADI. Integración Latinoamericana (Buenos Aires), año 6, no.62, octubre 1981, p.54-57

1095 BUSINESS INTERNATIONAL CORPORATION, New York
Trading in Latin America : the impact of changing policies. - New York : Business International Corporation, cop. 1981. IV,237p. (A Business International report)

1096 The CASE of LAIA. Bulletin for International Fiscal Documentation (Amsterdam), no.12, 1981, p.533-543

1097 COMPETENCIA desleal : criterios para un acuerdo de alcance regional en el marco de la ALADI. Integración Latinoamericana (Buenos Aires), (53), dec.1980, p.41-49

1098 DAGNINO PASTORE, José María VARTALITIS DE MACCALLUM, Ana María
Definiciones y mediciones de efectos de una zona de libre comercio. Integración Latinoamericana (Buenos Aires), año 7, no.69, junio 1982, p.49-60

Contents: Ordenamiento de datos sobre el comercio internacional. Medición del efecto de las negociaciones de la ALALC sobre el comercio intrazonal. Medición del efecto de las negociaciones de la ALALC sobre la liberalización y la preferencia arancelaria. Medición del efecto de las negociaciones de la ALALC sobre la multilateralización.

1099 DICCIONARIO de mercaderías NAB-NCCA/NABALALC. - Buenos Aires : Central de Estadísticas Nacionales de la República Argentina, 1982. 3 vols
Se actualiza mediante hojas renovables.

1100 ESTUDIO sobre el area de preferencias económicas establecida por el Tratado de Montevideo 1980. - Montevideo : ALADI, Asociación Latinoamericana de Integración, 1982. 78p.

1101 ESTUDIOS sobre la reestructuración de ALALC / Barros Charlin Raymundo, Armanet Pilar ed.; Universidad de Chile, Instituto de Estudios Internacionales. - Santiago : Editorial Universitaria, 1980. 104p. (Colección Estudios Internacionales)

1102 La EVALUACIÓN de Tratado de Montevideo 1980 y las perspectivas de las acciones de alcance parcial de la ALADI. Integración Latinoamericana (Buenos Aires), (50), Sept. 1980, p.4-29

1103 FAREWELL to LAFTA. South (London), (2), nov. 1980, p.51-42
|LAFTA| Latin American Free Trade Association

1104 From LAFTA to LAIA. Newsweek (New York), nov. 16, 1981

1105 GARCIA MARTINEZ, Carlos
ALADI : su creación y perspectivas. - Buenos Aires : Bolsa de Comercio, 1980. 18p.

1106 HUMMER, Waldemar
Die Lateinamerikanische Integrationsassoziation (ALADI) als Rechtsnachfolger der "Lateinamerikanischen Freihandelsassoziation" (ALALC). Verfassung und Recht in Uebersee (Hamburg), 13(4), 1980, p.361-370
Includes bibliographical references.

1107 IDENTIFICACION de modalidades instrumentales para el desarrollo del comercio y la cooperación agropecuaria y alimentaria en el marco del Tratado de Montevideo 1980 / FAO. Oficina Regional para América Latina. - Montevideo : ALADI, 1982. 170p.

1108 INTEGRACION en America Latina : la ALADI. - Caracas : Federación Venezolana de Cámaras y Asociaciones de Comercio y Producción, 1981. 64p.

1109 JORGE WITKER, V.
La Asociación Latinoamericana de Integración (ALADI) : sus objetivos, funcionamiento y texto del Tratado de Montevideo de 1980 comentado. - México : Guma, 1981, VIII,131p.

1110 JUNAC
Evaluación del patrimonio histórico de la ALALC y sus implicaciones para el Grupo Andino. (JUN/GAN.GA.ALALC/V/dt.3, 25 abril 1980)

1111 LAFTA : chronology of the main events and of the cooperation taking place within the integration schemes during 1979. Latin American Integration (Buenos Aires), April 1981, p.117-119
(Special English edition)

1112 LAFTA/ALADI: Asociación Latinoamericana de Integración. In: El Proceso de integración en América Latina en 1981. Buenos Aires : INTAL, 1982. p.27-63

1113 LAIA : a renewed hope. Integración Latinoamericana (Buenos Aires), año 5, no.47, Junio 1980.

1114 LAIA renews pact, continues to upgrade trade agreements. Business Latin America (New York), 22.9.1982, p.303-304

1115 LAIA takes hold as LAFTA accords are renegotiated. Business Latin America (New York), 21.1.1981, p.23-24

1116 LAIA'S first meeting analyses progress on trade accords. Business Latin America (New York), 13.5.1981, p.149-150

1117 LATEINAMERIKA : weitere ALADI-Aktivitäten. Nachrichten für Aussenhandel (Köln), 2.12.1981

1118 LAVUT, Anna
De ALALC a ALADI : evolución lógica. America Latina (Moskva), vol.55, no.7, July 1982, p.60-66

1119 A LONG road ahead for ALADI. Latin America Weekly Report (London), (37), 24.9.1982, p.9-10

1120 LONGO, Carlos A.
Indirect tax harmonization : the case of LAIA? Bulletin for International Fiscal Documentation International Bureau of Fiscal Documentation (Amsterdam), vol.35, 1981, no.12, p.533-543
mit dt.u.franz.Zsfassung.

1121 MAIRA, Luis I. de
Perspectivas de la preferencia arancelaria regional en la Asociación Latinoamericana de Integración. Integración Latinoamericana (Buenos Aires), año 7, no.70, julio 1982, p.12-20

Contents: El margen de preferencia ALALC. El margen de preferencia ALADI. Proyecciones del comercio intraregional.

1122 El MARGEN de preferencia arancelario y sus efectos en el comercio intra ALALC. Integración Latinoamericana (Buenos Aires), (49), Aug. 1980, p.5-12 ; Jan/Febr. 1981, p.12-17

1123 MONTEVIDEO TREATY 1980.
Latin American Integration (Buenos Aires), 1, April 1981, p.107-116 (Special English edition)

1124 MONTEVIDEO Treaty 1980 : instrument establishing the Latin American Integration Association (LAIA). - Montevideo : LAFTA, Secretariat, 1981. 41p.

Includes Resolutions CM/1 to 9 adcpted by LAFTA Council of Ministers of Foreign Affairs, Montevideo, August 1980

1125 MORALES DE MAREGA, Hebe Graciela
Evolución económica de la ALALC : tesis de doctorado. - Córdoba : Universidad Nacional, Facultad de Ciencias Económicas, 1982. 155p.

1126 MOTA PELEGRINO, Carlos Roberto
Evolution et perspectives de l'Association Latino-Américaine de Libre Commerce. - Nice : Copirex, 1975. 422p. (Thesis doctoral / Université de Nice. Institut du droit de la paix et du développement, Nice)
Bibl. p.339-407

1127 NUEVA etapa en la reestructuración de la ALALC. Integración Latinoamericana (Buenos Aires), (48), July 1980, p.30-40

1128 NUEVA guía ALADI. - Buenos Aires : Central de Estadísticas Nacionales de la República Argentina, 1982. 1 vol., suppl.

Se actualiza mediante hojas renovables.

1129 ORIA, Jorge Luis
La clausula de la nación más favorecida en el Tratado de Montevideo 1980. Integración Latinoamericana (Buenos Aires), 1981, año 6, no.62, octubre : parte 1, p.44-53, año 6, no.63, noviembre : parte 2, p.41-50

1130 ORREGO VICUÑA, Francisco
Las acciones parciales de integración y su compatibilización con el proceso de ALALC. Integración Latinoamericana (Buenos Aires), año 5, no.44, marzo 1980, p.74-86

1131 PEÑA, Felix
El régimen jurídico de la transformación de la ALALC en la ALADI. Integración Latinoamericana (Buenos Aires), año 7, no.65, enero-febrero 1982, p.33-36

Contents: Continuidad y cambio. Etapas de la transformación ALALC-ALADI. Renegociación del patrimonio histórico de la ALALC.

1132 PERSPECTIVAS de la preferencia arancelaria regional en la Asociación Latinoamericana de Integración. - Buenos Aires : INTAL, 1981. 24 leaves

1133 RENEGOCIACION de las ventajas comerciales de la ALALC. Sintesis (Montevideo), (137), Sept-Dec. 1980, p.2

1134 RESOLUCIONES del Consejo de Ministros de Relaciones Exteriores de la ALALC : CM/Resoluciones 1 a 9. - Montevideo : ALALC, 1980. 18p.

1135 RESULTADO de las negociaciones del patrimonio histórico de la ALALC. Comercio Exterior (Bogotá), vol.13, no.6-7, junio-julio 1981, p.17-64

1136 REUNION de la BANCA COMERCIAL, 1., 1982, Buenos Aires
La cooperación financiera y monetaria en el ámbito de la ALADI / Reunión de la Banca Comercial, 1., Buenos Aires, nov. 28-dic.1, 1982. - Montevideo : ALADI, 1982. 15p. (ALADI/BC/I/Di 2)

1137 REUNION DE DELEGADOS GUBERNAMENTALES DE ALTO NIVEL, 1981, Lima
Informe de la Reunión de Delegados Gubernamentales de Alto Nivel convocada por el primer período de sesiones extraordinarias de la Conferencia de Evaluación y Convergencia. - Lima : ALADI, 1981. 21p.

1138 SALAZAR SANTOS, Felipe
Asociación Latinoamericana de Integración. Nueva Sociedad (San José), (53), mar-abr. 1981, p.29-37

/LAFTA/ to LAIA, 1980 Treaty of Montevideo/, /regional/ economic integration/, /Latin America/.

1139 SALAZAR SANTOS, Felipe
The problem of convergence. Latin American Integration (Buenos Aires), no.1, April 1981, p.89-106.
(Special English edition)

Introduction. Background. Partial initiatives. Subregional agreements and sectoral agreements. The most-favored-nation clause. Relations with Third countries. Conclusions.

See also:
Convergencia de las Acciones parciales en el Marco de la ALADI. Integración Latinoamericana (Buenos Aires), no.50 y 62 respectivamente.

1140 SEMINARIO SOBRE INTEGRACION Y COMERCIO EXTERIOR EN AMERICA LATINA, 1982, Santiago de Chile
Informacion general, programa y discurso del Ministro de Economía y Hacienda de Chile, Rolf Luders / Seminario sobre Integración y Comercio Exterior en América Latina, Santiago, Chile, oct. 28-29, 1982. - Montevideo : ALADI, 1982. 14p. (ALADI/SEC/Memorandum 15.1)

1141 SLOAN, John W.
La Asociación Latinoamericana de Libre Comercio : un evaluación de sus logros y fracasos. Integración Latinoamericana (Buenos Aires), 4(42), dic. 1979, p.37-55

1142 The TARIFF margin of preference and its effects on intra-LAFTA trade. Latin American Integration (Buenos Aires), June 1982, p.8-10, Tabs.
(Special English edition)

Summary of a study prepared by Luis de Maira, Olga Bergalli de González, Jorge Augusto Torres Zorella, Alicia Alonso, Alfredo Smilges and José Maria Vacca, under the supervision of Martin Arocena.

1143 TRATADO de Montevideo 1980. - Montevideo : Secretaría de la ALALC, 1980 18p.

At foot of title: Instrumento que instituye la Asociación Latinoamericana de Integración (ALADI)

1144 TRATADO de Montevideo, 1980 = Montevideo Treaty, 1980 : instrument establishing the Latin American Integration Association (LAIA). - Montevideo : LAFTA Secretariat, 1981. 41p.

"Includes resolutions CM/1 to 9, adopted by LAFTA Council of Ministers of Foreign Affairs"

1145 El TRATAMIENTO preferencial a Bolivia y Ecuador en la ALALC : análisis crítico y evaluación de resultados. - Buenos Aires : INTAL, 1982. 118p.

1146 TUSSIE, Diana
Latin American integration : from LAFTA to LAIA. Journal of World Trade Law (Twickenham), vol.16, no.5, Sept./Oct. 1982, p.399-413. Ref. Tabs.

Abolition of the Latin American Free Trade Association (LAFTA) and its replacement by the Latin American Integration Association (LAIA) is related to the "opening-up" of the Latin America economies to the international market since the mid-seventies. Preliminary exploration of the relationship between this trend and the new conditions in international financial markets.

1147 WIONCZEK, Miguel S.
A comparative analysis of the 1960-1980 Montevideo Treaties. Latin American Integration (Buenos Aires), June 1982, p.74-78
(Special English edition)

Study prepared by Miguel S. Wionczek at the request of INTAL on "The Evaluation of the LAIA Treaty and the Outlook for Partial Scope Actions".

1148 WIONCZEK, Miguel S.
La evaluación del Tratado de Montevideo 1980 y las perspectivas de las acciones de alcance parcial de la ALALC. Integration Latinoamericana (Buenos Aires), vol.50, 1981.

1149 WIONCZEK, Miguel S.
The evaluation of the 1980 Treaty of Montevideo and the outlook for LAIA's partial actions. Latin American Integration (Buenos Aires), June 1982, p.14-15
(Special English edition)

Summary of a study prepared by Miguel S. Wionczek, INTAL consultant.

1150 WIONCZEK, Miguel S.
Evaluation of the Treaty of Acapulco and the outlook for the partial actions of the Latin American Integration Association (LAIA). Latin American Integration (Buenos Aires), no.1, April 1981, p.23-48
(Special English edition)

Introduction. World economic outlook for the 1980's. Probable trends in Latin American trade during the 1980's. General comments on the Treaty of Acapulco. Partial actions and their convergence in the Treaty of Acapulco. The instrumentation of the partial actions; economic complementation agreements with emphasis on the industrial sector; agricultural agreements; partial actions in the energy sector; regional and subregional financial matters. Sources.

ALADI Associación Latinoamericana de Integración

VIII-2.3. Andean Group—ANCOM

1151 ACUERDO de Cartagena y el trato preferencial en favor de Bolivia y Ecuador. - Buenos Aires : INTAL, 1982. 149p.

1152 AHO, Michael C. NUÑEZ del ARCO, José
United States direct investment in Latin America, 1966-67: an empirical analysis of the impact of the Andean Code (Decision 24). Latin American Integration (Buenos Aires), no.1, April 1981. p.49-62.
(Special English edition)

Introduction. The Andean Common Market and the Andean code. Authorization. Acquisition of national businesses. Access to internal credit. Transforming foreign-owned businesses into joint ventures. Profit remittance abroad. Transfer of technology. The impact of the Andean code: empirical evidence. 6 tabs. Methodology and data. Empirical results. Regressions 1-4. Conclusions. Bibliography.

1153 ALCALDE CARDOZA, Javier
Hacia una caracterización de las negociaciones en el Acuerdo de Cartagena. Integración Latinoamericana (Buenos Aires), año 7, no.71, agosto 1982, p.28-47

Contents: Introducción: concepción de las negociaciones en la teoría de la integración. Rasgos innovadores del Acuerdo de Cartagena como esquema de integración. El Acuerdo de Cartagena como sistema político institucional: los actores del sistema. Los actores de los países miembros y del exterior. Influencia de los actores externos: la negociación del Programa Automotor. Evolución reciente del Acuerdo de Cartagena : crisis, logros y temas de negociación. Conclusión : análisis de las negociaciones y del estado de la integración andina. Bibliografía.

1154 ALCANTARA SAEZ, Manuel JAMAR, Joseph
Le Pacte Andin. In: Intégrations régionales entre pays en développement. - Bruges : De Tempel, 1982. p.109-176
Bibliography: p.176-178

1155 ANALISIS del costo de transporte subregional andino y de las operaciones de comercio exterior. - Buenos Aires : INTAL, 1981. 153p.

1156 ANCOM rules interpretation signals Peru's commitment to attract foreign investment. Business Latin America (New York), 27.1.1982, p.25-30

1157 ANCOM will deemphasize broad integration efforts and focus on tariff cuts. Business Latin America (New York), 23.9.1981, p.297-298

1158 The ANDEAN Common Market : management implications of application of technology legislation / contributions by John D. Daniels .../et al./; edited by Fernando Robles. - New York : Council of the Americas, 1976. xxvii,167p.

Subjects: technology transfer - addresses, essays, lectures / Andes region - economic conditions -- addresses, essays, lectures.

1159 ANDEAN GROUP : chronology of the main events and of the cooperation taking place within the integration schemes during 1979. Latin American Integration (Buenos Aires), 1, April 1981, p.119-121
(Special English edition)

1160 ANDEAN GROUP : proposals on how the Pact should overcome the deadlock. Comercio Exterior (México), vol.27, no.4, April 1981, p.154

1161 ANDEAN pact members going their own separate ways. Latin American Regional Report (London), 27.2.1981, p.1

1162 ANDEAN pact : the pact's future under a cloud. The Andean Report (Lima), (1), Jan. 1981, p.16-17

1163 ANDEAN pact trade shows strong gains nontraditional exports up. Business Latin America (New York), 30.9.1981, p.310-311

1164 BACH, L.
Pacto Andino y la Integración Latinoamericana. - Buenos Aires : Tierra Nueva, 1976. 148p.

/Monograph/ analysing the background, scope, instruments and process of /economic integration/ in /Latin America/ and the/Andean region/. Includes selected fragments from the /international agreement/ of Cartagena and subsequent decisions which lay the basis for /regional/ development policy/, /bibliography: p.99-104 and /statistical table/s.

/Pacto Andino : el Perú, Colombia, Bolivia, Ecuador y Venezuela/

1165 BAENA, J., G.
Pacto Andino : su historia, su desarrollo, su futuro. - Bogotá : Glosa Pedagogíca, Didáctica, 1973.

/Política de desarrollo/, /desarrollo económico/, /integración económica/, /marco institucional/, /Grupo Andino/ - /aspectos jurídicos/, /cooperación regional/, /empresas multinacionales/, /inversiones extranjeras/, /mercado de trabajo/, /desarrollo industrial/, /desarrollo agricola/, /acuerdos arancelarios/, /datos estadísticos/.

1166 BASCON, Eduardo
Die Corporación Andina de Fomento als Entwicklungsbank des Andenpaktes. - Hamburg : Institut für Iberoamerika-Kunde, 1981. 111p. (Arbeitsunterlagen und Diskussionsbeiträge = Documentos de trabajo / Institut für Iberoamerika-Kunde ; 11)
Table of contents and summary also in Spanish.
Bibliography: p.89-94

1167 BOLIVIA and economic policy trouble the Andean pact. Latin American Regional Reports (London), Nov. 7, 1980, p.1

Problems with EEC due to political take-over in Bolivia threatens economic cooperation between Andean Group member. Automobile programme. Tariffs in Peru.

1168 BOLIVIA se retira del Pacto Andino : ataques diplomáticos de ambas partes. Visión. La Revista Interamericana (New York), vol.56, no.2, 26 enero 1981, p.15

1169 BRETON, R.
Groupe Andin : l'adoption et l'application du régime commun aux capitaux étrangers. - Laval, Qué. : Université Laval, 1978. 182p.

/Groupe Andin/, /analyse historique/, /régimes politiques/, /coopération régionale/ - /stabilité politique/, /idéologie politique/, bibliographie.

1170 BURELLI RIVAS, M.A.
Integración Latinoamericana y el Pacto Andino : los orígenes, las realizaciones, los desafíos. Mundo Nuevo (Caracas), 3(7-8),enero-junio 1980, p.7-22

1171 CAMACHO OMISTE, Edgar
Bolivia y la integración andina. - La Paz : Los Amigos del Libro, 1981. 437p.

1172 CARMONA ESTANGA, Pedro
El proceso de industrialización en el Grupo Andino. - LIMA : JUNAC, 1982. 18p. (JUN/di 690)

1173 CARMONA ESTANGA, Pedro
Trece años de un proceso de integración. - Lima : JUNAC, 1982. 18p.

1174 CARRAUD, Michel
L'intégration des pays andins. - Paris : Economica, 1981. 232p.
Bibliography: p./227/-230
ISBN: 2 7178 0309 2

1175 CASTAÑEDA ARRASCUE, Oscar
Decisión 24 : mito o realidad. - Lima : Universidad Nacional. Centro de Investigaciones para el Desarrollo. 1981. 151p.

1176 CHAPARRO, Alfonso Julio
Manual de integración andina. 4.ed., actualizada y ampliada. - Caracas : Monte Avila Editores, 1978. 431p. (Colección Estudios)

Subjects: Andes region - economic integration / Acuerdo de Cartagena.

1177 COMISION DEL ACUERDO DE CARTAGENA
Decisión 24 : régimen común de tratamiento a los capitales extranjeros y sobre marcas, patentes, licencias y regalías. - Lima : JUNAC, 1981. 46p.

Includes decisión: 47,48,103,109,110,118,124,125 and 144.

1178 COMISION DEL ACUERDO DE CARTAGENA. Sesiones extraordinarias, 30., 1981, Bogotá
Acuerdo de Cartagena : acta final / Comisión del Acuerdo de Cartagena, Trigésimo Período de Sesiones Extraordinarias, Bogotá. -Bogotá-Paipa : Comisión del Acuerdo de Cartagena, 1981. 14p.

1179 COMISION DEL ACUERDO DE CARTAGENA. Sesiones Ordinarias, 35., 1982, Lima
Evaluación del programa de reactivación y exámen de la situación actual y perspectivas del proceso de integración subregional / Comisión del Acuerdo de Cartagena, Periodo de Sesiones Ordinarias, 35., Lima, 4-6 oct. 1982. - Lima : Comisión del Acuerdo de Cartagena, 1982. 127p. (COM/XXXV/dt 2)

1180 CONVENIO de cooperación aduanera peruano-colombiano : protocolo modificatorio 1981 / Castañeda Arrascue Oscar, comp. - Lima : Centro de Documentación e Información Andina, 1981. 176p.

1181 COSTO de transporte y comercio subregional andino. - Buenos Aires : INTAL, 1981. 221p.

1182 CUEVAS RAMIREZ, Roberto
El Grupo Andino y la comunicación social. - La Paz : Asociación de Periodistas, 1981. 154p.

1183 DEERE, Carmen Diana LEON DE LEGAL, Magdalena
Women in Andean agriculture : peasant production and rural wage employment in Colombia and Peru. - Genève : ILO, 1982. 172p.

1184 DIFICIL trance para el Pacto Andino : urge reactivar el proceso de integración. Visión (New York), vol.59, no.4, 23 agosto 1982, p.43

1185 DOCUMENTOS presentados al Seminario sobre Cooperación Económica entre España e Iberoamérica con Especial Referencia al Grupo Andino. - Madrid : Centro Iberoamericano de Cooperación, 1979, 9 vol. en 1.

1186 DOLLFUS, Olivier
El reto del espacio andino. - Lima : Instituto de Estudios Peruanos, 1981. 141p. (Perú problema ; 20)

1187 ECHEVERRIA, Javier
Economic and industrialization policies in the Andean group of countries, 1970-1980. - Vienna : UNIDO, 21 April 1982. UNIDO/IS.313

ASEAN / Andean pact conference on regional industrial co-operation, Lima, Peru, 14-18 June 1982.

1188 EMERGENCY talks fact to rescue Andean pact from doldrums. Latin America Reports 12.12.1980, p.1

1189 ENCUENTRO ANDINO DE TRANSPORTISTAS DE CARTA POR CARRETERA, 1., 1982, Quito
Acta final / Encuentro Andino de Transportistas de Carta por Carretera, 1., Quinto, 29-30 nov. 1982. - Lima : JUNAC, 1982. 19p. (JUN/R.T.CC./I/Acta final)

1190 EVALUACION del proceso de integración 1969-1979. - Lima: Junta del Acuerdo de Cartagena, 1979. 11 vols.

/Evaluación económica/, /integración regional/, /Grupo Andino/ - /política comercial internacional/, /desarrollo industrial/, /comercio exterior/, /cambio tecnológico/,, /transferencia de tecnologías/, /estadísticas económicas/.

1191 EVALUACION económico financiera de la Corporación Andina de Fomento. - Lima : Ministero de Industria, Comercio, Turismo e Integración, 1981. 59p.

1192 FALCONI PUIG, Juan
Integración e inversión extranjera. Quito : Corporación de Estudios y Publicaciones, /1979/. 111p.

Subjects: Acuerdo de Cartagena /investments -- foreign investments - law and legislation - Andes region /industrial property - Andes region /Andes region - economic integration.

1193 FERNANDEZ, Javier
Colombia y el Grupo Andino : análisis de estrategias. Desarrollo y sociedad (Bogotá), no.3, enero, 1980, p.13-50
Includes bibliographical references.

1194 FERRIS, Elizabeth G.
The Andean Pact and the Amazon Treaty : reflections of changing Latin American relations. Journal of Inter-American Studies and World Affairs (Beverly Hills, Calif.), vol.23, no.2, 1981, p.147-175
Includes bibliographical references.

1195 FERRIS, Elizabeth G.
National support for the Andean Pact. Journal of Developing Areas (Macomb), vol.16, no.2, January 1982, p.249. Ref. Tabs.

It is examined why some member governments support the Andean pact more than the others, what the relationship is between the economic characteristics of a nation and its experiences in an integration scheme, and how the process of integration itself affects continued national support for integration.

1196 FISCHER, Hellmuth
Der Andenpakt: ein Versuch zur Verminderung aussenwirtschaftlicher Abhängigkeit.- Frankfurt a.M., Bern: Lang, 1981, II,183p. (Münchner Studien zur Internationalen Entwicklung; Bd 3)
Bibliography: p.153-183
ISBN: 3 8204 5898 0

1197 FLORES GUEVARA, Gustavo
Información tecnológica para la integración andina. Ciencia-Tecnología y Desarrollo, vol.5, no.1, enero-marzo 1981, p.105-127

1198 FUENTES TEJOS, Hugo ARIZA LOPEZ, Leopoldo
Manual del Pacto Andino y de la integración subregional. - Santiago de Chile : Talleras Gráficos García), 1976. XVI,565p.

1199 GARCIA GARCIA, Jorge
Programación industrial y el arancel externo común : un impuesto al sector agrícola del Grupo Andino. Coyuntura Andina (Bogotá), no.6, julio 1981, p.230-248

1200 GATT, Genève
Technical studies - Andean Group (Bolivia, Colombia, Ecuador, Perù, Venezuela) / note by the Secretariat.-/S.l. : s.n./, 1979. 148p. (LCD/TS/29)

1201 GENERAL overview of the ANDEAN group / prepared by the Board of the Cartagena Agreement. - Vienna : UNIDO, 21 April 1982. In: ASEAN/Andean pact conference on regional industrial co-operation, Lima, Perù, 14-18 June 1982. UNIDO/IS.312

1202 GIRALDO GONZALO, E. OLARTE, Miguel T.
Evaluación de la participación colombiana en el proceso de integración Andina en la década del 70. Revista de planeación y desarrollo (Bogotá), 12(2), mayo/agosto 1980, p.7-73

1203 GONZALES CANO, Hugo
Orientaciones para la armonización de los incentivos tributarios a las exportaciones no tradicionales en los países del Acuerdo de Cartagena. Integración Latinoamericana (Buenos Aires), no.59, julio 1981, p.31-69

1204 GROSSE, Robert
Codes of conduct for multinational enterprises. Journal of World Trade Law (Twickenham), vol.16, no.5, Sept/Oct., 1982, p.414. Ref. Tabs.

Survey of the codes concluded and in progress in various intergovernmental organizations which affect multinational enterprises. Discussion of the impacts of the Andean Pact Code on the OECD on MNC behaviour.

1205 GRUPO ANDINO. In: El proceso de integración en América Latina en 1981. Buenos Aires : INTAL, 1982, p.65-117

1206 GRUPO ANDINO. Reunión de Ministros de Agricultura, 3., 1979
Acta final de la tercera reunión de Ministros de Agricultura del Grupo Andino. (JUN/di 283/Rev.2, 3 abril 1979)

1207 GRUPO ANDINO. Reunión de Ministros de Agricultura, 4., 1980
Acta final de la cuarta reunión de Ministros de Agricultura del Grupo Andino. (COM/XXIX/dt 9, 27 mayo 1980)

1208 GUERRERO, M.
Diez años del Grupo Andino : memorias de un protagonista. - Ottawa : IDRC, 1979. 432p.

El libro es un estudio sistemático de las normas y decisiones del Acuerdo de Cartagena bajo la influencia del desarrollo político de los estados miembros. Analiza los orígenes del Acuerdo, la declaración de Bogotá y las reuniones del Comité de Expertos. Las decisiones sobre inversiones estranjeras.La aplicación de la política arancelaria. La armonización de la legislación económica industrial. Las bases para el desarrollo de tecnología y la industria petroquímica. La crisis y retiro de Chile. Los programas de la industria automotriz y del sector agropecuario.

1209 HERRERA, Beatriz
Grupo Andino y COMECON : crítica a la integración económica. - Lima : Pensamiento Crítico, 1982. 146p. (Serie tesis universitaria)

1210 HOJMAN, David E.
Andean Pact : failure of a model of economic integration? Journal of Common Market Studies (Oxford), vol.20, no.2, December 1981, p.139-160

1211 HORTON, Scott
Peru and ANCOM : a study in the disintegration of a common market. Texas International Law Journal (Austin, Tex.), 17(1), winter 1982, p.39-61

1212 HUBENE, Cecile
Los aspectos jurídicos de las relaciones entre la Comunidad Europea y el Grupo Subregional Andino. Integración Latinoamericana (Buenos Aires), no.68, mayo 1982, p.71-81

1213 INTAL
Grupo Andino : nuevo régimen de la empresa multinacional. Integración Latinoamericana (Buenos Aires), no.71, agosto 1982, p.48-50

1214 INTAL
El turismo en el Grupo Andino. Integración Latinoamericana (Buenos Aires), no.73, octubre 1982, p.69-71

1215 INTEGRACIÓN agropecuaria de Grupo Andino. Progreso (México City), marzo 1982, p.46

1216 INTEGRACIÓN Andina. - Bogotá : Fundación Friedrich Naumann, 1974, 375p.
Subjects: Acuerdo de Cartagena -- addresses, essays, lectures / Andes region - economic integration -- addresses, essays, lectures.

1217 JUNAC
Acciones y decisiones de los órganos principales del Acuerdo de Cartagena en el campo de la infraestructura física y los transportes. (JUN/di.498, 3 septiembre 1980)

1218 JUNAC
Acta final de la primera reunión del grupo de Alto Nivel de la Comisión para examinar la Propuesta 66/Mod.1 de la Junta. (COM/GAN.IS/Acta Final, 7 noviembre 1980)

1219 JUNAC
Acta final de la tercera reunión de presidentes, ministros y jefes de organismos de planificación del Grupo Andino. (JUN/R.MPL/III/Acta Final, 9 mayo 1980)

1220 JUNAC
Acuerdo de cooperación entre la Junta del Acuerdo de Cartagena y la Secretaría Permanente del SELA. (JUN/di.476, 20 junio 1980)

1221 JUNAC
Ampliación de los plazos para inicio de producción y reserva de mercado de productos de la Decisión 108 para ser producidos en Bolivia. (JUN/Propuesta 123, 10 diciembre 1980)

1222 JUNAC
Ampliación de los plazos para inicio de producción y reserva de mercado de productos de la Decisión 108 reservados para ser producidos en el Ecuador. (JUN/Propuesta 124, 10 diciembre 1980)

1223 JUNAC
Análisis de criterios correctivos del Arancel Externo Común de la Propuesta 96/Mod.1. (JUN/di 517, 27 noviembre 1980)

1224 JUNAC
Andean Pact technology policies / Junta del Acuerdo de Cartagena. - Ottawa : International Development Research Centre, /1976/ 58p. Bibl. Ref.

1225 JUNAC
Avances en la ejecución del plan andino de promoción de exportaciones de 1980. (JUN/RD.PE/IX/dt.4, 19 junio 1980)

1226 JUNAC
Ayuda memoria entre la Corporación Andina de Fomento y la Junta del Acuerdo de Cartagena en el campo de la promoción de exportaciones. (JUN/RD.PE/IX/di 2, 20 junio 1980)

1227 JUNAC
Bases para la elaboración de una propuesta modificada sobre arancel externo común y armonización de los instrumentos de comercio exterior. (COM/XXV-E/dt.2, 29 febrero 1980)

1228 JUNAC
Bases para la iniciación del complimiento del programa de liberación por parte de Bolivia y Ecuador. (JUN/dt.155, 2 diciembre 1980)

1229 JUNAC
Bases para la propuesta sobre el tratamiento de los programas industriales de los sectores electrónico y de telecomunicaciones farmoquímico y químico (JUN/dt.140, 13 agosto 1980)

1230 JUNAC
Caracterización de sectores industriales para determinar prioridades de racionalización industrial. (JUN/dt 126, 16 enero 1980)

1231 JUNAC
Compromisos que han asumido los países miembros y que deberán complirlos a partir de 1980. (J/PR/120/Rev.1, 19 mayo 1980)

1232 JUNAC
Consideración de la Junta del Acuerdo de Cartagena con respecto a la elaboración del Planteamiento de Orientación General del Proceso de Integración hasta 1990. (JUN/dt 132, 31 enero 1980)

1233 JUNAC
Contenido y descripción de la propuesta de la Junta sobre el programa de desarrollo de la industria siderúrgica. (COM/XXIX/dt 11, 23 mayo 1980)

1234 JUNAC
Décimocuarto informe sobre el cumplimiento de los compromisos derivados del Acuerdo de Cartagena y de las Decisiones de la Comisión. - LIMA : JUNAC, 1982. 75p. (COM/XXV/di 1)

1235 JUNAC
Decisión 126 : proyectos andinos de desarrollo tecnológico en el área de los alimentos. - Lima : /s.n./, /198-/. 1 vol.

1236 JUNAC
Las decisiones de la Comisión y el derecho interno de los países miembros. (JUN/R.EJ/I) di 1,4 febrero 1980)

1237 JUNAC
Declaración de los presidentes del Grupo Andino. (JUN/di 490, agosto 1980)

1238 JUNAC
Diagnóstico del sector transportes en el Grupo Andino. (JUN/dt. 139, 25 julio 1980)

1239 JUNAC
Evaluación del intercambio de Bolivia y Ecuador con los países andinos : (1969-1978). (J-PE-D-240, 29 octubre 1980)

1240 JUNAC
Evaluación del proceso de integración, 1969-1979 : Bolivia, Colombia, Perú, Venezuela / Grupo Andino. - Lima : JUNAC, 1979. 172p.

1241 JUNAC
Evaluación del programa petroquímico, 1975-1978. - Lima : La Junta, 1979. 173p. Bibl. Ref.

1242 JUNAC
Información estadística sobre los niveles mínimos de la franja del arancel externo común para 1983 y 1990 y aranceles nacionales vigentes. (COM/XXV-E/Dt 4, 5 marzo 1980)

1243 JUNAC
Informe de la Junta a la Comisión sobre relaciones entre el Grupo Andino y los Estados Unidos. (COM/XXX/dt 3, 10 octubre 1980)

1244 JUNAC
Informe de la Junta del Acuerdo de Cartagena al primer encuentro subregional andino de ciencia y tecnología. (JUN/ESA.CT/dt.1 Rev.1, 18 abril 1980)

1245 JUNAC
Informe de la Junta sobre la elaboración de programas sectoriales e intersectoriales de desarrollo industrial. (JUN/dt 127, 17 enero 1980)

1246 JUNAC
L'informe final de la cuarta reunión del Consejo de Planificación del Grupo Andino. (CPL/IV/Informe final, 7 mayo 1980)

1247 JUNAC
Mecanismos de la integración andina. 2.ed. - Lima : JUNAC, 1978. 80p.

1248 JUNAC
Orientaciones generales para el proceso de integración agropecuaria en el medio plazo. (JUN/R.MA/IV/dt 6, 14 junio 1980)

1249 JUNAC
Orientaciones para la armonización de los incentivos tributarios a las exportaciones no tradicionales. (J/PE/133, 23 septiembre 1980)

1250 JUNAC
Primera reunión del Consejo de Ministros de Relaciones Exteriores del Grupo Andino. (JUN/di 445, 30 enero 1980)

1251 JUNAC
Programa petroquímico del Grupo Andino / Junta del Acuerdo de Cartagena. - Lima : La Junta, Unidad de Comunicaciones, 1976. 40p. Ill. (Publicaciones oficiales de la Junta del Acuerdo de Cartagena)

1252 JUNAC
Programa sectorial de desarrollo de la industria automotriz. - Lima : Junta del Acuerdo de Cartagena, 1977 or 1978. 103p. Graphs.

Subjects: Acuerdo de Cartagena / automobile industry and trade - Andes region / industrial promotion - Andes region.

1253 JUNAC
Propuesta de la Junta para la actualización del Anexo XII de la Decisión 146. (JUN/Propuesta 116, 23 abril 1980)

1254 JUNAC
Propuesta de la Junta para la definición de los mecanismos aplicables a los productos que habiendo sido reservados para programas sectoriales de desarrollo industrial no fueron incluidos en ellos. (JUN/Propuesta 122, 26 noviembre 1980)

1255 JUNAC
Propuesta de la Junta para un Programa Andino de Desarrollo Tecnológico para el Medio Rural.- Lima : JUNAC, 1981. 222p.

1256 JUNAC
Propuesta de la Junta sobre el ajuste al programa sectorial del desarrollo de la industria petroquímica. (JUN/Propuesta 119, 24 junio 1980)

1257 JUNAC
Propuesta de la Junta sobre arancel externo común y armonización de los instrumentos de comercio exterior. (JUN/Propuesta 96/Mod.1, 17 mayo 1980)

1258 JUNAC
Propuesta de la Junta sobre normas especiales para la calificación del origen de las mercaderías. (JUN/Propuesta 39/Mod.2, 17 mayo 1980)

1259 JUNAC
Propuesta de la Junta sobre el programa sectorial de desarrollo de la industria siderúrgica. (JUN/Propuesta 66/Mod.2, 27 noviembre 1980)

1260 JUNAC
Proyecto específico de producción y agroindustrialización de palma africana. (JUN/R.MA/IV/dt 12, 15 marzo 1980)

1261 JUNAC
Resumen de la evaluación del proceso de integración 1969-1979. - /S.l. : s.n./, 1979, 41p. Ill. (J/PR/96/Rev.1)

1262 JUNAC
Reunión del Consejo de Ministros de Relaciones Exteriores del Grupo Andino con los ministros de relaciones exteriores de los Estados miembros de las Comunidades Europeas. (JUN/di 469, 14 mayo 1980)

1263 JUNAC
Reunión del Parlamento Andino. (J/RE/12, 27 octubre 1980)

1264 JUNAC
Sistema de coordinación permanente entre los convenios de la Integración Andina. (JUN/dt 147, 15 octubre 1980)

1265 JUNAC
Situación arancelaria en los países andinos para los productos sujetos a la applicación del Arancel Externo Común. (J/PE/102/Rev.1, 21 septiembre 1980)

1266 JUNAC
Términos de referencia para el estudio de la racionalización de la industria textil en el Grupo Andino. (JUN/dt 128, 17 enero 1980)

1267 JUNAC
Transferencia de tecnología de empresas extranjeras hacia el Grupo Andino. - Lima : JUNAC, 1979. 34p.
Bibliography: p.33

1268 JUNAC. Biblioteca
Bibliografía anotada sobre aplicación de la decisión 24 y comportamiento de la inversión extranjera en el Grupo Andino. - Lima : JUNAC, Biblioteca, 1981. 13p.

1269 JUNAC. Biblioteca
Bibliografía anotada sobre aspectos políticos de la integración andina : suplemento I, 1979-1980. - Lima : JUNAC, Biblioteca, 1981. 40p. 173 referencias.

1270 JUNAC. Biblioteca
Bibliografía sobre el integración subregional andina. 2a ed. - Lima : JUNAC, Biblioteca, 1977-
Indice de autores e instituciones.

1977. 1977. 83p.
1977. 1978. 28p.
1979/80 : supl. 1981. 37p.
1980/82 : supl. 1982. 25p.

1271 JUNAC. Biblioteca
Principales manuales sobre evaluación de proyectos de la Biblioteca JUNAC. - Lima : JUNAC, Biblioteca, 1981. 6p.

1272 JUNAC. Biblioteca
Tratamiento a la inversión extranjera y aplicación de la decisión 24 en el Perú : guía bibliográfica / elaborado por Araceli R. de Ramos Murga. - Lima : JUNAC, Biblioteca, 1982. 36p.

1273 JUNAC. Reunión de expertos gubernamentales de la industria siderúrgica, 4., 1980
Acta final de la cuarta Reunión de expertos gubernamentales de la Industria Siderúrgica. (JUN/REG.15/IVActa Final, 28 febrero 1980)

1274 JUNAC. Session, 30., 1980
Exposición del ministro secretario de Integración de Bolivia y presidente de la Comisión del Acuerdo al inaugurar el trigésimo período de sesiones ordinarias de la Comisión. (COM/XXX/di 5, 14 octubre 1980)

1275 KANN der Andenpakt seine Stagnation überwinden? : nationale Wirtschaftsinteressen treten stärker hervor. Nachrichten für Aussenhandel (Köln), 43, no.235, Dez.4, 1980, p.5

Scheiterungsmöglichkeit der Integrationsproblematik durch: Einführung eines gemeinsamen Aussenzolls, Realisierung des Kfz-Programms, Behandlung des Auslandskapitals. Unruhe. Ungewissheit, Rolle Boliviens.

1276 KRIEGER MYTELKA, Lynn
Restructuring the Andean Common Market. In: Equity, human rights and international interconnections. Latin American prospects for the '80s : what kinds of development? : deformation, reformation or transformation / eds D.H.Pollock, A.R.M.Ritter. - Ottawa, CA : Carleton University, Norman Paterson School of International Affairs, 1981, p.191-208
ISBN: 0 7709 0109 3
Conference on Latin American Prospects for the Eighties, Ottawa CA, 17 Oct-15 Nov. 1980.

Common market/ regional integration/ industrial planning/ foreign investments/ Andean Group.

1277 LESTIENNE, Bernard
Travailleurs face au Pacte Andin. Amérique Latine (Paris), no.7, automne 1981, p.72-78

1278 LEVIKIN, Eduard
La experiencia del Grupo Andino en la regulación de la actividad del capital extranjero. America Latina (Moskva), vol.55, no.7, julio 1982, p.67-72

1279 LLAMBIAS, Margarita
La integración andina. - Quito : Instituto Andino de Estudios Sociales, 1981.

1280 MAIRA, Luis de
Balance político y económico de la integración andina durante 1980. Estudios Internacionales (Santiago de Chile), 14(55), jul-sept. 1981, p.394-411
Includes bibliographical references.

1281 MAIRA, Luis de
El proceso de integración subregional andino durante 1979. Integración Latinoamericana (Buenos Aires), no.48, julio 1980, p.4-8

1282 MANUAL de procedimientos del inversionista extranjero : Decisión 24. - Lima : Ministerio de Industria, Turismo e Integración, 1981. 52p.

1283 MONTGOMERY, David
Nueva estructura para el Pacto Andino. Visión (New York), vol.59, no.4, 23 agosto 1982, p.28

1284 MORAWETZ, David
Destino del miembro menos desarrollado dentro de un esquema de países de menor desarrollo : Bolivia en el Grupo Andino. Integración Latinoamericana (Buenos Aires), no.69, junio 1982, p.4-20

1285 MORAWETZ, David
Fate of the least developed member of an LDC integration scheme : Bolivia in the Andean Group. - Cambridge, Mass.: Harvard University, Harvard Institute for International Development, 1979. 35p. (Development discussion paper / Harvard University. Harvard Institute for International Development ; 76)

/Regional integration/, /mining/, /Bolivia/, /Andean Group/ - /cost-benefit analysis, /trade volumen/, /trade structure/, /industrial integration/, /foreign capital/, /tariff agreements/

1286 MOSCOSO RUIZ, D.
Análisis jurídico de las normas de origen del Acuerdo de Cartagena.-/S.l. : s.n. 198-/. 105p.

1287 NEERSO, Peter
Peru, Andes-pagten og de transnationale selskaber. Nationaloekonomisk Tidsskrift (København), 119(1), 1981, p.64-77

1288 NUEVA estrategia del Pacto Andino. Visión (New York), vol.56, no.7, 6 abril 1981, p.29

1289 OTERO, Diego RODRIGUEZ V., Enrique SANCHEZ SIERRA, Gabriel
Análisis del balance energético del Area Andina. Boletín Energético, no.21, julio-agosto 1981, p.35-44

1290 PALOMINO ROEDEL, José
El tratamiento especial en favor de Bolivia y Ecuador en el Acuerdo de Cartagena. Integración Latinoamericana (Buenos Aires), año 7, no.69, junio 1982, p.21-33

Contents: El principio del desarrollo equilibrado en el Acuerdo de Cartagena. La magnitud del desequilibrio. La aplicación y el funcionamiento de los mecanismos de carácter comercial. La aplicación y el funcionamiento de los mecanismos de programación industrial. La aplicación y el funcionamiento de los demás mecanismos que contribuyen el trato preferencial. Conclusiones.

1291 PARRA-PEÑA, Isidro
De donde viene y para donde va el Grupo Andino. Desarrollo Indoamericano (Bogotá), 14(54), Dec. 1979, p.33-38

/Article/ analysing /economic integration/ results of the /Andean region/ during the 1970 decade. Describes the nature, objectives and scope of the Cartagena /Economic Agreement/, studies Andean economy/s, and discusses /market access/, /industrialization/, /foreign investment/, etc.

1292 La PARTICIPACION de los trabajadores en el proceso de integración Andina / introd. y selección de documentos Fernando Calero. - /Caracas/ : Instituto Latinoamericano de Investigaciones Sociales, /1981/. 6, 481p. Tabs.

ILDIS Instituto Latinoamericano de Investigaciones Sociales

1293 PETROLEO y transformación : Ecuador cambia su perfil. Visión (New York), vol.58, no.9, 3 mayo 1982, p.21-22

1294 PINGET, Paul
Oú en est le Pacte Andin? Projet (Paris), no.150, déc. 1980, p.1217-1225

/Article/ evaluating the impact of the Andean Pact, an attempt at /economic integration/ and /regional cooperation/ amongst five countries of the /Andean region/.

1295 POLITICA de promoción de exportaciones no tradicionales del Grupo Andino : 1969-1979. - Lima : Ministerio de Industria, Turismo y Integración, 1981. 160p. (Investigaciones socioeconómicas ; 2)

1296 PUYANA POLACIOS, Alicia de
Economic integration among unequal partners : the case of the Andean Group. - New York : Pergamon, 1982, XXVI,405p.: tabs. (Pergamon policy studies on international development). Notes, bibliography : p.277-389, Index : p.391-404. List of acronyms. ISBN: 0 802 8822 7

1297 REGIMEN común de tratamiento a los capitales extranjeros y sobre marcas, patentes, licencias y regalías. - Lima (Perú) : Junta del Acuerdo de Cartagena, /1979/, 46p. (Decisiones 24, 37, 37a y 70)

1298 Las RELACIONES económicas entre el Grupo Andino y los países del Caribe / JUNAC. Integración Latinoamericana (Buenos Aires), no.75, dic. 1982, p.74-80

1299 REUNION DE DIRECTORES DE PROMOCION DE EXPORTACIONES, 13., 1982, La Paz
Acta final / Reunión de Directores de Promoción de Exportaciones 13., La Paz, 6-8 dic. 1982. - Lima : JUNAC, 1982. 21p. (JUN/RD.PE/XIII/Acta Final)

1300 REUNION DE DIRECTORES DE PROMOCION DE EXPORTACIONES, 13., 1982, La Paz
Plan Andino de promoción de exportaciones para 1983. - Lima : JUNAC, 1982. 30p. (JUN/RD-PE/XIII/Acta Final)

1301 REUNION DE ORGANISMOS DE INTEGRACION Y COOPERACION ECONOMICA DE AMERICA LATINA, 2., 1982, Lima
Informe final / Reunión de Organismos de Integración y Cooperación Económica de América Latina, 2., Lima, 13-15 dic. 1982. - Lima : JUNAC, 1982. (JUN/R.OI/.CE.AL/II/Informe final)

1302 REUNION DE RESPONSABLES DE OFICINA DE INFORMACION DE ORGANISMOS DE AMERICA LATINA, 1., 1982, Lima
Acta final / Reunión de Responsables de Oficina de Información de Organismos de América Latina, 1., Lima, 8-10 dic. 1982. - Lima : JUNAC, 1982. 29p. (JUN/R.OI.Al/I/Acta final)

1303 REVISTA Peruana de Derecho Internacional (Lima), 32(76), dic. 1980, 156p.
Número especial dedicado al Grupo Andino. Contains source material.

1304 RIOSECO, Alberto
El proceso de retiro de Chile del Acuerdo de Cartagena. - Santiago de Chile : Universidad de Chile, Instituto de Estudios Internacionales, 1979. 84p. (Serie de publicaciones especiales / Universidad de Chile. Instituto de Estudios Internacionales ; 32)
Includes bibliographical references.

1305 RODRIGUEZ ELIZONDO, José
Dispute jars Andean Group : literally beneath the dispute between Peru and Ecuador is a controversial oil reserve : no matter what the outcome of the skirmish between the countries the real loser will be the Andean Group. South (London), no.6, 15 March-April 1981, p.40

1306 SEMINARIO SUBREGIONAL ANDINO DE GANADERIA BOVINA, 2., 1982, Guayaquil, Ecuador
Acta final / Seminario Subregional Andino de Ganadería Bovina, 2., Guayaquil, 4-6 oct. 1982. - Lima : JUNAC, 1982. 183p. (JUN/SEM.GB/II/Acta final)

1307 SOUTH America : why the Andean pact is falling apart. International Business Week, 21.9.1982, p.35-36

1308 TAMING foreign investment Andean style. South (London), (3) Dec. 1980, p.29-30

1309 TOBON LONDOÑO, Gustavo
Mirada al proceso andino. Universitas (Bogotá),50(58), Jun 1980, p.418-430
/Article/ analysing some of the mechanisms of /regional cooperation/ and /economic integration/ in the /Andean region/ gives an /evaluation/ of the integration process from the viewpoint of its /institutional framework/ and organisms, /references/.

1310 TRUCCO PADIN, Estela L.
El Pacto Andino, Acuerdo de Cartagena : una estrategia sub-regional de integración latinoamericana. 1.ed. - Buenos Aires : Editorial El Coloquio, 1974 or 1975. 387p.

Subjects: Acuerdo de Cartagena / Andes region -- economic conditions.

1311 URRUTIA, Miguel M.
Colombia and the Andean Group : economic and political determinants of regional integration policy. Quarterly Review of Economics and Business (Urbana/Illinois), vol.21, no.2, 1981, p.182-199

1312 URRUTIA, Miguel M.
Diversidad ideológica e integración andina. Coyuntura Andina (Bogotá, Col.), no.5, julio 1980, p.187-203

1313 VARGAS- HIDALGO, Rafael
Función de los transportes y las telecomunicaciones en la integración de los países andinos. Mundo Nuevo (Caracas), vol.3, nos 7-8, enero-junio 1980, p.132-148

1314 VENDRELL, Francisco José
Regime andin des capitaux étrangers et de la technologie. Genève : Institut Universitaire de Hautes Études Internationales, 1981. 127 leaves.

/Thesis/ on /foreign investment/ and /technology transfer/ in the /Andean Region/ in context with /economic integration/. Examines in and out /capital flow/, self-transformation of / foreign enterprise/s into /mixed enterprise/s or /public enterprise/s, objectives of /technological change/, /industrial property/, rights and the /commercialization/ of /technology/. /Bibliography: p.115 to 123

1315 VENEZUELA : a guide for foreign investment and technology licensing in the 1980's. Caracas : Superintendencia de Inversiones Extranjeras, 1980, VIII,57p., ill.

/Venezuela/ Andean Group/foreign investment/ /technology/ licencing/ common market/ economic growth/ international trade/ /labour legislation/ LDCs/

1316 VENEZUELA y el Pacto Andino : documentos y controversia / elaborado bajo los auspicios del Instituto de Comercio Exterior de Venezuela. - Caracas : Información Documental de América Latina, /1974/. xxii,/408/p.

1317 VINCES ZEVALLOS, Fausto KULJEVAN PAGADOR, Antonio
Estructura jurídica del Acuerdo de Cartagena. Lima : Oficina Nacional de Integración, 1974. 2 vols, XV,903p.

Includes the text of the Acuerdo de Cartagena and related documents issued by the Comisión del Acuerdo de Cartagena and the Junta del Acuerdo de Cartagena.

1318 WEINSTEIN, María Isabel Volochinsky
La Decisión 24 del Acuerdo de Cartagena en la jurisprudencia de la Contraloría General de la República. - Santiago de Chile : Universidad de Chile, Instituto de Estudios Internacionales, 1978. 170p. (Serie de publicaciones especiales / Universidad de Chile. Instituto de Estudios Internacionales ; 33)

"Monografía presentada en el programa de postgrado del Instituto, no.1". Bibliography: p.160-167

1319 WILLIAMSON, John
Comment on "Colombia and the Andean Group". Quarterly Review of Economics and Business (Urbana/Ill.), 21, 1981, 2, p.199-203

1320 WIRTSCHAFTSFLAUTE in Venezuela. Blick durch die Wirtschaft (Frankfurt a.Main), (24), no.38. Feb. 24, 1981, p.2

Interne Politik. Rolle der Gewerkschaften. Wirtschaftslage und Politik. Einfluss Anden-Pakt. Illegale Einwanderer. Arbeitslose. Produktion. Arbeitsmarkt. Budget, 1981. Export. Staatsschulden. Kredite. Inflation. Aussenhandel. Daten 1979-81

JUNAC Junta del Acuerdo de Cartagena, Lima, Perú

1321 ALCANTARA SAEZ, Manuel JAMAR, Joseph
Le Marché Commun de l'Amérique Centrale (MCAC). In: Intégrationes régionales entre pays en voie de développement. - Bruges : De Tempel, 1982. p.53-108
Bibliography: p.107-108

1322 AVANCES de la integración / Secretaría Permanente del Tratado General de Integración Económica Centroamericana. (no.1, 1981)- /Guatemala/ : SIECA, /1981/-
Irregular.

1323 BRODERSOHN, Victor
Problemática del empleo en Centroamérica. Trimestre Económico (México, D.F.), vol.49(2), no.194, abril-junio 1982, p.387-421

1324 CACERES, Luis René
Economic integration and under-development in Central America : dissertation. - /Utah : University/, 1978.

1325 CÁCERES, Luis René GONZALES U., H.R.
Investigación sobre los determinantes del ahorro en Centroamérica. Comercio Exterior (México, D.F.), 31(1), enero 1981, p.51-56

1326 CACM : chronology of the main events and of the cooperation taking place within the integration schemes during 1979. Latin American Integration (Buenos Aires), no.1, April 1981, p.121-122.
(Special English edition)

1327 CACM integration effort seeks new direction to bolster regional trade. Business Latin America (New York), August 25, 1982, p.266-277

1328 CACM is pursuing a variety of projects to offset oil imports. Business Latin America (New York), 19.11.1980, p.374

1329 The CACM situation after signing of the Peace treaty between Honduras and El Salvador. Comercio Exterior (México, D.F.), vol.27, no.5, 1981, p.194-195

1330 CACM/MCC-Mercado Comun Centroamericano. In: El Processo de integración en América Latina en 1981. - Buenos Aires : INTAL, 1982. p.119-158

1331 CALABRESE, José Luis UMANA QUESADA, Alvaro
Análisis del balance energético de América Central. Bolétin Energético, no.21, julio-agosto 1981, p.25-34

CACM Central American Common Market, Guatemala City, Honduras

VIII-2.4. Central American Common Market—CACM

1332 CATALAN ARAVENA, O.O.
De economische achtergrond van de Middenamerikaanse crisis. Internationale spectator ('s-Gravenhage), (35), no.6, juni 1981, p.319. Ref. Tabs.

Huidige politieke en economische situatie in Midden-Amerika. Gevolgen van de crisis van den jaren '30. Functioneren van de Middenamerikaanse gemeenschappelijke markt (MCCA). Rol van de Economische Commissie voor Latijns Amerika (CEPAL). Aanpassing aan nieuwe tendensen in de wereldeconomie. Toekomstperspectieven. Cijfers, 1960-1975.

1333 CENTROAMERICA : redefinición integracionista. Integración Latinoamericana. Revista mensual INTAL (Buenos Aires), no.51, octubre 1980.

1334 CONESA, Eduardo R.
La reestructuración del Mercado Común Centroamericano. Integración Latinoamericana (Buenos Aires), año 7, no.65, enero-febrero 1982, p.14-20

Contents: Introducción. La diferencias políticas, la preservación de los logros. Integración por proyectos. La distribución de los beneficios. Los incentivos fiscales y las desnaturalización del arancel externo comun. Vinculación con América Latina.

1335 DELGADO, Enrique
Evolución del Mercado Común Centroamericano y desarrollo equilibrado. - /S.l./ : Ciudad Universitaria "Rodrigo Facio", Costa Rica : Editorial Universitaria Centroamericana, Guatemala /?/ : ECID : SIECA, 1981. 232p. Ill. (Colección Integración)

1336 DOCUMENTOS sobre aspectos institucionales de la integración centroamericana. - San José, Costa Rica : Instituto Centroamericano de Administración Publica, 1973. 321p. (various pagings). ill.

Subjects: MCCA-Addresses, essays, lectures/ International economic integration -- Addresses, essays, lectures/Central America--Economic integration--Addresses, essays, lectures.

1337 FFRENCH-DAVIS, Ricardo
Integración económica y empleyo : algunos elementos para el caso Centroamericano. - Santiago : ILO, Regional Employment Programme for Latin America and the Caribbean, 1979. 33p. (ILO-PREALC/167)

/ILO publ./ /conference paper/ on the contribution of /economic integration/ to /employment creation/ in /Central America/. Analyses the effect of unified /trade policy/, /tariff policy/, /(customs union)/ and /investment policy/, etc. on /employment/ and shows that the /export/ of /labour intensive/ manufactures product/s to third countries should be regarded as complementary to /regional/ import substitution/.
/Bibliography/, p.32-33 and /reference/s.
/conf/ San José 1979 March.

1338 FRANK, C.R. SOTTO, M.A. SEVILLA, C.A.
The demand for labor in manufacturing industry in Central America. In: Economic integration in Central America / ed. W.R. Cline and E. Delgado. - Washington : Brookings Institution, 1978. p.126-180

1339 GUERRA BORGES, Alfredo
Las experiencias de la integración económica centroamericana : algunas reflexiones. Comercio Exterior (México), vol.32, no.12, diciembre 1982, p.1325-1331

Contents: Los primeros pasos. La experiencia en materia de libre comercio. El modelo adoptado. Tres concepciones diferentes. Principales resultados. Una lección aprendida. Logros y frustraciones en el desarrollo industrial. Los limites del crecimiento. Los obstaculos a la industrialización básica. El conflicto entre el interés regional y los intereses nacionales. La mejor experiencia : el futuro.

1340 HOLLY, Daniel A.
Le conflit du Honduras et du Salvador de 1979. Etudes Internationales (Québec), lo(l), mars 1979, p.19-51

1341 HORA de crisis en América Central. Visión (México), vol.56, no.9, mayo 1981, p.5

1342 LIZANO FAIT, Eduardo HUERTAS, Maritza
Bibliografía sobre el Marcado Común Centroamericano. Estudios Sociales Centroamericanos (San José, Costa Rica), no.24, set./dic. 1979, p.271-330

1343 LIZANO FAIT, Eduardo
Cooperación monetaria e integración económica en el Mercado Común Centroamericano. 1.ed. - México, D.F. : Centro de Estudios Monetarios Latinoamericanos, 1978. 235p.
Bibliography: p.221-232

Subjects: Mercado Comun Centroamericano / monetary policy -- Central America / Central America -- economic integration.

1344 MAYORGA QUIROS, Román
Aspectos institucionales de la integración centroamericana durante 1980. Integración Latinoamericana (Buenos Aires), vol.6, no.59. julio 1981. p.25-30

1345 MAYORGA QUIROS, Román
The social and economic outlook for Central America in the 1980's. Latin American Integration (Buenos Aires), no.1, April 1981. p.63-77.
(Special English edition)

General socioeconomic outlook: External sector. Fiscal sector. Financial intermediary sector. Agricultural structure. Political and social organization.
The outlook for central american integration : the success and stagnation of economic integration in Central America. Regression, stagnation, or progress in the 1980's? Our opinion and the conceptual basis thereof. First line of reasoning. Second line of reasoning. Stagnation scenario. Regression scenario. Progress scenario. Footnotes.

1346 MERCADO Comun Centroamericano. In: El proceso de integración en America Latina en 1981. Buenos Aires : INTAL, 1982, p.119-158

1347 MOLINA CHOCANO, Guillermo
Crisis política centroamericana y el nuevo cuadro internacional en la cuenca del Caribe. Revista Mexicana de Sociología (México, D.F.), vol.42, no.2, abril-junio 1980, p.711-730

1348 NECESIDADES de cooperación técnica subregional en el Istmo Centroamericano, 1982-1986 / Comité de Cooperación Técnica del Istmo Centroamericano. - México, DF : CEPAL, 1981. - 18 p.

1349 ORDOÑEZ FERNANDEZ, Hugo
Las industrias centroamericanas de integración : algunos aspectos de su problemática jurídica. Integración Latinoamericana (Buenos Aires), vol.7, no.62, octubre 1981, p.34-43

Origen y naturaleza del régimen. Incentivos y privilegios. Obligaciones y compromisos. Los productos de los industrias de integración y el libre comercio. Las industrias de integración y el capital extranjero. Consideraciones finales.

1350 ORDOÑEZ FERNANDEZ, Hugo
La resolución que crea la Comunidad Democrática Centroamericana : su naturaleza jurídica y alcances. Integración Latinoamericana (Buenos Aires), año 7, no.72, sept. 1982, p.46-52

1351 El PROCESO de integración económica centroamericana : evaluación crítica de algunas experiencias / SIECA. Integración Latinoamericana (Buenos Aires), vol.7, no.65, ene-febrero 1982, p.4-13

Palabras preliminares. La experiencia en materia de libre comercio. El modelo adoptado. Una lección aprendida. Logros y frustraciones en el desarrollo industrial. Los limites del crecimiento. La nueva etapa. El conflicto entre el interés regional y los intereses nacionales. El punto de vista teórico. Conflictos reales y supuestos. Conflictos en el intercambio. El caso de la competencia industrial. Reserva de oportunidades. Conflictos por falta de organización nacional para la integración. Las mejor experiencias : el futuro.

1352 REESTRUCTURACION del Mercado Común Centroamericano. Integración Latinoamericana (Buenos Aires), año 7, no.65, enero-febrero 1982. p.1-3

1353 REFLEXIONES sobre la situación actual y las perspectivas del proceso de la integración centroamericana / NU ; CEPAL. Integración Latinoamericana (Buenos Aires). vol.7, no.65- enero-febrero 1982, p.21-26

Contents: Presentación. 1. Algunas caracteristicas del proceso de la integración centroamericana. 2. Nuevos problemas a los que se enfrenta la integración. 3. Fundamentos para la adecuación del proceso de integración.

1354 RESTRUCTURING of CACM will be stalled by pervasive differences. Business Latin America (New York), 26.11.1980, p.379-380

1355 REUNION DE CONSULTA ENTRE LOS GOBIERNOS DEL ISTMO CENTROAMERICANO Y LOS DE CANADA, ESTADOS UNIDOS DE AMERICA, MEXICO Y VENEZUELA, 1981, San José, Costa Rica
Informe de la Reunión de consulta entre los Gobiernos del Istmo Centroamericano y los de Canada, Estados Unidos de América, México y Venezuela, San José, Costa Rica, 7 y 8 de septiembre de 1981 : versión provisional. - San José, Costa Rica : Ministerio de Relaciones Exteriores, 1981, 22p.

1356 REVISTA de la Integración y el Desarrollo de Centroamérica / Banco Centroamericano de Integración Económica. - Tegucigalpa : El Banco, 1976- no.20, (jul. 1976)-
Quarterly. - Continues. Revista de la Integración Centroamericana

1357 ROSENTHAL, Gert
Algunas reflexiones sobre el proceso de integración ecónomica centroamericana. Revista de la integración económica y el desarrollo de Centroamérica (Tegucigalpa, Honduras), vol.28, enero-junio 1981, p.3-18

1358 SENINGER, Stephen F.
Economias de escala y efectos de aglomeración regional en el mercado comun centroamericano. Revista de la Integración y el Desarrollo de Centroamérica (Tegucigalpa, Honduras), vol.28, enero-junio 1981, p.51-69

Contents: Formulación de Weber. Los enfoques funciones de producción. La ley de Verdoorn y la productividad del trabajo. Estimados preliminares de los parametros de Verdoorn. Referencias.

1359 SIECA
Legislación relacionada con el tratamiento a la inversión extranjera en los países centroamericanos / Secretaría Permanente del Tratado General de Integración Económica Centroamericana.- Guatemala : SIECA, 1978. 177p.

1360 SIECA
Noveno informe sobre el inventario de proyectos regionales de infraestructura en Centroamérica. - Guatemala : SIECA, 1980. (SIECA/79/INF./PF/28) p.6-8

|SIECA| Secretaría Permanente de Tratado de Integración Económica Centroamericana, Ciudad de Guatemala

1361 SIRI, Gabriel
Import tariffs, export taxes and trade policy options for Central America. - Buenos Aires : INTAL, 1981. 30p.

Documento presentado al Seminario sobre Políticas Comerciales Optimas, Buenos Aires, 22 al 24 junio 1981.

1362 La SOLUCION de conflictos en la integración latinoamericana. - Buenos Aires : Instituto para la integración de América Latina, Banco Interamericano de Desarrollo, 1972. IV,383p. (Estudios ; 8)

Subjects: Mercado Común Centroamericano/ALALC/ Latin American-economic integration

1363 TORRES RIVAS, Edelberto
Formación del estado y el sector público en Centroamerica y Panamá. Revista Méxicana de Sociología (México, D.F.), vol.42, no.2, abril-junio 1980, p.561-589

1364 TORRES RIVAS, Edelberto
Interpretación del desarrollo social centroamericano : proceso y estructuras de una sociedad dependiente. 6e ed. - Ciudad Universitaria Rodrigo Facio, Costa Rica : Editorial Universitaria Centroamericana, 1980. 319p. (Colección Seis)

Central America - economic conditions - social conditions / Central America - economic integration

1365 WILLIAMS, Robert G.
The Central American Common Market : unequal benefits and even development : dissertation. - /S.l./ : Stanford University, 1978

VIII-2.5. Caribbean Community—CARICOM

1366 ATKINSON, Glen W.
Economic integration in the Caribbean Community: a problem of institutional adjustment. Journal of Economic Issues. Michigan State University. Department of Economics, Graduate School of Business Administration, (East Lansing), vol.16, no.2, 1982, p.507-513

1367 AXLINE, Andrew W.
Sous-développement, inégalité et crise de coopération dans la Communauté des Caraïbes. Revue Canadienne d'Etudes du Développement, vol.1, no.1, 1980, p.84-74

/Integration régionale/, /coopération économique/, /sous-développement/, /Caraibes/, /CARICOM/ - /disparité régionale/, /redistribution du revenu/, /investissements étrangers/, /analyse économique/, /tableaux statistiques/.

1368 The CARIBBEAN Common Market : implications for U.S. business. Overseas Business Report (Washington), no.25, Sept. 1981, p.1. Tabs.

Caribbean Common Market. Caricom experience. Current developments. Investment and industrialization efforts. Information about Caricom members.

1369 CARIBBEAN Common Market : the new origin system / prepared by the Caribbean Community Secretariat. - Georgetown, Guayana : Caribbean Community, the Secretariat, 1977. 38 leaves.

Subjects: Caribbean Common Market / customs administration - Caribbean ores.

1370 CARIBBEAN Community in the 1980's : report / by a group of Caribbean experts appointed by the Caribbean Common Market Council of Ministers. - Georgetown, Guayana : The Caribbean Community Secretariat, 1981. XIX,157p.

/CARICOM/, /integrated development/, /development strategy/,/self-reliance/, /economic cooperation/, /regional integration/ - /production increase/, /institutional framework/, /trade relations/, /expert report/, /statistical tables/.

1371 CARIBBEAN DEVELOPMENT BANK, Bridgetown, Barbados
Annual report : 1980. - Barbados, St. Michael : CDB, 1981. Graph. Ill. Tabs.

Economic development in the region. Caribbean economic integration. Review of activities organisation and administration. Financial statements.

1372 The CARIBBEAN regional co-operation in shipping. The Courier (Bruxelles), December 1981, p.72
(Based on a CARICOM report).

1373 CARICOM. Secretariat
National accounts statistics of CARICOM countries, 1970 to 1977. 2nd ed. - Georgetown : The Caribbean Community Secretariat, 1977, 44p.

1374 CARICOM : chronology of the main events and of the cooperation taking place within the integration schemes during 1979. Latin American Integration (Buenos Aires), no.1, April 1981, p.122-124
(Special English edition)

1375 CARICOM nations plan summit meeting to revive integration. Business Latin America (New York), 24.2.1982, p.60-61

1376 CARICOM statistics year book : 1978. - Georgetown, Guayana : Caribbean Community Secretariat, Trade, Economics and Statistics Divison, 1980-
Annual

1377 CARICOM summit offers last chance for co-operation. Latin America Regional Reports-Caribbean (London), 5.11.1982, p.1-2

1378 COLOMBIA en el Caribe. Revista Cámara de Comercio de Bogotá (Bogotá), año 13, no.48/49, septiembre-diciembre 1982

1379 COMUNIDAD del Caribe (CARICOM), p.159-192.
In: El Proceso de integración en America Latina en 1981. Buenos Aires : INTAL, 1982.

1380 COMUNIDAD del Caribe : un grupo nuevo dentro de la CARICOM. Comercio Exterior (México, D.F.), vol.31, no.9, septiembre 1981, p.1066-1067

1381 COOPERACIÓN y desarrollo en el Caribe. Lecturas del CEESTEM, vol.1, no.4, 1981, p.5-123

1382 DUNDAS, Carl W.
Ensayos acerca del derecho y la práctica de la CARICOM incluyendo el Mercado Común. Integración Latinoamericana (Buenos Aires), 5(44), marzo 1980, p.49-73

1383 EAST CARIBBEAN COMMON MARKET
Customs tariff with list of conditional duty exemptions and reductions. - Antigua : /s.n./, /197-?/ (printed by ECCM/UNDP Printery). 1 vol. (loose leaf)

1384 ECONOMIC activity 1980 in Caribbean countries. - Port of Spain : ECLA Office for the Caribbean, 1981. 1 vol. (various pagings). (CEPAL/CARIB ; 81/10)

1385 FREYMOND, Jean P.
Political integration in the Commonwealth Caribbean : a survey of recent attempts with special reference to the associated states, 1967-1974 / translated by Paddy Summerfield and Roger Heacock. - Genève : Institut Universitaire de Hautes Études Internationales, 1980. 142p. Map. (Études et travaux / Institut Universitaire de Hautes Études Internationales ; 17)
Bibliography: p.131-138. Includes index.
ISBN: 2 8288 011 3

1386 GANNON, Francis X.
The Caribbean : removing United State and hemispheric blinders. Caribbean Life and Times, vol.1, no.4, 1980, p.61-64

1387 GARDENAS, Osvaldo
La viabilidad de la integración del Caribe. Estudios Sociales Centroamericanos (San José, Costa Rica), no.30, sept.-dic. 1981, p.33-49

1388 GREATBATCH, Bruce
Development problems in the Caribbean. The Round Table (London), no.280, October 1980, p.374-380

1389 A GUIDE to the common market origin rules / publ. by Caribbean Common Market. Caricom. - Guyana, Georgetown : CARICOM, Secretariat, 1981. 25p. Tabs.

General explanation of the new system for preferential treatment of goods produced within the Caribbean Common Market, into operation June 1981. Conditions of qualifications. Documentary evidence of origin. Other issues.

1390 JENKINS, M.
Social security trends in the English speaking Caribbean. International Labour Review (Genève), (120), no.5, sept./oct., 1981, p.631. Ref. Tabs.

Evolution, growth and administration of social security in the Caribbean regions. Overlapping between social security and other schemes. Regional co-operation of social security. Need for improvement of the quality of administration. It is argued that the scope and the coverage of social protection need to be further widened, particularly with regard to employment injuries and health care.

1391 KNOTTY problems on the agenda for CARICOM summit. Latin America Weekly Report (London), 12.11.1982, p.8

1392 KREST'IANINOV, V.
Karibskij bassein v planah Vašingtona. Meždunarodnaja žizn' (Moskva), 2, 1981, p.89-98

With some emphasis on CARICOM.

1393 LANDAU, Georges D.
El Grupo de Cooperación para el Desarrollo Económico del Caribe : un marco multilateral del progreso subregional. Commercio Exterior (México), vol.32, 1982, p.1332

1394 LATIN American regional reports : Caribbean. - London : Latin American Newsletters, /1979/-
ISSN: 0143 523 x

Weekly. Description based on: no RC-82-02 (19 Feb. 1982)

1395 LONG, Frank
CARICOM : the Caribbean Community in the 1980s : report by a Group of Caribbean Experts, 1981. Third World Quarterly (London), vol.4, no.4, 1982, p.827

1396 PAYNE, Anthony
The rise and fall of Caribbean regionalisation. Journal of Common Market Studies (Oxford), (19), no.3, March, 1981, p.255-280. References.

Problems concerning Third World integration movements examined by the rise and fall of CARICOM. Emergence of CARICOM. Impact of the community of the international economic crisis of 1973/74. Political limitations of Caribbean integration. Four conditions for CARICOM's existence : balance of power between memberstates. ideological consensus, rapport between the heads of government and united international interest in the region.

1397 PUBLIC sector issues in the Commonwealth Caribbean : (studies in Caribbean public enterprise) / Brown Adlith ed. Social and Economic Studies (Kingston), vol.30, no.1, March 1981, 252p.

1398 REUNION INTERGUBERNAMENTAL SOBRE EL PLAN DE ACCION DEL PROGRAMA AMBIENTAL DEL CARIBE, 1981, Montego Bay
Informe de la Reunión. - /S.l./ : PNUMA, 1981. 47p.

1399 ROSS, Murray
Economic integration in Caribbean. Latin American Integration (Buenos Aires), no.1, April 1981, p.78-88
(Special English edition)

Introduction. The region. Early integration efforts. Recent integrations directions. Caribbean group for cooperation in economic development. Second Conference of the Caribbean Group.

1400 ROSS, Murray
Integración económica en el Caribe. Integración Latinoamericana (Buenos Aires), 5(44), marzo 1980, p.4-17

1401 SACKEY, J.A.
Structure and performance of CARICOM : lessons for the development of ECOWAS. Canadian Journal of African Studies (Ottawa, Ont.), vol.12, no.2, 1978, p.259-277

/Regional integration/, /African organizations/, /income distribution/, /West Africa/, /CARICOM/, /Caribbean/ - /political aspects/, /ruling class/, /institution building/, /regional disparity/, /statistical data.

1402 STEPHANSKY, Ben
Human resources in the Commonwealth Caribbean. - Washington, DC : /s.n./, 1980, 40p.

Prepared for the task Force on Private Sector Activities of the Caribbean Group for Cooperation in Economic Development.

1403 TARASOV, Vladimir
Cambíos estructurales de la integración del Caribe. América Latina (Moskva), vol.55, no.7, julio 1982, p.73-81

1404 TURACK, Daniel C.
Freedom of movement in the Caribbean Community. Denver Journal of International Law and Policy (Denver, Co.), 11(1), fall 1981, p.37-49

1405 VARDI, J.
Coordination of energy policy in the Caribbean : revised report. - /S.l./ : UNDP, 1982. 122p.

1406 VILAS, Carlos M.
Campesinos y plantaciones en la agricultura del Caribe. Estudios Sociales Centroamericanos (San José, Costa Rica), año 10, no.29, mayo-agosto 1981, p.79-90

CARICOM	Caribbean Community and Common Market, Georgetown, Guyana

VIII-2.6. Amazon Pact

1407 AMAZON COOPERATION TREATY : chronology of the main events and of the cooperation taking place within the integration schemes during 1979. Latin American Integration (Buenos Aires), no.1, April 1981, p.124
(Special English edition)

1408 CHAVEZ CARRILLO, Luis
Implacable avance sobre la Amazonia : crueldad en los métodos de colonización. Visión. La Revista Interamericana (México), vol.57, no.9, noviembre 1981, p.41

... La fecha historíca que señaló un paso de vital importancia para la construcción de la "gran patria latinoamericana", según lo expresa el excanciller de Venezuela, Simón Alberto Consalvi, fue la del 3 de julio de 1978, con la firma del Tratado del Pacto Amazónico, en Brasilia, por delegados de Bolivia, Brasil, Colombia, Ecuador, Guyana, Perú, Surinam y Venezuela.

El documento precisa que se promovera el desarrollo armónico de esa zona a fin de permitir la distribución equitativa de sus beneficios entre las partes contratantes para "elevar el nivel de vida de sus pueblos y lograr la plena incorporación de esos territorios a las respectivas económias nacionales" ...

1409 DECLARACION de Belem. Integración Latinoamericana (Buenos Aires), no.52, noviembre 1980, p.101-103

Reunión de cancilleres de los países signatarios del Tratado de Cooperación Amazonica, 23 y 24 octubre 1980, Ciudad de Belem, Brasil

1410 FERRIS, Elizabeth G.
The Andean Pact and the Amazon Treaty : reflections of changing Latin American relations. Journal of Inter-American Studies and World Affairs (Beverly Hills, Calif.), vol.23, no.2, 1981, p.147-175

1411 INTAL : Tratado de Cooperación Amazónica. In: El proceso de integración en América Latina en 1980. - Buenos Aires : /s.n./, 1981. p.282-287

|INTAL| Instituto para la Integración de América Latina, Buenos Aires

1412 INTAL : Tratado de Cooperación Amazónica. In: El proceso de integración en América Latina en 1981. - Buenos Aires : /s.n./, 1982.

1413 LANDAU, George D.
The Treaty for Amazonian Cooperation : a bold new instrument for development. The Georgia Journal of International and Comparative Law (Athens, Ga), 10(3), 1980, p.463-489

1414 MORAN, Emilio F.
Ecological, anthropological and agronomic research in the Amazon basin. Latin American Research Review (Gainesville, Fla.), vol.17, no.1, 1982, p.3-41

1415 El PROCESO de integración en América Latina en 1981. - Buenos Aires : INTAL, Tratado de Cooperación Amazónica, 1982.

1416 PROGRAMAS multinacionales y otras formas de cooperación : Tratado de cooperación Amazónica, p.237-240. In: El proceso de integración en América Latina en 1981. - Buenos Aires : INTAL, 1982

1417 SCHERFENBERG, Ulrich
Der Amazonaspakt : Inhalt, Ziele und Probleme eines neuen Integrationsvertrags. - Hamburg : Institut für Iberoamerika-Kunde, 1979. 76p. Maps.
(Arbeitsunterlagen und Diskussionsbeiträge / Institut für Iberoamerika-Kunde ; 6)
Bibliography: p.74-76

1418 TRATADO de Cooperaçao Amazónica. - Brasília : Ministério das Relaçoes Exteriores, 1978. 150p. Ill.
Text also in Dutch, English and Spanish

1419 TRATADO de Cooperación Amazónica. Integración Latinoamericana (Buenos Aires), no.27, agosto 1978, p.62-64

VIII-2.7. River Plate Basin

1420 CUENCA del Plata / INTAL. In: El proceso de integración en América Latina en 1981. - Buenos Aires : INTAL, 1982. p.233-237

1421 CUENCA del Plata : Uruguay busca una mayor integración con sus vecinos. Comercio Exterior (México), vol.31, no.3, marzo 1981

1422 La EFICIENCIA del transporte fluvial en la Cuenca del Plata. - Buenos Aires : INTAL, 1981. 89p.

1423 HENDRICKS, David W. et al.
Modeling of water supply/demand in the South Plate River Basin, 1970-2020. Water Resources Bulletin. A journal of water resources research, planning, development and management (Minneapolis, MN), vol.18, no.2, April 1982, p.279-287

1424 NOHLEN, Dieter FERNANDEZ, Mario B.
Cooperación y conflicto en la Cuenca del Plata. Estudios Internacionales (Santiago de Chile), 14(55), jul.-sept. 1981, p.412-443

Concerns regional co-operation in Latin America

1425 PROGRAMAS multinacionales y otras formas de cooperación : Cuenca del Plata, p.233-237. In: El proceso de integración en América Latina en 1981. - Buenos Aires : INTAL, 1982

1426 REUNION DE CANCILLERES DE LOS PAISES DE LA CUENCA DEL PLATA, 12., 1981, Santa Cruz, Bolivia
Reunión de Cancilleres de los Países de la Cuenca del Plata, 12., Santa Cruz, Bol., 11-14 nov. 1981 : documentos de la reunión. - Santa Cruz : /s.n./, 1981, 1 vol. (various pagings)

1427 REUNION DE CANCILLERES DE LOS PAÍSES DE LA CUENCA DEL PLATA, 13., 1982, Brasilia
Reunión de Cancilleres de los Países de la Cuenca del Plata, 13., Brasilia, 6.-7 dic. 1982 : documentos de la reunión. - Brasilia : /s.n./, 1982, 455p.

1428 El RIO de La Plata : análisis del Tratado sobre limites fluviales y frente marítimo en la perspectiva de Argentina y Uruguay / Calixto Armas Barea ... /et al./. - Santiago de Chile : Universidad de Chile, Instituto de Estudios Internacionales, 1976. 160p. (Serie de publicaciones especiales / Universidad de Chile. Instituto de Estudios Internacionales ; 18)
Includes bibliographical references.

1429 El SISTEMA de la Cuenca del Plata / INTAL. In: El proceso de integración América Latina en 1980. - Buenos Aires : INTAL, 1981. p.273-281

VIII-3. AFRICA

1430 AFRIQUE du Centre : première conférence ministerielle de la CEEAC. Marchés Tropicaux et Mediterranéens (Paris), 38e année, no.1900, vendredi 9 avril 1982, p.970

CEEAC: Communauté Economique des Etats de l'Afrique Centrale

1431 ASANTE, S.K.B.
Economic integration in West Africa : some critical issues. Africa Development (Dakar), 5(2), Apr./June, 1980, p.67-83
Summary in French

1432 COBBE, James H.
Integration among unequals : the Southern African Customs Union and development. World Development (Oxford), 8(4), April 1980, p.329-336
Includes bibliographical references.

1433 COLLOQUE SUR L'INTEGRATION ECONOMIQUE DE L'AFRIQUE DE L'OUEST, 2., 1980, Conakry, R.P.R. Guinée
Deuxième colloque sur l'intégration économique de l'Afrique de l'Ouest, du 15 au 20 avril 1980. - Conakry : /s.n./, /1981/ (Conakry : Imprimerie de l'Education et de Culture). 2 vols

Vol.1. 367p.
Vol.2. 440p.

Contents:
1 : Discours d'ouverture du Président Ahmed Sékou Touré. p.6
2 : Perspectives de coopération et d'intégration économique en Afrique pour l'année 1980 / Adebayo Adedeji. p.19
3 : Organisation de l'Unité syndicale africaine / presenté par l'OUSA. p.74
4 : L'intégration régionale et le développement inégal en Afrique de l'Ouest / Abdoulaye Koita. p.96
5 : Sous-thème 1 : problématique de la region. p.104
6 : La libre circulation comme facteur d'intégration économique en Afrique de l'Ouest. p.133
7 : Stratégies pour le développement de l'industrie rizicole en Afrique de l'Ouest. p.153
8 : Intégration économique par la production : communication / présenté par Maīna Ari Adji Firgam. p.164
9 : L'agriculture dans le processus d'intégration économique de la région sahélienne. p.168
10 : Communication : l'intégration en Afrique : ses obstacles, sa dynamisation / présenté par Birame N'Diaye. p.185
11 : B.O.A.D. : le développement régional en Afrique de l'Ouest. p.214
12 : The role of women in economic development and integration / by Caryl M. Kline. p.235
13 : L'accroissement des échanges commerciaux grâce aux accords de règlements et de compensation : l'expérience de la C C A O. p.243
14 : Intervention du délégué de la C.E.E. p.250
15 : Sous-thème no. 8 "La politique d'intégration par la production identification des étapes". p.255
16 : West African lessons from East African failure in a Commun Market / by E. Chukwuma Anusionwu. p.276

cont.

cont´d

17 : Communication : l'intégration des économies africaines face au nouvel ordre international / présenté par Ely Madiodio Fall. p.291
18 : Communicaton : rôle des institutions financières dans l'intégration et problèmes monétaires de l'intégration économique / par F. Kouadio. p.306
19 : Le rôle des entreprises communautaires dans le processus d'intégration économique dans les pays en développement / par Tchabouré A. Gogue Esteg. p.321
20 : Sous-thème no. III : pour une politique integrée en matière de formation des cadres. p.334
21 : Commission II : some transport and communications policy issues in West Africa / by H.W. Yaidoo. p.343
22 : La liberté de circulation et l'établissement dans les communautés Ouest-Africaines / présenté par Ibrahim Fall
23 : Quelques réflexions sur la coopération inter-africaine en matière de transfer de technologie / présenté par I.A. Akinrele. p.3 /vol.2
24 : Prospects for increased economic cooperation and integration in Africa / by K.O. Pobbi Asamani. p.13
25 : La CEDEAO et la mer / Hibberd V.B. Kline. p.32
26 : Thème "Rôle des institutions financières dans l'intégration économique des pays de la CEDEAO. p.38
27 : Les expériences d'intégration économique en Afrique noire : évaluations et suggestions / Makhtar Diouf. p.51
28 : Intervention de Mamadou Bobo Camara, Sécrétaire Général de l'Union Panafricaine des Télécommunications (UPAT). p.64
29 : Communication : Ordre économique régional et stratégie de développement autocentre en Afrique de l'Ouest / par Mamadou Moustapha Kasse. p.74
30 : L'intégration des assurances : expérience de quelques pays d'Afrique noire francophone / Mamadou Racine Bathily. p.122-152
31 : Le point de vue de l'Union du fleuve Mano. p.153
32 : Les sociétés multinationales, la localisation des richesses spécifiques et le développement économique de l'Afrique de l'Ouest / par M.O.A. Adejugbe. p.160
33 : Club de Dakar : projet de recherche prospective en vue de l'établissement d'un schéma indicatif de développement intégré de l'Afrique de l'Ouest / par Mohamed T. Diawara. p.181
34 : "La libre circulation comme facteur de l'intégration économique en Afrique de l'Ouest / par Moussa Touré. p.206
35 : Le rôle des institutions de financement du développement dans l'intégration économique de l'Afrique / par Olabisi O. Ogunjobi. p.219
36 : Communication : la pêche dans l'ordre économique régional de l'Afrique de l'Ouest / par Oumar A. Berte. p.235
37 : Communication de Saidou Nourou Bah, Secrétaire Exécutif du Secrétariat Permanent Sénégalo-Gambien au Colloque sur l'Intégration Économique. p.263
38 : Economic integration in West Africa : the monetary problems / paper presented by Joseph I. Tommy, Shamsu M. Mustapha. p.269
39 : L'intégration régionale et le développement inégal en Afrique de l'Ouest : le partage des avantages de l'intégration. p.283
40 : Répartition équitable des avantages et coûts d'intégration en Afrique de l'Ouest / par M. Uka Ezenwa. p. 302
41 : Economic integration in the Economic Community of West African States (ECOWAS) - problems, progress and prospects / V.P. Diejomaoh. p. 312
42: Vers une intégration plus étroite des activités scientifiques et technologiques orientées - mission en Afrique. p.337
43 : Thème no. 2 : transports et télécommunications. p.360
44 : Rapport de la commission sur les problèmes monétaires et financiers. p.371

cont.

cont'd

45 : Rapport de la Commission II : Transports, communications et libre circulation. p.375
46 : Rapport de la Commission III : l'Intégration par la production et le partage des avantages. p.379
47 : Commission IV. p.388
48 : Raport final. p.394
49 : Motion spéciale. p.401
50 : Motion de remerciement. p.402
51 : Discours de clôture du Président Ahmed Sékou Touré. p.403

1434 CORTES, José Luis
La Organización para la Unidad Africana. - Madrid : G.I.D.A.F., 1982, 372p. Portr.

1435 DIOUF, Makhtar
Les problèmes-obstacles de la réussite de l'intégration économique en Afrique. - /S.l. : s.n./, 1981, 19 leaves.

Unpublished occasional paper submitted to the Preparatory Meeting of the UNITAR Programme on Regional and Interregional Co-operation in the 1980s, Berlin-West, November 18-21, 1981

1436 DIOUF, Makhtar
A propos de quelques problèmes qui se posent dans l'intégration économique. - /S.l. : s.n./, 1978. 8 leaves

Communication présentée au ler Colloque sur l'Intégration en Afrique de l'Ouest, Dakar 28 mars-2 avril 1978.

1437 GREEN, Reginald Herbold
Southern African development coordination : toward a functioning dynamics? IDS Bulletin (Brighton), vol.11, no.4, Sept., 1980

1438 HENIG, Michael WIONCZEK, Miguel S.
Systems approach to regional integration in West Africa. Journal of Common Market Studies (Oxford), vol.1/2, 1975

1439 KRIEGER MYTELKA, Lynn
New departures in Equatorial African Integration. Africa Today (Denver, Col.), vol.15, no.5, October/November, 1968, p.16-20

1440 KRINGS, Thomas
Strategien der integrierten ländlichen Entwicklung in den Sahelländern Westafrikas. Afrika Spectrum. Deutsche Zeitschrift für moderne Afrikaforschung (Pfaffenhofen/Ilm). H.2, 1978

1441 KUZNECOVA, M.
Ekonomičeskaja integracija v Zapadnoj Afrike. Azija i Afrika segodnja (Moskva), no.5, 1982, p.10-12

1442 LECHINI, Gladys
La integración : una perspectiva para el Continente Africano. Revista de Derecho Internacional y Ciencias Diplomáticas (Rosario, Argentina), 27/28 (48/49) 1979/1980, p.57-66

1443 LEYGNAC, G.
Aide extérieure et intégration économique régionale en Afrique de l'Ouest. - Paris : Centre d'Etudes et de Recherches sur le Développement International, 1976. 123p. Ill. (Cahiers de développement international ; 1)

Intégration régionale/ aide au développement, financement de l'aide/ Afrique de l'Ouest/ analyse économique/ implications économiques/ projets de développement/ PNUD/ CEE/ langues de développement/ infrastructure du transport/ coopération régionale/ bibliographie.

1444 NDONGKO, Wilfred A.
Central African regional co-operation in the context of the Lagos Plan of Action : The UDEAC. Africa Development (Dakar), vol.7, no.1/2, 1982. p.43-59

The Berg Report and the Lagos Plan of Action. Special double issue.

1445 SAID, Mohamed
Integration as a mode of ethnic conflict resolution in Africa. International Interactions (New York), 8(4), 1981, p.349-372
Includes bibliographical references.

1446 SCHMIDT, Gerold
The integration policy of 1977 in Africa. Internationales Afrikaforum (München), 13, 1977, 4, p.349-353

1447 TOURE, Ahmed Sekou
Economic integration of West Africa States. - Conakry : African Democratic Revolution, 1980. 62p. Ill.

1448 UNCTAD. TDB. Committee on Economic Co-operation among Developing Countries
Economic co-operation and integration among developing countries : a review of recent development in subregional, regional and interregional organizations and arrangement : report by the UNCTAD secretariat.-Genève : UNCTAD, 1982. - vols

Vol.1 : Latin America. 1982. X,110p. (TD/B/C.7/51)
Vol.2 : Africa. 1982. XI,108p. (TD/B/C.7/51)

1449 YADI, Melchiade
Les systèmes d'intégration régionale africaine : théorie, évolution, perspectives. - Genève : Georg, 1979. 373p.
Bibliography: p.351-369
ISBN: 2 8257 0062 2

VIII-3.0. Economic Community of West Africa—ECWA/CEAO

1450 CEAO. Marchés Tropicaux et Méditerranéens (Paris), 37e année, no.1864, vendredi 31 juillet 1981, p.1991-1992

Contents: Commerce: réunions tripartites sur les restrictions aux échanges intra-communautaires. Défense: adoption du protocole d'application de l'Accord de non-aggression et d'Assistance.

CEAO Communauté Économique de l'Afrique de l'Ouest, Ouagadougou, Haute Volta

1451 CEAO : aide extérieure de 50 milliards CFA pour plusieurs projets de développement. Marchés Tropicaux et Méditerranéens (Paris), 37e année, no.1884, vendredi 18 decembre 1981, p.3362

1452 CEAO approves projects. AED : Africa Economic Digest (London), vol.2, no.50, December 1981, p.14

1453 CEAO : les conclusions de la sixième session du Comité des administrateurs du FOSIDEC. Marchés Tropicaux et Méditerranéens (Paris), 37e année, no.1850, vendredi 24 avril 1981, p.1182

FOSIDEC Fonds de Solidarité et d'Intervention pour le Développement de la Communauté

1454 CEAO : coopération commerciale. Marchés Tropicaux et Méditerranéens (Paris), 37e année, no.1862, vendredi 17 juillet 1981, p.1879

(Voir détail en rubrique Courier de Bruxelles, p.1869: Etats membres de la CEAO. Programme de coopération commerciale régionale).

1455 CEAO : développement des échanges commerciaux : demande d'un soutien financier à la CEE. Marchés Tropicaux et Méditerranéens (Paris), 37e année, no.1836, vendredi 16 janvier 1981, p.133

1456 CEAO : dix milliards CFA pour la création à Bamako d'un centre régional d'énergie solaire. Marchés Tropicaux et Méditerranéens (Paris), 38e année, no.1917, vendredi 6 août 1982, p.2198

1457 CEAO : énergie solaire : projet de centre régional. Marchés Tropicaux et Méditerranéens (Paris), 37e année, no.1861, vendredi 10 juillet 1981, p.1822

1458 CEAO : Le FOSIDEC intervient pour des investissements au Mali, en Mauritanie et au Sénégal. Marchés Tropicaux et Méditerranéens (Paris), 37e année, no.1839, vendredi 6 février 1981, p.306

1459 CEAO : Institut des sciences halieutiques : mise en route du projet. Marchés Tropicaux et Méditerranéens (Paris), 37e aneée, no.1869, vendredi 4 septembre 1981, p.2272

1460 CEAO journal : Communauté Economique de l'Afrique de l'Ouest. Jeune Afrique (Paris), 22e anneé, no.1098, 20 janvier 1982, p.33-48

Contents: Un accent de vérité. Un tournant décisif. Le charme discret de Dakar. Une solidarité agissante. La conférence de l'ANAD. Les bailleurs de fonds. Un gage de crédibilité. Les rouages. Les objectifs. La Taxe de Coopération Régionale (TCR). Le Fonds de Solidarité et d'Intervention pour le Développement de la Communauté (FOSIDEC). Répondre aux besoins les plus urgents. Développement rural. Développement industriel. Développement des échanges. Le cadre juridique. Organigramme de la Communauté, adopté le 20 Octobre 1979 à Nouakchott (Mauritanie) par la 5e Conférence des chefs d'Etat. p.41

1461 CEAO-Länder verbessern ihre Kooperation : umfangreiche Unterstützung für Westafrikanische Wirtschaftsgemeinschaft. Nachrichten für Aussenhandel (Köln), vol.44, no.5, Jan. 8, 1981, p.5

Warenaustausch zwischen Mitgliedländern. Einheitlicher Zolltariff noch nicht erreichbar. Aussenhandel. Rolle "Fonds Communautaire de Développement (FCD)" und andere Institute. Projekte. Internationale Finanzierungsorganisationen zufrieden über regionale Wirtschaftsintegration der CEAO. Daten 1979-80.

1462 CEAO : mission d'information au Pérou auprès du Pacte Andin. Marchés Tropicaux et Méditerranéens (Paris), 38e année, no. 1890 vendredi 29 janvier 1982, p.256

1463 CEAO : prochain sommet de la Communauté à Dakar, en octobre prochain. Marchés Tropicaux et Méditerranéens (Paris), 37e année, no.1852, vendredi 8 mai 1981, p.1296

1464 CEAO : prochaine réunion des chefs d'Etat. Marchés Tropicaux et Méditerranéens (Paris), 38e année, no.1925, vendredi 1er octobre 1982, p.2653

1465 CEAO : projets communautaires : le financement de sept projets représentant 45 milliards de francs CFA. Marchés Tropicaux et Méditerranéens (Paris), 37e année, no.1877, vendredi 30 octobre 1981, p.2752

1466 CEAO : réunion d'experts à Ouagadougou avant le Conseil des ministres. Marchés Tropicaux et Méditerranéens (Paris), 37e année, no.1848, vendredi 10 avril 1981, p.998

1467 CEAO : réunion du Conseil des ministres à Dakar. Marchés Tropicaux et Méditerranéens (Paris), 37e année, no.1851, vendredi 1er mai 1981, p.1242

1468 CEAO : session d'experts à Ouagadougou pour préparer le "sommet" de décembre. Marchés Tropicaux et Méditerranéens (Paris), 38e année, no.1928, vendredi 22 octobre 1982, p.2833

1469 CEAO : situation et objectifs d'une communauté régionale africaine. Afrique contemporaine (Paris), no.120, 1982, p.8-17. Tabl.

1470 CEAO : Le sommet des chefs d'Etat se consacrera au problème des transports, les 19 et 20 décembre à Yamoussoukro. Marchés Tropicaux et Méditerranéens (Paris), 38e année, no.1936, vendredi 17 decembre 1982, p.3316

1471 CEAO : subvention de 750 millions CFA de la Communauté Economique Européenne. Marchés Tropicaux et Méditerranéens (Paris), 38e année, no.1888, vendredi 18 janvier 1982, p.135

1472 DIARRA, Eloi D.
Les dépenses de la CEAO (Communauté Economique de l'Afrique de l'Ouest). Marchés Tropicaux et Méditerranéens (Paris), 38e année, no.1953, vendredi 10 décembre 1982, p.3246-3249

Les dépenses des organes de fonctionnement. Les dépenses liées à l'application de la taxe de coopération régionale (TCR). Les dépenses d'intervention économique. Forces et faiblesses des finances de la CEAO.

1473 Dollars 2.6m for CEAO. West Africa (London), no.3363, 18 January 1982, p.206

1474 KÜHN, Rainer SEELOW, Frank
ECOWAS und CEAO : regionale wirtschaftliche Zusammenarbeit in Westafrika. Entwicklung and Zusammenarbeit (Bonn), H.3, 1980

1475 QUALI, Kamadini
Intégration africaine : le cas de la Communauté Economique de l'Afrique de l'Ouest. - Paris : Economica, 1981. 323p. Fig. Tabs. Dgms. Cartes

1476 SEPTIEME conférence de la CEAO, troisième de l'ANAD, troisième de l'UMOA : les 14 et 15 décembre à Dakar, trois conférences des chefs d'Etat de l'Ouest africain francophone. Marchés Tropicaux et Méditerranéens (Paris), 37e année, no.1885, vendredi 25 décembre 1981, p.3405

1477 YEROKUN, Olusegun
The Economic Community of West Africa : its evolution and scope. Indian Journal of International Law (New Delhi), vol.20, no.2, 1980, April/June, p.284-306

VIII-3.1. Economic Community of West African States—ECOWAS

1478 AGHAJI, J.C.
ECOWAS : is it a countervailing power for economic independence ? Journal of Asian and African Studies. Department of Sociology and Anthropology, York University (Toronto), vol.14, 1979, nos 1/2. p.109-120

ECOWAS Economic Community of West African States Lagos, set up on 28 May 1975

1479 ANYATONWU, G.N.
ECOWAS, an approach to sub-regional economic integration. Journal of African Studies (Los Angeles, Cal.), 9(1), spring 1982, p.30-38
Includes bibliographical references.

1480 ASANTE, S.K.B.
Studying ECOWAS. West Africa (London), no.3395, 30.8.1982, p.2223-2226

Review of a recent study of ECOWAS which 'addresses itself to almost all aspects of recent developments in the West African economic integration efforts'.

1481 CALLING ECOWAS - by phone / from a correspondent in Freetown. West Africa (London), no.3356, 23 November 1981, p.2767

1482 CEDEAO. Marchés Tropicaux et Méditerranéens (Paris), 37e année, no.1867, vendredi 21 août 1981, p.2158

CEDEAO Comunidad Económica de los Estados del Africa Occidental, Lagos

1483 CEDEAO : adoption à Cotonou du projet-cadre de développement agricole. Marchés Tropicaux et Méditerranéens (Paris), 38e année, no.1906, vendredi 21 mai 1982, p.1334

1484 CEDEAO: appel pour le règlement des contributions financières des Etats. Marchés Tropicaux et Méditerranéens (Paris), 37e année, no.1880, vendredi 20 novembre 1981, p.2942

1485 CEDEAO : chambre de compensation de l'Afrique de l'Ouest : réunion des gouverneurs des banques centrales. Marchés Tropicaux et Méditerranéens (Paris), 38e année, no.1909, vendredi 11 juin 1982, p.1507

1486 CEDEAO : chambres de commerce : réunion à Bamako. Marchés Tropicaux et Méditerranéens (Paris), 37e année, no.1878, vendredi 6 novembre 1981, p.2817

1487 CEDEAO : Conférence annuelle, 6., 1981, Freetown
Lettre d'information no 1 : CEDEAO-Communauté Économique des États de l'Afrique de l'Ouest. Jeune Afrique (Paris), no.1063, 20 mai 1981, p.45-50

A cette occasion, les chefs d'Etat et de gouvernement des seize pays membres vont s'engager dans une nouvelle étape décisive de la construction communautaire. Un défi raisonné. Des objectifs et des étapes. La volonté pour réussir. Non-agression. Les rouages. Premier pas. Par delà les frontières nationales. Le pilier financier pour assurer l'entraide et mobiliser les resources.

1488 CEDEAO : coopération : réunions à Freetown. Marchés Tropicaux et Méditerranéens (Paris), 37e année, no.1877, vendredi 30 octobre 1981, p.2753

1489 CEDEAO : création d'un fonds de resources énergétiques. Marchés Tropicaux et Méditerranéens (Paris), 38e année, no.1908, vendredi 4 juin 1982, p.1451

1490 CEDEAO : les décisions de la conférence des chefs d'Etat. Marchés Tropicaux et Méditerranéens (Paris), 37e année, no.1857, vendredi 12 juin 1981, p.1589

1491 CEDEAO : douane : réunion du Comité des experts. Marchés Tropicaux et Méditerranéens (Paris), 37e année, no.1869, vendredi 4 septembre 1981, p.2272

1492 CEDEAO : jeunesse et sports : un nouvel organisme. Marchés Tropicaux et Méditerranéens (Paris), 38e année, no.1895, vendredi 5 mars 1982, p.678

1493 CEDEAO : la libéralisation des échanges et le problème crucial de la prise de la participation des nationaux dans les sociétés. Marchés Tropicaux et Méditerranéens (Paris), 37e année, no.1846, vendredi 27 mars 1981, p.834

1494 CEDEAO : mission positive aux Etats-Unis. Marchés Tropicaux et Méditerranéens (Paris), 37e année, no.1852, vendredi 8 mai 1981, p.1296

1495 CEDEAO : les pays bailleurs de fonds ont examiné 138 projets de développement : télécommunications, transports aériens et routiers. Marchés Tropicaux et Méditerranéens (Paris), 37e année, no.1858, vendredi 19 juin 1981, p.1648

1496 CEDEAO : prochain sommet des chefs d'Etat du 27 au 29 mai à Freetown. Marchés Tropicaux et Méditerranéens (Paris), 37e année, no.1854, vendredi 22 mai 1981, p.1410

1497 CEDEAO : réunion du conseil des ministres. Relance des activités de la Communauté. Marchés Tropicaux et Méditerranéens (Paris), 38e année, no.1932, vendredi 19 novembre 1982, p.3071

1498 CEDEAO : réunions préparatoires au sommet des chefs d'Etat et de gouvernment. Marchés Tropicaux et Méditerranéens (Paris), 38e année, no.1904, vendredi 7 mai 1982, p.1206

1499 CEDEAO : le tournant? : la politique des petits pas a fait ses preuves. Jeune Afrique (Paris), no.1093, 16 décembre 1981, p.22-23

1500 CONSOMMATION des principaux hydrocarbures des pays de l'Union Monétaire Ouest Africaine, 1965-1979. Notes d'information et statistiques. Banque Centrale des États de l'Afrique de l'Ouest (Paris), no.289, déc. 1980, p.1. Tabs.

Evolution de la consommation pour l'Union, par catégorie d'hydrocarbure, comme essence auto, pétrole lampant, huiles lourdes. Consommation par pays: Bénin, Côte d'Ivoire, Haute-Volta, Nigeria, Sénégal, Togo, Chiffres 1965-80.

1501 CRONE, Donald
Industrialization and regionalism in ECOWAS and ASEAN : Nigeria and Indonesia in regional and world systems. -/East Lansing, Mich.?/:/Michigan State University?/, 1982?. 38p.

/Regionalization/, /industrialization/, /manufacturing/, /West Africa/, /South East Asia/ - /Nigeria/, /Indonesia/, /foreign investments/, /balance of payments/, /regional organizations/.

1502 DALIBOR, Gudrun
ECOWAS goes East. West Africa (London), no.3343, 24 August 1981, p.1923-1924

1503 DELAUNAY, Dominique
La Communauté Économique des Etats de l'Afrique de l'Ouest (CEDEAO). In: Intégrations régionales entre pays en voie de développement. - Bruges : Tempel, 1982. p.179-244
Bibliography: p.242-244

1504 DIABY-OUATTARA, Aboubacar
"ECOWAS is operational" : dr. Aboubacar Diaby-Ouattara talked with West Africa on the eve of the sixth Heads of State ECOWAS meeting in Freetown last week. West Africa (London), no.3331, 1 June 1981, p.1209

1505 ECONOMIC Community of West Africa-ECOWAS. West Africa (London), (3330), 25.5.1981, p.1153-1161

1506 ECOWAS approves ₦ 2.79m. West Africa (London), no.3408, 29 November 1982, p.3100

1507 ECOWAS currency convertibility sought. AED: Africa Economic Digest (London), vol.2, no.40, Oct. 1981, p.13

1508 ECOWAS : economic data of Economic Community of West African States. - Dakar : West Africa Industrial Forum, 1982 (Dakar : International Trade Fair). 116p. Ill. Tabs.

1509 ECOWAS energy : a correspondent reports from Bintumani in Sierra Leone in West African and other thoughts on energy and survival. West Africa (London), no.3358, 7 December, 1981, p.2918

1510 ECOWAS goes West. West Africa (London), no.3364, 25 January 1982, p.261

1511 ECOWAS microwave tenders disappoint. AED: Africa Economic Digest (London), vol.3, no.30, July 1982, p.12

1512 ECOWAS milestone. West Africa (London), no.3381, 24 May 1982, p.1395

1513 ECOWAS' missing money. West Africa (London), no.3359, 14 December 1981, p.2990

1514 ECOWAS 150 projects need investors. AED: Africa Economic Digest (London), no.28, 28.11.1980, p.1-7

1515 ECOWAS poised in advance. West Africa (London), no.3383, 7 June 1982, p.1492

1516 ECOWAS prepares for summit. AED: Africa Economic Digest (London), vol.3, no.19, May 1982, p.12

1517 ECOWAS ready to move forward : a correspondent looks at the state of the ECOWAS institutions, after last year's procedural and hierarchical problems, and assesses the prospects ahead of the organisation. West Africa (London), February 25, 1980, p.35

1518 ECOWAS telecoms make progress. AED: Africa Economic Digest (London), vol.2, no.50, December 1981, p.14

1519 ECOWAS trembling on the brink. West Africa (London), no.3383, 7 June 1982, p.1493

1520 ENERGY and ECOWAS. West Africa (London), no.3330, 25 May 1981, p.1181

1521 GHARBI, Samir
Paroles sans lendemain? : en dépit des professions de foi communautaires des uns et des autres, la grande organisation ouest-africaine marque le pas. Jeune Afrique (Paris), 22e année, no.1118, 9 juin 1982, p.30

1522 HARRELL-BOND, Barbara
ECOWAS: the Economic Community of West Africa States. Hannover/NH : /s.n./, 1979, 12p. (American Universities Field Staff. Reports. 1979/No.6 : Africa)

1523 IHONVBERE, Julius O.
ECOWAS revisited. West Africa (London), no.3399, 26 September 1982, p.2479

1524 INTEGRATIONSPERSPEKTIVEN der Wirtschaftsgemeinschaft westafrikanischer Staaten = (Economic Community of West African States - ECOWAS) / von Margit Scherb ... [et al.]. - Wien : Wiener Institut für Entwicklungsfragen, 1981.
Bibliography: p.218-225

1525 KÜHN, Rainer SEELOW, Frank
ECOWAS and CEAO : regional cooperation in West Africa. D and C : Development and Cooperation (Bonn), no.3, May/June 1980, p.11-13

1526 KÜHN, Rainer SEELOW, Frank
ECOWAS : regionale Zusammenarbeit in Westafrika. Entwicklung and Zusammenarbeit (Bonn), H.3, 1978

1527 KUMAR, Ashok OSAGIE, Eghosa
Problems of the Economic Community of West African States. In: Nigeria and the world : readings in Nigerian foreign policy / ed. A. Bolaji Akinyemi. - Ibadan : [s.n.], 1978

1528 LANGHAMMER, Rolf J.
Die Wirtschaftsgemeinschaft westafrikanischer Staaten (ECOWAS) - ein neuer Integrationsversuch. Europa-Archiv. Zeitschrift für internationale Politik (Bonn), Folge 5, 1975
Sonderdruck

1529 LOWO, Adeline
Sozioökonomische Aspekte des ECOWAS-Abkommens : wirtschaftswissenschaftliche Diplomarbeit.-Wien : Universität Wien, 1975.

1530 McLENAGHAM, John B. NSOULI, Saleh M. RIECHEL, Klaus-Walter
Currency convertibility in the Economic Community of West African States. - Washington, D.C. : International Monetary Fund, 1982. V,46p. tab. graph. (Occasional paper / IMF ; 13)
References
ISSN 0251 6365

1531 A MATTER of words. West Africa (London), no.3382, 31 May 1982, p.1453

1532 MENSAH, Dotè R. et al.
CEDEAO journal. Jeune Afrique (Paris), 22e année, no.1120, 23 juin 1982, p.51-60

Contents: Le sommet du défi. Sept ans après. Pour la Communauté Economique des Etats de l'Afrique de l'Ouest (CEDEAO), pour ses seize Etats membres, pour ses 150 millions d'habitants, c'est l'heure de relever le défi de la coopération et de la solidarité, d'engager la longue marche pour concrétiser ses idéaux du traité conclu en 1975 à Lagos. Cet engagement fraternel a été réaffirmé avec beaucoup de force par la conférence des chefs d'Etats et de gouvernment réunie les 28 et 29 mai 1982 à Cotonou (Bénin).

cont.

cont'd

Le sommet de la vérité et de l'action. Une cohérence sans faille. Un engagement résolu. Ils ont déclaré. Aboubakar Diaby-Ouattara : une confiance sereine. Le chemin parcouru. La stratégie agricole. Une entité viable. Le Fonds de la CEDEAO.

1533 NITSCH-TRABE, Ingrid
Transport- und Kommunikationswesen im Rahmen der ECOWAS. Neue Entwicklungspolitik. Wiener Institut für Entwicklungsfragen (Wien), vol.7, 1981, no.1, p.33-38

1534 "OBSERVE ECOWAS protocols". West Africa (London), no.3409, 6 December 1982, p.3182

1535 OSAGIE, Eghosa
Economic integration and ECOWAS. - Benin City/Ibadan : /s.n./, 1979

1536 PREPARING for ECOWAS meeting. West Africa (London), no.3380, 17 May 1982, p.1350
(See: Seven years of ECOWAS: no.1542)

1537 REUNION sectorielle agro-alimentaire du CDI pour la Cedeao en octobre à Bruxelles. Marchés Tropicaux et Méditerranéens (Paris), 38e année, no.1917, vendredi 6 août 1982, p.2189
CDI Centre pour le Développement Industriel

1538 ROBSON, Peter
The West African Economic Community : WAEC : a customs union in quest of an economic community. - /St. Andrew, U.K. : s.n., 198-/. 36p. /Unpublished paper/

1539 RONDOS, Alex
ECOWAS after Freetown : Alex Rondos looks at the practical progress towards ECOWAS' goals that was set in train at the recent summit meeting. West Africa (London), no.3334, 22 June 1981, p.1393-1395

1540 SACKEY, J.A.
Structure and performance of CARICOM : lessons for the development of ECOWAS. Canadian Journal of African Studies. Revue Canadienne des Etudes Africaines. (Ottawa, Ont.), vol.12, no.2, 1978, p.259-277

1541 SCHERTZER, Eliane
La place de l'économie nigériane dans la CEDEAO : étude. - Paris : Ministère de la Coopération, 1980. 222p. Tab. Diagr. Cartes. (Etudes et documents ; 42)
At head of title : Service des études et questions internationales.

/Coopération économique/, /organisations africaines/, /Afrique occidentale/, /Nigeria/ - /cadre institutionnel/, /aspects économiques/, /secteur agricole/, /secteur industriel/, /pétrole/, /infrastructure de transport/, /commerce extérieur/, /finances publiques/, /tableaux statistiques/.

1542 SEVEN years of ECOWAS. West Africa (London), no.3381, 24 May 1982, p.1364-1382

/1/ : The long road to the Treaty of Lagos
/2/ : Trade problems and prospects / Asante, S.K.B.
/3/ : Steps to monetary union
/4/ : Funding the Fund
/5/ : Benin : how to stay afloat
/6/ : Togo goes gently

1543 SIRCAR, Parbati K. DIBO EPIE, Maria
ECOWAS : The Economic Community of West African States. Africa Quarterly. Indian Council for Cultural Relations (New Delhi), vol.20, /1980/, nos.1/2, p.46-62

1544 STACY, M.
ECOWAS select readings, 1975-1981. - Washington, D.C. : African Bibliographic Center, 1982. 23p., ill. (Current reading list series ; vol.13 ; 4)

/Bibliography/, /economic cooperation/, /economic integration/, /regional organizations/, /West Africa/

1545 SYNGE, R.
African Development Bank asks for ECOWAS support. Africa Economic Digest (London), vol.2, no.22, May 29, 1981, p.16. Portr.

Plea for foreign participation in raising loans. ECOWAS (Economic Community of West African States) projects-planning. Tenders for telecommunication-programme. Infrastructure. Removal trade barriers.

1546 TANTON, Robert
La CEDEAO sera-t-elle dominée par la Nigeria? Europe-Outre-Mer (Paris), no.591, 1979

1547 UDOKANG, Okon
Nigeria and ECOWAS : economic and political implications of regional integration. In: Nigeria and the world : readings in Nigerian foreign policy / ed. A. Bolaji Akinyemi. - Ibadan : /s.n./, 1978

1548 WEST AFRICA INDUSTRIAL FORUM, Dakar
Economic data of Economic Community of West Africa States ECOWAS. Dakar : West Africa Industrial Forum, 1982. 16p., tab.

1549 WEST African cooperation and Development Fund beginning to work. BIS: Bank for International Settlements (Basel), (143), 28, July 1981, p.4-5

1550 Die WIRTSCHAFTSGEMEINSCHAFT Westafrikanischer Staaten "ECOWAS" : Zusammenarbeit zwischen Entwicklungsländern. Neue Entwicklungspolitik. Wiener Institut für Entwicklungsfragen (Wien), vol.7, 1981, no.1, 38p.
Beiträge verschiedener Verfasser

VIII-3.2. Central African Customs and Economic Union—UDEAC

1551 BEAC : un outil d'intégration économique régionale. Jeune Afrique (Paris), 22e année, no.1106, 17 Mars 1982, p.42

1552 DIALLO, Siradiou
Afrique Centrale : un marché commun impossible? : en rupture d'union depuis treize ans, le Tschad revient au bercail: mais les problèmes restent les mêmes après le sommet de l'UDEAC à Libreville. Jeune Afrique (Paris), 22e année, no.1096, 6 janvier 1982, p.54

1553 La GUINEE équatoriale devrait entrer dans l'Udeac. Marchés Tropicaux et Méditerranéens (Paris), 38e année, no.1937, vendredi 24 décembre 1982, p.3490

UDEAC Union Douanière et Economique de l'Afrique Centrale, Bangui

1554 JALLOH, Abdul Aziz
Foreign private investments and regional political integration in UDEAC. Cahiers Economiques et Sociaux. Université Nationale du Zaïre. Institut de Recherches Economiques et Sociales (Kinshasa), vol.17, no.2, 1979, p.174-197.
Bibliogr.: p.196-197

1555 KRIEGER MYTELKA, Lynn
Competition, conflict and decline in the Union Douanière de l'Afrique Centrale. In: African Regional Organization / ed. D. Mazzeo. /S.l./ : Longman, 1982

1556 LANGHAMMER, Rolf J.
Einige Probleme der gemeinsamen Aussenzolle der Westafrikanischen Zollunion. Die Weltwirtschaft. Halbjahresschrift des Instituts für Weltwirtschaft an der Universität Kiel (Kiel), 1, 1973, p.226-241

1557 UDEAC : M. Ambroise Foalem secrétaire général. Marchés Tropicaux et Méditerranéens (Paris), 38e année, no.1938, vendredi 31 décembre 1982, p.3550

1558 UNION Monétaire d'Afrique Centrale et UDEAC. Marchés Tropicaux et Méditerranéens (Paris), 37e année, 1981

BDEAC : réunion des organes directeurs à Bangui, p.30
La situation économique et monétaire en 1980, p.70
BEAC : évolution monétaire satisfaisante. p.315
BEAC : réunion de conseil d'administration à Libreville. p.1196
La situation économique et monétaire au 31 mars. p.1401
L'exercice 1979-1980 de la BDEAC. p.1486
Conseil d'administration de la BDEAC. p.1945
BEAC : amélioration de la conjoncture. p.2224

BDEAC Banque de Développement des Etats de l'Afrique Centrale, Brazzaville, Congo

BEAC Banque des Etats de l'Afrique Centrale, Yaoundé, Cameroun

VIII-3.3. East African Community—EAC

1559 ANJARIA, Shailendra J. EKEN, Sena LAKER, John F.
Payments arrangements and the expansion of trade in Eastern and Southern Africa. - Washington : International Monetary Fund, 1982. VII,52p. tab. (Occasional paper ; IMF ; 11)
ISBN 0251 6365

1560 COX, Thomas S.
Northern actors in a South-South setting : external aid and East African integration : draft. - New York City : /s.n./, 1981. 91p. Ref.

1561 DIOUF, H.
Marchés communs africains : des modèles viables ou des faux-fuyants? Moniteur Africain (Dakar), (747), aug-sep 1976, p.7-14

/Article/ on the viability of and /obstacles to /common market/s in /West Africa/ and the difficulties of the /EAC/ - includes /illustration/s.

1562 EAC assets talks scheduled. AED : Africa Economic Digest (London), vol.2, no.8, February 1981, p.10

EAC East African Community

1563 EAC ministers meet. AED : Africa Economic Digest (London), vol.2, no.50, December 1981, p.11

1564 EAC settlement expected by 1982. AED : Africa Economic Digest (London), vol.2, no.32, August 1981, p.8

1565 EAC states to meet again. AED : Africa Economic Digest (London), vol.2, no.44, Nov. 1981, p.7

1566 EAC states to meet in July. AED : Africa Economic Digest (London), vol.2, no.26, 26 June 1981. p.8

1567 EAST AFRICAN COMMUNITY. Office of the Registrar
The East African Industrial Court : special bulletin, 1970-1972 : a report and a review of Court's activities. - Nairobi : East African Literature Bureau, 1974. 132p.

1568 EST Africain : la réunion est-africaine de Kampala n'a rien résolu. Marchés Tropicaux et Méditerranéens (Paris), 37e année, no.1843, vendredi 6 mars 1981, p.625

1569 EST Africain : vers une reconstitution de la Communauté Economique. Marchés Tropicaux et Méditerranéens (Paris), 37e année, no.1834, vendredi 2 janvier 1981, p.36

... Certains estiment qu'une aide financière de quelque 100 millions de dollars fournie par des pays industrialisés pourrait contribuer à son démarrage et à son fonctionnement.

1570 GREEN, Reginald Herbold
East African Community : 1975 and after. In: Africa contemporary record, 1975-1976 / ed. Colin Legum. - New York : /s.n./, 1976

1571 HARD times push neighbours together. AED : Africa Economic Digest (London), (6), Febr. 1981, p.2-3

1572 INTEGRATION and disintegration in East Africa / edited by Christian P. Potholm and Richard D. Fredland. - Lanham : University Press of America. /1980/. x,219p.

Subjects: East African Community -- addresses, essays, lectures / Africa, East -- economic conditions -- addresses, essays, lectures.

1573 JENGO, Mukyusa
East African summit leaves questions. AED : Africa Economic Digest (London), vol.2, no.4, Jan. 1981, p.9

1574 KENYA's key to economic success. The East African Community : problems and potential banking in Kenya. - London : National and Grindlays Bank, 1973. Reprinted from the Banker, September 1973, p.1047-1063

1575 KÜHNHARDT, Ludger
Östliches Afrika : eine Region im Umbruch = Eastern Africa : a region in ferment. Aussenpolitik (Stuttgart), vol.32, no.2, 1981, p.186-197

Journal also available in English.

1576 MWASE, Ngila
The East African Community : a study of regional disintegration. - Dar es Salaam : University of Dar es Salaam, Economic Research Bureau, 1979. 59p. (Paper / Economic Research Bureau ; 77.10)
Bibliography: p.56-59

1577 MWASE, Ngila
Regional economic integration and the unequal sharing of benefits : background to the disintegration and collapse of the East African Community. Africa Development (Dakar), vol.4, nos.2/3, April/Sept., 1979, p.1-29

Summary in French

1578 NEIGHBOURS who miss one another. Africa (London), no.112, Dec. 1980, p.44

1579 NEW down for East Africa. Africa. An international business, economic and political monthly (London), no.114, Febr. 1981, p.12-13

1580 ODERO-JOWI, J.G.
East African oligarchs versus African Unity : history and politics on economic integration in East Africa. - /S.l. : s.n./, 1977. 1 vol.

The historical role played by leading groups in the demolition of East African Unity, and the idea of economic cooperation and interdependence among countries are analyzed in the context of East Africa's evolution.
/IDRC supported/, /economic cooperation/, /regional cooperation/, /political leadership/, /East Africa/ - /historical analysis/, /political aspects/, /regional integration/, /UN/, /nationalism/, /common market/, /government/, /African organizations/

VIII-3.4. Common Organization of African, Malagasy and Mauritian States

1581 SEMINAIRE OCAM/BIT SUR L'AMELIORATION DES CONDITIONS ET DU MILIEU DE TRAVAIL DES TRAVAILLEURS EN AFRIQUE, 1979, Cotonou
Incidences des changements technologiques sur les conditions de travail et de vie des travailleurs ruraux : quelques repères / J.M. Clerc. - Genève : ILO, 1979. 59p. (ILO-CONDI/T/1979/14)

/OCAM/-/ILO publ./- WHO publ./ - /Conference paper/ on the impact of /technological change/ on/working conditions/ and /living conditions/ of /agricultural worker/s in /Africa/ - Discusses /agricultural income/ at /poverty/ level, /hours of work/, /ergonomics/, /social adjustment/s required from a /traditional culture/ to adjust to new forms of /work organization/. Graphs. Maps. Ref. Statistical tables.

OCAM Organisation Commune Africaine et Mauricienne, Bangui

1582 SEMINAIRE OCAM/OMS/BIT SUR L'AMELIORATION DES CONDITIONS ET DU MILIEU DE TRAVAIL DES TRAVAILLEURS RURAUX EN AFRIQUE, 1979, Cotonou
Incidence des changements technologiques sur l'hygiène et la securité des travailleurs ruraux : aspects juridiques et institutionnels, formation / J.Castella. - Genève : ILO, 1979. 10p.

/OCAM/-/ILO publ./-/WHO publ./ /Conference paper/ discussing the relations between /technological change/, /occupational hygiene/ and /occupational safety/ of /rural worker/s in /Africa/ - /comment/s on/ILO recommendation/s, /EEC/ directives and /labour legislation/s and /vocational training/ to correspond with /agricultural mechanization/ in Africa. /Conf./ Cotonou 1979 Dec 3 to 7

1583 SEMINAIRE OCAM/OMS/BIT SUR L'AMELIORATION DES CONDITIONS ET DU MILIEU DE TRAVAIL DES TRAVAILLEURS RURAUX EN AFRIQUE, 1979, Cotonou
Inspection du travail et le secteur rural / D. Bonneau. - Genève : ILO, 1979. 5p.

/OCAM/-/ILO publ./-/WHO publ./ - /Conference paper/ on the role of /labour inspection/ in the /agricultural sector/-/comment/s on /ILO recommendation/s and /ILO convention/s and stresses need particularly in /developing country/s to cooperate at /national level/ and /local level/ in order to improve not only /occupational health/ and /occupational safety/ conditions but also /living conditions/ and /social protection/ of all /rural worker/s. Conf. Cotonou, Dec. 3 to 7

1584 SEMINAIRE OCAM/OMS/BIT SUR L'AMELIORATION DES CONDITIONS ET DU MILIEU DE TRAVAIL DES TRAVAILLEURS RURAUX EN AFRIQUE, 1979, Cotonou
Protection de la vie et de la santé des travailleurs ruraux en Afrique / S.Z. GANGBO. - Genève : ILO, 1979, 2p.

/OCAM/-/ILO publ./-/WHO publ./-/Conference paper/ on /occupational safety/ and /occupational health/ of /rural worker/s in /Africa/. Conf. Cotonou 1979 Dec. 3 to 7

1585 SEMINAIRE OCAM/OMS/BIT SUR L'AMELIORATION DES CONDITIONS ET DU MILIEU DE TRAVAIL DES TRAVAILLEURS RURAUX EN AGRIQUE, 1979, Cotonou
Risques d'accidents du travail dans l'agriculture / V. Toma. - Genève : ILO, 1979, 8p.

/OCAM/-/ILO publ./-/WHO publ./-/Conference paper/on the /occupational safety/ of /agricultural worker/s in /Africa/ - cites specific safety measures, emphasizes importance of /safety education/ and includes an /attainment appraisal / questionnaire/ Conf. Cotonou 1979 Dec. 3 to 7

1586 SEMINAIRE OCAM/OMS/BIT SUR L'AMELIORATION DES CONDITIONS ET DU MILIEU DU TRAVAIL DES TRAVAILLEURS RURAUX EN AFRIQUE, 1979, Cotonou
Rôle économique et social des femmes face à la technologie / M.C. Seguret. - Genève : ILO, 1979. 13p.

/OCAM/-/ILO publ./-/WHO publ./-/Conference paper/ on the impact of / technological change on the /social role/ of /rural women/ in /Africa/ - Considers the role of women in /agricultural production/ - /unpaid work/ and the /family/, and recommends increasing their /labour productivity/ by alleviating/ home-maker/s duties through appropriate /equipment/, /education/ and /rural worker organization/. Illustration. Ref. Statistics.

VIII-3.5. Economic Community of the Great Lake Countries—CEPGL

1587 GRANDS Lacs. Marchés Tropicaux et Mediterranéens (Paris), 37e année, no.1841, vendredi 20 février 1981, p.437

1588 GRANDS Lacs : Banque de Développement des Etats des Grands Lacs (BDEGL). Marchés Tropicaux et Mediterranéens (Paris), 38e année, no.1904, vendredi 7 mai 1982, p.1223

1589 GRANDS Lacs : coopération en matière d'énergie : le rôle de l'EGL. Marchés Tropicaux et Mediterranéens (Paris), 37e année, no.1840, vendredi 13 février 1981, p.383

1590 GRANDS Lacs : la deuxième assemblée générale de la Banque de Développement. Marchés Tropicaux et Méditerranéens (Paris), 38e année, no.1916, vendredi 3o juillet 1982, p.2154

1591 GRANDS Lacs : le financement de la centrale Ruzizi-2 est pratiquement assuré. Marchés Tropicaux et Méditerranéens (Paris), 37e année, no.1874, vendredi 9 octobre 1981, p.2579

1592 GRANDS Lacs : un nouveau secrétaire exécutif à la CEPGL. Marchés Tropicaux et Méditerranéens (Paris), 37e année, vendredi 2 janvier 1981, p.35

1593 GRANDS Lacs : un organisme commun de promotion économique - La Banque de Développement des Etats des Grands Lacs. Marchés Tropicaux et Méditerranéens (Paris), 38e année, no.1909, vendredi 11 juin 1982, p.1519

1594 GRANDS Lacs : présélection des entreprises pour la centrale "Ruzizi 2". Marchés Tropicaux et Mediterranéens (Paris), 37e année, no.1843, vendredi 6 mars 1981, p.624

1595 GRANDS Lacs : report de la conférence des chefs d'Etat. Marchés Tropicaux et Méditerranéens (Paris), 37e année, no.1881, vendredi 27 novembre 1981, p.3188 no. spécial

1596 GRANDS Lacs : réunion au sommet à Gisenyi. Marchés Tropicaux et Méditerranéens (Paris), 38e année, no.1891, vendredi 5 février 1982, p.332

1597 GRANDS Lacs : Ruzizi 2 : un investissement de 73 millions de dollars. Marchés Tropicaux et Mediterranéens (Paris), 38e année, no.1930, vendredi 5 novembre 1982, p.2965

1598 GRANDS Lacs : Ruzizi 2 : plan de financement complet. Marchés Tropicaux et Méditerranéens (Paris), 38e année, no.1919, vendredi 20 août 1982, p.2322

1599 GRANDS Lacs : Ruzizi 2 : prequalification reopened. <u>AED : Africa Economic Digest</u> (London), vol.3, no.34, September 1982, p.10

1600 GRANDS Lacs : Ruzizi 2 : les travaux devraient commencer cette année. <u>Marchés Tropicaux et Méditerranéens</u> (Paris), 38e année, no.1879, vendredi 19 mars 1982, p.802

1601 GRANDS Lacs : "sommet" a Gisenyi fin janvier. <u>Marchés Tropicaux et Méditerranéens</u> (Paris), 38e année, no.1889, vendredi 22 janvier 1982, p.203

1602 KAÏDI, Hamza
Entraide exemplaire : pour le Burundi, le Rwanda et le Zaïre, les Grands Lacs sont bien plus que voies de communication. <u>Jeune Afrique</u> (Paris), no.1046, 21 janvier 1981, p.46-47

1603 VOSS, Harald
Kooperation in Afrika : die Communauté Economique des Pays des Grands Lacs (CEPGL). <u>Afrika Spectrum.</u> Institut für Afrika-Kunde (Hamburg), vol.15, no.3, 1981, p.319-336. Map. Ref.

Ziele und Möglichkeiten der CEPGL (Zusammenarbeit seit 1976 von Burundi, Ruanda, Zaïre) im Kontext des Aktionsplanes von Lagos (der OAU, 1980). Perspektiven für das Jahr 2000.

1604 YADI, Melchiade
La Communauté Economique des Pays des Grands Lacs. <u>Studia Diplomatica</u> (Bruxelles), vol.34, no.6, 1981, p.709-752. Tabl.

CEPGL Communauté Economique des Pays des Grands Lacs

VIII-3.6. Mano River Union—MRU

1605 MANO River : plus de barrières douanières entre les trois pays membres. Marchés Tropicaux et Méditerranéens (Paris), 37e année, no.1855, vendredi 29 mai 1981, p.1474

1606 MANO River Union appeal. West Africa (London), no.3376, 19 April 1982, p.1907

1607 MANO River Union : breaking down barriers / by a correspondent in Freetown. West Africa (London), October 19, 1981

1608 MANO River Union starts trading. West Africa (London), no.3334, June 22, 1981, p.1399-1400

1609 NEUE Impulse für die Mano River Union : Beitritt Guineas stärkt Erfolgschancen. Nachrichten für Aussenhandel (Köln), 30.12.1980.

1610 PLANS for power project. Africa Research Bulletin (Exeter, Engl), no.6096. July 15-Aug 14, 1981. (WA 27/7)

1611 Le POINT de vue de l'Union du Fleuve Mano, p.153-159. In: Deuxième Colloque sur l'intégration économique de l'Afrique de l'Ouest, 1980. - Conakry, Guinée : /Imprimerie de l'Education et de la Culture, 1981/

1612 VERSTÄRKTES Auslandsinteresse an der Mano River Union : auch deutsche Handelsbeziehungen wachsen. Nachrichten für Aussenhandel (Köln), 7.1.1981.

/The MANO RIVER DECLARATION establishing the MANO RIVER UNION was signed on 3 October 1973 at Malema, Republic of Sierra Leone and Liberia. This unique experiment in subregional economic collaboration and integration was the vision of the two Heads of State inspired by the belief in the need to "accelerate the economic growth, social progress and cultural advancement" of the two countries and the overwhelming desire "to establish a firm economic foundation for lasting peace, friendship, freedom and social progress" between Liberia and Sierra Leone.

The MANO RIVER UNION is a Customs Union and its aims and objectives are (1) "to expand trade by the elimination of all barriers to mutual trade; by cooperation in the expansion of international trade; by the creation of conditions favorable to an expansion of mutual productive capacity, incl. the progressive development of a common protective policy and cooperation in the creation of new productive capacity; (2) to ensure a fair distribution of benefits from economic cooperation"./

MRU Mano River Union

VIII-3.7. Organization of Senegal River States—OMVS

1613 BESSIS, Sophie
Faut-il construire les barrages sur le Sénégal. Jeune Afrique (Paris), no.1072, 22 juillet 1981, p.53-56

1614 DAM plans materialise : Adama Gaye writes from Dakar about the proposed OMVS project for the construction of two new-dams on the river Senegal. West Africa (London), no.3409, 6 December 1982, p.3140

OMVS Organisation pour la Mise en Valeur du fleuve Sénégal

1615 DURAN, Bernard
Une foire pas comme les autres : à la 5e FIDAK, il y aura des discours, des produits à vendre mais, surtout, une volonté de promouvoir les PME en Afrique de l'Ouest. Jeune Afrique (Paris), 23 année, no.1140, 10 novembre 1982, p.26

FIDAK Foire Internationale de Dakar

1616 Le FLEUVE Sénégal au Parlement européen. Afrique-Asie (Paris), no.271, du 5 au 18 juillet, 1982, p.25

1617 GRANDS barrages pour l'industrie, eau pourrie pour les villageois : au fleuve Sénégal une population entière est menacée. - Montreal,Qué.CA : Centre international de solidarité ouvrière, fév. 1981. 24p. illus.

Décrit le contexte ou se situe le projet de mise en valeur du fleuve Sénégal. Fait part de l'ampleur des travaux envisagés et dégage les effects anticipés sur les conditions de vie et de travail de la population tout en comparant les avantages et désavantages de ces grands travaux.

1618 MANANTALI foundation stone laid. AED : Africa Economic Digest (London), vol.3, no.20, May 1982, p.13

The présidents of Mali,Mauritania and Senegal attended the 11 May ceremony to lay the foundation stone of the Manantali dam on the Bafing river ...

1619 OMVS : aide américaine pour la repartition des frais du programme de barrage. Marchés Tropicaux et Méditerranéens (Paris), 37e année, no.1858, vendredi 19 juin 1981, p.1648

1620 OMVS : barrages : financement européen. Marchés Tropicaux et Méditerranéens (Paris), 38e année, no.1894, vendredi 26 février 1982, p.613

1621 OMVS : bouclage difficile du plan de financement. Marchés Tropicaux et Méditerranéens (Paris), 37e année, no.1836, vendredi 16 janvier 1981, p.133

1622 OMVS : certaines difficultés pourraient retarder le démarrage effectif des travaux. Marchés Tropicaux et Méditerranéens (Paris), 37e année, no.1860, vendredi 3 juillet 1981, p.1765

1623 OMVS : la Communauté européenne et l'aménagement du fleuve Sénégal. Marchés Tropicaux et Méditerranéens (Paris), 38e année, no.1929, vendredi 29 octobre 1982, p.2849

1624 OMVS : les conclusions de la 19e session extraordinaire (à Dakar) du Conseil des ministres. Marchés Tropicaux et Méditerranéens (Paris), 38e année, no.1925, vendredi 1 octobre 1982, p.2653

1625 OMVS : confirmation de l'aide du Fonds d'Abu Dhabi. Marchés Tropicaux et Méditerranéens (Paris), 37e année, no.1861, vendredi 10 juillet 1981, p.1822

1626 OMVS : crédit français de 4616 millions CFA pour le financement du barrage de Diama. Marchés Tropicaux et Méditerranéens (Paris), 37e année, no.1869, vendredi 4 septembre 1981, p.2272

1627 OMVS : crédit koweitien de 30 milliards CFA. Marchés Tropicaux et Méditerranéens (Paris), 38e année, no.1910, vendredi 18 juin 1982, p.1567

1628 OMVS : Diama : nouveau financement français de 600 millions CFA. Marchés Tropicaux et Méditerranéens (Paris), 38e année, no.1901, vendredi 16 avril 1982, p.1023

1629 OMVS : lancement des premiers travaux cette année. Marchés Tropicaux et Méditerranéens (Paris), 37e année, no.1847, vendredi 3 avril 1981, p.941
Numero spécial.

1630 OMVS : Manantali : aide de la BID. Marchés Tropicaux et Mediterranéens (Paris), 38e année, no.1898, vendredi 26 mars 1982, p.846

1631 OMVS : Manantali : début des travaux avant la fin du premier trimestre 1982. Marchés Tropicaux et Méditerranéens (Paris), 37e année, no.1885, vendredi 25 décembre 1981, p.3424

1632 OMVS : Manantali : pose de la première pierre le 4 mai prochain. Marchés Tropicaux et Mediterranéens (Paris), 38e année, no.1902, vendredi 23 avril 1982, p.1090

1633 OMVS : un plan directeur pour la santé. Marchés Tropicaux et Méditerranéens (Paris), 38e année, no.1909, vendredi 11 juin 1982, p.1507

1634 OMVS : prêt d'environ $ 7o millions du Fonds d'Abou Dhabi. Marchés Tropicaux et Mediterranéens (Paris), 38e année, no.1899, vendredi 2 avril 1982, p.906

1635 OMVS : réunion des chefs d'Etat et lancement des travaux du barrage de Manantali. Marchés Tropicaux et Méditerranéens (Paris), 38e année, no.1906, vendredi 21 mai 1982, p.1334

1636 OMVS : réunion du Conseil des ministres. Marchés Tropicaux et Méditerranéens (Paris), 38e année, no.1905, vendredi 14 mai 1982, p.1269

1637 OMVS : session ministérielle à Dakar. Marchés Tropicaux et Méditerranéens (Paris), 38e année, no.1924, vendredi 24 septembre 1982, p.2593

1638 OMVS : les travaux du barrage de Diama commenceront en novembre. Marchés Tropicaux et Mediterranéens (Paris), 37e année, no.1872, vendredi 25 septembre 1981, p.2437

1639 OMVS : les travaux du barrage de Diama se poursuivent selon le programme fixé. Marchés Tropicaux et Méditerranéens (Paris), 38e année, no.1926, vendredi 8 octobre 1982, p.2711

1640 OMVS works to start in autumn. AED : Africa Economic Digest (London), vol.2, no.21, May 1981, p.21

1641 PLATON, Pierre
La mise en valeur du bassin du flueve Sénégal. Marchés Tropicaux et Méditerranéens (Paris), (37), no.1849, avril 17, 1981, p.1061. Ill. Maps. Tabs.

Organisation pour la mise en valeur du fleuve Sénégal (OMVS). Evolution des conceptions. Objectifs de l'OMVS. Programme à réaliser. Fleuve Sénégal et son environnement. Couverture des financements.

1642 REICHOLD, Walter
The Senegal River : life-line of three nations : an economic geographical study of the utilization of the Senegal River and its surroundings. - München : Weltforum-Verlag, 1978. XIV,383p, 13 maps, 12 phots. (Ifo-Institut für Wirtschaftsforschung, Afrika-Studien ; 102)

Translation of: Der Senegalstrom : Lebensader dreier Nationen : eine wirtschaftsgeographische Studie des Senegals und seiner Umwelt.

VIII-3.8. Organization for the Management and Development of River Gambia Basin

1643 OMVG to admit Guinea-Bissau, AED : Africa Economic Digest (London), vol.3, no.26, 25 June 1982, p.13

OMVG Organisation pour la Mise en Valeur du fleuve Gambie

1644 OMVG : transfer à Dakar du siège de l'organisation. Marchés Tropicaux et Mediterranéens (Paris), 38e année, no.1891, vendredi 5 février 1982, p.316

1645 ROSS, C.G.
Development of the Gambia River : a planning methodology. Economic planning (Montreal), vol.18, no.2, March-April 1982, p.3-8

/Planning methods/, /development strategy/, /development plans/, /Gambia/, /Senegal/, /Guinea/ - /development projects/, /scenarios/, /obstacles to development/, /agricultural sector/, /livestock/, /water management/.

VIII-3.9. Organization for the Management and Development of the Kagera River Basin

1646 GENERAL background information on the planning for the development of the Kagera River Basin / prepared by the Secretariat of the Kagera Basin Organization. - /Kigali, Rwanda/ : Organization for the Management and Development of the Kagera River Basin, 1979. 41 leaves

OKB Organisation for the Management and Development of the Kagera River Basin

1647 UNCTAD. TDB. Committee on Economic Co-operation among developing Countries Economic co-operation and integration among developing countries : a review of recent development in subregional, regional and interregional organizations and arrangement : report by the UNCTAD secretariat. - Genève : UNCTAD, 1982-.-vols

Vol.1 : Latin America. 1982. X,110p. (TD/B/C.7/51)
Vol.2 : Africa. 1982. XI,108p. (TD/B/C.7/51)

VIII-4. ASIA

VIII-4.1. General

1648 ALIM, Abdul
Agriculture in East Asia : requisites, technology, and integration for ESCAP region. 1st ed. - Dacca, Moona Alim : Oriental Book Service, 1977. XX,170p.

1649 COOPERATION for development in South Asia : a programme of sub-regional collective self-reliance / by Marga Institute, Colombo. IFDA Dossier (Nyon, Suisse), no.18, July/Aug., 1980, p.45-58

1650 NUGENT, Jeffrey B.
Toward a feasible path to economic cooperation and integration in Western Asia. - Los Angeles, Ca. : University of Southern California, 1981. 177p.
(Economics working paper ; 81-020)
Bibliography: p.169-177

1651 PROBLEMS surrounding Pacific Basin cooperation. Asia Pacific Community (Tokyo), no.9, summer 1980, /41p./

VIII-4.2. Association of South-East Asian Nations—ASEAN

1652 AMJAD, R.
Development of labour intensive industry in ASEAN countries. - Bangkok : Asian Employment Programme, ILO, 1981. 337p.
ISBN: 92 2 102751 1

/Industrial development/, /employment creation/, /small-scale industry/, /Philippines/, /Indonesia/, /Singapore/, /Thailand/, /Malaysia/ - /industrial policy/, /development strategy/, /labour intensity/, /industrial economics/, /industrial statistics/, /list of participants/.

1653 ANIN, F.
ASEAN pod pricelom japonskoj diplomatii. Meždunarodnaja žizn' (Moskva), no.2, 1982, p.45-50

ASEAN Association for Southeast Asian Nations

1654 ANNUAL report of the ASEAN Standing Committee : 1980/1981- . - Jakarta : ASEAN Secretariat, 1981- (ASEAN documentation series).
Annual.

1655 ARIFF, Mohamed
The development of the ASEAN industrial projects (AIP's). - Wien : UNIDO, 1982. 78p. (Studies on regional co-operation in the field of industry) (UNIDO/IS.281)

/UNIDO publ./ Study on /ASEAN/ /industrial project/s (AIPs) (references : / regional cooperation/) covers (1) concept and potential for AIPs (2) /trade/ and /industrialization policy/s of /member states/ /Indonesia/, /Malaysia/, /Philippines/, /Singapore/ and /Thailand/ ; /trend/s in ASEAN manufactures (3) the ASEAN /institutional framework/ and mechanisms for AIPs ; project experience concerning /urea/, rock /salt/, /fertilizer/, /diesel engines/, /tyres/, /machine tools/, /newsprint/, /tin plate/s, colour TV /electronic tubes/, /potash/ and /fishery/, (4) problems and prospects. Additional references; /manufacturing/, /market/.

1656 ARIFF, Mohamed
Malaysia and ASEAN economic co-operation. - Singapore : Institute of Southeast Asian Studies, 1980. 177p. (Current issues / Institute of Southeast Asian Studies. ASEAN Economic Research Unit ; 9)

/Economic co-operation/, /foreign trade/, /industrial development/, /Malaysia/, /ASEAN/ - /balance of trade/, /protectionism/, /trade negotiations/, /trade relations/, /industrial projects/, /regional co-operation/, /economic indicators/, /industrial statistics/, /statistical tables/, references.

1657 ARIFIN, M.A.
ASEAN environment bibliography. - Serdang : Perpustakaan, Universiti Pertanian Malaysia, 1981. 41p.

/Bibliography / environment / environmental management / energy / health / ASEAN 1970-1980.

1658 ASEAN at a glance. Far Eastern Economic Review (Hongkong), vol.117, no.33, August 13, 1982, p.70

1659 ASEAN chemical club proposes tariff cut and industrial joint venture. Business Asia. Weekly report to managers of Asia (Hongkong), (36), 3.9.1982, p.285

1660 ASEAN co-operation in the field of industry : a background study on past and present activities / prepared by the Regional and Country Studies Branch Division for industrial studies. - Wien : UNIDO, 1981. 58p. Tabs. Diagr. (UNIDO/IS.204)

/UNIDO publ./ /Report/ on /regional cooperation/ for /industrial development/ among /ASEAN/ member states (/Indonesia/, /Malaysia/, /Philippines/, /Singapore/, /Thailand/) - covers (1) economic characteristics of the ASEAN countries (2) establishment of ASEAN and organizational structure (3) activities in the /industrial sector/ ; /regional project/s (4) cooperation/ in /trade/ and industrial /financing/ (5) /economic relations/ with other groups of countries (6) technical assistance/ and cooperation. Annexes text of ASEAN declarations and a /bibliography/.

1661 ASEAN cooperation with Third Countries and International Organizations. ASEAN Newsletter (Jakarta), vol.2, no.2, July 1981, p.5

1662 ASEAN documentation series. - 1980- . - Jakarta : ASEAN Secretariat, 1980- Irregular.

1663 ASEAN '82. Far Eastern Economic Review. Focus (Hongkong), vol.117, no.33, August 13, 1982, p.39-86

1664 ASEAN food process seeks tariff barriers. Business Asia (Hongkong), (23), 4.6.1982, p.184

1665 ASEAN heute - Ihr Partner von morgen : Vorträge der Internationalen Wirtschaftsplanung, 28-30 September 1981 = ASEAN today - your partner of tomorrow : proceedings of the International Business Conference, 28-30 September 1981.- Rüschlikon/Zürich : Gottlieb Duttweiler Institut, 1981

1666 ASEAN, Hong Kong, South Korea and Taiwan economies : their structure and outlook into the 1980s. - London : Economist Intelligence Unit, 1980. 422p.

/Economic conditions/, /primary sector/, /industrial sector/, /service industry/, /Indonesia/, /Malaysia/, /Philippines/, /Singapore/, /Thailand/, /Hong Kong/, /Korea R./, /Taiwan/ - government/, /employment/, /national accounts/, /economic planning/, /economic development/, /trends/, /agricultural production/, /energy resources/, /mining/, /industrial production/, /public finance/, /foreign trade/, /export earnings/, /imports/, /exports/, /balance of payments/, /tourism/, /foreign investments/, /transport/, /ASEAN/, /economic indicators/.

1667 ASEAN in a changing Pacific and world economy / Ross Garnaut editor. - Canberra ; Miami, Fla. : Australian National University Press, 1980. XXIII,557p.

Papers and proceedings of the Tenth Pacific Trade and Development Conference, held at the Australian National University in Canberra in March 1979.
Bibliography: p.537-547. Tabs.
ISBN: 0 7081 1302 8

1668 ASEAN investments in the 80's. Philippine Industry & Investment, 4 th q. 1980, p.1

1669 ASEAN marks 15th year. Trade, Industry and Investments Development Digest (Makati, Metro Manila), vol.2, no.8, August 1982, p.11

1670 ASEAN Ministerial Meeting. - Jakarta : ASEAN Secretariat, /1968/- . (ASEAN documentation series).
Annual. - Description based on: 12th (1979).

1671 ASEAN projects face high hurdles but move slowly ahead. Business Asia (Hong Kong), vol.13, no.16, 1981, April 17, p.123

1672 The ASEAN report / prepared and written by Thomas W. Allen of the Implementation and Management Group ; edited by Barry Wain. - Hong Kong : The Asian Wall Street Journal, cop. 1979. 2 vols.
ISBN: 962 7022 01 2

1 : A comparative assessment of the ASEAN countries. 225p. tabs. map.
2 : The evolution and programs of ASEAN. 167p. tabs. map.

1673 ASEAN um engere Kooperation bemüht : Spezialisierung im Reedereiwesen empfohlen. Nachrichten für Aussenhandel (Köln), 43, no.249, Dez. 29, 1980, p.1

Rolle der FASA (Federation of ASEAN Shipowners' Association) und der RIASEAN (Rubber Industries Association of South East Asian Nations) in der Regionalkooperation der ASEAN. Energieprojekte Colombo-Plan-Staaten.

1674 ASEAN-U.S. BUSINESS COUNCIL, Washington, D.C.
Guide to U.S. generalized system of preferences for ASEAN exporters / prepared by ASEAN-U.S. Business Council. - Washington, D.C. : Chamber of Commerce of the United States, 1981. 55p.

1675 The ASEAN year in review. ASEAN Newsletter (Jakarta), vol.2, no.2, July 1981, p.2

1676 ASEAN'S debate : strength within or ties without. Far Eastern Economic Review (Hong Kong), vol.118, no.50, December 10, 1982, p.70-72

1677 ASEAN'S motto is very simple : every man for himself. Far Eastern Economic Review (Hong Kong), vol.113, no.32, 1981, July 31, p.47

1678 ASHER, Mukul G.
Revenue systems of ASEAN countries. - Singapore : University Press, /1980/. 66p. Ill.

1679 ASHER, Mukul G.
Structural features of sales taxes in ASEAN countries. Bulletin for International Fiscal Documentation (Amsterdam), vol.35, no.5, May, 1981, p.207. Ref. Tabs.

Structure and role of sales taxes of the ASEAN-countries. Methods of avoiding multiple taxation. Valuation problem. Coverage and exemption structure. Treatment of domestic-, imported-, and exported goods. Rate differentiations.

1680 AUSTRALIA-ASEAN INDUSTRIAL COOPERATION CONFERENCE, 1978, Melbourne
Report of the Australia-ASEAN Industrial Co-operation Conference, Melbourne, Australia, June 1978 / sponsored by the Australian Government. - Canberra : Australian Government Pub. Service, 1978. 158p. Maps.
ISBN: 0 642 01525 2

1681 AUSTRALIA and ASEAN : report from the Senate Standing Committee on Foreign Affairs and Defence. - Canberra : Australian Govt. Pub. Service, 1980. 82p. Map. (Parliamentary paper / The Parliament of the Commonwealth of Australia ; 270/1980). ISBN: 0 642 05706 0

1682 AUTOMOTIVE scheme sets course for ASEAN integration. Business Asia (Hong Kong), vol.13, no.40, 1981, Oct. 2, p.313

1683 AWANOHARA, Susumu
ASEAN '82 : we manufacture more new ideas than things. Far Eastern Economic Review (Hong Kong), vol.117, no.33, August 13, 1982, p.46

1684 AWANOHARA, Susumu
ASEAN's push into petrochemicals. Far Eastern Economic Review (Hong Kong), vol.111, no.6, Jan. 30, 1981, p.40. Fig. Ill.

By oil and natural gas resources, Asean a petrochemical power in the 1980's. Investment climate. World demand, since 1960. Capacity. Petrochemical products. Projects. Figures 1960-90.

1685 AWANOHARA, Susumu
Finance for Asean - at last : after several years of talks, a finance group will be formed to promote regional industrial cooperation. Far Eastern Economic Review (Hong Kong), vol.111, no.6, 1981, Jan.30, p.46

1686 AWANOHARA, Susumu
The Five take up the chase. Far Eastern Economic Review (Hong Kong), vol.113, no.37, 1981, Sept. 4, p.56

1687 AWAHONARA, Susumu
Suzuki : give some, get some. Far Eastern Economic Review (Hong Kong), vol.111, no.4, 1981, Jan. 16, p.48

As the Japanese prime minister begins his Asean tour, he finds his hosts unwilling to make too many guarantees.

1688 BEDLINGTON, Stanley S.
Laos in 1980 : the portents are ominous. Asian Survey (Berkeley, Ca.), vol.21, no.1, 1981, Jan., p.102-111

1689 BHATTACHARYA, S.S.
India and the ASEAN. Strategic Analysis (New Delhi), 5(8), November 1981, p.368-372

With some emphasis on the Kampuchea.

1690 BIN AWANG, I. HUONG KHE LEE, J. et al.
L'Asie du Sud-Est en 1981 : bilan et perspectives. Sudestasie. Magazin d'Information (Paris), no.8/9, jan./fév., 1981, p.35. Ill. Maps. Portrs. Tabs.

Le développement économique et politique de Birmanie, Indonésie, Kampuchea, Laos, Malaysia, Philippines, Singapour, Thailande, Vietnam. Consommation d'énergie. Rôle d'ASEAN et ASPAC. Histoire. Aide internationale. Climat politique. Climat d'investissement. Plans économiques. Chiffres 1958-84.

1691 BOOTH, Anne
The economic impact of export taxes in ASEAN. The Malayan Economic Review (Singapore), 25(1), April, 1980, p.36-61

1692 BOWRING, Philip
ASEAN'S dark horse : on a medium-term view Thailand is the one to watch. Far Eastern Economic Review (Hong Kong), vol.118, no.43, October 22, 1982, p.85-90. Ill.

1693 BRUCH, Mathias
Lohnsatzdifferenzen zwischen grossen und kleinen Industriebetrieben : eine Untersuchung für die ASEAN-Länder. - Kiel : Institut für Weltwirtschaft an der Universität Kiel, 1982. 55p. (Arbeitspapier ; 137)

1694 BRUCH, Mathias
Zur Finanzierung kleiner Industriebetriebe in den ASEAN-Ländern. - Kiel : Institut für Weltwirtschaft an der Universität Kiel, 1982. 70p. (Arbeitspapier ; 138)

1695 BURNS, Brigid
The Association of South East Asian Nations (ASEAN). In: Intégrations régionales entre pays en voie de développement. - Bruges : De Tempel, 1982. p.1-52
Bibliography: p.50-72

1696 A CALL for greater cooperation. Trade, Industry and Investments (Makati, Manila), vol.2, no.5, May 1982, p.3

Key-note address of President Ferdinand E. Marcos before the 13th Meeting of the ASEAN Economic Ministers, Philippines, International Convention Center, 20 May 1982.

1697 CHANDA, Nayan RICHARDSON, Michael
First round to Asean : the UN conference highlights differences between the Five and China as Son Sann and Sihanouk delegates attend the talks. Far Eastern Economic Review (Hong Kong), vol.113, no.30, 1981, July 17, p.13

1698 CHANDA, Nayan
Hanoi tightens up : sensing a weakening of Asean's stand, Vietnam hardens its own approach, apparently hoping to win more concession. Far Eastern Economic Review (Hong Kong), vol.112, no.17, 1981, Apr. 17, p.12

1699 CHIA SIOW YUE
ASEAN economic co-operation : ASEAN Economic Research Unit Workshop Proceedings. - Singapore : Institute of Southeast Asian Studies, ASEAN Economic Research Unit, 1980. IV,164p. Includes bibliographical references. Proceedings of International and Regional Conferences
ISBN: 9971 902 060

/Economic co-operation/, /ASEAN/, /South East Asia/ - /economic integration/, /international trade/, /trade agreements/, /regional co-operation/, /political aspects/, /commodities/, /commodity agreements/, /export earnings/, /food production/, /food supply/, /energy consumption/, /power demand/, /energy resources/, /foreign investments/, /list of participants/.

1700 CHIA SIOW YUE
Do Australia and New Zealand to be polite to Southeast Asia? Asean Business Quarterly (Singapore), vol.4, no.4, 4e kw., 1980, p.7. Graphs. Ill.

Comparison of ASEAN and Australian-New Zealand economies, economic relations and major issues. Foreign trade. Investment climate. Commodity trade. World commodity trends. Development aid. Trade balance. ICAP-issue. ASEAN industrialisation. Australian restructuring. Figures 1980-'82.

1701 CHIN KIN WAH
A new assertiveness in Malaysian foreign policy. Southeast Asian Affairs, 1982, p.273-282

1702 CHOUDHURY, G.W.
ASEAN and the Communist world. Asia Pacific Community (Tokyo), no.13, summer 1981, p.34-49

1703 CONFERENCE OF THE ASEAN ECONOMIC ASSOCIATIONS, 3rd, 1978
Papers / Conference of the ASEAN Economic Associations, 3rd, Nov.2, 1978. - /S.l. : s.n./, 1978. 1 vol. (unpaged)

/IDRC supported/, /ASEAN/, /New International Economic Order/, /economic cooperation/ - /foreign investments/, /technology transfer/, /commodity market/, /informational sector/, /programme planning/, /industrial planning/, /trade liberalization/, /sea transport/, /conference report/.

1704 COUNTRIES and firms lose interest in ASEAN. Business Asia (Hong Kong), (29), 2.8.1982, p.215

1705 CRONE, Donald
Emerging trends in the control of foreign investments in ASEAN. Asian Survey (Berkeley, Calif.), vol.21, no.4, April 1981, p.417-436

1706 DANUSAPUTRO, Munadiat St.
Toward regional arrangement on legal development : an ASEAN perspective with extended reference to environmental law. - Jakarta : Badan Pembinaan Hukum Nasional, Departemen Kehakiman Bandung, 1978 (distributed by Litera). vi,257p. 1 leaf of plates. Ill.

Subjects: Association of South East Asian Nations / law -- Asia, Southeastern.

1707 DAS, K.
Threat? What threat? : Mahathir causes a diplomatic stir by implying that Vietnam is not the biggest danger to Asean. Far Eastern Economic Review (Hong Kong), vol.113, no.35, 1981, Aug. 21, p.11

1708 The DEVELOPMENT of labour intensive industry in ASEAN countries / edited by Rashid Amjad. - Bangkok : Asian Employment Programme, ILO-ARTEP, 1981. 337p.
Includes bibliographical references and index.
ISBN: 92 2 102751 1

1709 DIAMOND, J.
Reserve pooling as a development strategy : the potential for ASEAN. - Cambridge, Mass. : Harvard University, Harvard Institute for International Development, 1979. 36p. (Development discussion paper / Harvard University, Harvard Institute for International Development ; 80)

/Regional development/, /foreign exchange reserve/, /ASEAN/ - /industrial integration/, /economy of scale/

1710 DODSWORTH, J.R. DIAMOND, J.
Monetary co-operation as a source of development finance : the ASEAN case. Journal of Development Economics (Amsterdam), 7(3), Sept., 1980, p.409-425
Includes bibliographical references.

1711 DONGES, Juergen B.
Die konjunkturelle Weltlage und ihre Auswirkungen auf den deutschen Export (insbesondere nach Italien, Saudi-Arabien und in die ASEAN-Staaten), p.23. In: Bericht über die Exportkonferenz 1982. Veranstaltet vom RKW, Eschborn und Düsseldorf, und dem Wirtschaftsmagazin "Impulse", Köln, am 10. und 11.5.1982 auf der Godesburg. Eschborn 1982.

1712 DRUMMOND, Stuart
Fifteen years of ASEAN. Journal of Common Market Studies (Oxford), vol.20, no.4, June 1982, p.301-319

1713 ECONOMIC co-operation in ASEAN outlined. Overseas Trading (Canberra), vol.33, no.21, Oct. 23, 1981, p.672, Ill. Tabs.

Stimulation measures for intra-ASEAN-trade. Possible trade implications. Preferential trading arrangements. Industrial co-operation. Role "ASEAN Industrial Projects". Basic agreement. Opportunities. Figures, 1977.

1714 EXCERPTS of messages on the occasion of the inauguration of the New Secretariat building. Jakarta, May 9, 1981. ASEAN Newsletter (Jakarta), vol.1, no.9, May 1981, p.2

1715 FALLON, Padraic
The ascetic of Lee Kuan Yew. Euromoney (London), July 1978, nos.16, 18, 21, 25, 27

In an interview the Prime Minister of Singapore discusses his economic policies, the prospects for ASEAN, international banking in Asia and the political situation in Southeast Asia.

1716 FIFIELD, Russell Hunt
ASEAN and the Pacific Community. Asia Pacific Community. Asian Club (Tokyo), no.11, 1981, p.14-22

Discusses what the concept of a Pacific Community is and examines how the Association of South Asian Nations can fit into a larger scheme of economic integration.

1717 FIFIELD, Russell Hunt
ASEAN, the perils of viability. Contemporary Southeast Asia (Singapore), 2(3), December 1980, p.199-212

1718 FIFIELD, Russell Hunt
National and regional interests in ASEAN : competition and co-operation in international politics. - Singapore : ISEAS, 1979. 83p. (Occasional paper series ; 57)

The major issue in the future of ASEAN centres around national versus regional interests. Against a background of the revolution of ASEAN, the national interests of the five partners are identified and their regional interests, as reflected in the Association, are considered. The prospects for ASEAN over its second decade are analysed in terms of competition and co-operation in regional and international politics. Considerable attention in the study is given to the "Indochinese Connection".

1719 The FIVE are growing faster than Japan. Far Eastern Economic Review (Hong Kong), vol.116, no.24, June 11, 1982, p.76-80

1720 FOERDERUNG der Produktion von Kfz-Vergasern in Thailand und im ASEAN-Raum. Nachrichten für Aussenhandel (Köln), (44), no.99, Mai 25, 1981, p.1

Kooperationsmöglichkeit für eine Investition zur Herstellung von Kfz-Vergasern. Vorteile und Einzelheiten. Uebrige Projekte der Ergänzungsproduktgruppen von Kfz-Teilen im ASEAN-Raum.

1721 FOUNDATIONS of ASEAN economic growth. Asia Research Bulletin. Monthly economic reports with political suppl. (Singapore), (11), no.4, Sept. 1981, p.842(1) Graphs. Tabs.

Economic development. Commodity prices. Agricultural production. ASEAN-growth rates comparisons with leading countries. Developments in Indonesia, Malaysia. Foreign trade. Figures, 1959-79.

1722 FUKUDA, Takeo
"Heart to heart understanding is necessary in regional cooperation". ASEAN Newsletter (Jakarta), vol.2, no.4, September 1981, p.8

1723 The GENERAL products directory of Singapore 1982 / publ. by Lee J. - Singapore : Singapore General Trade Directories, 1982. /348p./. Ill. Tabs.

Singapore overseas missions. Government bodies. Economic strategy and performance (geography, people, strategies, policies, economics, Asean co-operation (GSP). Classified directory of products with manufactures (name, address, telephone, telex, nature of business). Banking and finance. Insurance. Shipping agencies/ companies. Freight forwarders.

1724 GETTING ASEAN into top gear. Thailand Business (Bangkok), vol.4, no.5, March 1981, p.22

Contents: Merely a symbol. US pullout. Excerpts from Boonchu's speech. Political factors. Integration process.

1725 GHAZALI SHAFIE, Tan M.
ASEAN, contributor to stability and development. The Fletcher Forum (Medford, Mass.), 6(2), summer, 1982, p.355-373

1726 GLENN, John
ASEAN and the United States : partners for progress and security. Indonesian Quarterly (Jakarta), 8(4), October 1980, p.21-27

1727 HAVRYLYSHYN, Oli
From cooperation to liberalisation. Far Eastern Economic Review (Hong Kong), vol.118, no.52, December 24, 1982, p.36-37

1728 HERRES, Franz R.
ASEAN : Ein Weg aus der Unterentwicklung? Grenzen und Möglichkeiten regionaler wirtschaftlicher Zusammenarbeit. - München : Simon & Magiera, 1981. 160p.
Bibliography
ISBN: 3 88676 004 3

1729 HORI-ANDROUAIS, Anne
Les investissements japonais dans les pays de l'A.S.E.A.N. : stratégie des firmes multinationales japonaises en Asie du sud-est. - Paris : Presses Universitaires de France, 1979. 288p. (Bulletin de la Maison franco-japonaise. Nouvelle série ; t.10, 2)
Bibliography: p.285-288

1730 INDONESIA 1981 : an official handbook. - Jakarta : Department of Information, 1982. 277p., ill., map.

1731 INDONESIAN Foreign Affairs (Jakarta), vol.1, no.2, 1981, p.3-48

Contents: Future prospects of Asean / Ali Moertopo. Documents: ASEAN Peace Plan I: A zone of peace, freedom and neutrality / Sumaryo Suryokusumo. Inauguration of the ASEAN Secretariat: Statement of General Carlos P. Romulo, as chairman of the ASEAN Standing Committee at the conclusion of the informal meeting of the ASEAN Foreign Ministers, Jakarta, 8 May 1981. Opening Address by the President of the Republic of Indonesia. Statement of the Minister for Foreign Affairs of the Republic of Indonesia. Speech by the Foreign Minister of the Republic of the Philippines. Statement of the ASEAN Secretary General.

Eleventh Meeting of the ASEAN Economic Ministers: Opening address by the President of the Republic of Indonesia. Joint press statement.

Fourteenth Annual ASEAN Ministerial Meeting: Press release by the General Chairman of the ASEAN Standing Committee, Manila, 15 June 1981. Opening Statement by the Minister for Foreign Affairs of the Republic of Indonesia. Closing Statement by the Minister for Foreign Affairs of the Republic of Indonesia. Joint communiqué.

1732 INVESTMENT incentive laws of ASEAN countries / compiled and edited by Zenaida S. Reyes. - Quezon City : U.P. Law Center, 1978, vi,177p.

Subjects: Association of South East Asian Nations / investments -- law and legislation -- Asia, Southeastern

1733 JACOB, Eleanore BERND, Wolf
Länder der ASEAN : Ergebnisse der kapitalistischen Industrieentwicklung im Einflussbereich des Auslandskapitals. Wirtschaftswissenschaft (Berlin), 28(8), August 1980, p.966-978

1734 JENKINS, David
The singer, not the song : Asean leaders seem satisfied with Suzuki's recent trip though they are still wary on some fronts. Far Eastern Economic Review (Hong Kong), vol.111, no.7, 1981, Feb. 6, p.26

1735 JENKINS, David
You can't fool us, says Asean : Vietnam's initiative on Kampuchea fails to impress Asean leaders who still want a solution through the UN resolution. Far Eastern Economic Review (Hong Kong), vol.111, no.8, 1981, Feb. 13, p.8

1736 JOHNSON, Oakley
U.S. business looks at ASEAN. Asia Pacific Community (Tokyo), no.12, spring 1981, p.34-41

1737 KANAPATHY, V.
Development strategies in ASEAN. UMBC Economic Review (Kuala Lumpur), vol.6, no.2, 1980

1738 KARUNARATNE, Neil Dias
Growth euphoria, academia and the development paradigm. Third World Quarterly (London), vol.4, no.2, April 1982, p.268-289

Concerns ASEAN

1739 KATANO, Hikoji
Japanese enterprises in ASEAN countries : statistical outlook. - Kobe, Japan : Kobe University, Research Institute for Economics and Business Administration, /1981/. II,371p. (Kobe economic and business research series ; 8)

1740 KONINCK, Rodolphe de   COMTOIS, Claude
L'accélération de l'intégration du commerce extérieur des pays de l'ASEAN au marché mondial. Etudes Internationales (Laval-Quebec, Can.), vol.11, no.1, mars 1980, p.46-63
ISSN 0014 2123

Postule que le faible degré d'intégration économique interne des pays de l'ASEAN est précisement le résultat de l'accroissement de l'intégration externe au marché mondial. Examine, dans ce contexte, l'évolution quantitative et qualitative du commerce extérieur de ces pays de l'Asie du Sud-Est et insistant sur le rôle crucial de Singapour.

1741 KOREAN-ASEAN ties mean boost to investment and trade. Business Asia (Hong Kong), vol.13, no.25, 1981, June 19, p.194

1742 KROEF, Justus M. van der
Afghanistan and the Middle East : new dimensions of ASEAN security. Contemporary Southeast Asia (Singapore), vol.2, no.4, March 1981, p.295-307

1743 KROEF, Justus M. van der
Asean, Hanoi, and the Kampuchean conflict : between "Kuantan" and "third alternative". Asian Survey (Berkeley, Ca.), vol.21, no.5, 1981, May, p.515-535

1744 KUWAHARA Yasuo HARADA TERUO MIZUNO YOSHIHIRO
Employment effects of foreign direct investments in ASEAN countries. - Genève : ILO, 1979, 118p. Tab. (Multinational enterprises programme. Research on employment effects of multinational enterprises) (Working paper ; 6)
Bibliography: p.115-118
ISBN: 92 2 102270 6

/Foreign investments/, /employment/, /Indonesia/, /Malaysia/, /Philippines/, /Singapore/, /Thailand/ - /wages/, /industrialization/, /statistical data/, /Bibliography/.

1745 KUZ'MICHEV, Ju.
ASEAN v farvatere čuždoj politiki. Novoe Vremja (Moskva), no.29, 1982, p.10-11

1746 LANGHAMMER, Rolf J.
ASEAN manufactured exports in the EC markets : an empirical assessment of common and national tariff and non-tariff barriers confronting them. p.125-/193/
In: Proceedings of a Conference on ASEAN-EEC Economic Relations / edited by Narongchai Akrasanee and Hans Christoph Rieger. - /S.l./ : ISEAS, Institute of Southeast Asian Studies, /198-/. - (Proceedings of international and regional conferences / ASEAN Economic Research Unit)

1747 LANGHAMMER, Rolf J.
Nationaler Protektionismus im Rahmen der EG-Handelspolitik, dargestellt am Beispiel der Industriegüterimporte aus ASEAN-Ländern. Weltwirtschaft (Tübingen), no.1, 1981, p.74. Tabs. Ref.

EG Staaten werden identifiziert, die mit nationalen Importquoten beziehungsweise Länderquoten überdurchschnittlich stark ausländische Konkurrenten an Marktzugang hindern. Auswirkungen für die Asean-Staaten. EG Importe aus Asean-Ländern im Rahmen der Zollpräferenzen 1978. Ursachen protektionistischer Alleingänge innerhalb der Gemeinschaft. Beschäftigungseffekte. Implikationen für die Zukunft der gemeinsamen Handelspolitik.

1748 LASSERRE, Philippa BOISOT, Max
The transfer of technology from European to ASEAN enterprises : strategies and practices in the chemical and pharmaceutical sectors. Fontainebleau : INSEAD, 1980. 109,VIp.
Bibliography: V-VI

At head of the title: Euro-Asia Centre

1749 LAU TEIK SOON
ASEAN and the Cambodian problem. Asian Survey (Berkeley, Ca.), vol.22, no.6, June 1982, p.548-560

Contents: ASEAN's main objectives. The threat to Thailand's security. Indochina's response. Toward a United front in Cambodia. The role of the major powers.

1750 LAURIAT, G.
Refining in ASEAN. Insight. Asia's business monthly (Hong Kong), June 1981, p.12, Ill. Tabs.

Developments of ASEAN refineries. Singapore as important refining centre. Prospects. Middlemen to Singapore. Developments and refining capacity of ASEAN countries.

1751 LEE BOON HIOK
Constraints on Singapore's foreign policy. Asian Survey (Berkeley, Ca.), vol.22, no.6, June 1982, p.524-535

Contents: Size, level of development, and foreign policy. Conclusion. Notes.

1752 LEE POH PING
The Indochinese situation and the big powers in Southeast Asia : the Malaysian view. Asian Survey (Berkeley, Ca.), vol.22, no.6, June 1982, p.516-523

1753 LEWIS, John
A sleeping giant emerges : Japanese officials see the prime minister's Asean trip as evidence of the country's active new role in world affairs. Far Eastern Economic Review (Hong Kong), vol.111, no.7, 1981, Feb. 6, p.26

1754 LIM CHONG YAH
Brunei : what changes will independence bring? Asean Business Quarterly (Singapore), 4, no.4, 4e kw., 1980, p.25. Ill. Maps. Tabs.

Monarchy and British protectorate. Independence at 1.1.1984. Political climate. Participation problems in ASEAN and ASEAN-projects. Oil wealth. External policy-role Shell. Third Five-Year Plan (1975-79). Economic indicators. Figures 1974-84.

1755 LIM PENG CHEE
Big problems for small-scale industries. ASEAN Business Quarterly (Singapore), (4), no.4, 4e kw., 1980, p.43. Ill. Ref.

Developing small business sector in ASEAN countries. Different definitions of small industries. Role of small industries in ASEAN-economies. Investment incentives advantages for larger industries. Tax structure. Access to credit. Role of commercial banks. Figures, 1958-80.

1756 LIM, Robyn
Perceptions of ASEAN in Australia. - Brisbane : Griffith University, School of Modern Asian Studies, Centre for the Study of Australian-Asian Relations. 1981. 31,Vp. (CSAAR Research Paper ; 12)
ISBN: 0 86857

1757 LUBIS, Mochtar
ASEAN : van droom tot werklijkheid? Internationale Spectator ('s-Gravenhage), 34(12), December 1980, p.747-752

1758 LUGOVSKOJ, Ju.
Kto nagnetaet naprjažennost' v Jugo-Vostočnoj Azii. Meždunarodnaja žizn' (Moskva), 2, 1981, p.99-105

Concerns ASEAN and political situation in South East Asia.

1759 MACBETH, John
The dangerous option : Vietnam could strike again at the KNPLF if Asean and others decide to increase military aid to Son Sann. Far Eastern Economic Review (Hong Kong), vol.116, no.23, June 4, 1982, p.10

1760 MAJOR issues confronting ASEAN countries in the New Year : part 2. Business Asia (Hong Kong), vol.13, no.2, 1981, Jan. 9, p.10

1761 MAJOR issues for ASEAN : firms to track in the New Year. Business Asia (Hong Kong), vol.13, no.1, 1981, Jan. 2, p.7

1762 MEHTA, Pradeep Kumar SARMA, Atul
Role of foreign capital in ASEAN countries. Economic and Political Weekly (Bombay) vol.15, no.51, 20 December 1980, p.2152-2156
Includes bibliographical references.

1763 MENG, L.Y.
On the wings of ASEAN solidarity. ASEAN Business Quarterly (Singapore), (5), no.2, 2nd quarter, 1981, p.11. Ill.

ASEAN bankers' meeting resulting in "ASEAN Financial Corporation" (ACF). Basic formula. Economic potential. Intra-ASEAN investments. Help of ASEAN-banks.

1764 MIR v Azii : obščaja zabota stran kontinenta. Problemy Dal'nego Vostoka (Moskva), 4, 1981, p.3-17

Concerns ASEAN and NATO

1765 MOGGIE, Datuk Leo
Prospects in ASEAN's energy efforts. ASEAN Newsletter (Jakarta), vol.2, no.4, September 1981, p.6

1766 MORGAN, Joseph
ASEAN navies : new missions and old problems. Marine policy (Guildford, U.K.), 6(3), July 1982, p.236-237

1767 NEWTON, Donald C.
Co-operation in import procurement among selected Asian developing countries / UNCTAD, UNDP, ESCAP. - /S.l. : s.n/. III,/88/ leaves. Tabs.
(Asian Trade Expansion Programme ; Project RAS 71/722)

1768 NICHOLAS, Rhondda M.
ASEAN and the Pacific Community debate : much ado about something? Asian Survey (Berkeley, Ca.), 21(12), December 1981, p.1197-1210
Includes bibliographical references.

1769 NIKSCH, Larry A.
Thailand in 1980 : confrontation with Vietnam and the fall of Kriangsak. Asian Survey (Berkeley, Ca.), vol.21, no.2, 1981, Feb., p.223-231

1770 NO one envies Asean's political climate. Far Eastern Economic Review (Hong Kong), vol.114, no.43, 1981, Oct. 16, p.63

1771 NON-OIL exporting developing economies. NRI Quarterly Economic Review (Tokyo), (11), no.2, Apr. 1981, p.10. Graphs. Tab.

Expected growth rates for 1981 and 1982. Terms of trade. Current accounts deficits and implications. Strong performances in Asia. Turning points in Hong Kong and Northeast Asian economies. Asian countries' outlook. Figures.

1772 NOONAN, R.
Schooling in the ASEAN region : primary and secondary education in Indonesia, Malaysia, the Philippines, Singapore and Thailand. Third World Quarterly (London), vol.3, no.3, 1981, p.565

1773 NOR, Z.A.B.M.
Some comments on the role of the banking sector in Asean countries. UMBC Economic Review (Kuala Lumpur), (18), no.1, 1982, p.62. Ref. Tabs.

Controversy regarding the positive/negative role of the financial system in economic development. Analysing the performance of the banking sector in ASEAN countries, it is shown that this sector can contribute to economic growth if non-repressive monetary policies are pursued. Statistics, 1961-81.

1774 OCAMPO, Sheilah
Asean's hunt for funds : a meeting of the group's Council on petroleum studies capital requirements and foreign investors' concerns. Far Eastern Economic Review (Hong Kong), vol.114, vol.43, 1981, Oct. 16, p.103

1775 OOI GUAT TIN
The ASEAN preferential trading arrangements (PTA) : an analysis of potential effects on Intra-ASEAN trade. - Singapore : ISEAS ASEAN Economic Research Unit, 1981. 34 leaves. Ref. (Research notes and discussion paper ; 26)
References.
List of the publication in the Series.

ISEAS Institute of Southeast Asian Studies

1776 OUHIB, Slimane
Le ventre du volcan. Afrique-Asie (Paris), no.279, du 11 octobre au 24 octobre 1982, p.38

"S'il fallait lutter contre la corruption il ne resterait plus personne" ; c'est ce qu'a déclaré un des généraux hauts responsables du régime ...

1777 PACIFIC TRADE AND DEVELOPMENT CONFERENCE, 10th, 1979
ASEAN in a changing Pacific and world economy / Ross Garnaut editor. - Canberra Miami, Fla. : Australian National University Press, 1980. xxiii,557p.

ASEAN -- congresses / Asia, Southeastern -- foreign economic relations -- congresses / Asia, Southeastern -- industries, congresses.

1778 PANGLAYKIM, Jusuf
ASEAN Finance Corporation : prospects and challenge : studies on regional cooperation in the field of industry. - Wien : UNIDO, 1982. 20p. Diagrs. (UNIDO/IS.291)

/UNIDO publ./ describing an /ASEAN/ /development bank / (reference : /regional cooperation/) - covers (1) creation and purpose of the ASEAN Finance Corporation (AFC) ; /administrative aspects/ (2) shareholders, /management/ and headquarters ; /organizational aspects/ (3) the AFC as an ASEAN vehicle for external industrial /cooperation/ ; co-operation AFC- /Japan/ (4) the AFC as a vehicle for advancing industrial /investment/ among/member states/ (5) identification of /industrial project/s and availability of /financing/ (6) process of /decision making/. Diagram.

1779 PARK, Ungsuh K.
The economic relationship between ASEAN and Korea. Asian Perspective (Seoul), 4(2), fall/winter, 1980, p.224-232

1780 PARK, Ungsuh K.
The economic relationship between ASEAN and Korea. Korea and World Affairs (Seoul), 5(1), spring 1981, p.53-60

1781 PATERNO, Vicente T.
ASEAN industrial complementation : studies on regional co-operation in the field of industry. - Wien : UNIDO, 1982. 154p. Tabs. Diagrs. (UNIDO-UNIDO/IS.282)

Study of /ASEAN/ /regional cooperation/ through complementary /industrial project/s - covers (1) need for industrial complementation in ASEAN (AIC) ; /institutional framework/ and new products and proposals for existing products (3) the potential for AIC programmes: /motor vehicle industry/, /electrical industry/ and /electronics industry/, light /machinery/, /steel/ and other /metals/, /pulp and paper industry/, /chemicals/, /glass/, /rubber/ products, /food industry/, /textile industry (4) major constraints to increased cooperation (5) general outlook and /recommendations / for future activities. /Diagrams/s.

1782 PATHAMANATHAN, Murugesu
The Pacific settlement of disputes in regional organisations : a comparative perspective of the OAS, OAU, and ASEAN. - /Kuala Lumpur/ : /s.n./, 1978. 54 leaves

Subjects: Pacific settlement of international disputes / Organization of American States / Organization of African Unity.

1783 PEYMAN, Hugh
An Asean embarrassment : Muslims from southern Thailand flee south, posing a delicate problem for Kuala Lumpur and Bangkok. Far Eastern Economic Review (Hong Kong), vol.112, no.16, 1981, April 10, p.30

1784 PROBLEMS ahead for ASEAN/Japan trade. Business Asia (Hong Kong), vol.13, no.46, 1981, Nov. 13, p.368

1785 PROCEEDINGS of a Conference on ASEAN - EEC economic relations / ed. by Narongchai Akrasanee, Hans Christoph Rieger ; ASEAN Economic Research Unit. - /S.l./ : Institute of Southeast Asian Studies, /1980/. 171p., 22 tab.
ISBN 9971 902 47 8

1786 PROCEEDINGS of the conference on the ASEAN : problems and prospects in a changing world, December 18-20, 1975, Chulalongkorn University, Bangkok, Thailand / edited by Sarasin Viraphol, Amphon Namatra, and Masahide Shibusawa. - Bangkok : The University, /1976/. x,254p.

Association of South East Asian Nations -- congresses / Asia, Southeastern - politics and government - congresses / Asia, Southeastern -- economic conditions - congresses.

1787 QUEK WAN YUE
Asean banks : how do they fare? Singapore Business (Singapore), (6), no.7, July 15, 1982, p.11. Tabs.

Overview of the financial performance of South East Asia's Asean top 12 commercial banks (country of incorporation, total assets, loans, deposits, net profits), of the 10 top foreign banks in Asean, as well as of Euro-money's ranking of Asean banks. Statistics, 1980-81.

1788 RASTALSKY, H.J.H.
Projekte : Mehr ASEAN-Kooperation in der Energiepolitik : Grossvorhaben zur Wassernutzung Sarawak. Nachrichten für Aussenhandel (Köln), 44, no.4, Jan. 7, 1981, p.1

Tagung des "Asian-African Legal Consultative Committee". Das Elektrizitätsverbundsystem anscheinend rentabel. Wasserkraftwerke in Malaysia. Oil and gas exploration in Indonesia. Technology transfer. Entwicklungschancen. Daten 1980-81.

1789 RICHER, Philippe
L'Association des Nations du Sud-Est Asiatique, 1975-1980 : éveil de la coopération économique ? Relations Internationales (Paris), no.26, été 1981, p.241-254

1790 ROMULO, Carlos P.
The progress of ASEAN : its steady growth in 14 years. ASEAN Newsletter (Jakarta), vol.1, no.7, March 1981, p.7

1791 ROSENO, Bambang
Imperialistische Rivalitäten um die ASEAN. Wirtschaftswissenschaft (Berlin), 28(8), August 1980, p.952-965
Summaries in English and Russian

1792 ROWLEY, Anthony
The unspecific Pacific : ASEAN shows signs of impatience over proposals to set up a community like EEC, while experts want more research. Far Eastern Economic Review (Hong Kong), vol.112, no.24, 1981, June 5, p.51

1793 RULES and regulations. - Tokyo : ASEAN Centre, ASEAN Promotion Centre on Trade, Investment and Tourism, 1982. 117p.
Cover title

Contents: Agreement establishing the ASEAN promotion Centre on Trade, Investment and Tourism. The plan of operation and work programme of the Asean Promotion Centre..., adopted by the Council at its Inaugural Meeting held on June 30-July 1, 1981. Rules of procedure of the Council of the ASEAN Promotion Centre ..., adopted by the Council ... 1981. Financial regulations, adopted by the Council ..., 1981. - Staff regulations and rules, adopted by the Council at its Annual Meeting held in December 11-12, 1981.

1794 SACERDOTI, Guy
ASEAN'82 : what's in it for us : not all that much. Far Eastern Economic Review (Hong Kong), vol.117, no.33, August 13, 1982, p.65

1795 SACERDOTI, Guy
A doctrine of suspicion : a Japan-Asean symposium in Jakarta airs Asean's lingering fears over Tokyo's growing defence capabilities. Far Eastern Economic Review (Hong Kong), vol.113, no.38, 1981, Sept. 11, p.36

1796 SACERDOTI, Guy
Putting a spoke in : Malaysia's car-making plans could upset ASEAN's complementation scheme and damage the industry regionwide. Far Eastern Economic Review (Hong Kong), vol.118, no.52, December 1982, p.32-34

1797 SACERDOTI, Guy
Setting the scene for Manila : while Hanoi is welcome to attend, a conference on Kampuchea should not wait, say Asean foreign ministers. Far Eastern Economic Review (Hong Kong), vol.112, no.21, 1981, May 15, p.20

1798 SACERDOTI, Guy
Silence on success : resolution of Asean's air war with Australia is unpublicized. Far Eastern Economic Review (Hong Kong), vol.112, no.25, 1981, June 12, p.94

1799 SALIM, Z.
ASEAN and the United Nations. Indonesian Quarterly (Jakarta), vol.9, no.2, 1981.

1800 SAMOJLENKO, V.V.
ASEAN : politika i ekonomika. - Moskva : Nauka, 1982. 191p.

1801 SCHWEIKART, J.A. CHOI, F.D.S. BAVISHI, V.B. et al.
International accounting. Management Accounting (New York), (63), no.2, Aug. 1981, p.15. Ports. Ref. Tabs.

Four contributions by Schweikart, Choi, Bavishi, and Berry. Plea for method of segment reporting that preserves domestic information to take the place of foreign subsidiary consolidation. Plea for international cost accounting harmonization, part. a cluster approach to bridge the gap between international standards and those of LDCs (example: ASEAN). Capital budgeting practices at multinationals.

1802 SEAH CHEE-MEOW
ASEAN and its perceptions on Western Pacific security. Asian Perspective (Seoul), vol.5, no.2, fall/winter 1981, p.170-181

1803 SELVARATHAM, V.
Malaysia in 1981 : a year of political transition. Southeast Asian Affairs, 1982, p.245-272

1804 SHENG-YI LEE
ASEAN industrial joint ventures (AIJVs) in the private sector. - Vienna : UNIDO, 21 April 1982. (Studies on regional co-operation in the field of industry). UNIDO/IS.310

1805 SHIM JAE HOON
ASEAN here we come! : more South Koreans are travelling for pleasure as the Seoul Government looses controls on overseas visits. Far Eastern Economic Review (Hong Kong), vol.114, no.44, October 1981, p.26

1806 SHIM JAE HOON
ASEAN's accolade for Chun : the South Korean leader achieves major diplomatic objectives in his tour and marvels at Singapore's blueprint for society. Far Eastern Economic Review (Hong Kong), vol.113, no.29, 1981, July 10, p.14

1807 SHIM JAE HOON
Exchanging complements :it was all give and take and tit for tat on the Indonesian leg of South Korean President Chun's Asean grand tour. Far Eastern Economic Review (Hong Kong), vol.113, no.28, 1981, July 3, p.12

1808 SHIM JAE HOON
Getting to know how : the band plays "Tea for Five" as South Korean exporters meet Asean visitors in a follow-up to Chun's tour. Far Eastern Economic Review (Hong Kong), vol.114, no.45, 1981, Oct. 30, p.52

1809 SHIM JAE HOON
Mission accomplished : South Korean president Chun's Asean tour raised his nation's diplomatic profile and strengthened regional ties. Far Eastern Economic Review (Hong Kong), vol.113, no.30, 1981, July 17, p.8

1810 SHIM JAE HOON
Self-help, Seoul style : South Korean officials show the relevance of their village movement to the Asean countryside. Far Eastern Economic Review (Hong Kong), vol.113, no.29, 1981, July 10, p.44

1811 SHIM JAE HOON
The southward drive : Chun's Asean tour marks a new era in South Korea's economic ties. Far Eastern Economic Review (Hong Kong), vol.113, no.30, 1981, July 17, p.38

1812 SILVA, Manik de
Don't call us, we'll call you : Premadasa sees economic advantages in Asean membership, but the application from Colombo embarrasses the Five. Far Eastern Economic Review (Hong Kong), vol.112, no.24, 1981, June 5, p.14

1813 SIMON, Sheldon W.
The ASEAN states and regional security. - Stanford, Cal. : Hoover Institution Press, /1982/. /175/p. Maps. Tabs.
Bibliography

1814 SIMON, Sheldon W.
Cambodia and regional diplomacy. Southeast Asian Affairs, 1982, p. 196-207

1815 SMITH, Patrick
Asean's victory roll : a new fares structure opens up the Australia-London run, allowing regional airlines to compete with Quantas and BA. Far Eastern Economic Review (Hong Kong), vol.112, no.23, 1981, May 29, p.68

1816 SMITH, Patrick
ASEAN'82 : Vietnam's claims cause most trouble. Far Eastern Economic Review (Hong Kong), vol.117, no.33, August 13, 1982, p.66

1817 SMITH, Patrick
More issues than answers : Asean ministers leave some stones unturned as they work out a united approach to world economic difficulties. Far Eastern Economic Review (Hong Kong), vol.115, no.4, January 22, 1982, p.56

1818 SOLIDUM, Estrella D.
Philippines perceptions of crucial issues affecting Southeast Asia. Asian Survey (Berkeley, Ca.), vol.22, no.6, June 1982, p.536-547

Contents: Philippines - China relations. Philippines - U.S. relations. Vietnam, Laos, Kampuchea. Kalayaan Island Group ... Pan-Pacific cooperation. Middle East. Conclusion.

1819 SRICHARATCHANYA, Paisal
Dust-up over soda ash : Indonesia's bid to build a plant similar to one long delayed in Thailand strains Asean ties. Far Eastern Economic Review (Hong Kong), vol.113, no.32, 1981, July 31, p.82

1820 SRICHARATCHANYA, Paisal
Paper over the cracks : differences are put aside as the Five discuss Cambodia. Far Eastern Economic Review (Hong Kong), vol.114, no.52, 1981, Dec. 18, p.8

1821 SRICHARATCHANYA, Paisal
Self-help in Asean : the grouping's Aluminium Industry Club looks to increased cooperation to ease difficulties. Far Eastern Economic Review (Hong Kong), vol.116, no.25, June 18, 1982, p.62

1822 SRI LANKA's trade patterns with ASEAN. Central Bank News Survey, vol.1, no.2, August 1981

1823 SUBHAN, Malcolm
ASEAN'82 : The EEC : the duty to back other groupings. Far Eastern Economic Review (Hong Kong), vol.117, no.33, August 13, 1982, p.46

1824 SUDARMADJI, Slamet
Food consumption and production patterns in ASEAN (forthcoming). - /Singapore : ISEAS, 1980/. (Research notes and discussions paper series ; 14)

1825 SUHRKE, Astri
ASEAN Association of Southeast Asian Nations : adjusting the new regional alignments. Asia Pacific Community (Tokyo), no.12, spring, 1981, p.11-33

Examines implications of the Sino-Vietnamese conflict and the expansion of Soviet and Vietnamese power for the Association of South East Asian Nations and the security of its members.
Includes bibliographical references.

1826 SULITSKAJA, T.I.
ASEAN i meždunarodnye otnošenija v Jugo-Vostočnoj Azii. Narody Azii i Afriki (Moskva), no.6, 1981, p.98-105

1827 SYCIP, David
ASEAN-Japan economic cooperation. Asia Pacific Community (Tokyo), no.13, summer 1981, p.10-15

1828 TAN, Gerald
Intra-ASEAN trade liberalisation : an empirical analysis. Journal of Common Market Studies (Oxford), vol.20, no.4, June 1982, p.320-331

1829 TANTER, Richard
The militarization of ASEAN : global context and local dynamics. Alternatives. A Journal of World Policy (New Delhi), vol.7, no.4, spring 1982, p.507-532

Contents: Introduction. Militarization in ASEAN : government and social structure. Military in economic life. Militarization of civilian institutions. Repression and human rights. Counterinsurgency. International aggression. National security ideologies. Government spending, the trade in arms. Explanations of militarization in ASEAN. Threat perceptions and the integrity of the nation-state. Structure and consequences of the arms industry. Militarization and the reproduction of social formations. Conclusion.

1830 TASKER , Rodney CHANDA, Nayan SUBHAN, Malcolm et al.
ASEAN'82 : Musyawarah gets the key of the door. Far Eastern Economic Review (Hong Kong), (117), no.33, August 13, 1982, p.39. Ill.

Historical and political background of the ASEAN group. Indochina's impact on the grouping. Importance of ASEAN for each country. Relations of ASEAN with the EEC and UN. Trade and industry of Asean countries.

1831 TASKER, Rodney
The wooing of Asean : after success in the US, Chun looks to Southeast Asia. Far Eastern Economic Review (Hong Kong), vol.112, no.27, 1981, June 26, p.28

1832 TAX sparing : another obstacle to Australian-ASEAN relations. In: Industrial development news-Asia and the Pacific. - Bangkok : UN, Economic and Social Commission for Asia and the Pacific, 1982, no.14, p.63-67. (ST/ESCAP/183)

This paper was prepared by David Flint, Senior Lecturer in Business Law, New South Wales Institute of Technology. It is reproduced in the form in which it was received and has not been edited. The views expressed are those of the author and do not necessarily reflect the views of the Secretariat of the United Nations.

1833 TEXTILE and fiber situation in the ASEAN countries. Cotton. Monthly review of the world situation (Washington, D.C.), (34), no.10, May 1981, p.9. Tabs.

Analysis of the markets for textile and fiber in the ASEAN region by country. Production and consumption trends by sector. Cotton consumption, production and imports 1970/71-1980/81 by country. Man-made fiber production 1970-1979 and production capacity 1970-1981 by country.

1834 THAMBIPILLAI, Pushpa
Brunei in ASEAN : the viable choice ? Southeast Asian Affairs, 1982, p.105-112

1835 TOBA, Reijiro
ASEAN favors Reagan's hard-line foreign policy. Asia Pacific Community (Tokyo), no.11, winter 1981, p.55-68

Examines the Reagan Administration's policy toward Southeast Asia. Discusses the role of ASEAN in Reagan's strategy in Southeast Asia. Stresses the difficulty of applying Western standards of parliamentary democracy to developing countries and suggests that security concerns should take priority over human right issues.

1836 TOUGH trade issues : slow growth of ASEAN EEC ties. Business Asia (Hong Kong), vol.13, no.42, 1981, Oct. 16, p.333

1837 TYMOWSKI, Maciej
Reconciliation and standardization of the foreign trade statistics of ASEAN member states. - Genève : UNCTAD/UNDP/ESCAP/, 1980. 1 vol., (various pagings), 27 tabs. (ECDC/48)

Project RAS/77/015 : ASEAN trade development and co-operation

1838 UNDERSTANDING ASEAN / ed. by A. Broinowski. - New York : St. Martin's Press /1982/, (15), 323p. charts, map, tabs, with bibliography

1839 UNITED STATES. International Trade Administration
A business guide to the Association of Southeast Asian Nations. - Washington : U.S. Govt. Print. Off., 1980. 58p.

Partial contents: ASEAN - what is it? Development plans and major projects. Best prospects in ASEAN. Doing business in ASEAN. Country data.

1840 US-ASEAN trade : aiming for fast growth with new ties. Business Asia (Hong Kong), vol.13, no.37, 1981, Sept. 11, p.296

1841 VIKSNINS, G.J.
Financial deepening in ASEAN countries. - Honolulu, Hawaii : Pacific Forum, 1980. 76p. (Pacific community series)
ISBN: 0 8248 0745 6

/Financial institutions/, /economic development/, /growth rate/, /money market/, /South East Asia/ - /Indonesia/, /Malaysia/, /Philippines/, /Singapore/, /Thailand/, /banks/.

1842 WANANDI, Jusuf
Conflict and cooperation in the Asia-Pacific region : an Indonesian perspective. Asian Survey (Berkeley, Ca.), vol.22, no.6, June 1982, p.503-515

Internal problems. Developments in the Asia Pacific region. Great power relations in Southeast Asia.

1843 WANANDI, Jusuf
Dimensions of Southeast Asian security. Indonesian Quarterly (Jakarta), 8(1), January, 1980, p.39-52

1844 WANG LOOK KEAH
Is ICAP viable with Quantas still in the red? ASEAN Business Quarterly (Singapore), (4), no.4, 4e qw., 1980, p.3. Ill. Map.

Australian new government policy, the ICAP "International Civil Aviation Policy". Low fare travel policy for a new market of tourists. Attitude of ASEAN-countries. Role of Quantas airlines. Kangaroo-route. ASEAN-negotiations. Figures, 1979-81.

1845 WELLS, Raymond J.G.
ASEAN commodity trade. Asia Pacific Community (Tokyo), no.13, summer 1981, p.50-67 Includes bibliographical references.

1846 WELLS, Raymond J.G.
ASEAN : how to ensure self-sufficiency in energy needs. ASEAN Business Quarterly (Singapore), (4), no.4, 4e kw., 1980, p.32. Ill.

Problems of exploration resources. Energy consumption policy. Oil production. Self-sufficiency. Energy prices. Indonesia, OPEC-member. Prices. World Bank role. Diversification energy economy. R. and D. ASEAN energy programm. Figures, 1979-80.

1847 XUTO, Somsak
How to disagree without being disagreeable : ASEAN meeting in Singapore earlier this year. Far Eastern Economic Review (Hong Kong), August 13-19, 1982, p.22

1848 YAO, R.
Canada and ASEAN : a preliminary analysis.–Toronto, Ont. : Joint Centre on Modern East Asia, 1981. 57p. (Working paper series / Joint Centre on Modern East Asia)

Presents an overview of the political and economic development of ASEAN since its formation in 1967. Discusses Canada's relations with its members in terms of trade and aid, and a number of issues which are not only prominent in Canadian-ASEAN relations, but also significant in their world-wide implications.

VIII-4.3. Pacific Basin

1849 AIMING to mate ASEAN with the Pacific Basin. Far Eastern Economic Review (Hong Kong), vol.116, no.24, June 11, 1982, p.71-74

1850 ASIA-PACIFIC in the 1980s : toward greater symmetry in economic interdependence / Center for Strategic and International Studies, Jakarta, eds. - Jakarta : CSIS, 1980.

These papers and the report, contained in a separate booklet, were the result of the CSIS conference held at Bali in January 1980. In the main, the papers are concerned with economic interdependence in the Asia-Pacific region and with suggesting better ways in which this interdependence might be managed. Discussion of the Pacific Community concept is implicit in all of the papers and explicit in quite a few. Papers by H. Edward English, Goh Chok Tong, Robert Keatley, Mahathir bin Mohamad, William V. Roth, Jr., and Lester L. Wolff. The separate report contains rapporteurs' report on each conference session.

1851 An ASIAN-Pacific regional economic organization : an exploratory concept paper / Congressional Research Service, Library of Congress, ed. Prepared for the Committee on Foreign Relations, United States Senate. - Washington : Government Printing Office, 1979, 74p.

Contents: This 74-page booklet had an important catalytic effect on debate on the Pacific Community concept. It includes a study by Peter Drysdale and Hugh Patrick, entitled "Evaluation of a Proposed Asian-Pacific Regional Economic Organization", which presents the most complete outline to date of the rationale for an intergovernmental "Organization for Pacific Trade and Development "(OPTAD). This study is summarized separately in this bibliography. There is a very brief addendum by Alfred Reifman of the Congressional Research Service expressing a sceptical view of the need for an OPTAD. Reifman points out that proposed members now participate in ESCAP and argues that a new Pacific organization could run counter to the traditional U.S. "universalist approach" to economic issues. A forward to the booklet by Senator John Glenn, then Chairman of the Asian and Pacific Subcommittee of the Senate Foreign Relations Committee, calls the Patrick/Drysdale thesis "generally persuasive" and the Reifman arguments unconvincing. The major part of the space of the booklet is taken up by several appendices providing trade and economic statistics on the region generally and on the U.S. interaction with the region and presenting descriptive summaries of existing Asian and Pacific regional organizations.

1852 AUSTIN, R.W.L.
An Australian view of the Pacific Basin. In: La Comunidad del Pacifico en perspectiva /Instituto de Estudios de la Universidad de Chile, eds. - Santiago de Chile : Editorial Universitaria, 1979. 2 vols. vol.2, p.78-88

Contents: This paper attempts to give a broad overview of Australia's interest in the Asia-Pacific region and examines progress to realize a Pacific Community organization. The author argues that since the American withdrawal from the region in 1975, Australia has had to stand alone and search for its own place in the region. At the present, its position appears at best ambivalent. The economic dynamism of the Asia-Pacific area is examined and efforts to promote a Pacific cooperative organization. The paper concludes that structural adjustments to industries in the region will be necessary and that change in the Basin is inevitable.

1853 La COMUNIDAD del Pacifico en perspectiva / Instituto de Estudios Internacionales de la Universidad de Chile, eds. - Santiago de Chile : Editorial Universitaria, 1979. 2 vols.

Contents: These two volumes consist of papers presented at a conference on the Pacific Community concept held at Easter Island, Chile, in October 1979. The main topics include historical relationships between Latin America and East Asia; political and economic relations in the Pacific; ASEAN and the Pacific Community; the Pacific island nations and the Pacific Community; the role of Japan, Canada, Australia, China, and India in a Pacific Community; and resource issues in the Pacific. Papers by R.W.L. Austin, R.G. Crocombe, Mitsuro Donowaki, Javier Illanes, Rosewati Ismail, Lau Teik Soon, Guy J. Pauker, Walter Sanchez, Dante Simbulan, and Jusuf Wanandi.

1854 CRAWFORD, John
The Pacific Basin cooperative concept. In: Pacific Economic co-operation / Crawford, Sir John and Seow, Greg., eds. - Selangor, Malaysia and Singapore : Heinemann Educational Books (Asia), 1981. p.35-40

Contents: Sir John maintains that despite the diversities existing among nations of the Pacific Basin, the complementarity of resources and trade which have contributed to interdependence necessitate the establishment of a Pacific Community organization. Bilateral approaches are insufficient to deal with these relationships and the author argues that the establishment of ASEAN itself is a recognition of this inadequacy. Sir John discusses the form such a new organization might take and focusses on the Commonwealth model and the proposed OPTAD. He rejects the former since political and security issues could too easily be imported into the agenda. OPTAD, however, is favored since it would deal with strictly economic issues. Strategic and economic issues are not so intertwined as to warrant "confusing them" in one body. Aspects of membership and leadership of the organization are discussed.

1855 DRYSDALE, Peter PATRICK, Hugh
Evaluation of a proposed Asian-Pacific regional economic organization. In: An Asian-Pacific regional economic organization : an exploratory concept paper, prepared for the Committee on Foreign Relations, United States Senate. - Washington: Government Printing Office, 1979.

Contents: This study, prepared for the U.S. Senate Foreign Relations Committee, presents the rationale for the creation of an intergovernmental "Organization for Pacific Trade and Development" (OPTAD) from the standpoint of the authors' perceptions of U.S. national interests. The study describes the growth of economic interdependence in the Pacific region and its implications for the United States. It argues that the U.S. has a "major interest in preserving a leadership role in commitment to a liberal international economic order which promotes relatively free, multilateral flows of goods, services, and capital" on a global and a Pacific regional basis. Existing global trade institutions are regarded as increasingly directed toward protection of the existing economic order, and a new Pacific organization is deemed attractive to deal with problems inherent in the dynamic growth of the Pacific region, particularly problems of structural adjustment. The history of the OPTAD proposal is outlined and the authors discuss possible membership options, favoring an initial membership including the five developed countries of the Pacific region, the ASEAN group, South Korea, Taiwan, Hong Kong, Papua New Guinea

cont.

cont'd

and the Pacific island states as a group. The authors suggest that the administrative apparatus of and OPTAD be confined to a small permanent secretariat and that issues be handled by specific functional task forces. They suggest six task forces on the following subjects: free and fair trade, trade restructuring, financing of regional development, foreign direct investment, resource and energy security, and trade with non-market economy countries.

1856 ESTANISLAO, Jesus P.
The Philippines and the Pacific Community Concept. In: The Pacific Community concept : views from eight nations / Japan Center for International Exchange, ed. - Tokyo : JCIE : Japan Center for International Exchange, 1980. (The JCIE Papers ; 1)

Contents: Estanislao sets out nine principles which he feels should guide any Pacific Community that may be established, involving policies for mutual benefit in the fields of resources, matters relating to multinational corporations, foreign aid and greater harmonization of economic and industrialization policies. In order for these principles to be attuned to reality, the author proposes five steps to clarify the concept: conceptualizing an identity for the Pacific region; agreeing on the purpose of a Pacific regional organization; defining the input to such a body by countries in the area; clarifying mechanics for action and formulating programs every four years. The Philippines, according to Estanislao, looks particularly forward to strengthening ties with Latin America.

1857 FABIANI, Oberto
Problemi del Sud-Est asiatico e del Pacifico. Rivista di studi politici internazionali (Firenze), vol.47, no.4, ottobre/dicembre 1980, p.503-522

1858 GOH CHOK TONG
The role of national governments in strengthening economic interdependence in the Asia-Pacific region. In: Asia-Pacific in the 1980s : toward greater symmetry in economic interdependence / Center for Strategic and International Studies, Jakarta, eds. - Jakarta : CSIS, 1980.

Contents: Much of this article is devoted to showing that economic interdependence based on international specialization is associated with growth. The role of national governments, according to Singapore's Minister for Trade and Industry, is largely confined to creating the right kind of climate and economic philosophy that will facilitate free interaction among the private sectors of the region. In closing, Goh suggests that Asia-Pacific cooperation among governments begin "with the lowest form - a forum of like-minded countries in the region". Such a forum would provide for regular consultations among leaders of market-oriented economies.

1859 HARA, Yasushi
How to make a concept real : the idea of Pacific Basin cooperation. Japan Quarterly (New Delhi), vol.17, no.4, 1980, p.471-478

Contents: One outstanding contribution this paper makes to the Pacific Community debate is in its emphasis on the method of Japanese policy-making. Hara points out that Ohira's Pacific Basin proposal initially received a lukewarm reception by the Japanese bureaucracy, since the policy was initiated at Prime Ministerial level and

cont.

cont'd

was seen as an undermining of traditional ways. In addition, "the various ministries feared an encroachment on their areas of authority." The author discusses the report of the Japanese Pacific Basin Cooperation Study Group and attempts to suggest reasons why Japan was motivated to promote the concept.

1860 ILLANES, Javier
El rol internacional de la India y su efecto en la relación Transpacífico al nivel de países en desarrollo. In: La Comunidad del Pacifico en perspectiva / Instituto de Estudios Internacionales de la Universidad de Chile, eds. - Santiago de Chile : Editorial Universitaria, 1979. 2 vols., vol.2, p.98-127

Contents: Illanes discusses the internal strengths and weakness of India and its foreign policy. Much of the paper is devoted to India's relations with Latin America. The author believes that India will continue to be basically a regional power in the Subcontinent, but that gradually it will play a more important global role. The Pacific Ocean has served as a barrier between India and the Latin American countries.

1861 INDUSTRIAL development news : Asia and the Pacific. - New York : United Nations, Economic and Social Commission for Asia and the Pacific, 1982. no.14, 96p. tabl. (ST/ESCAP/183)

1862 KOJIMA, Kiyoshi
Economic co-operation in a Pacific Community. - Honolulu, Hawaii : East-West Center, 1980. mimeo. 22p. Paper presented as part of the (Pacific Community Lecture Series)

Contents: One of the "fathers" of the Pacific Community concept examines the reasons for the establishment of such a body and comments on the various organizational forms proposed to date. Kojima points to three basic concepts of a Pacific Community: the first envisages a high degree of institutional integration and is based on a customs union like the EEC; secondly, there is the humanistic conception with a lesser degree of institutional integration; and thirdly, the proposal for an Organization for Pacific Trade and Development, with a less rigid organizational framework than the first alternative. The author inclines toward the third proposal as it focusses on a clear objective - the development of cooperation to utilize economic potential for mutual benefit. The reasons for closer economic cooperation are listed and Kojima recommends the creation of an ASEAN-Pacific Forum to foster a functional approach toward economic development. This is due to the fact that he believes it is premature to establish an organization such as OPTAD at the present time. Therefore, an approach to sub-regional issues is preferred over a region-wide body. The possible benefits to be derived from this grouping are listed.

1863 LEE POH PING
Reflections on the Pacific Community concept. Asia Pacific Community (Tokyo), no.8, 1980, p.35-43

Contents: Beginning with a brief attempt to analyze the motivations of the developed countries' interest in the idea, Lee moves on to raise the organizational problems associated with the concept. Thereupon follows a digression on the applicability or otherwise of various models of development to ASEAN and a chastisement of the Japanese for their behavior in Southeast Asia. Finally, the article concludes that if the proposed organization were basically economic, "then there might be a case for it."

1864 MORRIS-SUZUKI, Tessa
Japan and the Pacific Basin Community. World Today (London), vol.37, no.12, December 1981, p.454-461.

1865 MORRISON, Charles E.
American interest in the Pacific Community concept. In: The Pacific Community concept : a view from eight nations / Japan Center for International Exchange, ed. - Tokyo : JCIE, 1980. p.17-31 (The JCIE Papers ; 1)

Contents: Written before the 1980 Presidential elections, this paper seeks to describe American interest in the concept at the private, bureaucratic and Congressional levels. The author sees the two most compelling factors being first, that this interest is still very new and confined to a small group of individuals and second, that interest is growing. Development of this interest is traced to the mid- and late 1960s, when policy matters pertaining to Asia and the Pacific occupied the attention of many U.S. scholars and policy-makers. After the U.S. withdrawal from the Asia-Pacific region following the Vietnam war, American interest rapidly declined. However, the late 1970s saw a rekindling of interest due to: increased American trade links with East Asia and appreciation by Americans of their importance; dissatisfaction amongst Americans involved in Asian affairs with the conduct of U.S. foreign policy toward the region in the 1970s; and that the political climate in the Pacific region had shifted and this new climate welcomed American participation. The author concludes that whether or not an institutionalized Pacific Community will be realized depends upon whether a "critical mass" of nations find the concept beneficial in terms of their respective national interests.

1866 OKITA, Saburo
The Pacific Community idea. In: Three dialogues with Saburo Okita. East Asia Program of the Woodrow Wilson International Center for Scholars. - /s.l. : Woodrow Wilson International Center for Scholars, 1979. 24p. (Occasional paper, May 1979)

Contents: Dr. Okita's thoughts on the Pacific Community concept are presented here as part of a dialogue held at the Wilson Center to which scholars, journalists, diplomats, legislators and policy-makers with an interest in Asian affairs were invited. Main discussants included Congressman Lester Wolff, Dr. Alan K. Henrikson of the Fletcher School of Law and Diplomacy and William Watts of Potomac Associates. The accommodation and role of ASEAN in a Pacific Basin organization, how to reconcile a regional organization with U.S. and Japanese global economic policies and the question of membership are all discussed.

1867 PACIFIC Basin development : the American interests / Harald B. Malmgren, ed. - Lexington, Massachusetts : Lexington Books, 1972. 138p.

Contents: This collection of papers was published in an effort to stimulate American policy thinking on the Asia-Pacific region in the wake of the Guam Doctrine. Some of this material, although outdated, is still applicable to the situation in the Asia-Pacific area today. The two papers by Malmgren, particularly, contain insights relevant to the current Pacific Community debate. Malmgren, in the first chapter, urges U.S. policy-makers to take more of an interest in the region and not just in security terms. While rejecting a PAFTA, Malmgren points out that

cont.

cont'd

cooperation can take various forms and at various levels. In this area, the author believes there is an avenue for the U.S. to take a leading role in encouraging cooperation. Soedjatmoko, in another chapter, points to the necessity for an international forum in order for a "dynamic equilibrium" to be maintained in the Asia-Pacific region. Seiji Naya and Richard Schatz examine the role of U.S. and Japanese development assistance to the region and investigate the role a regional organization could play in this process. J. Alexander Caldwell looks at Japanese economic involvement in the area from 1950-1970, while Robert d'A. Shaw and Donald R. Sherk examine the role of labour and multinational corporations in the Basin. Bernard K. Gordon contributes a brief piece on regionalism in the Asia-Pacific region.

1868 The PACIFIC Community concept : views from eight nations / Japan Center for International Exchange, eds. - Tokyo : JCIE, 1980. 108p. (The JCIE Papers ; 1)

Contents: This collection of papers was originally presented at a symposium at Osio, Japan, as part of the Japan Center for International Exchange's (JCIE) Asian Dialogue program. The first paper by Miyashiro and Morisson summarizes the proceedings of the symposium and the papers that follow. Papers by Narongchai Akrasanee, Jesus P. Estanislao, Carl S. Green, Hang Sung-Joo, Lee Poh Ping, Charles E. Morrison, Pang Eng Fong, Takeshi Watanabe and Albert Widjaja.

1869 PACIFIC Community News Letter.- Washington, D.C.: Pan Pacific Community Association (PPCA), vol.1, no.1, 1981. (Particular issue)

Contents: Incorporated in 1980, the PPCA was established to serve as a clearinghouse, liaison office and symposia organizer for the Pacific Community concept. This newsletter collects information on current developments in relation to the concept and reports on conferences and symposia to be held in the near future. This particular issue includes a report on the PPCA Planning Session held in Honolulu in February 1981.

1870 PACIFIC economic cooperation : suggestions for action / John Crawford and Greg. Seow, eds. - Selangor, Malaysia and Singapore : Heinemann Educational Books (Asia), 1981. 246p.
ISBN: 9971 64 023 6

Contents: This book contains the proceedings and summary recommendations of the Pacific Community Seminar held in Canberra in September 1980. Convened pursuant to a request by the Japanese and Australian Prime Ministers in January 1980, the seminar was a private, non-governmental symposium which brought together one government representative and two persons from the academic/private sector of the five developed countries of the Pacific Basin--U.S., Japan, Canada, Australia and New Zealand-the ASEAN five--Indonesia, Malaysia, Thailand, Singapore and the Philippines --South Korea and the Pacific island states (as a group). Chaired by Sir John Crawford, the seminar was organized along four discussion questions: What are the forces promoting the Pacific Community idea? (comments by Don Brash and Hadi Soesastro); What are the issues for substantive cooperation? (comments by Han Sung-Joo and Lawrence Krause); Which countries are interested to participate and in what form? (comments by Amado Castro and Seizaburo Sato); What steps could be taken? (comments by Snoh Unakul and Eric Trigg). Statements by Thanat Khoman, Sir James

cont.

cont'd

Vernon, representing PBEC, and the International Steering Committee of PAFTAD are included. The six page summary report of proceedings and recommendations follows, proposing the setting up of the Pacific Cooperation Committee (PCC) to establish task forces on specific issues where cooperation could be facilitated. The other 211 pages of this volume are taken up with "readings", that is, excerpts from 34 papers previously published elsewhere.

1871 PACIFIC trade and development, II : Papers and proceedings of the second PAFTAD conference held at the East-West Center, Honolulu, Hawaii, in January 1969 / Kiyoshi Kojima, ed. - Tokyo : The Japan Economic Research Center, 1969. 409p.

Contents: In this volume, papers by Harry G. Johnson, Sperry Lea, and H. Edward English explore the general world economic situation, including North-South relations. Bruce W. Wilkinson, L.V. Castle, Kojima and I. Yamazawa look at the concept of a Pacific Free Trade Association (PAFTA) and its implications for Asian trade and development. I.A. McDougall, Peter Drysdale, and L.V. Castle consider some of the costs and benefits of a smaller free trade area consisting of Japan, Australia, and New Zealand. Proposals for regional monetary cooperation are dealt with by Robert Triffin, and Masaru Fukuda outlines the potential contribution of the Asian Development Bank. Kuo-shu Liang and Subroto examine the aid, trade and development experiences of Taiwan, South Korea, and Indonesia. The final paper, by Hiroshi Kitamura, considers regional economic cooperation and integration in Southeast Asia, focussing on the potential of the newly formed ASEAN.

1872 PANG ENG FONG
The concept of a Pan-Pacific Community and ASEAN : a view from Singapore.
In: The Pacific Community concept : views from eight nations / Japan Center for International Exchange, ed. - Tokyo : JCIE, 1980. (The JCIE Papers ; 1)

Contents: A summary of the development of the concept of Pacific cooperation is presented and a statement of the major issues for discussion before such a body could be formed. Pang adheres to the view that ASEAN is skeptical of the concept and points out that, at the present time, ASEAN would prefer to consolidate its own strength and concentrate on developing bilateral ties with developed countries. Of the ASEAN countries, however, it is predicted that Singapore would be the most favorable to the idea.

1873 PAUKER, Guy J.
Managed interdependence : some limits. In: Day after tomorrow in the Pacific region / Lee, Hongkoo et al.-/s.l./ : The Asia Society and Worldview, 1981, p.24-26

Contents: This article points out that oil-importing countries of Asia and the Pacific are vitally dependent on the Middle East for petroleum and will have an increasing difficulty finding the foreign exchange to pay for their growing petroleum requirements. Asia is also increasingly dependent on food imports, adding to the balance of payments burdens of food-importing countries. The advanced countries of the region are finding it increasingly difficult politically to provide more than limited assistance to the developing countries. There is no indication that the creation of a Pacific Community would affect this situation other than possibly to provide improved statistical information.

1874 PBEC papers / Pacific Basin Economic Council, eds. - /s.l./ : SRI International, California, 1980.

Contents: A series of occasional papers published by the Pacific Basin Economic Council (PBEC), comprising papers presented at the annual general meetings of PBEC and other matters of interest to PBEC members. PBEC was formed in 1967 to further the links between businessmen in the Asia-Pacific region. Recent issues of PBEC Papers, of particular interest to those involved in the Pacific Community debate, include: Irving Leibson, "Energy Resource Use in the Pacific Basin Countries"; Nicholas Marian, "Trade and Technology in the Pacific Rim Countries in the 1980s;" Harold Charles Schmidt, "Food, Agriculture and Interdependence in the 1980s;" and Sir John Vernon and M. Mark Earle, Jr., "Summary of the Pacific Community Canberra Seminar."

1875 SUN CHEN
Toward regional co-operation and prosperity. In: New foundations for Asian and Pacific security / Joyce E. Larsen, ed. - Papers and report of a conference held at Pattaya, Thailand, December 1979, p.152-162

Contents: A brief analysis of economic trends in the region is supported by lengthy tables on economic indicators, trade, export and import commodities, primary resources and manufactured products of the Asia-Pacific region. Sun outlines the deleterious repercussions of protectionism and the growth of trade in the area. He advocates further development of trade among Asia-Pacific nations, with the exception of the U.S. In addition, tariff and non-tariff barriers should be reduced to facilitate trade growth. The author maintains that the Asia-Pacific region has avoided many political and economic disturbances and has, in the main, "maintained peace, order and prosperity."

1876 TRADE and employment in Asia and the Pacific. Papers and proceedings of the Eighth Pacific Trade and Development Conference, Pattaya, Thailand, 1976, Honolulu / Narongchai Akrasanee, Seiji Naya and Vinyu Vichit-Vadakan, eds. - Honolulu : The University Press of Hawaii, 1977. 451p.

Contents: The Eighth PAFTAD conference was the first to be held in a developing Asian country and participants from virtually all the developed and developing nations of the Asia-Pacific region were included. The focus of the conference was on trade and employment issues affecting Asia-Pacific nations. Robert E. Baldwin presents an overview of world trade, limits to economic growth and employment and examines the implications of the NIEO. An assessment of alternative trade strategies, growth and employment is undertaken by Anne O. Krueger and country studies of trade and employment in developed nations, developing nations and in particular Korea, Brazil, Thailand, Malaysia and Indonesia are included. In addition, studies on trade and stabilization policies are presented by Yoichi Okita, Olarn Chaiprawat, Norma O. Alban and Harry G. Johnson. Heinz W. Arndt provides a summary paper on trade and employment generally. Comments and floor discussions on each paper are included plus an opening address by Dr. Snoh Unakul, then Governor of the Bank of Thailand.

1877 WHITLAM, Edward Gough
A Pacific Community. - Cambridge and London : Harvard University Press, 1981. 122p.

Contents: Originally, three of the four offerings in this book were presented as lectures by Gough Whitlam, Australian Prime Minister 1972-75, when he occupied the chair of Australian Studies at Harvard University in 1979. All four essays provide a comprehensive and wide-ranging discussion of critical issues affecting the Asia-Pacific region as well as prescribing lessons which should be derived from recent history by policy makers. The first paper, "Resources of the Pacific," discusses the natural resources of China and Mexico, fishing zones in the region and the new Law of the Sea. In "Western Pacific Trade," the second chapter, Whitlam turns his attention to the growing interdependence among economies of the region and discusses the Pacific Community concept. It is recommended that governments become more involved in the concept, although Whitlam believes that the time for an OPTAD is not yet ripe and proposes a forum modelled after the Commonwealth. In "Politics of the Western Pacific" the history of Australian and U.S. involvement in the Vietnam conflict, the division of Korea and the newly won independence of Pacific island states are discussed. The final paper on Japan and Australia examines Japan's economic success and relations, on an economic and political level, between the two nations. Throughout, the book provides interesting insights into Australia's foreign relations and her interaction with the region.

1878 ZAKARIA, Haji Ahmad
The Pacific Basin and ASEAN : a note on problems and prospects. Contemporary Southeast Asia (Singapore), 1980, 20p.

Contents: Zakaria cautions that optimism with regard to Pacific area economic growth must be mitigated with concern at the potential for instability. He sees the proposed Pacific Community as arising from the needs of certain developed nations for greater security. The paper proceeds to discuss the founding of ASEAN and then expresses commonly articulated ASEAN fears of the concept. Zakaria raises a multitude of questions without attempting to provide any answers and concludes that the ASEAN states would only find the Community attractive if ASEAN's strength is not weakened by its membership.

OPTAD Organization for Pacific Trade and Development

PAFTA Pacific Free Trade Association

VIII-4.4. Bangkok Agreement

1879 SHUKLA, Shrirang Purushottam
Long-and medium-term contracts : past experience and future possibilities in the context of the Bangkok Agreement. - /S.l. : s.n./, 1980. 1 vol. (various pagings). Graphs. Tabs.
(UNCTAD/ESCAP/UNDP) (RAS/71/722)

ESCAP Economic and Social Commission for Asia and the Pacific, Bangkok

UNCTAD United Nations Conference on Trade and Development, Geneva

UNDP United Nations Development programme, New York

VIII-5. ARAB WORLD

VIII-5.1. General

1880 ABDUL-MOHSEN, Assem
Economic integration more feasible in unity drive. Middle East (London), no.53, March 1979, p.14-18

1881 AGHA, Ismail Sateh
Etude analitique de l'expérience arabe d'Union économique. Revue Egyptienne de Droit International (Le Caire/Al Qahira), vol.27, 1971, p.107-120

1882 AL-ALWAN, Kadhim Hussain
The future of the Arab World and an Integrated Investment Bank for OAPEC surplus funds (AWIIB): unpublished doctoral dissertation. - /S.l./ : Mississippi State University, 1980, 207p.

1883 ALLAM, Ezzat
Les fonds inter-arabes de développement du Moyen-Orient.- Lausanne : Piantanida, 1979. 419p.

1884 AL-SABAH, Duayj
The League of Arab States as an agent of Arab integration : realities and prospects.-Beirut : Department of P.S.P.A.-A.U.B., 1975. (Thesis MA)

1885 ARAB economic integration : a distant goal. The Arab Economist (Beirut), vol.11, no.120, September 1979, p.13-14

1886 ARAB food experts say : co-operate or starve. The Middle East (London), no.49, November 1978, p.132

1887 ARAB Monetary Fund provide loans : technical assistance to member states. IMF Survey (Washington), vol.7, March 6, 1978, p.69-71

1888 ARAB shipping 1981 : a seatrade guide / ed. by G. Gimson. 4th ed. - Colchester, UK : Seatrade Publications, 1981. 180p. Graphs. Ill. Maps. Tabs.
ISBN: 0 905597 18 4

Articles on: Energy, Suez Canal, Inter-Arab trade. Intermodalism. Insurance. Country by country survey with information on: area, population, currency, main exports/imports, notes for travellers, government departments and associations, banks and finance houses, insurance companies, shipowners and managers, fleet growth, ship repairers, shipping agents, classifications societies, marine services, ports and terminals, shipping lines. Company index (alphabetical).

1889 The ARAB world. The Arab Economist (Beirut), vol.13, no.146, November 1981, p.3

1890 The ARAB world. The Arab Economist (Beirut), vol.13, no.147, December 1981, p.2

1891 AREAS of economic cooperation among Islamic Countries / Statistical Economic and Social Research and Training Centre for Islamic Countries. - Ankara : Organisation of the Islamic Conference, 1980.

1892 AWANOHARA, Susumu
The Arabs find Asia - at last. Far Eastern Economic Review (Hongkong), vol.113, no.31, 1981, July 24, p.38

1893 BANI-HANI, Mohammad Suleiman
Economic integration in the Arab world : application of some economic concepts: Unpublished doctoral dissertation. - /Riverside/ : University of California, 1979, 296p.

1894 BEAUCÉ, Th. de
Trois fonds arabes de coopération. Politique Etrangère (Paris), vol.41, no.1, 1976, p.43-56

1895 BERTAND, Jean-Pierre BOUDJIKANIAN, Aida PICAUDOU, Nadine
L'industrie libanaise et les marchés arabes du Golf. - Beirut : CERMCC, 1979. VII,159,(1)p. Ill. Map. (Publications du CERMCC ; 4)
Bibliography: p.159-/1/
ISBN: 2 7297 0060 9

1896 BOUTROS-GHALI, B.
Les fonds arabes pour le développement économique. Annuaire Français de Droit International (Paris), vol.21, 1975, p.65-72

1897 BURELLI RIVAS, M.A.
Conflict and cooperation in the Persian Gulf / Mughisuddin Mohammad ed. Third World Quarterly (London), vol.1, no.2, 1979, p.175

1898 The CHARTER on the integration of the Arab Republic of Egypt and the Democratic Republic of Sudan. - /Khartoum : s.n., 1982/. 21p.

1899 DAJANI, Burhan
Les difficultés qui entravent la croissance économique du monde arabe. Syrie et Monde Arabe (Damascus), vol.27, no.317, June 25, 1980, p.53-68

1900 DAMIANI, N.
Arab Economic Council steps up efforts towards Unity. The Arab Economist (Beirut), vol.11, no.115, April 1979, p.16-17

1901 DJAVED, Abdolhassan Djavadi
Economic integration in the Middle East: unpublished doctoral dissertation. - Claremont, Ca. : University Center, Claremont Graduate School, 1977. 319p.

1902 ECONOMIC integration requires political will. The Arab Economist (Beirut), vol.14, no.153, June 1982, p.10-13

1903 EL MALLAKH, Ragaei et al.
Implications of regional development in the Middle East for U.S. trade : capital flows, and balance of payments. - Boulder, Colorado : International Research Center for Energy and Economic Development, 1977. 64p.
"A summary report on findings of National Science Foundation, RANN, Grant no. Apr. 75-22411."

Examine present and future possibilities for economic integration of the Arab countries. Analyze U.S. relations with the Arab countries and their effect on the U.S. economy. Also discuss U.S. energy policy alternatives.

1904 EL-SAADI, Ahmed
Aspects of Arab cooperation and coordination in the energy field. Contemporary Review (London), vol.237, no.1374, July 1980, p.13-18

1905 FINANCIAL experts stress Inter-Arab co-operation. The Arab Economist (Beirut), vol.12, no.129, June 1980, p.33-35

1906 GHANTUS, Elias T.
Arab industrial integration : a strategy for development. - London; Canberra : Croom Helm, 1982, 240p.
ISBN: 0 7099 1117 3

Contents: Part 1: A theoretical framework. 1. Economic integration a. development. 2. An approach to industrial integration. Part 2: Arab industrial integration. 3. Arab economic regionalism. 4. Arab economic framework. 5. Arab industrialization : problems and prospects. 6. Possibilities for industrial integration. 7. Integration potential in the fertilizer industry. 8. Conclusions and prospects.

1907 GLAUBITT, Klaus LAGEMAN, Bernhard
Arab economic integration, which way? - Bochum : Institut für Entwicklungsforschung und Entwicklungspolitik, 1980. 29 leaves. (Materialien und kleine Schriften / Ruhr-Universität Bochum. Institut für Entwicklungsforschung und Entwicklungspolitik)

1908 HAMED, Osama
Egypt's open door economic policy : an attempt at economic integration in the Middle East. International Journal of Middle East Studies (London), vol.13, no.1, February 1981, p.1-9

1909 HARIK, Bassam Elias
Economic integration in less developed countries : prospects for six arab countries: unpublished doctoral dissertation. - /S.l./ : Wayne State University, Mich., 1978. 191p.

1910 HASEEB, K. MAKDISI, Samir A.
Arab monetary integration: issues and prerequisites. - London : Croom Helm, 1982. 224p.

1911 HASHIM, Jawad
An understanding of the importance of Arab Islamic Funds available for development projects and economic support. OAPEC News Bulletin (Kuwait), vol.5, April 1979, p.29-35

1912 JOINT SYMPOSIUM ON LONG-RANGE PLANNING AND REGIONAL INTEGRATION WITH SPECIAL REFERENCE TO THE ARAB REGION, 1976, Cairo
Joint symposium on long-range planning and regional integration with special reference to the Arab region, 14-21 January, 1976, Cairo. - /s.l.: s.n./, 1976. (Papers)

1913 KAWAR, Suheil
Arab institutions for development aid. Pakistan Economist (Karachi), vol.19, February 24, 1979, p.21-24

1914 KELIDAR, Abbas
The integration of modern Iraq. - London : Croom Helm, 1979. 208p.

1915 KUEPPERS, N.F.
Regionale Absatzstrategie im VAE-Geschäft : zielgruppeninterne Differenzierungen. Nachrichten für Aussenhandel (Köln), (44), no.118, Juni 25, 1981, p.1

Probleme der Verschiedenartigkeit der sieben Emirate, bei regionalen Lieferungen und Exporten. Ungleichgewichtige Bevölkerungsstruktur. Erwerbstätige. Regionale Kaufkraftverteilung. Betriebe und Gehälter in der Industrie.

1916 MAKDISI, Samir A.
Arab economic co-operation. In: Arab industrialization and economic integration, edited by Roberto Aliboni.-New York : St. Martin's Press, 1979. p.90-133

1917 MAKDISI, Samir A.
Commerce extérieur et intégration économique des pays arabes. Le Commerce du Levant (Beirut), vol.51, no.4727, 1979, p.12-17

1918 MAMMERI, Ali M.
Possibilités et formes d'intégration économique régionale Egypte-Lybie-Syrie-Alger. - Alger : Université d'Alger, Institut des Sciences Economiques, 1978. 142p. Tabs.

1919 METWALLY, M.M.
The case for Arab economic integration. L'Egypte Contemporaine. Société Egyptienne d'Economie Politique, de Statistique et de Législation (Al Qahira), vol.70, no.376, April 1979, p.205-225

1920 METWALLY, M.M.
The case for Arab economic integration. L'Egypte Contemporaine (Al Qahira), vol.71, no.379, 1980, p.71-100

1921 MONDE arabe. Syrie et Monde Arabe. Étude Mensuelle. Politique et Statistique (Damask), vol.27, no.322, déc. 25, 1980, p.11. Tabs.

Importations des produits sidérurgiques et échanges commerciaux des pays de l'OECD, 1975-1978 (par pays et produits).

1922 MONDE arabe et développement économique / coordonné par Bichara Khader. - Paris : Le Sycomore, 1981. 227p.

1923 MURSEY, Alfred
First steps toward Arab economic integration. International Development Review (Roma), vol.13, no.1, 1971, p.13-18

1924 Los ORGANISMOS económicos de la Liga Arabe. Medio Oriente Informa, vol.20, December 1981, p.48-53

1925 PROGRES dans l'exploitation des ressources minières arabes. Economiste Arabe. L'économie et les finances des pays arabes (Beirut), 23, no.264, nov. 1980, p.15

Rôle et les investissements de l'Arab Mining Company (ARMICO). Développement des ressources minières. Des projets en commun : projets dans Maroc, Mauritanie, Yemen Nord, Somalie et Tunisie. Investissements en Jordanie.

1926 REFLECTIONS on regional development finance and the intercountry project financing approach to integration in the Arab world : presented to the Second World Scientific Banking Meeting "International Financing of Economic Development", Dubrovnik, Yugoslavia, May 26 to 31, 1980 / by Mohammed Imady ... /et al./. - /S.l. : s.n., 1980/. /24/ leaves

1927 The ROLE of the air transport sector in Arab economic integration. The Arab Economist (Beirut), vol.13, no.144, September 1981, p.11

1928 SAADEDDINE, Fawzi
Die arabische Wirtschaftsintegration : Darstellung und kritische Untersuchung ihrer Rolle zur Förderung des Industrialisierungsprozesses der arabischen Staaten.- Tübingen : Erdmann, /1977/. XIII,255p. (Bochumer Materialien zur Entwicklungsforschung und Entwicklungspolitik ; 5)

1929 SAADEDDINE, Fawzi
Integrationsansätze im Arabischen Raum und ihre mögliche Weiterentwicklung. In: Entwicklungsprobleme der arabischen Erdöl-Staaten. - Hamburg : Deutsches Orient-Institut, 1977. p.62-73

1930 SAYIGH, Jusif A.
Arab economy : past performance and future prospects. - Oxford : Oxford University, 1982. 175p., ill.
ISBN: 0 19 877188 6

/Economic development/, /Arab countries/ - /historical analysis/, /agricultural aspects/, /educational aspects/, /petroleum/, /industrialization/, /financial aspects/, /economic relations/, /economic structure/, /regional co-operation/, /future/, /statistical tables/.

1931 SAYIGH, Yusif A.
The economics of the Arab world. - New York : St. Martin's Press, 1978. 726p.

1932 SAYIGH, Yusif A.
The integration of the oil sector with the Arab economies. OPEC Review (Wien), (4), no.4, winter, 1980, p.20-41. Ref.

Development of the Arab oil industry in the 1930s and 1940s. Oil as financial pump-primer: 1950s and 1960s. Loans of decision-making with respect to important oil policies. Contribution of the oil to the financial resources, utilization of oil revenues. Oil sector promoted development.

1933 SAYIGH, Yusif A.
New economic framework. Arab Perspectives, vol.2, November 1981, p.46-51

1934 SCHART, Traute
Arab development funds and banks. - Paris : Development Center of the Organization for Economic Co-operation and Development. - Washington, D.C. : OECD Publication Center, 1978.

1935 UNIDO
Comparative study of development plans of Arab states. - New York : UN, 1976. 268p.

1936 UNITED STATES OF AMERICA. Congress. Joint Economic Committee
The political economy of the Middle East, 1973-78 : a compendium of papers submitted to the Joint Economic Committee, Congress of the Unites States. - Washington, D.C. : U.S.G.P.O., 1980, V,575p. Ill.

At head of title: 96th Congress, 2nd session. Committee print

1937 ZERAOUI, Zidane
El mundo arabe : imperialismo y nacionalismo. - México : CEESTEM : Editorial Nueva Imagen, 1981. 218p. Bibliography: p.217-218.

CEESTEM Centro de Estudios Económicos y Sociales del Tercer Mundo

VIII-5.2. Arab Common Market—ACM

1938 ALBAR, Ahmad
Le Marché Commun Arabe. - Cairo : ALESCO, 1978, 191p.

1939 ARAB Common Market. Current Notes on International Affairs (Canberra), vol.36, no.6, June 1965, p.314-318

1940 ARAB Common Market still at square one. The Middle East (London), no.57, July 1979, p.90

1941 Les ETAPES franchies pour le Marché Commun Arabe. - Damascus : Office Arabe de Presse et de Documentation, 1979.
/Congrès des Chambres de Commerce, d'Industrie et d'Agriculture des Pays Arabes, 21. Session, Damascus/

1942 GUINE, Antoine
Etude sur le Marché Commun Arabe et sur la coopération économique inter-arabe.– Damascus : Office Arabe de Presse et de Documentation, 1972. 368p.

1943 Le MARCHE Commun Arabe après neuf ans. Syrie et Monde Arabe (Damascus), vol.21, no.244, May 1974, p.38-41

1944 MUNRO, John
Towards economic integration : the case of Arab Common Market. The Arab Economist (Beirut), vol.9, no.90, March 1977, p.8-14

1945 NEED to revive the Arab Common Market. The Arab Economist (Beirut), vol.11, no.112, January 1979, p.20-21

1946 OU en est le Marché Commun Arabe? Syrie et Monde Arabe (Damascus), vol.21, nos.240-241, January-February 1974, p.1-19

1947 SAADEDDINE F. Fawzi
Der Arabische Gemeinsame Markt : ein Erfolg? Orient (Hamburg), vol.17, no.1, 1976, p.87-107

VIII-5.3. Maghreb Permanent Consultative Committee

1948 GUEN, Moncef
Ce Maghreb uni qui ne dépend que de nous. Jeune Afrique (Paris), no.1038, 26 novembre 1980, p.17

1949 Le MAGHREB et l'Afrique subsaharienne / par Slimane Chikh... /et al./; avant-propos de B.Etienne ; coordination, S.Chikh, H.Michel. - Paris : Editions du Centre national de la recherche scientifique, 1980. VIII,263p., maps. (Collection Etudes de l'Annuaire de l'Afrique du Nord)
"Extrait de l'A.A.N. 1978". At head of title: Centre de recherches et d'études sur les sociétés méditerranéennes.
Includes bibliographical references.
ISBN: 2 222 02870 1

1950 ORTNER-HEUN, I.
Tunesien fördert Wirtschaftskooperation im Maghreb-Raum. Nachrichten für Aussenhandel (Köln), (44), no.158, Aug. 20, 1981, p.5

Abstimmung der industriellen und handelspolitischen Aktivitäten. Seit 1980 intensive diplomatische Aktivität zwischen Tunesien, Marokko und Algerien. Zusammenarbeit. Wirtschafts-Annäherung mit kleinen Schritten. Lieferverträge im Bausektor.

VIII-5.4. Gulf Co-operation Council—GCC

1951 ARAB economic cooperation agreement. The Arab Economist (Beirut), vol.13, no.142, July 1981, p.4

... Customs duties would be abolished and financial and banking regulation harmonized with the aim of creating a common Gulf currency. The agreement is part of plans by the six members of the new Gulf Cooperation Council to form a group similar to the EEC to safeguard Gulf stability ...

1952 CREATION du Conseil de Coopération du Golfe, Abu Dhabi. L'Economiste Arabe. Centre d'Etudes et de Documentation Economiques, Financières et Sociales (Beirut), vol.24, no.271, 1981, p.15-16

1953 ENCOURAGEMENT a l'initiative privée. L'Economiste Arabe (Beirut), vol.25, no.278, janvier 1982, p.21

... Les libertés consenties dans le nouvel accord, conclu par les six Etats-membres du Conseil de Coopération du Golfe (Arabie Séoudite, Koweit, Qatar, Bahrein, les Emirats Arabes Unis et Oman) comprennent le droit de propriété dans n'importe lequel de ces Etats ...

1954 ENERGY : GCC delays oil talks. Meed : Middle East Economic Digest (London), vol.27, no.1, 7-14 Jan. 1983, p.3

1955 The GULF Cooperation Council economic agreement. The Arab Economist (Beirut), vol.14, no.150. March 1982, p.36-37

1956 GCC : Gulf Cooperation Council : first steps towards integration. The Arab Economist (Beirut), vol.14, no.153, June 1982, p.6

1957 GUECIOUEUR, Adda
Problems and prospects of economic integration among the member countries of the Arab Gulf Co-operation Council. The Arab Gulf Journal (London), vol.2, no.2, October 1982, p.43-54. Notes and references.

1958 GULF states : formation of Gulf Co-operation Council. Keesing's Contemporary Archives (Edinburgh), no.30982, July 24, 1981

1959 GULF states organization similar to EEC. The Arab Economist (Beirut), vol.13, no.138, March 1981, p.7

1960 HOW the Emirates are beating the odds. World Business Weekly (London), no.34, Aug. 31, 1981, p.29. Ill. Map. Tab.

The United Arab Emirates a prosperous state of seven small sheikdoms. Abu Dhabi, the only rich oil-country. Creation of the "Gulf Cooperation Council". US-role. Protection oil. Industry. Housing. Figures, 1980.

1961 MAAREK, Gilles
Du Marché Commun Arabe au Conseil de Coopération du Golfe. Défense Nationale (Paris), vol.37, août/sept., 1981, p.65-78

1962 A MOVE towards Gulf Unity. Financial Times (London), 3.6.1981

GCC Gulf Co-operation Council

IX

Bibliographies, Documents, and Statistical Sources

1963 AFRICAN international relations : an annotated bibliography / Mark W. DeLancey. - Boulder, Colo.: Westview 1981. XVIII,365p. (Westview special studies on Africa)
Includes index.
ISBN: 0 89158 680 6

1964 AFRIKA, Latijns Amerika, Azie : integration / edited by Didier van Houts, /assisted/ by Erik van Deun. - Antwerpen : Universiteit, R.U.C.A., College voor de Ontwikkelingslanden, 1981. 315p. (Bibliography ; 2)

1965 ANALYTICAL compendium of developing countries' decisions and recommendations on ECDC/TCDC, 1976-1981 / research team : Boris Cizelj, Bojan Zidarič, Metka Fuks. - Ljubljana : Research Centre for Co-operation with Developing Countries, 1981. 194p.
Prepared for the ECDC/TCDC promotion workshop, Bled (Yugoslavia), November 2-7, 1981

1966 ARIFIN, M.A.
ASEAN environment bibliography. - Serdang : Perpustakaan, Universiti Pertanian Malaysia, 1981. 41p.

/Bibliography/, /environment/, /environmental management/, /energy/, /health/, /ASEAN/, 1970 -1980.

1967 ASEAN Documentation Series / ASEAN Secretariat. - Jakarta : ASEAN Secretariat.

1968 ASEAN Newsletter / Association of Southeast Asian Nations. - Jakarta : ASEAN Secretariat

1969 BIBLIOGRAFIJA knig, brošjur i statej po problemam Afriki i stran tret'ego mira, opublikovannyh v SSSR. - Moskva : Akademija nauk SSSR, Institut Afriki, /1982/.

1970 BIBLIOGRAPHY on Technical Co-operation among Developing Countries : /documents of the organizations of the United Nations Development System and other international organizations/. - New York : /United Nations/, 1981. 28 leaves

1971 CENTRAFRIQUE : données statistiques sur les activités économiques, culturelles et sociales. - Paris : Ministère de la Coopération, Service des Etudes et Questions Internationales, 1979. 127p. Tab. Cartes

1972 COMMISSION ECONOMIQUE POUR L'AFRIQUE
Rapport annuel 1980 / Commission Economique pour l'Afrique. Documents officiels, 1980 / Conseil Economique et Social. - New York : Nations Unies, 1980. V,131p. (Supplément ; 7) (E/CN.14/781/Rev.1)

1973 DAMIAN, Ana
Bibliography of selected books and articles on non-alignment. - Beograd : Institute of International Politics and Economies, Research Center for International Relations, 198o. 115p.

1974 DEVINDEX 198- : index to selected literature on economic and social development = index d'ouvrages sur le développement économique et social. - Ottawa : International Development Research Centre-IDRC, 198-.
ISBN: 0 88936 379 X
ISSN: 0708 2533
Microfiche edition available

1975 DOCUMENTOS presentados a la "Conferencia sobre Perspectivas de Comercio entre las Américas". Estudios Económicos, vol.11, no.2, abril-junio de 1981, p.1-185

1976 DOCUMENTOS sobre aspectos institucionales de la integración centroamericana. - San José, Costa Rica : Instituto Centroamericano de Administración Publica, 1973. 321p. in various pagings ; ill.

1977 ECONOMIC cooperation and integration among developing countries = Cooperación económica e integración entre los países en desarrollo = Coopération économique et intégration entre les pays en développement = Ekonomska saradnja i integracija medju zemljama u razvoju : a select annotated bibliography 1979-1980 / compiled and edited by Nada Verbič. - Ljubljana : Center za proučevanje sodelovanja z deželami v razvoju, 1981. X, 310 p.

1978 ECONOMIC titles / abstracts. Semi-monthly journal providing concise information of interest to business, trade, industry, economic libraries and research institutes.-The Hague : Martinus Nijhoff, 1981, 1982

1979 FERRIS, Elizabeth G.
Andean Pact : a selected bibliography. Latin America Research Review (Austin), 13(3), 1978, p.108-124
Covers primarily Spanish language sources.

1980 INFORPRESS Centroamericana, nos.375-424, 1980

1981 INTERNATIONAL trade documentation : annotated list of publications received by the International Trade Centre. - /Geneva/ : International Trade Centre UNCTAD/GATT. Documentation Section, 1983. IVp, 32 leaves (ITC/TD/DS/61)
Appendix: ITC publications issued in 1982.

1982 JUNAC. Biblioteca
Bibliográfia anotada sobre aplicación de la decision 24 y comportamiento de la inversión extranjera en el Grupo andino. - Lima : Biblioteca, 1981. 13p.

1983 JUNAC. Biblioteca
Bibliografía anotada sobre aspectos políticos de la integración andina : suplemento I, 1979-1980. - Lima, Peru : Biblioteca, 1981. 40p. 173 referencias.

1984 JUNAC. Biblioteca
Bibliografía sobre la integración subregional andina. 2a ed. - Lima : JUNAC Biblioteca, 1977-
Indice de autores e instituciones.

1985 JUNAC. Biblioteca
Principales manuales sobre evaluación de proyectos de la Biblioteca JUNAC. - Lima : Biblioteca, 1981. 6p.

1986 JUNAC. Biblioteca
Tratamiento a la inversión extranjera y aplicación de la decisión 24 en el Peru : guía bibliográfica / /elaborado por Araceli R. de Ramos Murga/. - Lima : JUNAC, Biblioteca, 1982. 36p.

1987 MONEY, banking and finance in Africa : bibliography / Association of African Central Banks. - Dakar : African Centre for Monetary Studies, 1979. 257p.

1988 MOVIMIENTO de países no-alineados : bibliografía / Ministerio de Relaciones Exteriores. - La Habana : Dirección de Documentación, 1979. III,213p.
Accompanied by: Suplemento bibliográfico, 1980. - Includes indexes.

1989 NEITZEL, Hartmut NÖTZEL, Renate
Afrika und die arabischen Staaten : Dokumentation zur Entwicklung der politischen und wirtschaftlichen Beziehungen seit 1973 = Africa and the Arab States : documentation on the development of political and economic relations since 1973. - Hamburg : Institut für Afrika-Kunde, Dokumentations-Leitstelle Afrika, 1979. 458p., maps. (Aktueller Informationsdienst Afrika.Sondernummer / Institut für Afrika-Kunde, Dokumentations-Leitstelle Afrika ; 1)
Includes documentation in English, French or German. Includes bibliographies

1990 The NEW international economic order : a selective bibliography = Le nouvel ordre économique international : bibliographie sélective / Dag Hammarskjöld Library. - New York : United Nations, 1980. 128p.
(ST/LIB/SER.B/30)

1991 Newsletter / ISEAS, Institute of Southeast Asian Studies. ASEAN Economic Research Unit. - Singapore : ISEAS
Periodically

1992 PLANIFICACIÓN regional en América Latina : bibliografía / Lucía Alzamora C. - Quito : Sección Publicaciones, JUNAPLA, 1977. 55p. (Serie Materiales de trabajo / ILDIS ; 13)
On cover: Instituto Latinoamericano de Investigaciones Sociales, Fundación Friedrich Ebert, Junta Nacional de Planificación y Coordinación Económica.

1993 REGIONALISMUS und regionale Integration : Bibliographie 1970-1980 : Afrika, Karibik, Lateinamerika, Südostasien / von J. Günther Doeker /et al./. - Frankfurt a.M. : Lang, 1981. 107p. - (Völkerrecht und internationale Politik ; 6)
ISBN: 3 8204 6982 6

Contents: Günther Doeker, Wolfgang S.Heinz, Thomas Koll, Mark B.M. Suh et Abdullahel Masud Syed ont uni leurs efforts pour présenter une étude bibliographique sur le régionalisme et l'intégration régionale de 1970 à 1980. Dans ce travail sont présentées l'Afrique, la zone Caraïbe, l'Amérique Latine, l'Asie du Sud-Est.

1994 RESEARCH CENTRE FOR COOPERATION WITH DEVELOPING COUNTRIES, Ljubljana
Bibliography on technical Co-operation among developing countries : (draft) Ljubljana : Research Centre for Co-operation with Developing Countries, 1981. 28p. (Suppl. to the basic Centre's Bibliography on ECDC/TCDC, covering 1970-1978)

1995 SELA noticias. Caracas : Secretaría Permanente del SELA, 1980- . Monthly

1996 SELA. Secretaría Permanente
Lista de documentos de trabajo e informativos presentados a la VIII reunión ordinaria del Consejo Latinoamericano. - Caracas : SELA, 1982. (SP/CL/VIII.O/Di.12)

1997 SELECT bibliography of documents on transfer and development of technology that have been prepared by or for the UNCTAD secretariat / United Nations Conference on Trade and Development. Trade and Development Board. Committee on Transfer of Technology. - Genève : UNCTAD, 1980. 18p. (TD/B/C.6/INF.2/Rev.2)

1998 SELECTIVE bibliography on integration / Institute for Latin American Integration. - Buenos Aires : Institute for Latin American Integration, 1977. 1 vol. (Bibliographical series ; 1)

/Bibliography/ on /economic integration/, with emphasis on / Latin America/. Includes a list of /periodicals/ which frequently include articles on integration.

1999 SIECA
Carta informativa / Secretaría Permanente del Tratado General de Integración Económica, Ciudad de Guatemala : SIECA. Nos.219-228, 1980

2000 STACY, M.
ECOWAS select readings, 1975-1981. - Washington, D.C. : African Bibliographic Center, 1982. 23p. ill. (Current reading list series ; vol.13, no.4)

2001 ŠTAJNER, Vera
Zemlje u razvoju i novi ekonomski poredak : Bibliografija 2 : Zagreb : Ekonomski institut Zagreb, 1983. XII,244p.

2002 TAN SOK JOO
ASEAN : a bibliography. - /Singapore/ : /ISEAS/, 1976. 116p. (Library bulletin ; 11)

2003 UNCTAD 1963-1983 : Bibliography = CNUCED 1963-1983 : Bibliographie. - Geneva : United Nations Library = Nations Unies, Bibliothèque, 1983. II,81p. (Special Bibliographies, Repertoires and Indexes = Bibliographies spéciales, Répertoires et Index, Series C ; 4)

2004 UNIDO
Directory of industrial information services and systems in developing countries / prep. for Industrial and Technological Information Bank INTIB by UNIDO Technology Programme, Industrial Information Section. - Wien : UNIDO, 1981. /121/p.

List of information services, arranged by country in alphabetical order, with information on: address, telephone/telex, language used, type of activity, services provided, subject coverage, geographic scope, publications. Indexes of subjects, acronyms and institutions.

Author Index

A

B

C

Č

D

E

F

G

H

I

J

K

L

LL

M

N

O

P

Q

Š

T

U

V

W

X

Y

Z

List of Periodicals

A

ACIER ARABE. Union Arabe du fer et de l'acier, Alger
AED, see AFRICA ECONOMIC DIGEST
AFRICA. An international business, economic and political monthly, London
AFRICA DEVELOPMENT, Dakar, Senegal
AFRICA ECONOMIC DIGEST-AED. Weekly business news, analysis and forecast, London
AFRICA GUIDE
AFRICA QUARTERLY. A journal of African affairs. Indian Centre for Africa, New Delhi
AFRICA REPORT, New Brunswick, N.J.
AFRICA RESEARCH BULLETIN, Exeter, Engl.
AFRICA TODAY, Denver, Colorado
AFRICAN AFFAIRS, London
AFRICAN BUSINESS, London
AFRIKA SPECTRUM. Deutsche Zeitschrift für moderne Afrikaforschung, Pfaffenhofen/Ilm
AFRIQUE-ASIE, Paris
AFRIQUE CONTEMPORAINE. Documents d'Afrique noire et de Madagascar, Paris
AFRIQUE INDUSTRIE INFRASTRUCTURES, Paris
ALTERNATIVES, New Delhi
AMERICA LATINA, Moskva
AMERICAN ECONOMIC REVIEW, Nashville, Tenn.
AMERICAN STUDIES AND WORLD AFFAIRS, Beverly, Ca
AMERICAS, Washington
AMERIQUE LATINE, Paris
ANDEAN REPORT, Lima
ANNEE AFRICAINE. Centre d'Etude d'Afrique Noire de Bordeaux, Paris
ANNUAIRE FRANÇAIS DE DROIT INTERNATIONAL, Paris
ARAB ECONOMIST. Center for economic, financial and social research and documentation, Beirut
ARAB GULF JOURNAL, London
ARAB PERSPECTIVES
ASEAN BUSINESS QUARTERLY, Singapore
ASEAN DOCUMENTATION SERIES, Jakarta
ASEAN NEWSLETTER, Jakarta
ASIA PACIFIC COMMUNITY. Formerly-until 1978: Pacific Community, Tokyo
ASIA RESEARCH BULLETIN, Singapore
ASIAN AFFAIRS, New York
ASIAN PERSPECTIVE, Seoul
ASIAN SURVEY, Berkeley, California
ASIEN, AFRIKA, LATEINAMERIKA, Berlin
ASLIB PROCEEDINGS, London
AUSSENPOLITIK. Zeitschrift für internationale Fragen, Stuttgart
AZIJA I AFRIKA SEGODNJA, Moskva

B

BANK FOR INTERNATIONAL SETTLEMENTS-BIS, Basle
BIS, see BANK FOR INTERNATIONAL SETTLEMENTS
BLICK DURCH DIE WIRTSCHAFT, Frankfurt a. Main

BOLETIN ENEGERTICO
BULLETIN FOR INTERNATIONAL FISCAL DOCUMENTATION, Amsterdam
BUSINESS ASIA. Weekly report to managers of Asia, Hong Kong
BUSINESS LATIN AMERICA, New York

C

CAHIERS DU CEDAF
CAHIERS ECONOMIQUES ET SOCIAUX, Zaire, Kinshasa
CANADIAN JOURNAL OF AFRICAN STUDIES, Ottawa
CARIBBEAN LIFE AND TIMES
CASE WESTERN RESERVE JOURNAL OF INTERNATIONAL LAW, Cleveland, Ohio
CEMLA BOLETIN, Mexico
CENTRAL BANK NEWS SURVEY
CEPAL REVIEW, Santiago de Chile
CHAMBER NEWS. Metropolitan Chamber of Commerce and Industry, Dacca, Bangladesh
CIENCIA-TECNOLOGIA Y DESARROLLO
CIENCIAS ADMINISTRATIVAS, La Plata, Arg.
COLUMBIA JOURNAL OF WORLD BUSINESS, New York
COMERCIO EXTERIOR, México
COMMERCE, Bombay
COMMERCE DU LEVANT, Beirut
CONTEMPORARY CHINA, Boulder, Colorado
CONTEMPORARY REVIEW, London
CONTEMPORARY SOUTHEAST ASIA, Singapore
COTTON. Monthly review of the world situation, Washington, D. C.
COURIER, Bruxelles
COYUNTURA ANDINA, Bogotá
CRITIQUE DE L'ECONOMIE POLITIQUE, Paris
CURRENT BIBLIOGRAPHICAL INFORMATION. Dag Hammarskjøld Library-UNBIS, New York
CURRENT NOTES ON INTERNATIONAL AFFAIRS, Canberra
CURRENT RESEARCH ON PEACE AND VIOLENCE, Tampere, Finland

D

D and C: DEVELOPMENT AND CO-OPERATION, Bonn
DEFENSE NATIONALE, Paris
DEMOGRAFIA Y ECONOMIA, México
DENVER JOURNAL OF INTERNATIONAL LAW AND POLICY, Denver, Colorado
DESARROLLO ECONOMICO, Buenos Aires
DESARROLLO INDOAMERICANO, Barranquilla, Colombia
DESARROLLO Y SOCIEDAD, Bogotá
DEVELOPMENT AND CHANGE, London
DEVELOPMENT AND PEACE, Budapest
DEVELOPMENT SEEDS OF CHANGE

DOCUMENTALISTE, Paris
DRITTE WELT, Koenigstein, Meisenheim, F. R. G.

E

ECONOMIC AND POLITICAL WEEKLY, Bombay
ECONOMIC BULLETIN FOR ASIA AND THE PACIFIC, Bangkok
ECONOMIC DEVELOPMENT AND CULTURAL CHANGE, Chicago
ECONOMIC PLANNING, Montreal
ECONOMIC TITLES/ABSTRACTS, The Hague
ECONOMICS, Tübingen
ECONOMISCH EN SOCIAAL TIJDSCHRIFT, Antwerpen
ECONOMISTE ARABE, Beirut
EGYPTE CONTEMPORAINE, Al Qahira
ENTWICKLUNG UND ZUSAMMENARBEIT. Deutsche Stiftung für internationale Entwicklung, Bonn
ESTRATEGIA, Buenos Aires
ESTUDIOS ECONOMICOS
ESTUDIOS INTERNACIONALES, Buenos Aires, Santiago de Chile
ESTUDIOS PUBLICOS, Santiago de Chile
ESTUDIOS SOCIALES CENTROAMERICANOS, San José, Costa Rica
ESTUDOS ECONOMICOS, Sao Paulo, Brazil
ETUDES INTERNATIONALES, Québec, Canada
EURE. Revista latinoamericana de estudios urbano regionales, Santiago
EUROMONEY. The Monthly journal of international money and capital markets, London
EUROPA ARCHIV. Zeitschrift für internationale Politik, Bonn
EUROPE OUTRE-MER. Formerly: Europe France Outremer, Paris
EX LIBRIS. International Development Research Centre. Monthly list of documents ..., Ottawa, Ontario

F

FAR EASTERN ECONOMIC REVIEW, Hongkong
FINANCE AND DEVELOPMENT, Washington, D. C.
FINANCIAL TIMES, London
FLETCHER FORUM, Medford, Mass.
FOOD POLICY, London
FOREIGN TRADE REVIEW, New Delhi
FORO INTERNACIONAL, México
FUTURABLE, Buenos Aires

G

GEORGIA JOURNAL OF INTERNATIONAL AND COMPARATIVE LAW, Athens, Ga, USA
GLASNIK PRIVREDNE KOMORE JUGOSLAVIJE, Beograd
GLOBE AND MAIL, Toronto, Can.

I

IDB NEWS. Inter-American Development Bank, Washington, D. C.
IDS BULLETIN-Institute of Development Studies, Brighton, Engl.
IFDA DOSSIER, Nyon, Suisse
IMF SURVEY, Washington
INDIA QUARTERLY, New Delhi
INDIAN JOURNAL OF INTERNATIONAL LAW, New Delhi
INDIAN JOURNAL OF POLITICAL SCIENCE, New Delhi
INDONESIAN FOREIGN AFFAIRS, Jakarta
INDONESIAN QUARTERLY, Jakarta
INSIGHT. Asia´s business monthly, Hong Kong
INTEGRACION LATINOAMERICANA, Buenos Aires
INTER-AMERICAN STUDIES AND WORLD AFFAIRS, see Journal of Inter-American Studies ...
INTERCIENCIA, Caracas
INTERECONOMICS, Hamburg
INTERNATIONAL BUSINESS WEEK
INTERNATIONAL DEVELOPMENT REVIEW, Roma
INTERNATIONAL INTERACTIONS, New York
INTERNATIONAL JOURNAL, Toronto
INTERNATIONAL JOURNAL OF MIDDLE EAST STUDIES, London
INTERNATIONAL LABOUR REVIEW, Genève
INTERNATIONAL ORGANIZATION, Madison, Wisc.
INTERNATIONAL PROBLEMS, Tel Aviv, Israel
INTERNATIONAL RELATIONS, Tokyo
INTERNATIONAL REVIEW OF INDUSTRIAL PROPERTY AND COPYRIGHT LAW, Weinheim, F.R.G.
INTERNATIONAL SOCIAL SCIENCE JOURNAL, Paris
INTERNATIONAL TRADE FORUM, Genève
INTERNATIONALE SPECTATOR, ´s-Gravenhage/The Hague
INTERNATIONALES AFRIKAFORUM, München

J

JAPAN QUARTERLY. India Committee for Studies on Economic Development in India and Japan, New Delhi
JERUSALEM JOURNAL OF INTERNATIONAL RELATIONS, Jerusalem
JEUNE AFRIQUE, Paris
JOURNAL DU DROIT INTERNATIONAL, Paris

JOURNAL OF AFRICAN STUDIES, Los Angeles, Cal.
JOURNAL OF ASIAN AND AFRICAN STUDIES. Department of Sociology and Anthropology, York University, Toronto
JOURNAL OF COMMON MARKET STUDIES, Oxford
JOURNAL OF DEVELOPING AREAS, Macomb, Illinois
JOURNAL OF DEVELOPMENT ECONOMICS, Amsterdam
JOURNAL OF DOCUMENTATION; devoted to the recording, organization and dissemination of specialized knowledge, London

JOURNAL OF ECONOMIC CO-OPERATION AMONG ISLAMIC COUNTRIES, Ankara
JOURNAL OF ECONOMIC ISSUES, East Lansing, Mich.
JOURNAL OF INTER-AMERICAN STUDIES AND WORLD AFFAIRS, Beverly, California
JOURNAL OF INTERNATIONAL LAW AND POLITICS, New York
JOURNAL OF MODERN AFRICAN STUDIES, London
JOURNAL OF SOCIAL AND POLITICAL STUDIES, Fairfax, Va.
JOURNAL OF WORLD TRADE LAW, Twickenham

K

KEESING´S CONTEMPORARY ARCHIVES. Weekly record of world events, Edinburgh
KOREA AND WORLD AFFAIRS, Seoul

L

LATEINAMERIKA: Herrschaft, Gewalt und internationale Abhängigkeit, Bonn
LATIN AMERICA REPORTS
LATIN AMERICA WEEKLY REPORT, London
LATIN AMERICAN INTEGRATION, Buenos Aires
LATIN AMERICAN REGIONAL REPORTS, London
LATIN AMERICAN RESEARCH REVIEW, Gainesville, Florida
LATINSKAJA AMERIKA, Moskva
LAW AND STATE, Tübingen
LECTURAS DEL CEESTEM-Centro de Estudios Económicos y Sociales del Tercer Mundo

M

MALAYAN ECONOMIC REVIEW, Singapore
MAN AND DEVELOPMENT
MANAGEMENT ACCOUNTING; formerly: NAA Bulletin-Management, New York
MARCHES TROPICAUX ET MEDITERRANEENS, Paris

MARINE POLICY, Guildford, Engl.
MARKSISTIČKA MISAO, Beograd
MARKSIZAM U SVETU, Beograd
MEDIA DEVELOPMENT, London
MEDIO ORIENTE INFORMA
MEDJUNARODNA POLITIKA, Beograd
MEDJUNARODNI PROBLEMI, Beograd
MEDJUNARODNI RADNIČKI POKRET, Beograd
MEED, see Middle East Economic Digest
MERCADO DE VALORES, México
MEŽDUNARODNAJA ŽIZN', Moskva
MIDDLE EAST, London
MIDDLE EAST ECONOMIC DIGEST-MEED: weekly news, analysis and forecast, London
MIROVAJA EKONOMIKA I MEŽDUNARODNYE OTNOŠENIJA, Moskva
MONDE ARABE, Damascus
MONITEUR AFRICAIN; mensuel économique des cadres d'Afrique noire, Dakar, Senegal
MONTHLY REVIEW, New York
MUNDO NUEVO, Caracas, Venezuela
MUNICH RADIO FREE EUROPE, München

N

NACHRICHTEN FÜR AUSSENHANDEL, Köln
NARODY AZII I AFRIKI, Moskva
NATIONALOEKONOMISK TIDSSKRIFT, København/Copenhagen
NATURAL RESOURCES FORUM, New York
NEUE ENTWICKLUNGSPOLITIK, Wien
NEW AFRICAN, London
NEW LEADER, New York
NEWSWEEK, New York
NOTES d'INFORMATION ET STATISTIQUES. Banque Centrale des Etats de l'Afrique de l'Ouest, Paris
NOVEDADES ECONOMICAS, Cordoba
NOVOE VREMJA, Moskva
NRI QUARTERLY ECONOMIC REVIEW, Tokyo
NUEVA SOCIEDAD, San José, Costa Rica

O

OAPEC NEWS BULLETIN, Kuwait
OCCASIONAL PAPER. Vienna Institute for Development, Wien
OPEC BULLETIN, Wien
OPEC REVIEW, Wien
ORBIS, Philadelphia
ORIENT, Hamburg
OVERSEAS BUSINESS REPORT, Washington, D. C.

OVERSEAS TRADING, Canberra/Melbourne, Australia
OXFORD BULLETIN OF ECONOMICS AND STATISTICS, Oxford

P

PACIFIC AFFAIRS, Vancouver
PACIFIC COMMUNITY NEWSLETTER
PAKISTAN DEVELOPMENT REVIEW, Islamad
PAKISTAN ECONOMIST, Karachi
PAKISTAN HORIZON, Karachi
PHILIPPINE INDUSTRY AND INVESTMENT
POLITICA INTERNACIONAL, Beograd
POLITIČKA MISAO, Zagreb, Jugoslavia
POLITIQUE ETRANGERE, Paris
PROBLEMES POLITIQUES ET SOCIAUX: articles et documents d'actualité mondiale, Paris
PROBLEMY DAL'NEGO VOSTOKA, Moskva
PROBLEMY MIRA I SOCIALIZMA, Praga
PROGRESO: comercio-industria-finanzas-desarrollo, Mexico City
PROJET, Paris
PUBLIC ADMINISTRATION AND DEVELOPMENT, New York
PUBLIC ENTERPRISE QUARTERLY JOURNAL, Ljubljana

Q

QUARTERLY REVIEW OF ECONOMICS AND BUSINESS, Urbana, Illinois

R

RABELS ZEITSCHRIFT FÜR AUSLÄNDISCHES UND INTERNATIONALES PRIVATRECHT, Tübingen
REGIONAL DEVELOPMENT DIALOGUE
RELATIONS INTERNATIONALES, Paris
REPERES: Cahiers du C.E.R.E.S., Paris
REVIEW OF AFRICAN POLITICAL ECONOMY, London
REVIEW OF CONTEMPORARY LAW, Bruxelles
REVIEW OF INTERNATIONAL AFFAIRS, Beograd
REVISTA ANDI
REVISTA CAMARA DE COMERCIO DE BOGOTA, Bogotá
REVISTA DE LA CEPAL, Santiago
REVISTA DE DERECHO INTERNACIONAL Y CIENCIAS DIPLOMATICAS, Rosario, Argentina
REVISTA DE ECONOMIA LATINOAMERICANA, Caracas, Venezuela

REVISTA DE LA INTEGRACION ECONOMICA Y EL DESARROLLO DE CENTROAMERICA, Tegucigalpa, Honduras
REVISTA DE PLANEACION Y DESARROLLO, Bogotá
REVISTA INTERAMERICANA DE PLANIFICACION, Buenos Aires
REVISTA MEXICANA DE SOCIOLOGIA, México
REVISTA PERUANA DE DERECHO INTERNACIONAL, Lima, Peru
REVUE CANADIENNE d'ETUDES DU DEVELOPPEMENT
REVUE DE POLITIQUE INTERNATIONALE, Beograd
REVUE EGYPTIENNE DE DROIT INTERNATIONAL, Le Caire
REVUE ROUMAINE D'ETUDES INTERNATIONALES, Bucureşti
RIVISTA DI STUDI POLITICI INTERNAZIONALI, Firenze
ROUND TABLE, London

S

SADEX: THE SOUTHERN AFRICA DEVELOPMENT INFORMATION, Washington, D. C.
SELA NOTICIAS, Caracas
SINGAPORE BUSINESS; supersedes: Singapore Trade & Industry, Singapore
SINTESIS, Montevideo, Uruguay
SOCIAL AND ECONOMIC STUDIES, Kingston
SOCIAL AND POLITICAL STUDIES, Buenos Aires
SOCIAL INDICATORS RESEARCH, Dordrecht, Netherlands
SOCIALISMO Y PARTICIPACION
SOCIALIST THOUGHT AND PRACTICE, Beograd
SOCIJALIZAM, Beograd
SOCIOLOGIA RURALIS, Assen, Netherland
SOUTH. The Third World Magazine, London
SOUTHEAST ASIAN AFFAIRS, Singapore
The SOUTHERN AFRICA DEVELOPMENT INFORMATION/DOCUMENTATION, Washington, D. C.,See: SADEX
SOVETSKOE GOSUDARSTVO I PRAVO, Moskva
STRATEGIC ANALYSIS, New Delhi
STUDIA DIPLOMATICA. Formerly: Chronique de Politique Etrangère, Bruxelles
SUDESTASIE. Magazin d'information, Paris
SYRACUSE JOURNAL OF INTERNATIONAL LAW AND COMMERCE, Syracuse, N. Y.
SYRIE ET MONDE ARABE. Etude mensuelle économique, politique et statistique, Damascus

T

TEORIJA IN PRAKSA, Ljubljana
TERCER MUNDO Y ECONOMIA MUNDIAL
TEXAS INTERNATIONAL LAW JOURNAL, Austin, Texas
THAILAND BUSINESS, Bangkok
THIRD WORLD, México City
THIRD WORLD QUARTERLY, London
TIERS-MONDE, Paris

TIJDSCHRIFT VOOR ECONOMISCHE EN SOCIALE GEOGRAFIE-TESG, Leiden
TRADE AND DEVELOPMENT. An UNCTAD review, Genève
TRADE, INDUSTRY AND INVESTMENTS, Makati, Manila
TRIMESTRE ECONOMICO, México, D. F.

U

UMBC ECONOMIC REVIEW: United Malayan Banking Corp. Berhad, Kuala Lumpur, Malaysia
UNIVERSITAS; ciencias juridicas y socio-economicas, Bogotá
UTAFITI, Dar es Salaam

V

VERFASSUNG und RECHT in UBERSEE, Hamburg
VISION. La revista inter-americana, New York

W

WATER RESOURCES BULLETIN, Minneapolis, MN
WELTWIRTSCHAFT. Halbjahresschrift des Instituts für Weltwirtschaft an der Universität Kiel, Kiel
WEST AFRICA, London
WEST AFRICAN ECONOMIC JOURNAL, Ibadan, Nigeria
WIRTSCHAFTSWISSENSCHAFT, Berlin
WISSENSCHAFTLICHE BEITRÄGE, Berlin
WORLD BUSINESS WEEKLY, London
WORLD DEVELOPMENT, Oxford
WORLD MARXIST REVIEW, Toronto
WORLD OF INFORMATION, Essex, England
WORLD TODAY, London

Y

YUGOSLAV SURVEY, Beograd

Z

ZBORNIK TRETJEGA PROGRAMA RADIO ZAGREBA, Zagreb

About the Book

Bibliography on Economic Cooperation Among Developing Countries, 1981–1982: With Annotations

compiled and edited by Nada Verbič

Covering the period 1981-1982 and containing more than 2,000 entries of books, articles (from 283 periodicals in nine different languages), studies, reports, and official documents, this international bibliography on economic cooperation and regional integration among developing countries includes annotations for many entries, an alphabetical list of periodicals, an author index, and a number of selected entries of earlier publications. It is intended to serve a wide range of readers from various fields: researchers, policymakers, professors, and students, as well as people involved in business in developed and developing nations.

The RCCDC Series on South-South Cooperation each year introduces new studies and reference materials on economic cooperation among developing countries. The series is directed by an international editorial board and coordinated by the RCCDC director, Dr. Boris Cizelj.

Nada Verbič, an economist, has dealt with various economic subjects as reference librarian in the Central Economic Library of the Faculty of Economics, University of Ljubljana, Yugoslavia. She also compiled and edited the 1970-1978 and 1979-1980 RCCDC bibliographies on economic cooperation and regional integration among developing countries.

For Product Safety Concerns and Information please contact our EU representative GPSR@taylorandfrancis.com Taylor & Francis Verlag GmbH, Kaufingerstraße 24, 80331 München, Germany

Batch number: 10725979

Printed by Printforce, the Netherlands